Artifacts and the American Past

THE AMERICAN ASSOCIATION FOR STATE AND LOCAL HISTORY

★ ★ ★ 1940 ★ ★ ★

Artifacts

and the American Past

THOMAS J. SCHLERETH

American Association for State and Local History

Nashville, Tennessee

Library of Congress Cataloguing-in-Publication Data

Schlereth, Thomas J
    Artifacts and the American past.

    Bibliography: p.
    Includes index.
    1.   United States—Antiquities—Addresses, essays, lectures.   2.   United States—
Civilization—Addresses, essays, lectures.   3.   Historical museums—United States—
Addresses, essays, lectures.   4.   Photography in historiography—Addresses, essays, lec-
tures.   I.   Title.
E159.5.S34   973   80–19705
ISBN 0–910050–47–3

First Edition 1980
Second Printing 1981

Publication of this book was made possible in part by funds from the sale of the Bicentennial State Histories, which were supported by the National Endowment for the
Humanities.

Author and publisher make grateful acknowledgment to the following, for permission to
use in this book the materials credited to them:

Exposure: The Journal of the Society for Photographic Education, Fall 1980, for "Mirrors of
the Past: Historical Photography and American History."
    The Newberry Library Papers in Family and Community History, Fall 1980, for "Past
Cityscapes: Uses of Cartography in Urban History."
    History News 33, no. 4 (April 1978), for "Historic House Museums: Seven Teaching
Strategies."
    The Museologist 141 (June 1977), for "The Historic Museum Village as a Cross-
Disciplinary Learning Laboratory."
    Hayes Historical Journal 1, no. 3, (Spring 1977), for "The 1876 Centennial: A Model for
Comparative American Studies."
    Environmental Review 4, no. 1 (November 1980), for "Vegetation as Historical Data: A
Historian's Use of Plants and Natural Material Culture Evidence."
    American Studies International, (Autumn 1974), for "Regional Studies in America: The
Chicago Model."
    Understanding Local History, edited by Thomas Krasean (Indianapolis: Indiana Historical
Society, 1979), for "Above-Ground Archaeology: Discovering a Community's History
through Local Artifacts."
    Roundtable Reports, Summer/Fall 1978, for "Collecting Ideas and Artifacts: Common
Problems of History Museums and History Texts."

For

the students in American Studies 484:
American Material Culture
past, present, future

Contents

Artifacts and useful objects are a part of all recorded history. They are devised, invented, and made as adjuncts to the human being's ability to accomplish work or enjoy pleasure. A close examination of any object is a graphic description of the level of intelligence, manual dexterity, and artistic comprehension of the civilization that produced it. It can reflect, as well, the climate, religious beliefs, form of government, the natural materials at hand, the structure of commerce, and the extent of man's scientific and emotional sophistication.

—R. Latham, "The Artifact as Cultural Cipher," in *Who Designs America?*

Introduction

History outside the History Classroom

IN the past two decades, many historians have talked about and sought to practice what some call "the new history." Motivated by an urgent desire to reinvigorate the teaching of history in both its formal and informal learning contexts, the new history endeavors to embrace a pedagogical philosophy that puts principal emphasis on learning as intellectual inquiry rather than rote memorization; seeks to involve students in the process of first-hand research investigations using primary sources; and attempts to recognize that much historical evidence, knowledge, and understanding exists outside the traditional history classroom.[1] In the essays that follow, I hope to make a contribution to this current historiographical, pedagogical, and methodological emphasis in history teaching and research.

Of course, I recognize that the "new" history is not new at all. The inquiry learning that many of us espouse actually rests on a very old Socratic premise: people learn by asking questions. The Italian scholar Benedetto Croce put the idea most succinctly for the history teacher: "Every line of history should ask a question."[2] So should every photograph, road map, craftsman's tool, domestic residence, or city neighborhood.

John Dewey and Francis Parker, American progressive educators teaching at the turning of this century in Chicago, acknowledged as much in their pioneering development of the inquiry approach in history education. The inquiry pedagogy sees every artifact—textbook, school, museum, community—as a learning environment. Dewey—who, eighty years later, is still worth rereading on the role of history, historical museums, and history teaching in public education—envisioned a student's entire world as a learning laboratory where "experiments in history teaching" should take place.[3] A similar philosophy animates my historical research and teaching with American artifacts.

I find the concept of the school, the museum, and the community as "learning laboratories" a most appropriate analogue for the institutional

1

contexts (the plural is important) in which many contemporary historians work. The analogue—where students should be subjected to more labor and less oratory—considers such environments with their diverse graphic, documentary, and physical evidence as places where the original Greek meaning of the word *history* ("to investigate," "to inquire") applies in its fullest sense.

In my own quest to investigate the American past, I have frequently found myself making inquiries outside my history classroom. Since I teach American urban, architectural, and cultural history, much of the evidence for these aspects of our past are, understandably, found in museums, historical societies, living-history farms, towns, and cities, as well as in libraries, archives, municipal record offices, and academic lecture halls. In recent years, historians, borrowing a nomenclature from anthropologists and archaeologists, have begun to use the term *material culture* to describe the entire natural and man-made environment with which researchers can interpret the past. Such evidence underscores each of the nine techniques I am proposing here whereby we can analyze various graphics (chapters 1-3), historic sites (chapters 4-6) and whole landscapes (chapters 7-9) as artifacts.

Inasmuch as material culture evidence informs much of my approach to the history outside the history classroom, permit me to give it a working definition. Material culture, it is often said, is something of a contradiction in terms; that is, material culture is not culture, but its product. Culture entails socially transmitted rules for behavior, ways of thinking about and doing things. Consequently, culture can be defined as "that complex whole which includes artifacts, beliefs, art and the other habits acquired by man as a member of society, and all products of human activity as determined by these habits."[4]

Material culture, when defined by a cultural anthropologist such as Melville Herskovits, is usually considered to be roughly synonymous with the totality of artifacts in a culture, with the vast universe of objects used by humankind to cope with the physical world, to facilitate social intercourse, to delight our fancy, and to create symbols of meaning.[5] The proper study of mankind, to paraphrase Alexander Pope, is man *and* what man has made—a Brooklyn Bridge, a William Faulkner novel, a computer, a Thomas Cole painting, a field pattern, a toleware container, a dog-trot house, a Walt Whitman poem, a highway clover-leaf, a John Rodgers sculpture group, a college campus, a city plan.

James Deetz would have us also consider a somewhat broader definition of material culture that, in addition to including artifacts from the simplest (e.g., a common pin) to the most complex (e.g., an interplanetary space vehicle), would also press the historian to investigate "cuts of meat as material culture, since there are many ways to dress an animal, plowed fields, even the horse that pulls the plow, since scientific breeding of livestock involves the conscious modification of an animal's form according to culturally derived ideals. Our body," argues Deetz, "itself is a part of our physical environment, so that such things as parades, dancing, and all aspects of kinesics—human motion—fit within our definition. Nor is the definition limited only to matter in the solid state. Fountains are liquid examples, as are lily ponds, and material that is partly gas includes hot-air balloons and neon signs." Deetz has also suggested, in *Invitation to Archaeology*, that even language is a part of material culture, a prime example of it in its gaseous state. Words, after all, are air masses shaped by the speech apparatus according to culturally acquired rules.[6]

An equally catholic definition, much in debt to the Deetzian perspective, pervades my own use of material culture as historical evidence. I view the study of artifacts and the American past as a thoroughly historical study and, hence, a totally humanistic enterprise. "Great nations write their autobiographies in three manuscripts," insisted Ruskin: "the book of their deeds, the book of their words, and the book of their arts. Not one of these books can be understood unless we read the two others; but, of the three, the only trustworthy one is the last."[7] While I would certainly not claim that artifacts possess the only veracity as historical evidence, I do wish to make a strong case for the potential of this largely unexamined (at least by many historians) data. Utilizing Leslie A. White's three main subdivisions of culture—material, social, and mental—I would argue that American material culture has received far less systematic attention as a field for pioneering historical research and teaching than the other two subdivisions of social and mental culture.[8]

Material culture study attempts to explain why things were made, why they took the forms they did, and what social, functional, aesthetic, or symbolic needs they serve. Moreover, a basic assumption underlying such teaching and research is that artifacts are cultural statements, whether the artifact is a stereograph view, a historical house interior, an Osage orange hedge-row, a mail-order catalog, or a White Tower restaurant. The historian's primary purpose in using artifacts is always to interpret them in their cultural history context. My suggestions below operate on that assumption.

Several other axioms permeate these ideas of ways to explore the history outside the history classroom. One dictum, perhaps obvious even by now, is that the historian should confront material culture evidence *directly* whenever possible. Reproductions will do, in a pinch, but nothing can substitute for the real thing. "The historian should consider looking at artifacts to be so much a part of his trade," urges Eugene S. Ferguson, "that he will, over the years, develop a keen critical sense regarding the authenticity and significance of the artifacts and restorations that he sees. To be used effectively, the artifacts must mean something to the historian directly, not once removed through the mind and eye of the curator."[9] To have first-hand, experiential confrontation with the artifacts of the American past requires that most of us (teachers and students) depart our traditional academic haunts for other locales of historical learning—history museums, historical societies, outdoor history museum villages, farms and towns, suburbs and cities. A corollary to that injunction to do more, as it were, teaching on location, is that we consider the entire American environment as a historical museum. Landscapes are artifacts, cultural documents of the ways we were and are.

Artifacts enable us to gain an understanding of the uncommon history of common things. Hence a second axiom defining this book is that material culture data provides us with one abundant source for gaining historical insight into the lives of those who left no other records. Long ago, Emerson told those of us who would be American scholars that we should study "the meal in the firkin; the milk in the pan; the ballad in the street."[10] More recently, other cultural interpreters, such as Siegfried Giedeon, have argued that artifacts are often the historian's best approach to "anonymous history."[11] The past lives of most men and women, while numerically dominant, have left little or no self-conscious literary records. We know the craftsman, the slave, the homemaker, the common individual of America ofttimes only by their physical remains—their tools, their homes, their cities; in short, the extant material evidence that offers some clue as to their cultural history.

Such a cultural history is considerably broader than Matthew Arnold's frequently quoted definition of high culture (the best that has been thought and said primarily by artists, scholars, writers, political and religious elites) and is, instead, particularly attentive to the historical experiences of Americans who were nonliterate, or literate but who did not leave behind any writing, or, for various reasons, who have not figured prominently in traditional political or economic narratives written by historians.[12] These Americans deserve our attention, for, as Warwick in Shakespeare's *Henry IV* reminds us, "There is a history in all men's lives."[13] One way to know their history is through their artifacts.

The need for methodological rigor and precision is a third teaching and research axiom that I hope an interest in material culture studies nurtures among historians. I have proposed no new or novel interpretative models, but I have tried to elucidate those that have surfaced to date and those whose hypotheses deserve further testing. I feel very strongly, however, that research on artifacts and the American past must now move beyond the merely descriptive stage of investigation into the more problematic area of historical analysis and interpretation. Methodological innovation must be on the agenda in the future. Henry Glassie, a folklorist who has already contributed to this much needed dialogue about the relationship of theory and practice in several experimental studies,[14] pinpoints a fundamental principle that must underlie whatever research strategy is adopted by the historian working with material culture data: "Artifacts, being human products, are always comprehensible if thought about them proceeds in an orderly way," argues Glassie; "if, that is, observation is systematic and the synchronic description is complete before diachronic problems are approached."[15] It is not necessary to adopt Glassie's structuralist method of interpreting material culture, but it is vital for the historical investigator to adapt or create a research design that seems most appropriate to the questions he or she wishes to address to the artifactual data under study. Again, the essays below attempt to suggest—within a limited range of material culture evidence—the spectrum of questions that might be asked and some of the current methods employed to answer such historical inquiries.

In that sense, this book is a sampler, a collection of teaching and research techniques that I have tried, revised, and tried again over the past half decade. By design, it is an eclectic volume that reflects a multiplicity of perspectives and techniques. No one orthodoxy or approach has been imposed upon what I hope is a thoughtful miscellany of experiments in history teaching and research. These techniques aspire to be what Marc Bloch, author of *The Historian's Craft*, once called "the memorandum of a craftsman who has always liked to reflect over his daily task." I consider technique to be particularly crucial to my task of approaching history, be it history researching, history writing, history teaching, or history exhibiting. By technique, I mean what T. S. Eliot meant: "Any selection, structure . . . and form of rhythm imposed upon the world of action by means of which . . . our apprehension of the world of action is enriched and renewed."[16]

Technique, in terms of history teaching and research with American material culture, is plural; I am persuaded that there should be several variations on the historian's basic method. Yet, I believe these essays all attempt to involve the students, be they eight or eighty, not only in the discovery, identification, and classification of material culture evidence, but also in the analysis and interpretation of such artifacts in the broad context of American cultural history.

I hope that the techniques that I have proposed will help inculcate and promulgate this basic premise of the historical method. My own thinking on historical method has been stimulated through the assortment of crucibles in which these essays have been forged. Most of these studies first appeared as spoken presentations—papers delivered at professional meetings or addresses given to historical conferences. I learned much from those who listened to my ideas, supporting some, challenging some, offering me many of their own. Then, in emulation of many a nineteenth-century lyceum or chautauqua lecturer, I published those platform pieces as articles in various journals. Another dialogue ensued. In the correspondence and discussion that followed upon publication, generous readers gave me additional advice and assistance. I am particularly indebted to those editors noted on the copyright page of this volume, not only for permission to reprint these chapters that first appeared in their journals, but also for their editorial help in preparing them for publication.

With the initial encouragement of Robert Richmond, chairman of the American Association for State and Local History Committee on Publications, and the continuing assistance of Gary Gore, director of the AASLH Division of Publications, these ten essays have now been conjoined as a brood of ideas that I hope will prompt still further interest among historians in using artifacts to interpret the American past.

Inasmuch as these chapters have already had two lives—as public lectures and as scholarly articles—there may be occasional repetition of a concept or a citation in their collective appearance in this volume. I have tried to eliminate such duplication, but sometimes, when I thought the repeated emphasis was essential to my argument, I have allowed it to remain. These various techniques for the teaching historian, despite their disparate conception, share a common paternity. The occasional overlap in methodological focus or evidential base can be attributed, quite simply, to my intersecting research, teaching interests, and approaches, as well as my current intellectual heroes and mentors in American material culture scholarship.

I am certain that one common birthmark that definitely identifies each of the techniques proposed in this book is that each aspires to help others think historically, to become their own historians, capable on their own of reading history books, visiting history museums, doing research about their own past with perspicacity and pleasure for the rest of their lives. For most of them, that will mean studying history outside the classroom. Finally, although I recognize that ancient wisdom has it that teaching cannot be taught, I hope that my fellow teaching historians, whatever their institutional affiliation, will find methods, sources, and ideas that they, in turn, can either adapt in full form for immediate use or modify to their own particular teaching needs and style.

In my own continuing education in material culture teaching and research, I have borrowed from many generous teachers who have repeatedly shared with me their own techinques for understanding artifacts and the American past. What I have learned from these enormously talented historians who practice their craft in universities and high schools, historical museums and historical societies, historic preservation organizations and public history agencies, is truly one of my best personal examples of what I mean by the vitality of "the history outside the history classroom."

My intellectual debts to these many men and women who have taught me via their published books, articles, lectures, and exhibits, as well as through personal contacts, extended correspondence, and encouraging conversations, are recorded in the notes to my essays. Some of these colleagues have taught me so much about the possibilities and the pitfalls of material culture research that they deserve my special gratitude. To Kenneth Ames, Scott Swank, Beno Foreman, Marianna James, Bill Moore, Nancy Malan, Jay Anderson, Richard Brown, Richard Candee, Cary Carson, Barbara Carson, Lizabeth Cohen, E. McClung Fleming, Roger Fortin, Charles Hummel, William Stapp, Claudia Kidwell, Lilly Koltun, Felice Jo Lamden, Larry Lankton, Myron Marty, Zane Miller, Bernard Mergen, Susan Myers, Patricia O'Malley, Tim Parks, Charles Peterson, Barbara Riley, Rodris Roth, Suzanne Schell, Philip Speiss, Fred Schroeder, Richard Haupt, Martin Sullivan, Joseph Trimmer, Dana White, Wilcomb Washburn, Joanna Schneider Zangrando, Ron Ronsheim, Barnes Riznik, John Stilgoe, Wendy Clauson Schlereth, James Bellis, George Talbot, Gerry Danzer, Glen Holt, Harold Skramstad, John Zukowsky, Peirce Lewis, Peter Cousins, J. B. Jackson, Thomas Frye, and William Alderson—I owe more than I can say. These historians, plus those students to whom this volume is dedicated, have consistently enlivened and expanded my own interest in and sensitivity to the American past, a past from which we continually borrow experience (individually and communally) whereby to fashion our strategies for coping with the present and the future.

Part I
Graphics as Artifacts

1

Mirrors of the Past: Historical Photography and American History

"I HAVE seized the light, I have arrested its flight!" With this bouyant explanation, Louis J. M. Daguerre of France announced his success in capturing a photographic image on silver-coated copper plate in 1839. As is often the case in the history of invention, William H. Fox Talbot of England, practically simultaneously with Daguerre's breakthrough, perfected a different photographic technique known as the calotype process that produced a negative image on paper, which could then be used to reproduce an unlimited number of paper prints by contact exposure.[1] Photography had been born. Now, fourteen decades later, we have a surfeit of historical evidence in the diverse forms of photographic images that is without precedent and without peer: a special kind of knowledge—vivid, dramatic, concrete—that provides practically anyone with a novel opportunity to witness the past as if it were, momentarily, present.

Men and women with a historical consciousness recognized this unique potential of the photograph from its earliest days. Following the lead of Lady Elizabeth Eastlake's 1857 essay on "Photography," Oliver Wendell Holmes urged historians to preserve photographs as visual records of change for their future counterparts.[2] Holmes, a medical doctor, essayist, and noted American philosopher, confessed himself enraptured by the new medium, smitten by its uncanny "appearence of reality that cheats the senses with its seeming truth." Photographs were magical illusions. But even more than that, he explained, they were matchless pieces of information, descriptions of things, scenes, and persons infinitely more vivid than words. Eventually, he foresaw, photography would reproduce the entire world, reducing all solid objects to thin film images.

Holmes followed up his observation by a proposal to establish a national photographic archive that would especially collect stereographs,

an important and extremely popular photograph type in whose development he had played a small part.[3] Unfortunately, nothing came of his plan
for a National Stereographic Library. In 1883, however, Holmes's fellow
New Englanders in the Boston Camera Club initiated one of the early
systematic historical surveys of extant structures and farmsteads for various local historical societies and archives. Consequently, their undertaking can be considered as one of the early attempts by "above-ground
archaeologists" to use photography as a fieldwork research tool.[4] Photographer George E. Francis, in an 1888 essay delineating "Photography as
an Aid to Local History," inadvertently recognized that in claiming: "No
words can adequately bring to our minds the chain of little gradual
alterations in the houses, the roads, fields, woods, water courses, as
would a series of accurate pictures taken at short and regular intervals:
something like the family photograph album, where are treasured all the
likenesses, it may be, of the youngest son from his infancy to his man-
hood."[5] The comparative approach, contrasting American landscape photographs over time, as envisioned by Francis, continues as one of many
teaching techniques employed by historians in both museums and in
classrooms. In published format, this approach surfaces in numerous
"then-and-now" photobooks of urban history.[6]

Paralleling this nascent interest in historical photography in New
England was similar activity in Old England. There, Sir Benjamin Stone
founded the National Photographic Record Association in 1897 with an
aspiration to mount a national effort "for collecting photographic records
of objects and scenes of interest throughout the British Isles." Stone
sought to have this ever-expanding cache of historical evidence deposited
in the British Museum.[7]

Back on this side of the Atlantic, a Chicago publisher, recognizing the
photograph's pedagogical potential, introduced at the turn of the century
a semimonthly magazine entitled *History Study Pictures*. Each issue of the
magazine contained ten reproductions intended to aid teachers in illustrating to "their pupils some of the chief topics in history, geography, and
literature, by means of reproductions of paintings and photographs of
historic scenes and persons of note."[8] Unfortunately, *History Study Pictures* ceased publication after ten issues; yet its purpose and, to an extent,
its format continue in certain modern media history-slide sets and photograph portfolios such as *Photo-Documents of American History* and *The
American Experience*, a pictorial history of America from the Smithsonian
and Scholastic Book Services.[9]

Such sporadic instances of awareness of the historical potential of

Figs. 1 and 2. An 1860s stereograph (above), by John Carbutt, showing Chicago's East Eleventh Street, with its collection of prestigious apartments and large single-family homes. Compare with the photograph below, a 1910 view of the same site by a talented amateur, Charles R. Clark, noting the remarkable transition in this particular streetscape of the city.—Courtesy Chicago Historical Society photographs among historians and photographers in the second half of the nineteenth century are symptomatic of a similar relationship in the first half of the twentieth century. Only occasionally did a historian such as Ralph Henry Gabriel venture forth with a publication like his fifteen-volume history, *The Pageant of America*, which drew upon various kinds of graphic evidence including photographs.[10] Although this excellent source collection has gone largely unnoticed by the majority of historians, Gabriel, an intellectual historian at Yale, could take a degree of solace in one of its historiographical influences. A colleague at Columbia, Professor Harry Carman, recommended these volumes to colleagues and students, one of whom, Roy Stryker, became head of the Farm Security Administration Historic Section.[11] The FSA, of course, became one of the most prolific sources of documentary photography of Depression America. The Gabriel-Carman-Stryker story has an important sequel. In 1939—significantly the centenary of Daguerre's public announcement of his photographic process—the American Historical Association devoted one of the sessions at its national convention to the topic of "Sources and Materials for the Study of Cultural History: Documentary Photographs." The principal speaker was Roy Stryker, along with Paul H. Johnstone. At that meeting, their analysis of nine photographs still remains one model survey of the possibilities and pitfalls of using photography in historical research.[12]

As several historiographers of historical photography (e.g., Bernard Mergen, Glen Holt, Walter Rundell) have documented,[13] the acceptance of photography as historical evidence has come begrudgingly in the forty years since Stryker made his appearance at an AHA rostrum. If historians used photographs at all in their published research, or, more probably, in their textbooks, it was usually only to provide materials for illustrative relief from the authors' narrative. Since textbook writers tend to plagiarize from one another in both idea and image, there have been a series of "most favored photos" (e.g., Dorothea Lange's *White Angel Breadline* [1933] or *Migrant Mother* [1936], depicting the Depression) replicated ad nauseam in American history texts. An interesting research exercise for students would be to examine the photographs used in their various history texts, attempting to decide why particular photographs were chosen, what conditioned their particular placement in the book, and what might be their effect in conveying historical information and insight. Clues for such an analysis—as well as the basis for a comparison of visual and verbal content in American histories—can be gleaned from Frances FitzGerald's *America Revisited*.[14]

Such critical analysis should demonstrate to students the more obvious reasons for historians' traditional distrust or neglect of photographic sources: most topics of interest to political, economic, and diplomatic historians have had an abundance of written sources; the kinds of questions asked by historians have usually not been phrased in ways that photographic data can answer directly; since the nineteenth century and the coming of pictures (e.g., lithographs or photographs) as either replacements for written words or as enticing and subversive supplements to them, such graphic evidence has seemed to many thoughtful people to be artistically and intellectually suspect. As students of the word, with a large investment in careful verbal analysis, many historians, like other academicians, have tended to deprecate new types of visual evidence that threaten the primacy of printed communication. If historians are to use photographs as data, they should be aware of these caveats as well as others raised by perceptive critics. To be sure, historical photography has significant limitations as historical evidence: it can distort, bias, abbreviate, and misrepresent reality. So do other forms of historical evidence. Yet, after all the methodological rejoinders have been issued, all questions of veracity and representativeness raised, and all the problems of adequate citation and verification noted, historical photography still survives as an important evidential mode enormously valuable to the historian in his or her teaching and research.

Such a perspective informs this discussion of one of the most characteristically American of artifacts. Here a *historical photograph* is defined as a photograph[15] offering: "a believable image of times past . . . capable of supporting the study or the interpretation of history." The apparent reality of any photographed instant of time, Robert Weinstein and Larry Booth assure us, "can be verified and illuminated by the historical photograph made of it. The moment after it is made, it becomes a visual artifact, although it is not always valued as a historical source."[16] I value every historical photograph as a potential historical source, but I also value certain photographs more than others. Make no doubt about it, some photographs tell us much about the past, ofttimes much more than the proverbial thousand words; a great many tell us hardly anything at all. The historian must judge.

In this essay, such judgments will exclusively entail what historians of the medium call *still photography.*[17] Although they are equally important evidence for the American history of the modern period, motion pictures, television, and other multimedia data are not analyzed save as they may relate to the use or abuse of historical photography. For guides on how historians should use this visual evidence, I recommend Paul Smith's *The Historians and Film*; John O'Connor and Martin Jackson's *Teaching History with Film*; the quarterly journal *Film and History*; and Steven Schoenherr's *Multimedia and History*. [18]

To acquire a rudimentary knowledge of both the potential and the problems of using still photography as historical evidence, one needs to recognize that photography is many things at once: a branch of chemistry, a form of art, an aesthetic language, and an endeavor involving a process, a product, and, most important of all, persons. Given the complexity and multiplicity of this material culture, I propose to discuss its historical evidential value in three categories wherein photography is studied as historical process, as historical data, and as historical analysis. In the first category, a quick review is offered of the history of photographic technology, typology, aesthetics, and styles followed by a brief enumeration of the major depositories, sources, and collections where historical photographic data can be located and thereby used in historical research. A third section takes note of the literature of visual communication, then surveys the interpretive models and methodological techniques that some American historians, who have made extensive use of photographic evidence, have developed. A final review of the limitations of photography as historical data, as well as a sketch of the needs and opportunities for using such material culture conclude the essay.

Photography as a Historical Process

"A photograph is a document, and the historian's first business is to ask of it, as he would of any other record, who made it, to whom it was addressed, and what was it meant to convey." [19] How historical photographs were actually made is an absolutely essential body of knowledge that the historian must master before he can competently begin to classify and then interpret photographic images. Such images resulted from a wide assortment of chemical processes producing negatives and prints and involving equally diverse types of cameras. One simply has to understand how photography happens. If one does not, perhaps the best place to find such elementary but indispensable information is from the primer of an American master: Ansel Adams's *Basic Photo: Camera and Lens*. [20]

Basic technical works on photography are abundant, attesting to the importance of photography in contemporary American cultural history. These would-be resources for the historian of technology range from the simplest of how-to-do pamphlets to the most intricate realms of the lens and film esoterica. For the neophyte photo historian encountering the bewildering nomenclature that is part and parcel of historical and contemporary photography, the *Focal Encyclopedia* and the fourteen-volume *Life Library of Photography* are excellent explanatory and reference works.[21] Detailed treatments of technical history (e.g., from the dry plate to Ektachrome) and photographic scientific history (e.g., from "sun artists" to satellite images) are also available.[22] Although in the past decade a pioneering literature has emerged on the history of cameras, material-culture students need to devote much more attention to this fact and symbol of American life. In that context, Eaton Lothrop's *A Century of Cameras*, tracing as it does the historical development of the camera from the original Daguerre model to the beginning of today's miniature forms, provides an approach worthy of imitation in its relating of photography to the equipment of a particular historical milieu.[23]

To apply the history of photography as process to doing research in historical photography, one can divide the technological territory into several separate but related categories. Each category, in turn, can be organized by historical sequence. In the first group, photographic historians usually classify photographs according to the kind of *processes* produced by different photographic media invented around 1839: the direct-positive process, or the negative-print process. Another typology can be constructed as to the various *images* resulting from those processes. As the reference chart in Appendix I suggests, knowing the chronology of *processes* and *images* used in photographic reproduction, together with the ability to recognize them, is as essential to the photographic reseacher as the similar mastery of ceramic types or architectural styles is to the archaeologist or the architectural historian. The ability to recognize the different processes and images is a vital skill but a very specialized one; there are many images, for example, that are quite difficult to distinguish one from another. With a solid understanding of the processes employed and the images produced (ranging from well-known daguerreotype to the more obscure aristotype), the historian has an invaluable tool for beginning to identify and date his evidence.[25] Two excellent applications of this tool to raw photographic data are case studies by William Parker on a single person and William Peterson on single place.[26]

The techniques of producing certain photographic images have been both ways of classifying historical photography and ways of analyzing such data as historical evidence. Among the assortment of early, direct-positive process techniques (e.g., ambrotype, tintypes),[27] none has captured our imagination in the past two decades as has Daguerre's original process and its pictures of fine detail, exquisite tonality, and unique illusion of an image reflected as if in a mirror.[28] American fascination with the daguerreotype began early in photography's career, as is evident from the fact that it was only slightly more than a decade after Samuel F. B. Morse brought the technique to the United States that Nathaniel Hawthorne, in his novel *The House of the Seven Gables,* made his hero, Holgrave, a daguerreotypist.

The daguerreotype became a revered object—one is tempted to say icon—in many nineteenth-century households. The attractively embossed cases made of gutta percha, pressed paper, and leather provide additional artifactual evidence to the cultural historian of the esteem in which the daguerreotype was held.[29] Two comprehensive works—*Mirror Image* by Richard Rudisill and *Facing the Light* by Harold F. Pfister [30] detail the enormous technical and symbolic impact of this technique practiced by the first generation of American photographers.

The collodion version of the negative-positive process introduced in 1851 rapidly eclipsed the daguerreotype. This "wet-plate" process, forming as it did the basis for all modern photography, provided a negative image on glass, from which an unlimited number of prints of high quality could be made.[31] Photographers everywhere rushed to use the wet plate. Until the perfection of the commercially manufactured gelatin dry plate in the 1880s, the wet plate remained the standard negative material. Moreover, with the perfection of the collodion process, commercially produced photographic prints became widely available, and an increasing number of amateurs became attracted to photography. Gradually, photography was becoming an American folk art—perhaps the most democratic art the world has ever known.

This gradual democratization of photography in America deserves much more careful study by historians. Three popular nineteenth-century photographic forms made possible by the collodion process were the *carte de visite,* the cabinet card, and the stereograph. Because of easy, multiple reproduction at relatively cheap cost, the *carte de visite* revolutionized portrait photography. Parents regularly took their children to *carte de visite* studios to have their growth recorded for relatives and posterity. As people acquired more and more of the photographic cards, a way was needed to preserve and present them. Hence the origin of the *carte de visite* or cabinet card album, a precursor of the family snapshot album and a significant artifact of American social and cultural history.[32] The exchanging of *carte de visite* and cabinet card photos in the nineteenth century might also have a twentieth-century analogue in the annual ritual wherein high school and sometimes college students exchange "wallet-size" photographs with their peers. Those photographs, of course, are intended to be preserved in official yearbooks, types of communal albums, that are still another form of photographic material culture to which history students might pay attention.

By the 1880s, no well-appointed American parlor could afford to be without a *carte de visite* album or a cabinet card album and stereograph cards and viewer (stereoscope) and album. The stereograph's role in American life is the subject of an innovative publication of the Visual Studies Workshop called *Points of View: The Stereograph in America—A Cultural History*.[33] Following up on the work of earlier scholars on the topic,[34] a collaborative team of historians, museum curators, sociologists, and art historians has explored, in interdisciplinary fashion, "the stereograph as a primary source of visual history," as well as the "modes of presentation and display of such photographic evidence in order to develop a possible alternative to the traditional historiography" of museum photographic exhibition.[35] While this catalogue does not fulfill all its promises, it is an exciting experiment in both historical methodology and history museum practice.

Stereographs became so popular that large companies were formed dealing exclusively with this new form of photography. Companies such as the Keystone View Company helped feed the public's seemingly insatiable appetite for more and more views. The Keystone photographic corpus—one of the world's greatest archives of three-by-six-inch stereograph cards and negatives, now housed as the Keystone-Mast Collection at the Museum of Photography of the University of California[36]—contains more than 140,000 items and all sorts of fascinating photographic data, such as the *Teacher's Guide to the American History Set of Stereographs* (1927). Perhaps the single most prominent champion of the stereograph was Oliver Wendell Holmes, who boasted that he had viewed more than one hundred thousand stereographs. Holmes, who called the daguerreotype "the mirror with a memory," became so enamored of the stereograph as a means of recording American history that, as we have seen earlier, he recommended the establishment of national and city stereographic libraries throughout the United States.[37]

Unfortunately, Holmes's recommendation never came to fruition, but the perfection of the techniques of the dry-plate process[38] in the 1860s and of roll film ("American film," as it was called) plus the Kodak box camera by George Eastman in the 1880s guaranteed that the next one hundred years of American history would be visually documented as never before.

Eastman's achievement looms as a watershed in the history of American photography. As Daniel Boorstin reminds us, "Photography could not become universal until there was some simpler way of taking a picture." Eastman found the way. Photography for the millions became possible to such an extent that, by 1980, photography has become the most popular American hobby, and the United States manufactures more film (especially Kodak) than any other nation on earth. In the absence of a modern historical biography of George Eastman, Boorstin's analysis of him as one of those inventive entrepreneurs (e.g., Thomas A. Edison, Edwin H. Land) who made experience repeatable by mass-producing the moment, provides the student with many provocative insights.[39]

With the advent of Eastman's hand-held Kodak and later the Brownie (designed for Eastman by Frank Brownell, creator of more hand cameras than any other man of his time) came the form of historical photography probably known best to most of us: the snapshot.[40] Amid the clutter of material culture to be found filling cupboards and drawers in an average American household, the ubiquitous snapshot must surely rank among the most commonplace. Yet, to date, this most prolific and most democratic of American popular art forms is the least studied by photography historians. Although such visual evidence would appear invaluable to the "new" social history, only slowly have scholars begun to investigate this enormous cache of unpretentious photographic data, most of which is still in the hands of its creators or their descendants. This enormous uncollected and uncatalogued archive may prove to be one of the most productive research frontiers for academic and museum historians and their students. Suffice it to note here that the snapshot, which some cultural historians propose may be the appropriate visual equivalent of modern experience, has received only minimal discussion in either the historical or photographic literature. An English publication, The Snapshot Photograph, traces the social background and contents of British snapshots from 1888 to 1939, and an Aperture paperback, simply titled The Snapshot, provides the beginning researcher with a series of articles, interviews, and portfolios examining the vitality and ambiguity of the snapshot photograph in this country.[41]

In addition to knowing the principal photographic materials, process techniques and forms, the historian should be well informed about two other typologies: photographic subjects and photographic conventions. Probably the photographic subject genres most familiar to historians would be portraits, landscape and city views, warfare, and the rather amorphous categories of documentary and reform photography. What history text does not include a Matthew Brady portrait of Lincoln, a Timothy O'Sullivan view of the frontier west, an Alexander Hesler panorama of early Chicago, an Alexander Gardner perspective of the aftermath of a Civil War battlefield, an Arthur Rothstein documentary of Dust Bowl Oklahoma or a Jacob Riis exposure of a Robbers' Roost?[42]

Individual studio portrait photographers have been studied by several scholars, both here and abroad, providing us with valuable material for initiating students in the comparative analysis of images and interpretations.[43] The bibliography on American landscape photographs has grown so enormously in the past decade that it deserves to be analyzed separately below. To begin preliminary documentation of American war photography (figs. 3 and 4), a woefully neglected source of cultural as well as military history, see work from George Barnard to David Douglas Duncan.[44]

Inasmuch as every photograph is indeed a document, the precise classification of documentary photography is a particularly slippery task. Any classification of the genre, however, would have to include the surviving photographic evidence of those photographers who sought to make a conscious record of life and conditions in places all over America. While coined in 1926 by John Grierson, the term came into popular usage during the Depression, when the telling pictures of poverty-stricken farmers taken by Roy Stryker, Margaret Bourke-White, Russell Lee, and Walker Evans awakened Americans to the needs of social reform. In many minds, the first mention of documentary photography connotes only westering "Okies" or southern sharecroppers.

In America, the reform tradition in documentary photography extends backwards at least to Jacob Riis, whose life and work can be evaluated as a case study of what David Noble has called the "paradox of progressive reform." Coupling Riis's own writings and photographs with a general historical interpretation like Noble's and recent cultural-history analyses of Riis himself,[45] yields a provocative picture of the progressive temper. In an American history survey course, careful study of Riis can be followed by work on Lewis Hine (whose work has been suddenly rediscovered in the last decade),[46] and then any of the FSA photographers whose work is widely known and widely published. If one were to go back into the nineteenth century to add two other giants—Matthew Brady and Edward S. Curtis—[47] one could teach an intriguing seminar in general American cultural history (1850–1950) from the camera work of Brady, Curtis, Riis, Hine, and, say, Arthur Rothstein.

Other teaching and research possibilities exist in the historical study of lesser-known documentarians such as Francis Greenwood Peabody,

Joseph Byron, Jessie Tarbox Beals, Solomon Butcher, Erwin Smith, Arnold Genthe, and Francis Benjamin Johnston. Much conscious documentary photography of local life survives unexamined in small historical societies, commercial photographers' files, newspaper morgues, and government offices. As a new exhibition catalogue[48] suggests, the federal government produces much photographic documentary evidence—five million photographs are presently (1980) retained in the National Archives alone. Historians probably know best the FSA achievement in the 1930s, but there are equally important documentary photographic records produced by the Office of Economic Opportunity (OEO) agencies in the 1960s and by the Environmental Protection Agency (EPA) in the 1970s.[49]

Fig. 3. Running Water Bridge in Whiteside, Tennessee, as photographed by George N. Barnard in 1865. Executed with a glass-plate negative, the image illustrates several characteristics of both American landscape photography and Civil War photography.— Courtesy University of Notre Dame Archives

Fig. 4. Another type of "war" photograph, documenting the campus dissent over American involvement in Vietnam, was taken by an undergraduate student, William Mitchell, on the University of Notre Dame campus in May 1969.—Thomas Schlereth Collection

Three other subjects of photography little exploited as historical evidence are the group photograph, the news (or journalism) photograph, and the commercial photograph. Neal Slavin's *When Two or More Are Gathered Together* explores the contemporary group portrait and how that photographic genre (Slavin calls it "an American icon") can communicate "the desire to belong in America in the mid-1970s and the conflicts caused by that wish." Slavin's visual investigation of the relationship of the one to the many—a principle ever problematic in democratic societies—provides the historian with a slate of questions by which to interrogate those formal pictures of past clubs, singing societies, fraternities, sports teams, troupes, occupational groups and associations, or informal groupings of people around a dinner table, on outings, on the front porch.[50]

Photo-journalism, considered by some historians of photography as a subspecies of the documentary, has a century-long history, beginning with the development of inexpensive methods of reprinting photographs in magazines and newspapers. This reprinting capacity, plus the availability of faster lenses, faster film, portable cameras, and, later, flashlighting via flashbulbs, made modern news photography possible. Cameramen who practiced this trade quested after "newsworthy" events. While the impact of such photography has begun to be assessed at the level of the national picture magazines (e.g., *Life, Time, Look*) and from the idiosyncratic perspective of the acclaimed "great news photos and the stories behind them," cultural historians have yet to evaluate American news photography in the aggregate.[51] John Szarkowski's *From the Picture Press* (New York: Museum of Modern Art, 1973), with chapter headings such as "Ceremonies," "Losers," "Winners," "Disasters," "Heroes," "Good News and the Good Life," could serve as a starting point for making more extensive and interpretive use of photo-journalism as social history.

A similar argument should be mounted for commercial photography. Since the vast majority of these images were made for money, there is a major bias running through most collections of photographs made by commercial photographers. Despite the inherent biases of commercial photography, nineteenth-century business photographers, such as John W. Taylor and George Lawrence, in Chicago, are a boon to urban historians. They contracted with architectural firms to portray their latest and highest buildings, with real estate developers who were promoting new suburbs, with capitalists erecting industrial and manufacturing plants, and with civic groups detailing particular features of the city for advertising promotions and tour guides.

In addition to basic processes, materials, techniques, types, and subjects, there are also photographic conventions that must be understood in interpreting historical photography. Or, to put it another way, to be able to use photographs as documents, the historian must establish a framework for analyzing the organization of visual documents: that is, what is in the foreground, middle distance, background? Is the perspective elevated or eye-level?—and so on. He may work with various analytical tools that other scholars (largely art historians) have already devised,[52] or, given the type of photography he wishes to use as historical evidence, he may have to prepare a research design of his own devising.

No one, to date, has developed a universally satisfactory model for analyzing the internal forms by which a picture informs. Perhaps one cannot adapt the concept of model-building to the elusive, multifaceted images that photographs present, especially those taken by unknown photographers of unknown people. Much research in this area of "convention detection" deals exclusively with aesthetic principles and tends to ignore the content of the image as also being an arrangement of historical information. However, one approach pioneered by John Szarkowski in *The Photographer's Eye* (New York: Museum of Modern Art, 1966) can be adapted to the historian's purposes for two reasons: first, in attempting to categorize the basic elements of photographic vision, he defines some of the biases inherent in photographs that every historian using such visual data as evidence should be cognizant of; and second, Szarkowski delineates five components he maintains to be essential elements in photographic vision. These include "The Thing Itself," or the subject on which the camera focused and whose three-dimensional reality has been transformed into a quite different two-dimensional artifact; "The Detail," or the recognition that, outside of the photographer's studio (where he can, more or less, control the content of an image), photographs never can tell a complete story, they merely document a fragment of a scene; "The Frame," or what a photographer sees in the camera's view-finder, which defines what he considers most important, thereby making photography by its very nature selective; "Time," which became increasingly important as advanced photographic technology enabled photographers to capture movement and thereby segregate and stop time; and a finally, "Vantage Point," or the range of visual choices (e.g., bird's-eye view, view from behind, at an oblique angle, etc.) a photographer can make when deciding how to photograph a subject.

Szarkowski's primer, when supplemented with other basic works on the conventions of photographic communication,[53] provokes a set of questions that the historian must keep in mind when interrogating historical photography. We become aware, for example, of the various nineteenth-century conventions of posing for the camera. As frontier Kansas photographer G. D. Freeman recalled, in 1892, cowboys liked to pose deliberately in outlandish costumes, with large sombreros, leather leggings, and weaponry. Amateur photographers were urged by popular writers to "visit all available art-galleries, and carefully study poses by the great masters of portraiture."[54] Bernard Mergen, who has investigated the conventions of portrait and group-photograph posing, argues that we must remember at least three important points in analyzing nineteenth-century views: that there was a large element of play involved in being photographed; that the subjects of photographs often had definite ideas about the image they wanted to create; and that the photographer often conceived of himself as an artist, creating a portrait.[55]

Historians have only begun to establish the most rudimentary frameworks for interpreting the basic conventions of posing or being posed in photography. As Neil Harris reminds us, pictorial analysis, often called iconography, demands a careful monitoring of the changing inclusions and exclusions, placements, techniques, and visual formulations found in a particular photographic genre. Harris is persuaded, however, that students who combine research in both cultural/social history and material culture studies might be best suited to carry out this intriguing historical task. "The ability to detect changes in the manipulation of images quite obviously rests on familiarity with established conventions," he insists. "The requisite discriminations belong to those who are habituated to the analysis of pictures and objects."[56]

A guide to such analysis, and perhaps the most famous of the American historical surveys of the processes of photography, the photographers, and the phenomenon of photographing, is Beaumont Newhall's *History of Photography from 1839 to the Present Day* (New York: Museum of Modern Art, 1964). Used extensively as a basic text in university art courses, Newhall's survey portrays the history of photography almost exclusively as the history of an art medium, reproducing only those images that have telling aesthetic effect. While art photography and photographic aesthetics are assuredly an important dimension of American cultural history and should be studied as such,[57] historians should not be misled by specialized art history studies of photography that afford them little help (outside of the history of high style or elite aesthetic conventions) in classifying and explaining the type of historical information that can be found in an aesthetically insignificant mass of photographs.

More germane to the historian's quest for the single survey study that can introduce the novice to the history of American photography without being overdetailed or lacking adequate chronological and typological coverage are works by Helmut and Alison Gernsheim, Robert Taft, and Reese Jenkins. *The History of Photography from the Camera Obscura to the Beginning of the Modern Era* (New York: McGraw-Hill, 1969) by the Gernsheims should be on every photographic historian's reference shelf. Surveying historical developments in photographic systems throughout the world, it is an encyclopedic reference text of immense use. Inasmuch as the Gernsheims' volume has a stated emphasis toward English innovations, Robert Taft's perceptive panorama of *Photography and the American Scene: A Social History, 1839–1889* (New York: Dover Publications, 1938, 1964) should also be part of the American historian's library. As Lilly Koltun points out, Taft, a chemist, enlivens his book with wry and humorous references to the reactions of post-Civil War Americans in the face of the bewildering new scientific artifacts and processes that photography entailed. For example, she notes, "he refers to 'the 10,000 cackling Yankee hens' whose co-operation was needed to produce enough egg albumen to coat the photographic paper of Edward Anthony."[58] *Images and Enterprise: Technology and the American Photographic Industry, 1838 to 1925* (Baltimore: The Johns Hopkins Press, 1975), by Reese V. Jenkins, concentrates on the economic significance of photography in American commerce and industry. A detailed examination of the production and marketing of photographic material culture in the United States, this sourcebook also traces the development of monopolies, the legal struggles over patent restrictions, new techniques of business management and corporate structures (particularly as developed by crafty George Eastman), and the interaction between the demands of American society and the supply of the American photographic industry.

Photography as Historical Data

The exact number of photographs with which the American photographic industry has supplied the American populace (and hence historians) since 1839 will remain, of course, forever unknown. What is becoming apparent, however, is that a staggering mass of historical photographic data survives in published and unpublished, identified and unidentified, public and private collections in this country; that millions of photographic images and negatives are extant in governmental and public agencies, in private businesses and trade organizations, in newspaper and magazine offices, in old photograph studio files and the collections of individual photographers, and in family bureau drawers and albums.

How does the historian find such photographic evidence? Where are such photographic resources located? What finding aids are available?

Several model directories listing many of the public and private depositories where historical photographs might be found in a particular geographical area include Ann Novotny's *Picture Sources 3,* published (1975) and sold by the Picture Division of the Special Libraries Association in New York City; Shirley L. Green's compilation of *Pictorial Resources in the Washington, D.C., Area,* published by the Library of Congress in 1976; the *Oregon Historical Society's Union Guide to Photograph Collections of the Pacific Northwest,* published in 1978; and the Atlanta Historical Society's *Atlanta Images: A Guide to the Photo Collection of the Atlanta Historical Society,* published in 1980.[59] Other clues as to where to find historical photography for researching neglected aspects of American history would be Weinstein and Booth's chapter three on "Sources" and Steven Schoenherr's advice on "Teaching with Audiovisual Documents: Resources in the National Archives."[60]

Picture Sources 3 is the third edition of an invaluable photography directory listing the special collections of photographs (and prints) on all subjects in 1,084 institutions in the United States and Canada. In the majority of these public collections, the pictures are regarded as visual documents, as sources of information, rather than as works of art. Divided by subject matter into fifteen chapters and indexed four ways (alphabetically, geographically, numerically, and topically), this reference work, when used in conjunction with Renata V. Shaw's bibliography on *Picture Searching: Techniques and Tools* (Special Libraries Association Bibliography Number 6: 1973), constitutes the closest counterpart to a comprehensive national research guide currently available to the historian on unpublished photographic resources.

Among the major repositories discussed in *Picture Sources 3* but not as yet mentioned in this essay are the Metropolitan Museum of Art, in New York; the American Antiquarian Society, in Worcester, Massachusetts; the University of Texas, at Austin; Columbia University, New York; the Museum of the City of New York; the Chicago Historical Society; the New York Historical Society, in New York City; the Missouri Historical Society, in St. Louis; and the State Historical Society of Wisconsin.

Published collections of photographs become more abundant each year. For the historian's use, such collections might be divided into two types:

the single-book format, reprinting the photographs of a single photographer (e.g., Nickolas Muray, *Muray's Celebrity Portraits of The Twenties and Thirties*); a single place (William Lee Younger, *Old Brooklyn in Early Photographs, 1865–1929*); a single event (David Lowe, *The Great Chicago Fire*); or a single subject (Children's Aid Society, *New York Street Kids*).[61] A second format would be the prepackaged sets of visual materials distributed by commercial firms, such as Light Impressions, and research centers like the International Museum of Photography at the George Eastman House.[62] Two excellent examples of these formats produced by the same agency, the National Archives, are the earlier-cited paperback volume on *The American Image* and the National Archives' slide sets of historical photography on the American West, the Civil War, American Indians, and the City.[63] Commercial houses have also reproduced elaborate slide-set teaching kits on various aspects of nineteenth-century America and the Great Depression. Helpful in initiating a beginning class or seminar into the methodology of using photography as historical evidence, they can also be employed to prompt cross-cultural historical comparisons and research when used in conjunction with similar projects, such as *Canada's Visual History*, prepared by the National Museum of Man.[64]

Occasionally, private collectors either publish selections from their personal collections of historical photography or permit selected researchers limited access to study the visual data they have amassed.[65] Here, for instance, one is reminded of the work of David Phillips on American western history.[66] Perhaps the most famous private American collection of photographs, sketches, cartoons, advertisements, paintings, and movie stills is the Bettmann Archive, begun by German refugee Otto Bettmann in 1941. A credit line found at least a dozen times in most American history textbooks, the Bettman Archive has also periodically published samples of its own holdings.[67] Location and terms of access to certain other private repositories can be found in Max and Tina Lent's *Photography Galleries and Selected Museums: A Survey and International Directory* (Venice, California: Garlic Press, 1978).

No matter whether the historian uses unpublished or published, public or private photographic sources, he should watch for the professional curator's or private collector's hand upon the form and content of the collection that he intends to use as evidence. The historian must be sensitive to the assortment of systems that professional archivists and dedicated amateurs have developed for classifying and analyzing their photographs. In the best photographic archives, accession control has expanded far beyond the photograph's provenance and general description to include description of image content, physical format, the photographer, the purpose of the photograph, copyright, physical condition, location, and circulation history.[68] In any photographic research in which students are involved while pursuing material culture studies, they should be encouraged to include such complete documentation with every photograph that they, as historians, take or use as evidence in their investigations of the past.

Such an exercise, in addition to providing accurate documentation of their photography for future historians, should reinforce an awareness that both private and public accumulations of historical photography vary in purpose, content, and time frame. In this context, Marie Czach's caveat is well taken:

That a philosophy of collecting can change the perception of the history of the medium is often overlooked. Without collections, there would, of course, be no possibility of history. But in an area of inquiry as malleable as photography, the sensibilities of the curator, reflected in the selections made for inclusion in an archive, even within an institution with a well-defined directive for collecting, has a greater than normal bearing on the direction of the history of printmaking. In general, it is difficult to know how much of the history of photography is attributable to curatorial selection and effective public relations, and how much, on the other hand, is attributable to inherent quality.[69]

Despite this difficulty inherent in any collection of historical data, photocurators, archivists, and librarians provide invaluable assistance to the historian in their careful preparation of finding aids to past photography. Three discussions of their work are particularly worth the American historian's attention: a series of articles by Renata V. Shaw in *Special Libraries*; Paul Vanderbilt's essay, "On Photographic Archives" in *Afterimage*; and periodic bibliographical pieces in *Picturescope*, the quarterly newsletter of the Picture Division of the Special Libraries Association.[70]

Writings on photography by photographers and others form a final general resource that historians should consult in their research. Two anthologies, one edited by Beaumont Newhall and another compiled by Nathan Lyons, afford us a study of critical source material written by established photographers on their craft.[71] Of the two, the Newhall is the more useful to historians, since the volume focuses on nineteenth-century developments, whereas Lyons treats only the twentieth century. Newhall also includes inventors, scientists, and cultural critics in his anthology. While a comprehensive reader documenting the changing intellectual, social, and cultural import of photography as seen by contemporaries remains to be compiled, William Welling's *Photography in America: The Formative Years, 1839–1900: A Documentary History* (New York: Thomas Crowell, 1977) contains a rich selection of facsimile materials, correspondence, articles, and reminiscences for use in the integration and interpretation of the visual and the verbal elements of photographic history.

Photography as Historical Interpretation

As with verbal literacy, visual literacy requires rigorous and analytical techniques, specifically a knowledge of the logic, grammar, syntax, and epistemology of what Rudolf Arnheim calls "visual thinking," Jurgen Reusch and Welden Kees label "non-verbal communication," and Estelle Jussim terms "visual information."[72] These theorists of "how we see" offer the historian an assortment of principles of visual perception applicable in constructing an appropriate methodology for using photographic evidence to construct a historical interpretation.

One must learn to study a historical photograph, warn these theorists, with the care and attention to detail and nuance that an archaeologist might give to a single potsherd, a chemist to a scientific paper, or a literary scholar to a complicated symbolist poem. "Every part of the photographic image carries some information that contributes to its total statement," insists Howard Becker. "The viewer's responsibility is to *see* every thing in the most literal way, everything that is there and respond to it. To put it another way, the statement the image makes—not just what it shows you, but the mood, moral evaluation, and causal connections it suggests—is built up from those details."[73]

Becker, a sociologist, and John Collier, an anthropologist, provide historians with two excellent overviews wherein abstract visual communication theory is translated into specific research techniques and models for historical analysis. Karin Becker Ohrn, in a short essay on "Re-Viewing Photographs: Unexplored Resources For Communications Research," also contributes a cogent digest of approaches to the historical photograph as a special representation of reality, a communication system worthy of careful and critical interpretation.[74]

What is the current state of the art of scholarly historical interpretation using photographic evidence as an important data base? What are the best models and methods of such historical interpretation? What historical topics have been particularly suitable for interpretation by means of historical photography?

One can answer the first question easily. Use of historical photography is increasing rapidly in all its genres. Perhaps the most prolific and, unfortunately, least sophisticated, in terms of methodological rigor, has been the pictorial history. Ever since the perfection of the half-tone reproduction process in the 1890s, historians and especially their editors have combed picture archives for striking and colorful images to enliven history texts, or, occasionally, as in Ralph Gabriel's *The Pageant of America* (1929) and Frederick Lewis Allen's *American Procession* (1933), to construct a panorama of the national experience.

Usually, pictorial histories use photographs merely to illustrate the text, rather than to instruct the reader. A few historians have attempted to demonstrate how, in Glen Holt's estimate, pictorial histories can "use photographs as documents." Holt's claim receives further explanation in his perceptive methodological statement that introduces Harold Mayer and Richard Wade's *Chicago: Growth of a Metropolis*, published by the University of Chicago Press in 1968. Prefaces, forewords, and introductions to books using photographs are often a significant source of insight and ideas about photography as historical interpretation. They should always be consulted for a historian's methodological premises. In my own initial venture into using nineteenth-century photography as historical documentation, I used an introductory essay ("Discovering the Past in Print, Person, and Photography") to apprise my readers of my method of investigation and interpretation.[75] Journal articles, case-studies, and periodical essays are other places to scour for innovative research techniques and explanatory models employing historical photography as a primary evidential base.[76] Several journals are devoted exclusively to photography—*Afterimage, History of Photography, Exposure, Image,* and *Aperture*—and contain the most *au courant* scholarship.[77]

To date at least four major history subfields (landscape, urban, architectural, and social history) have employed photographs to interpret the American past. Photographic documentation of the landscape began with the introduction of photography into this country in 1839. It was, however, the period from 1860 to 1885 that is considered the first "golden age of landscape photography," when men such as Robert H. Vance, Carleton E. Watkins, Eadweard J. Muybridge, Alexander Gardner, Andrew Joseph Russell, Timothy O'Sullivan, and William Henry Jackson framed the American West in images that allowed Americans to view parts of their country and its peoples that they would otherwise never have seen.[78] The land, particularly the western landscape, has always been a source of special fascination for the American imagination. Even before Frederick Jackson Turner, American historians shared this interest. Only recently, however, has the historical potential of landscape photography begun to be realized. Some observers have interpreted this photography as typically American, focused as it was, physically and aesthetically, on a primeval land. Of course, these western photographers and the images they created became a significant part of the American myth and symbol of a virgin landscape replete with vast open space and awesome natural features.

The photographic process of the "taming of the West," as David Phillips has labeled it, deserves more careful study by American historians,[79] for it had a significant impact on American literature (the poet Henry Wadsworth Longfellow), art (nineteenth-century landscape painting),[80] and ecological politics. When F. V. Hayden, leader of one of the western land surveys, sent nine of W. H. Jackson's best 1871 photographs of the Yellowstone region in Wyoming to each member of the United States Senate and House of Representatives, he set in motion a legislative process that resulted in the country's first national park in 1872. Other interdisciplinary research can be done by students to compare the important nineteenth-century American literature and literary criticism of the West with the published photography of the western survey photographers, their writings (e.g., W. H. Jackson, *Time Exposure: The Autobiography of William Henry Jackson*), and the historical interpretations of their achievements. Here one can also contrast the work of Richard Rudisill, Maisie and Richard Conrat, and Weston Naef and James Wood with that of Walter Prescott Webb, Henry Nash Smith, and William Goetzman.[81] Gary F. Kurutz's finding aid to "Pictorial Resources: The Henry E. Huntington Library's California and American West Collections" (*California Historical Quarterly* 54, no. 2 [Summer 1975]: 175–182) offers historians a beginning guide to primary resources for such research.

The changing look of the American land across time can also be traced by exploring the innumerable archives of federal, state, and local governmental agencies. Perhaps most widely published (and hence available for classroom use and student research projects) is the work of the documentary movement of the 1930s. Roy Stryker and Nancy Wood's *In This Proud Land* (Boston: New York Graphic Society, 1973); Erskine Caldwell and Margaret Bourke-White's *You Have Seen Their Faces* (New York: Viking, 1937); Arthur Rothstein's *A Vision Shared* (New York: St. Martin's Press, 1976); Dorothea Lange and Paul Taylor's *An American Exodus* (New Haven, Conn.: Yale University Press, 1969); James Agee and Walker Evans's *Let Us Now Praise Famous Men* (Boston: Houghton Mifflin, 1941); and the U.S. Farm Security Administration's own chronicle of *The Years of Bitterness and Pride* (New York: McGraw-Hill, 1975) have probably shaped our historical image of a depressed nation struggling against the man-made physical environment as much as any of President Franklin Delano Roosevelt's fireside chats or Congress's New Deal legislative acts. William Stott, in a brilliant and seminal work on the meaning of *Documentary Expression and Thirties America* (New York: Oxford University Press, 1973), provides us with a persuasive interpretation of this visual evidence. Stott demonstrates that the "documentary expression" that emerged in nonfiction, social science writing, and film, as well as photography, enabled the country to see its social and physical landscape in a totally new way. His choice of photographs goes far beyond any usual decorative function and instead forms an integral part of establishing his central thesis.

Another innovative application of the historical photograph has been put forth by Peter Daniel in his study, *Deep'n as It Come: The 1927 Mississippi Flood* (New York: Oxford University Press, 1977). Some of the historical photography on which Daniel based his interpretation of this catastrophe was secured from the personal albums of flood victims. In addition to gathering this primary data, he also conducted oral history interviews with flood refugees. Daniel found that the snapshots made by the survivors revealed what they thought was important to record at the time and served as an additional stimulus to their memories of the event a half-century after it occurred.

In addition to turning to the extant landscape photography of the recent past,[82] historians are both using and creating photographic documentation of the land and its use. David Plowden's chronicling of *The Hand of Man on America* (Riverside, Conn.: Chatham Press, 1973) is one form that this enterprise has assumed; collective endeavors such as the Environmental Protection Agency's Documerica and the *Nebraska Photographic Documentary Project, 1975–1977: Images of Nebraska* (Lincoln, Neb.: Nebraska Historical Society, 1977) are others. Established in April 1972 "to document photographically America's environmental concerns," Documerica employed over a hundred photographers and produced some 16,000 images. Under the direction of Gifford Hampshire, Documerica conceived of the environment in the broadest sense and undertook projects such as Gary Truman's study of German immigrant culture in New Ulm, Minnesota, and Jonas Dozydenas's study of Indian reservation life in Nevada. Although much of the work is in color (a radical departure from the documentary tradition), some of it recalls the photography of the Farm Security Administration.[83]

Understandably, photographic documentation of the historical landscape also provides the historian of the built environment with significant data. As Phyllis Lambert has demonstrated, the visual recording of build-ings as expressions of society has a long European tradition, originating in France in the 1850s. Many early masters of photography—Hippolyte Bayard, Charles Negre, Henri le Secq, Edward Baldus, and the Bisson brothers—made extensive records of buildings and the great engineering works for various government departments under the Second Empire. For instance, Baldus's photographic record of the new Louvre, erected be-tween 1852 and 1868, had a profound trans-Atlantic impact on public architecture throughout North America.[84]

Despite extensive nineteenth-century European precedents for ar-chitectural photography and a less well-known corpus of Eastern land-scape views, many Americans remained largely preoccupied with the landscape photography of the West until the 1890s, a chronological bench-mark Turner took to be the closing of the frontier. The historian of domestic architecture, however, finds some exceptions to that statement in sources like Austin A. Turner's *Villas on the Hudson: A Collection of Photo-lithographs of Thirty-One Country Residences* (1860); Henry Hobson Richardson's *The New York Sketch Book of Architecture* (1874) and James Corner's *Examples of Domestic Colonial Architecture in New England* (1891).[85]

Researchers can also turn to photographs as historical evidence of the evolution of a single building type, be it the barn, fast-food restaurant, or state capitol.[86] When conducting a historical investigation of a specific building type, the research is immediately defined and encompassed; therefore, sequential graphic evidence of various buildings of a type constructed at different times and places provides an incisive view of changing architectural values that are, of course, expressions of changes in the values of society. When a building's physical evidence or original plans no longer survive, photography often affords us the only clues by which to conduct architectural research.[87]

If building evidence does exist in sufficient abundance but is far too large (as are most structures) to study under laboratory conditions, sys-tematic photography of such data *(in situ)* by historians becomes both an act of evidence collection (again, for future historians) as well as an act of historical interpretation. In a model study, highly adaptable to other public buildings such as fire and police stations, post offices and city halls, Richard Pare has shown what can be done on the history of the American county courthouse. For an explanation of his methodology, one should consult his essay, "Creating the Photographic Record: The United States Court House Project" (*Archivaria* 5 [Winter 1977–78]: 78–91), and for his historical in-terpretation, see his final work, *Court House: A Photographic Document* (New

York: Horizon Press, 1978). Beginning with the earliest (1725) surviving courthouse in continuous use in King William County (Virginia) and tracing the evolution of the building type up until our own time, Pare and twenty-four other photographers made more than eight thousand images of 1,054 buildings.

Pare's work, along with that of other professional architectural photographers,[88] should be read carefully by historians, to better understand the common problems (e.g., lighting, distortion, clients' demands) peculiar to architectural photographs. Pare's confession that "even under the best conditions, the photographer of architecture is the slave of circumstance" likewise applies to past photography of buildings. "Much depends on the time of day, time of year, and seasonal change. . . . Thus it is understandably difficult to capture the sense of a building through photographs and yet maintain a sense of its environment."[89]

Despite these limitations, it must be acknowledged that pictures can often be a mine of historical information about architecture in an environmental context, not isolated from its surroundings, as are the illustrations in most contemporary architectural magazines. During the past 135 years, photographic documentation has been increasingly recognized as an indispensable tool for studying and understanding the social art of building in its fullest expression, which is to say as components of a city, rather than as isolated formal structures.

Historians now investigate the photographic imagery (see figs. 1 and 2) of the American city with increasing frequency. In addition to several methodological assessments of photography's potential for urban historical studies,[90] a number of classic texts have been written that can serve as interpretive models. Harold Mayer and Richard Wade's innovative use of graphics of all types—especially photographic imagery from daguerreotypes to aerial views—in their *Chicago: Growth of a Metropolis*, published by the University of Chicago Press in 1968, currently reigns as perhaps the most creative use of urban photography as actual historical evidence. Older histories by E. H. Chapman on Cleveland, J. H. Cady on Providence, and J. A. Kouwenhoven on New York also offer the current researcher a sense of the available evidence and its interpretive potential.[91]

Speaking of New York City, it may be the American city with the most published urban photography. Thanks to the aggressive publishing policies of the Pictorial Archives of the Dover Press, the teaching historian can create a small paperback research library of historical photography on New York, ranging from Mary Black's *Old New York in Early Photographs* to Allan Talbot's *New York in the Sixties*.[92]

The published New York corpus is rich in one form of urban imagery—reform photography—but deficient in another—aerial photography. That is not without reason. Almost everywhere in the United States, urban historians researching the nineteenth-century city are confined to urban views from the ground or from elevated structures.[93] The 1860 wet-plate exposure of "Boston as the Eagle and Wild Goose See It" by Black was the first aerial photograph made of an American city and one of the only ones made until the late nineteenth century. In the twentieth century, however, photographs taken from the air abound for both rural and urban America.[94] Used heretofore primarily by geographers, aerial photography—particularly when researched in concert with extant cartography—provides the urban historian with a storehouse of geological, ecological, architectural, and town-planning data, as well as political, economic, and sociological information.[95]

Historians have made extensive use of reform photography, unlike their lack of attention to aerial photography. In addition to the much-acclaimed work of urban progressives such as Riis and Hine, Thomas Garver has shown there was even "an urban America as seen by the photographers of the Farm Security Administration."[96] In addition, urban social change documented through photography did not, of course, end with World War II. The movement's message assumed varied forms and degrees of political and social radicalism, ranging from Robert Frank's The Americans (New York: Grossman, 1969), with an introduction by Jack Kerouac, and Lorraine Hansberry's The Movement: Documentary of a Struggle for Equality (New York: Simon and Schuster, 1964) to Leonard Freed's Black in White America (New York: Grossman, 1965) and Benedict J. Fernandnez's In Opposition: Images of American Dissent in the Sixties (New York: DaCapo Press, 1968).

In addition to their conscious and unconscious documentation of urban historical phenomena such as housing, sanitation, transportation, immigration, work, and neighborhood life, such historical evidence contains a subtle but powerful political interpretation of modern American history. As Sam Walker and Victor Greene have persuasively argued, this photography is imbued with the tradition of liberal reform.[97] And as Steven Schoenherr notes, the misinterpretation of such photographic evidence has, on occasion, distorted historical research on working-class life as well as stereotyped scholarship on ethnicity.[98]

Mention of working-class and ethnic-group culture introduces the subject of social history, a final special historical field that investigators have begun to explore in earnest but one almost totally neglected until twenty-five years ago. Attempts at collecting historical evidence of social behavior via photographs was begun by photographers such as Edward S. Curtis, whose twenty volumes of *The North American Indians* (Seattle: University of Washington Press, 1907) sought to document the vanishing culture of the native American. Curtis's extensive visual and verbal evidence can be contrasted with the photographic legacy of other American ethnographers, such as A. C. Vroman,[99] and then evaluated in light of the methodology of anthropologists, folklorists, and social scientists who use photographs as analytical tools for ascertaining the patterning of societal values, attitudes, and behavior.[100] Joanna Scherer, "You Can't Believe Your Eyes: Inaccuracies in the Photographs of North American Indians," (*Studies in the Anthropology of Visual Communication* 2, no. 2 [1976]: 67–78) reminds us, however, of the potential bias present in such supposedly social scientific images, particularly in the staged and manipulated photographs of Curtis.

Photographs have also perpetuated stereotypes in their depiction of immigrants. At the same moment that American immigration reached epic proportions, in the period from 1890 to 1920, photography matured technically to provide an extensive pictorial record of that generation. Reformist photographers such as Lewis Hine concurrently found immigrant ghettos and poor blue-collar workers to be excellent sources for compositions. Modern social history research now suggests, however, that Hine's familiar compositions, reproduced repeatedly in histories of American labor, and those of his liberal colleagues probably have created an inaccurate impression, in that these now-classic photographs fail to give the viewer much of an idea of the dynamic, multifaceted social community of which the immigrants were a part.

To be sure, these Eastern and Southern Europeans were primarily working-class populations and photography remains a superb primary resource in researching the social history of work and working. Nevertheless, as Victor Greene's analysis of ethnic photographs concludes, "The workers were also individuals who functioned in definitely stratified societies; that is, among complex groupings with middle- and even upper-class members."[101] Historians using such photography must recognize and examine the visual record left by the anonymous masses (e.g., construction workers, garment workers, mine laborers), the "middling sorts" (shopkeepers, businessmen, fraternal heads), and the ethnic elite (religious leaders, politicians, newspaper editors). To date, American Jewry, in its multiple historical and geographical features, probably has been studied the most comprehensively by historians using its diverse photographic evidence.[102]

George Talbot, curator of the Visual and Sound Archives at the State Historical Society of Wisconsin and an innovative pioneer in the historical interpretation of local, amateur, or "vernacular photography," together with Majorie Mellon, has launched an exciting research project into the themes of ethnicity, continuity of traditions, self-identity and family process through the interpretation of rural life in a Pommeranian farming neighborhood near Watertown, Wisconsin. Working extensively with the photographs, artifacts, and the oral folk traditions of the Krueger family, Talbot and Mellon are working on a State Historical Society of Wisconsin museum exhibit—"Six Generations Here: A Family Remembers Ethnicity and Change on a Wisconsin Family Farm, 1851–1978"—that, while recognizing the many pitfalls involved in interpreting photographs as social history, shows their enormous value because they simultaneously give information about the substantive content of family life (dress style, architecture, environment) and the subtle (sometimes unconscious) images that the photographer and his human subjects wish to project.[103]

Talbot's current ethnicity research grows out of an earlier work (*At Home: Domestic Life in the Post-Centennial Era, 1876–1920* [Madison, Wisc.: State Historical Society of Wisconsin, 1976]) in the two final subtopics— family and community history—that presently intrigue so many social historians seeking to extract new historical insight by consulting photographic evidence. *At Home*, in addition to two short but excellent methodological essays that are essential primers for any historian venturing forth into the social history of American domestic life via photography,[104] affords a concise summary of the topical subdivisions of historical domesticity. Whereas architectural historians using photographs tend to be interested in exteriors, social historians, like Talbot, research interiors. The meanings of house, home, hearth, and household can be explored, he suggests, in the extant photographs of nineteenth- and twentieth-century interiors. Preliminary investigations can be executed as to arrangement of artifacts, furniture styles, and general ambience of the room. But no single photograph of an interior can be trusted as complete evidence if one wishes to do careful social history with visual material culture. Many interior photographs must be examined, cross-examined, and re-examined. Talbot, Bernard Mergen, and William Seale suggest that the social historian should do this, primarily by interrogating large collections of interior photographs (see fig. 12) with such questions as:

How did individuals organize and utilize space? Did arrangement of rooms, furniture, and artifacts influence relationships among family members? Was there a specific woman's place in the home? Children's place? Servant's place? Are there typical or novel features to be discovered in the ways that different socio-economic classes in society chose to organize their homes and households? If people are included in the photographs, in what rooms are they shown most often and in what relationship to the assorted material culture around them?[105]

To provide a general context for initial exploration of these broad research inquiries, the beginning student can consult any number of overviews that attempt to survey *The American Family* via an *American Album* or *The Family Album* in *Home Town, U.S.A.*[106] More concretely rooted in a specific historical time and place are the edited catalogues of commercial photographers' collections, wherein can be found much evidence for the history of American domesticity. *The Smith and Telfer Photographic Collection,* published by the New York State Historical Association in 1978, is a typical example. What Washington Smith (1828–1893) and his successor Arthur Telfer (1859–1954) unconsciously did in Cooperstown, New York, and what other relatively unknown commercial photographers (e.g., Henry Koopman, E. A. Scholfield) did in hundreds of other American cities,[107] was to produce something close to the kind of photographic archive that the *British Journal of Photography* had pleaded for in 1889, an archive "containing a record as complete as it can be made of the present state of the world."[108]

In pursuing the potential of commercial studio photographs as social-history evidence, we also need a thorough social history of the American commercial photographer. We need far more detailed information—ascertainable through traditional historical sources such as city directories, tax records, census reports, business directories, newspapers, and genealogical registers—about how photographers worked, about their relations and commercial arrangements with clients, about their ways of presenting pictures to particular publics. We need to know much more than we do about how people behaved toward such "public" pictures (leaving aside the even more complex matter of their private use of photographs within family circles or personal life), whether they preserved them (and how), exhibited them (and where), or inscribed them (and in what manner).

Social historians have begun to put such questions to what assuredly is the largest cache of photographic evidence of any type, form, or subject—the kind variously called "nonprofessional photography," "amateur vernacular photography," or, simply "family or home photography."[109] The bulk of these family images, stored in shoeboxes, film processors' envelopes, or family albums, remains uncatalogued, unclassified, unedited, unresearched, and uninterpreted. Often the historian must act as his own archivist, attempting to bring some order to such a body of material before ascertaining if it is to be of use historically. Thomas L. Davis has prepared a beginner's primer called *Shoots: A Guide to Your Family's Photographic Heritage* (Danbury, N. H.: Addison House, 1977), but two superb methodological articles by Karin Becker Ohrn and Steven Ohrn are essential to understanding how a family photograph collection can serve as an "archive" of family life—a way of remembering people and events and also a way of passing on these memories to other members of the family.[110]

Social historians such as Judith Mara Gutman have maintained that it may also be possible to decipher specific functional and psychological roles that different family members may have performed, roles that we may have overlooked in family-history research. Gutman argues that, in most American family photographs, there is a kind of inward, propelling action led by the mother—not by the sister, daughter, or wife, but by the mother—whose "look, clothes, hand, or face becomes the fulcrum for the [family] photograph's movement."[111] Gutman's hypothesis deserves empirical testing before it can be awarded the status of a satisfactory explanation in social-history research, but it is the kind of question that social historians should be asking of extant photographic data.

We should likewise be trying to differentiate what constitutes family photography and what may be more properly community photography. Perhaps wedding and funeral photographs, although undoubtedly involving family members, are really more concerned with community history than familial activity. Barbara Norfleet's historical assessment of American *Weddings* demonstrates that this type of group imagery can tell the historian a great deal about American social behavior within a cultural institution such as marriage. In what she candidly subtitles "a brief and highly speculative history of wedding photographs in America, based on pictures found in attics, basements, professional photograph negative files, historical societies, and interviews," Norfleet suggests the multiple provenance of wedding photographs and then outlines their historical evolution in four major chronological periods from 1850 to 1970. Her comparative analysis of wedding photographs (ca. 1855 and 1905), showing changing aesthetic styles as revelatory of changing behavioral patterns, indicates still another of photography's uses to social historians.[112]

So does the innovative work currently being done by Karin Ohrn, Jonathan Garlock, and Amy Kotkin on family photograph albums. While the family photograph album may be the single history book that each of us has had a hand in creating, only recently have repositories dedicated to the collection of historical photography shown the slightest interest in this abundant visual legacy of the American Everyman. There are only about sixty family albums in the George Eastman House in Rochester, New York, but Jonathan Garlock's survey of that same community turned up evidence that more than half the people surveyed possessed family photographs (numbering between one and five hundred) in drawers and envelopes, and especially in albums.[113]

From 1974 to 1976, the Family Folklife Program at the Smithsonian Institution conducted oral history interviews with more than five thousand local residents and visitors to Washington, D.C. The folklorists asked those interviewed about the stories, expressions, and traditions that encapsulated their families' past experiences and could characterize their relationships in the present. The researchers also asked people how their families preserved shared experiences. Keeping family photos, family photo albums, along with home movies, slides, and forms of needlework were among the most frequent methods of historical preservation.

Recognizing that the family album is the most common and in many cases the only unified, conscious document of a family's history, Amy Kotkin (who worked on the Family Folklife Program) recommends that we interrogate this text as we would any other work of history: Who made the album? When was it made? How was it made? Where is it kept? What can we say about the way that images are arranged, in terms of pose and setting? What processes of selection of images have taken place from the total number of images available? What processes of editing and juxtaposition have been imposed upon the images? Is it possible to know what kind of emotional attachment there was (is) to the album?[114]

Historians have only scratched the surface of the enormous potential of vernacular photographs found in family photograph albums. Their research value probably lies not in their proclivity to detail life as it is, but in their tendency to express communal ideals, beliefs, and attitudes. On an immediate level, they seem to represent shared notions of appropriate moments to photograph. Stanley Milgram, a social psychologist, recognized this phenomenon and notes that, while we are free to photograph anything we want, we in fact do not. "Photography," he claims, "extends two psychological boundaries, perception and memory. . . . It is essentially a future-oriented art."[115] Milgram's observation, in addition to being a valuable caveat to remember when critically evaluating photographic imagery, may also help explain photography's enormous popularity in America, a nation that Alexis de Toqueville thought to be the most future-conscious in the history of mankind.

Acknowledging that we tend to take photographs according to what we want to remember, and how we want to be remembered, it must be admitted that family photographs represent a stylized reality. The researchers at the Family Folklife Program still concluded that, on at least three levels, social historians can legitimately use photography as evidence of domestic life.

Viewed over time, photographs evoke stories and expressions, and may even serve as the basis for family legends. As part of our material culture, their similarities in pose and setting suggest that they derive from widely shared values and aesthetics. Finally, photographs not only capture the common folkloristic events in the family, such as weddings, birthdays, and holidays, but become part of the rituals they record. Today, the act of picture-taking itself is a central part of holiday celebrations.[116]

Photography as Historical Distortion

"Cameras Don't Take Pictures," warns Paul Byers. In a perceptive article,[117] he dispells the persistent folk notion that the camera records objectively what is there for it to record, no matter the purposes, attitudes, biases, or preconceptions of the person who pushes the button. Yet, not without cause, people appear more prone to "believe" in the factual accuracy of a supposedly "impersonal" photograph than they are of a painting, drawing, or engraving. Photographs quickly became, and still are, acceptable legal evidence. That trust, of course, is often naive; the camera *can* lie, as often and as cleverly as any other tool wielded by people intent on telling lies. And even in the best of cases, where the photographer is as honest as one can wish, his picture will inevitably show only what the particular lens on the camera is capable of showing in the way of depth, clarity, and spatial relations. The very frame of the photograph is itself something of a distortion or imposition of artificiality; had we been present at the scene, standing where the camera stood, we all know that we would have seen more than what the frame or the exposure allows us to see. Cropping of a scene cuts off the viewer from other details that may well be relevant to an understanding of the picture.

In the past, the lengthy exposures and high sensivity to the blue end of the color spectrum required by the wet collodion process prevented the simultaneous recording on the same negative of both geographical features and meteorological phenomena such as clouds. Other exposure liabilities minimized motion and curtailed picture-taking in inclement weather and at night. Until the development of panchromatic films, photographic records could not reveal accurate color relationships. To this day, photographic technology other than holography cannot easily record true perspective and scale or exact spatial relations of one object to another. Thus, historians using photographs as evidence must ever remember a simple, obvious, commonplace (yet often forgotten) truth: a photograph is not a facsimile of a total past reality; it is only a partial reflection of that past reality. Moreover, the photographer exerts enormous control over that reflection and the information and insight it conveys.[118]

These inherent limitations in the truth-telling capacities of historical photography point up, however, one of its essential characteristics and one of its major differences from paintings, maps, drawings, and other originally hand-produced images: the photograph could not have been made had not a camera been present at the scene of its making. Photographs cannot be made from memory. A photographer does not retire to a studio to render a scene he has witnessed; he makes the rendering at the same time that he witnesses the scene. Of course, many artists also paint or draw before a living scene, but the painting's "past" is the imagination of the painter, not the light rays that once passed through a lens on to a plate or film. Unlike the painter's brush, the camera makes its exposure and its record on film almost instantaneously.

To be sure, the photographer has considerable leeway in the darkroom to alter tones and to crop the negative or print even further; he may also retouch or manipulate the image in other ways. To paraphrase Byers, cameras don't develop or print pictures. But when the photographer does airbrush, "dodge," "burn," or "outline," he is altering a picture that already exists: a picture formed in a chemical change on emulsified film in the fraction of a second measured by the click of the shutter. Any straight, single-negative photograph tells us that at the very least a camera was there at some point in past time.[119]

Since every photograph is altered or manipulated in some manner by the intention of its creator, the nature of the camera apparatus, the film, the developing and printing, a historian must account for all of these variables in his or her interpretation, recognizing that the manipulation of the images can be either honest or dishonest. As Richard Huyda reminds us, knowing which is the case becomes critical for any accurate interpretation of any photographic record:

> Honest manipulation·is present in the inherent bias of the person taking the photograph for a purpose and is restricted only by the limits of photographic technology and the practical and aesthetic concepts of the photographer and his clientele. Dishonest manipulation involves, for example, removing the subject of the photograph from its proper context. This can be done by simulating events and presenting the photographs taken as records of another event—a common practice of some photojournalists. Deliberate distortion occurs when the photographer records only those realities which support his viewpoint, for example, a passing smile during an otherwise sombre occasion.[120]

One way to unmask deliberate distortion in photographic evidence is to make a careful distinction between a photographer's negatives, the positive prints made therefrom, and the photomechanical prints reproduced from the positives in the magazines and books where most of us derive our knowledge of historical photography. Among photographic data, negatives are unrivalled as historical documents, because from them alone can we derive record of the forms and textures first recorded by the camera. When they survive, the historian should always go to the negatives, since they are the primary source of his photographic evidence. Alterations, even in their most sophisticated forms, are usually detectable on a negative, whereas they might pass unnoticed on a positive print or a published photograph.[121]

Yet even when a negative is available, the image it records is a storyless fragment; photographs are basically nonnarrative, as well as nonfictitious. What have historians—whose function has always been that of narrative storytellers—made of such evidence? How have the historical interpretations of historical photography promoted or perpetuated historical distortions? How can historians overcome the range of nettlesome methodological dilemmas such as measurement of change, evidential veracity, sampling, modes of communicating research, reactivity, representativeness, and objectivity? How do we surmount the fecklessness of historical preservation that, quite by accident, salvages certain photographs and confines others to oblivion?[122]

Answering the first question is relatively easy, since, with the exception of the model works cited previously in the discussion of "Photography as Historical Interpretation," most of the serious historical scholarship that has used photography to tell American history has been descriptive or analytical, rather than narrative. Issues of using photographic imagery to monitor change over time, to ascertain its meaning in a broad cultural context, and to relate such understanding, in an appropriate narrative form, should be on the future agenda of every historian intrigued by the abundant yet elusive evidence that is American historical photography.[123]

What should *not* be permitted on that agenda is the tendency, encouraged by pop psychologists and some psycho-historians, to overinterpret "the hidden psychological meaning of personal and public photographs."[124] Too often, interpreters of a historical photograph move from the literal content of a single document to its alleged symbolic meaning, deducing, from such symbolism, far-reaching conclusions supposedly applicable (despite the limited data base) to a vast expanse of historical time and universal human experience. Without a doubt, the historian should attempt to get inside the mind of the photographer, to ferret out his intentions, or to point out ways in which his picture may say even more than he realized or intended. But as Alan Trachtenberg (one of the most astute practitioners of the myth-and-symbol, interpretive school of American Studies and material culture scholarship) acknowledges, "Symbolic interpretation is an enterprise full of risks, not the least of which is the temptation to be reckless, to venture guesses without evidence. Like all pictures, photographs invite interpretations, but the interpreter needs some controls upon his own imagination, some limits, and a boundary between sense and non-sense."[125]

Michael Lesy's much-touted *Wisconsin Death Trip* (New York: Pantheon, 1973) has been severely critized by his fellow historians for overstepping those limits and that boundary in his use of historical imagery. To present enlarged images of the staring eyes in photographs taken during the 1890s in Black River Falls, Wisconsin, as definitive evidence of the suffering and mental illness resulting from an economic depression, complains one interpreter, "is bad history, whatever it may be as surrealistic self-expression on the part of the author. Those images of staring eyes are not primary evidence for the psychic history of a bleak, isolated, small midwestern town; they are the visual documentation of average people's difficulties holding still during the long exposures required by available lenses and emulsions." A second lesson to be learned from Lesy's interpretation, remarks still another critic, concerns his overinterpretation (and hence historical distortion) of photographs of the dead as evidence of the morbid world-view of the entire Black River Falls community. In so doing, Lesy overlooked the changing conventions of sepulchre photography, a widespread and appropriate ritual event of the past now considered by us to be a rather bizarre practice.[126]

Wisconsin Death Trip, despite its methodological naivete and evidential distortion, attempted to analyze a large aggregate of vernacular photographs in the Charles Van Schaick Collection at the State Historical Society of Wisconsin. If historians are to overcome the multiple factors that can distort their research in historical photography, one technique will be to use as wide a data base as possible. Another method should involve juxtaposition of certain types of images with other related images in order to evolve a comparative historical approach. Use of oral history to correct misinterpretations and to point out myopias should likewise be employed. Methodological skills can be tested and refined—in concert with students—on the abundant photographic data close at hand to all of us: the family album, or its academic counterpart, the school yearbook. Finally, historians themselves should become photographers; there is no better way to equip oneself to interpret the processes, the photographers, and the photographs of the past. In so doing, the historian, in addition to expanding his teaching and research skills, should also consider adding to the future's historical record by contributing his own photographs to any of the current research programs for historical photography sponsored by local historical museums and municipal documentation projects.[127]

*

Both photographers and historians attempt to arrest time. A photograph is a fragment snipped from the film of history, a physical impression of light bouncing off the surfaces of a past event; a history is a narrative created from both the stuff and the spirit of past and present human moments. Photography and history, while seemingly sharing a common objectivity in interpreting the past, turn out to be similar provocateurs in portraying the ambiguity and obscurity of the past human experience. Reading photography is assuredly analogous to pursuing history. Inquiry is crucial to both. One question, whether it is raised by a family letter or by a family photograph, invariably leads to another. Of course, many questions raised by the historian's inquiries or the photographer's pictures are never answered, but part of the challenge lies in the chase. That important questions are raised by historical photography cannot be denied. The validity of the photograph's enormous value as historical evidence, despite its necessary qualifications, remains intact. "If the historian will be faithful to the photograph," concludes Beaumont Newhall, "the photograph will be faithful to history."[128]

2

Mail-Order Catalogs as Resources in Material Culture Studies

"THERE'S a Haynes-Cooper catalog in every farmer's kitchen," remarks a Wisconsin woman in *Fanny Herself*, Edna Ferber's 1917 novel, depicting the Chicago mail-order industry. "The Bible's in the parlor, but they keep the H.C. book in the room where they live."[1] Harry Crews, in his autobiography of his boyhood in Bacon County, Georgia, recalls a similar centrality accorded the secular "Big Book" or "Farmer's Bible" in his family's tenant-farmer shanty. The highest form of entertainment for him was to thumb through the Sears, Roebuck catalog with his black friend Willalee and make up fantasies about the models on the book's pages. Writes Crews: "Without that catalog our childhood would have been radically different. The federal government ought to strike a medal for Sears, Roebuck Company for sending all those catalogs to farming families, for bringing all that color and all that mystery and all that beauty into the lives of country people."[2]

Numerous other interpreters of the American experience have recognized what Ferber and Crews claim: mail-order catalogs have had an enormous impact on American life. Maintaining that the mail-order business is "very nearly indigenous to America," one of its historians insists that "nowhere else in the world has the catalog house assumed the unique status it enjoys in the United States."[3] Daniel Boorstin has argued that the mail-order catalog is a "characteristically American kind of book," like the almanac or the how-to-do-it manual,[4] and that we are something of a catalog civilization. To wit: today you can send away for *The Dance Catalog, The Whole Sewing Catalog, The New England Catalog,* and *The Whole Sex Catalog.* Of course, there exist both a finding aid to such modern wishbooks *(The Catalog of Catalogs)* and a self-help manual *(Mail Order Moonlighting),* "satisfaction guaranteed or your money back," to bring out the Richard W. Sears in every one of us.[5]

Boorstin contends that rural and small-town Americans viewed the nineteenth-century mail-order catalog as a "Farmer's Bible," the secular gospel of what he calls "the new rural consumption communities." For many Americans, urban as well as rural, the catalogs of the Chicago giants—Ward's and Sears—probably did express some of their hopes for salvation. There is, for example, the oft-quoted folk tale of the little boy who, upon being asked by his Sunday School teacher where the Ten Commandments came from, unhesitantly replied, "From Sears, Roebuck, where else?"[6]

Let us define the mail-order catalog industry as a method of merchandising that distributes goods to consumers upon receipt of orders, placed not in person but by mail after they examine a catalog that lists the products for sale, and that delivers the goods to the customers by some established shipping service such as express, freight or post.[7] The origins of this business practice, then, can be traced (the claims of Montgomery Ward notwithstanding)[8] to D. H. Lawrence's "sharp, little, snuff-colored" Ben Franklin, the only one of the Founding Fathers also to have a chain store named after him. Although relatively few eighteenth-century mail-order catalogs have been recorded in Charles Evans's twelve-volume *American Bibliography* (1903–1934), Lawrence Romaine is persuaded that hundreds were printed and that Franklin's 1744 mail-order promotion of his Pennsylvania fireplaces and other items was, indeed, the first American example of this genre.[9] Appropriately enough, both Sears and Ward's catalogs still list Franklin stoves as available for purchase by mail.

Franklin stoves are not the only historical reproductions sold in post-Bicentennial America. Reprint publishers and remainder houses currently sell any number of replicas of an 1897 Sears, Roebuck catalog or an 1895 Montgomery Ward catalog, advertised, more often than not, by modern mail-order catalogs.[10] This nostalgia craze, in addition to being a significant cultural activity for scholars who study contemporary American popular culture, can also be a boon for those of us in American Studies who wish to introduce our students to the uses of material culture evidence to study the past. Presently, I am aware of at least eight different reproduction editions of the Sears, Roebuck catalog, extending from the 1890s to the 1930s.[11] A reprint edition of one of Sears, Roebuck's specialized regional catalogs prepared directly for the American southwest market will be published in 1980 by the University of Oklahoma Press, with an introductory essay by Patrick Butler. To date, only one reprint of a Ward catalog (the 1895 Spring/Summer edition) has appeared, but that reproduction is a valuable, completely unabridged facsimile.[12] To my knowledge, no one has yet marketed reprints of the vintage catalogs of

Aldens, Speigel's, or J. C. Penney, the three other giants of the U.S. industry. But there have been reprints of the major Canadian mail-order houses (Woodwards, Eatons, Hudson Bay), providing us with the opportunity to attempt cross-cultural analyses.[13] Finally, Sears, Roebuck has deposited complete microfilm reproduction sets of their semiannual catalogs in 130 public libraries, colleges, and universities around the country. These microfilmed editions begin with the 1896 Sears catalog and are brought up to date each year.[14] Hence, in addition to the proliferation of reprint mail-order catalogs now available, most teachers also have easy access to an expansive yet heretofore largely unexploited primary source, rich in word and image, detailing numerous facets of late nineteenth- and twentieth-century American experience.

At the present time, I know of only a few instances of teaching historians using the Big Book as a casebook, sourcebook, textbook, or "question book" of American history. One of these instances, located, appropriately enough, in the state where Richard Sears (a native of Stewartsville) got his start, is an exercise developed by the Education Department of the Minnesota Historical Society. A second is a learning activity developed by the Education Department staff at the Chicago Historical Society; a third and fourth include William R. Smith's work with mail-order catalogs in secondary school social studies courses and Jame Kavanaugh's efforts at Hobart and William Smith College.[15] A fifth is what I am proposing here.

Actually, I would like to suggest two major teaching and research strategies whereby this important and prolific resource might be employed. One I will call "Mail-Order Catalogs as Resources in American Studies." The other, in some ways a subset of the first, but in other ways an independent field of inquiry, I will label "Mail-Order Catalogs as Resources in American Material Culture Studies." Before beginning to offer several illustrative research and teaching techniques for using catalogs in each of these categories, I should note at the outset that I will also be considering the mail-order catalog itself as an artifact. Although it is a verbal document, it is also a physical object, a form of American material culture. As such, the mail-order catalog is a historical artifact that, like all artifacts, both answers and raises questions about the past. Hence, for me, the American mail-order catalog, in addition to being the "wishbook" that Nick Westbrook and others have so thoroughly analyzed,[16] is also a most provocative "question book," extremely useful in the inquiry approach to history teaching.[17] Nonetheless, despite this principal emphasis on mail-order *catalogs* as such, I recognize that they cannot be studied apart from at least two other contexts; that is, the products they describe (i.e., mail-order *goods*), and the processes that create them (i.e., mail-order *merchandising*).[18]

Mail-Order Catalogs as Resources in American Studies

Under the broad umbrella of the American Studies movement, several disciplines and their subfields can make ample use of the mail-order catalog. On the level of popular literature, for example, mail-order catalogs deserve serious attention inasmuch as they have inspired at least two novels—Ferber's earlier mentioned *Fanny Herself* and George Milburn's *Catalogue, A Novel* (1936). The mail-order catalog has been critically reviewed by Lovell Thompson in *The Saturday Review of Literature* and, in 1946, was selected by the Grolier Society as one of the hundred outstanding American books having the most impact on American life and culture.[19] Catalogs have also been the subject of hilarious satire and parody, such as the *Rears and Robust Mail Order Catalogue for Spring/Summer/Fall/Winter* (1940)—a six-hundred-page volume interlarded with lessons about sex gleaned from pages advertising underclothing and the pharmacy in real catalogs, numerous spoofs on WPA workers and FDR's New Deal, plus textural samples of every type of toilet tissue that you would expect a complete mail-order supply house to offer, from cellophane ("For People Who Like to See What They are Doing") to ditto sheets ("For People Who Like to Make an Impression").[20]

All written literature—popular, folk, or classic—is simultaneously a commodity, a physical art object, a cultural window, an example of communications theory and practice, and a medium for imaginative and abstracted expression. Recognizing these multiple dimensions of literature, Fred Schroeder has evaluated the mail-order catalog as a prime example of a popular literary document. Catalog terminology, grammar, and syntax, he argues, served to standardize the American language, inasmuch as the dialect of the Chicago-based mail-order houses homogenized the nomenclature of much American material culture. For example, what is still known in the rural South as a "sling-blade" or "slam-bang" must be ordered from Sears by recognizing a catalog picture in which it is labeled a "weed-cutter."[21]

Much like the New England primer of the seventeenth century, the Sears catalog of the nineteenth doubled as a school reader, text, and encyclopedia (see fig. 5) in many one-room schoolhouses. From it, children were drilled in reading and spelling; they practiced arithmetic by filling out orders and adding sums; they did geography from its postal-zone maps; and tried drawing by tracing the catalog models. Novelist Harry Crews credits the Sears catalogs of his youth with being a primary catalyst for his literary career: he claims he spent all his childhood making up outlandish stories about the people he found on the catalog's pages.[22]

Researchers might consider mail-order catalogs as another form of the American almanac, since the "Big Books" often contained inspirational readings, bits of verse, cracker-barrel wisdom, epigrams, farming and household tips, all interlaced with pictorial materials and merchandising advertisements. Sayings from Franklin's "Poor Richard"—"A good workman requires good tools," or "He who hesitates is lost"—abound throughout the catalogs. Montgomery Ward, upon realizing this characteristic of his catalogs, began issuing a separate publication called the *Almanac For 1897: A Book of Practical Information for the Farmer and the Stock Raiser.*[23]

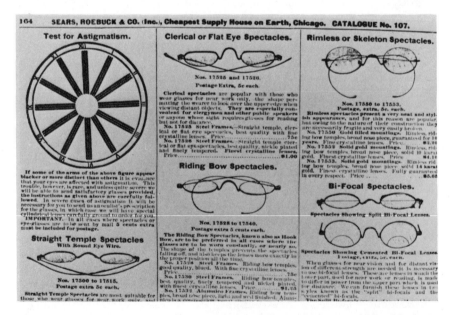

Fig. 5. Appealing to the American penchant for self-help, the Sears, Roebuck Catalog of 1898 provided do-it-yourself optical care for astigmatism. Catalogs also contained detailed instructions on taking measurements for ready-made clothing.—Courtesy Sears, Roebuck and Company Archives

First and foremost, mail-order catalogs were (and are) vehicles to sell things. Consequently, they are textbooks of American economic history that demonstrate several important trends in late nineteenth- and early twentieth-century macro- and micro-economics. Since few corporate records prior to World War II of either Sears or Ward's survive, scholars have had to depend primarily on their catalogs as a key source for documenting the entrepreneurial or internal history of these firms and their founders.[24] Exposing students to the catalogs invariably leads them to investigate the business history that has been written about the companies. Such a perspective enables them to grasp what an enormous economic transformation, to use Robert Heilbroner's phrase,[25] took place in America between the Civil War and World War I—an overwhelming change involving mass production, mass marketing, mass advertising, mass transportation, mass communication, and mass consumption. Moreover, the catalogs indirectly hint at other economic forces at work during the period: the decline of the small towns, cyclical national depressions and recessions, the national debate over Rural Free Delivery (RFD) and parcel post mail service, plus the prolonged and vitriolic antimail-order campaigns waged by local merchants and country storekeepers.[26] In the last instance, general store merchants and editors, such as R. E. Ledbetter in Milburn's novel, instigated townspeople and farmers to bring their catalogs to a "Home Town Industry Jubilee and Bonfire," whereupon local merchants paid a bounty of one dollar in trade for every new catalog turned in to fuel the grand *auto-da-fe* staged in the town's public square.[27] This bitter, but as yet largely unresearched, example of economic conflict prompted, among other things, the epithets surrounding mail-order merchandising that have become part of the American language: "Monkey Ward's," "Rears and Robust," "Shears and Sawbuck," "Shears and Rears."[28]

If interrogated carefully, the mail-order catalog (particularly the book's order instructions and explanation of business policies) provides evidence of what two revisionist historians, one writing at the peak of mail-order merchandising (Ida Tarbell, *The Nationalizing of Business, 1878–1898*) and one our contemporary (Robert Wiebe, *The Search For Order, 1877–1920*), have recognized as a central tendency of modern American corporate enterprise.[29] The search for order, efficiency, rational planning, automation, and high productivity is nowhere more graphically or unashamedly portrayed than in successive catalogs containing detailed descriptions and illustrations of these Chicago firms' growth in national business. Sears even marketed fifty stereograph views of its "mail-order army," thousands of men and women shown working at their desks, receiving orders, processing orders, mailing orders. These "Views of Sears, Roebuck and Company" were first sold complete with a leatherette case and a stereoscope for fifty cents.[30] Extant in many local historical society collections, this set of fifty stereographs provides an excellent pictorial source for illustrating the internal operations of a national corporation (at least as projected by company management) and a graphic example of Frederick Taylor's principles of *Scientific Management.*[31]

Unfortunately, we know little about those people who purchased Sears' stereographs or any of the thousands of other items for sale in the 1908 catalog. Without a doubt, the biggest questions raised by the "Big Book" for the economic historian are: Who were its customers? Who bought what, when, where, how often, and in what quality? Were customers as rural, as midwestern, as agrarian as our conventional wisdom and history textbooks suggest? In brief, is it possible, in addition to gaining insight into entrepreneurial history and mercantile history, to achieve some understanding of consumer history? Can the self-proclaimed, semiannual "Consumers' Guide" (as the Sears catalog began to be labeled, with the 1894 edition) provide us with new historical information about past American consumers?

In the almost total absence of complete purchase order forms for any period before the computerization of that kind of data, the catalogs are the only available resource for reconstructing a tentative social, economic, or cultural profile of the past mail-order consumer. Neither Sears nor Ward's has retained any significant number of their past purchase orders, primarily because it was their policy to return the order form to the customer along with the merchandise purchased. If purchase orders had survived, such data would be invaluable for the social historian interested in demography and quantification. Random orders do exist in private papers and manuscript collections in historical societies and museums, as well as in mail-order company archives. I doubt, however, even if they would be examined collectively, that they would yield an adequate sample for creating a statistical portrait of the material needs and wants of late nineteenth-century lower/middle class American consumers. They simply lack the comprehensiveness of, for instance, the household inventories and probate records that are being used by social historians to research consumers in the late seventeenth century.[32]

Nonetheless, the mail-order catalog can be a heuristic tool in teaching social history within an American Studies context. Deborah and William Andrews, Susan May Strasser, Elizabeth Baker, and Ruth Schwartz

Cowan offer us scholarly approaches to domestic material culture evidence equally applicable to mail-order research.[33] Cowan's study ("The 'Industrial Revolution' in the Home: Household Technology and Social Change in the Twentieth Century"), for example, investigates assorted domestic artifacts—washtubs and washing machines, vacuum cleaners and electric irons—asking the question: Is it primarily technology that influences how we live, or is it principally our changing social values that prompt innovations in our technology? Cowan's research objective is to explore the relationship between technology and social change, particularly as those forces have affected the history of the family and the history of women.

I would argue that mail-order catalogs can also be employed to investigate such questions. Moreover, the catalogs are a data base wherein one can research several corollaries of the Cowan thesis; that is, the decline of domestic service; a proliferation of child-care requirements for mothers; the unprecedented expansion of the cosmetics industry after World War I; an increase in (rather than a liberation from) domestic activities in the home; and the mechanization, electrification, and specialization of American household technology.[34] To cite a single example: when one discovers—by a systematic examination of the catalogs from 1890 to 1930—that there is a very rapid decline in the availability of an item such as sewing pattern books (particularly in the 1920s), coupled with a marked increase in machine-made ladies' clothing (advertised by repeated injunctions to "Buy Ready-Made"), a significant question is raised regarding what such a shift in material culture history might mean in social history.[35]

Social historians should also consider mail-order catalogs as etiquette books, advice manuals, and self-improvement primers. We have studied the influence of *Godey's Lady's Book* (1830–1898) and other forms of late nineteenth-century normative literature, but neglected mail-order catalogs as still another type of guide to social conduct, proper fashion, and acceptable personal behavior befitting either the status that a person had achieved or the status to which he or she aspired.[36] For some recently arrived immigrants, catalogs also served as guides in the process of assimilation and Americanization. In short, the catalog-as-conduct-book offered its semiannual readers a series of mobility patterns, role models, and even heroes to emulate. For instance, some of the most persuasive examples of evidence to substantiate John William Ward's claims for the spontaneous, highly symbolic, public fascination with Charles Lindbergh's 1927 solo trans-Atlantic flight can be found in mail-order catalogs. Here one finds artifacts such as "Lucky Lindy" aviator caps and "Spirit of St. Louis" model-airplane kits appearing almost immediately following the historic event.[37] Fred Schroeder proposes that the catalogs lend themselves to this American Studies "fact-and-symbol" approach, or, as his essay title suggests, that they can be read as "a popular icon."[38]

Mail-Order Catalogs as Resources in Material Culture Studies

As I hope is evident, I am persuaded that mail-order catalogs, whether analyzed individually, researched sequentially, or studied comparatively, afford us numerous approaches for an interdisciplinary study of the past. In my judgment, catalogs also rank as an important resource in American material culture studies, a field of research and teaching that, since the 1950s in this country, has found its most hospitable academic home within American Studies programs and departments.[39] The mail-order catalog can be used as a resource in material culture studies in at least five ways: as a reference work; as a graphics and advertising library; as a primer for artifact exercises; as a paperback museum; and as a resource for assorted case studies.

Mail-order catalogs contain immense quantities of information for the researcher seeking to identity and to date extant late nineteenth- and early twentieth-century artifacts. What Kenneth Ames has written of trade catalogs can also be said of mail-order catalogs: "They can provide a scholar with more images of thoroughly documented artifacts than he could hope to gather in years of scouring museums, historical societies, and private collections."[40] Like the analogous trade catalog (a genre of evidence that Lawrence Romaine has collected and classified and that the Pyne Press has reprinted in its American Historical Catalog Collection),[41] mail-order catalogs provide accurate evidence of objects actually in production or available on order. As Emilie Tari, Curator of Collections at Old World Wisconsin (see fig. 13), suggests: "The range of material handled by these [mail-order] companies is almost all-inclusive and covers a complete range of domestic as well as farm ware. Objects in these categories are by and large rarely illustrated elsewhere. . . . Descriptions also frequently provide valuable tidbits such as material, type of construction, color choices, and price range."[42] Consulted as reference works, mail-order catalogs therefore can yield answers to questions such as: How long were certain articles manufactured? How did design and cost change over time? How, and to what extent, were certain styles reflected in given classes of objects?

In the past, the "Big Book" has answered these and other questions common to material culture studies for a diverse lot of researchers: set designers at Warner Brothers Studios (where a complete run of Sears catalogs is maintained); scholars writing books on toys as indices of American social history; antique collectors; university drama departments;[43] historic preservationists; exhibit designers at the Louvre; directors of research at living history farms and their collection curators, such as those responsible for restoring the German Rankinen House (ca. 1898) and the Finnish Ketola farmstead (ca. 1918) at Old World Wisconsin[44] (see fig. 13). In many historical museum exhibitions, the catalog has been an essential reference tool; such was the case in two Smithsonian exhibits: "Suiting Everyone: The Democratization of Clothing in America," and the "Hall of Everyday Life in the American Past." Claudia Kidwell, Curator of the "Suiting Everyone" exhibit, found mail-order catalogs of immense value in determining what ready-made clothing was being offered and when.[45] In the historical reconstruction and refurnishing of a tenant-farmer's house from Prince Georges County, Maryland, for exhibition in the Smithsonian's Hall of Everyday Life, George McDaniel also used mail-order catalogs. McDaniel tracked down some of the former occupants of the house, as well as neighbors and then, armed with catalogs, he asked his informants to select from the books the various domestic artifacts that they recalled using in the house.[46] Understandably, in several of Chicago's historical museums depicting that city's urban history, the mail-order catalog has been used as both artifice and artifact.[47]

Oftentimes the mail-order catalog is the only comprehensive source by which a student can establish an accurate, detailed, design chronology, particularly for more mundane objects still unresearched in the modern period. Take the instance of the stove: we know a great deal about the stove's design history in the nineteenth century, but little of its development in the twentieth. A design chronology reconstructed from Sears catalogs would show that Sears offered the first gas-burning stoves to the public in 1895. Enamelled porcelain gas ranges made their first appearance in 1915; table-top ranges were brought out in 1931, with the Kenmore line of built-ins (gas and electric) introduced in the 1966 fall line. The 1972 spring book first advertised the Kenmore range with a ceramic cook-top by Corning. Any number of valuable methodological exercises can be developed by the imaginative teacher with access to a substantial chronological run of catalogs. An excellent model for developing such exercises can be adapted from Craig Gilbert's essay, "Pop Pedagogy: Looking at the Coke Bottle," where techniques are found for analyzing a commonplace object's diagnostic attributes, temporal sequence and duration, and stylistic evolution.[48]

As Nicholas Westbrook and Joan Siedl have shown on a panel in the "Mail Order in Minnesota" exhibition, the catalog can be an aid in the analysis of historical photographs.[49] Photographs of domestic interiors can become fascinating exercises in material culture research when their contents are identified and interpreted with the aid of the catalog's pictorial images and descriptive text. Local historical societies and family albums abound with such photographs. But should these sources be unavailable, there are now numerous pictorial anthologies that teachers can use, such as William Seale's *Tasteful Interlude: American Interiors through the Camera's Eye, 1850–1917* or George Talbot's *At Home: Domestic Life in the Post-Centennial Era, 1876–1920*.[50] Mail-order catalogs can sometimes provide us with a method of establishing a relative chronology by which to classify unidentified late nineteenth- and early twentieth-century photography. A photograph of a Nebraska farm family, posed in front of their sod house, for example, can be dated to the 1880s, since that was the decade that Ward's first introduced the particular type of "Montgomery Ward's calico" from which the mother in the picture made her dress and the blouses of her three boys[51] (see fig. 6).

In addition to being pictorial sources for basic artifact research, catalogs are comprehensive collections of graphic art, advertising techniques, and first-hand examples of the changing technology of printing. Under the pressure of competition, the catalog developed rapidly, not only in size but in techniques of presentation. In point of fact, the mail-order catalog can be cited as the vehicle for introducing several new developments in the graphic arts.[52] For instance, the first commercial use of the patent binding process was the Ward catalog of 1896, an edition that also included four pages of half-tone photographs showing baby bonnets and corsets worn by "live models." Curtains, shoes, and carpets were shown in color photographs in 1889, the year when the Ward's catalog also represented the first commercial use of the rotary printing press.[53] By 1903, Sears had set up its own printing plant, turned to four-color printing, which required an improved ink to dry rapidly without smearing. The firm then had to produce a new paper that would take color printing and still be lightweight enough for cheap mailing even when bound into a 600-page catalog. Despite the numerous changes in mail-order printing technology, as late as 1905 more than half the illustrations were still woodcuts, leading art historians to suggest that it was the mail-order catalog that kept alive the art form of wood engraving.[54]

Fig. 6. Curators at the Minnesota Historical Society, in their 1979 exhibition on "Mail Order in Minnesota," used a large photomural (left) of an 1880s Nebraska farm family to depict typical Midwestern mail-order consumers beside the artifacts that they might have purchased from the "Big Book."—Photograph by T. J. Schlereth

"Advertisements of artifacts" could easily serve as a shorthand description of mail-order catalogs that were, simultaneously, automatic marketing research devices, laboratories of salesmanship, and vivid pictorial archives of advertising graphic art. Only a few historians (e.g., David Potter, Daniel Boorstin) have explored the interrelationship between artifacts and advertising; most have ignored Marshall McLuhan's forecast that "historians and archaeologists will one day discover that the ads of our times are the richest and most faithful daily reflections that any society ever made of its entire range of activities."[55] In the catalogs, however, students can explore the often symbiotic relationship between artifacts and their advertisements in a number of ways.

With the methodology provided by Erving Goffman in his book *Gender Advertisements*, material culture students can evaluate mail-order catalogs as a resource in an aspect of women's history.[56] They can investigate "Advertising and Material Civilization," as does American Studies scholar Donald McQuade and others in the recent book *Edsels, Luckies, and*

Frigidaires: Advertising the American Way.[57] Or they might compare mail-order depiction of objects with illustrations of similar items advertised in other contemporary media, such as those collected in sourcebooks like Edgar Jones's *Those Were the Good Old Days* or Victor Margolin, *et al., The Promise and The Product* (e.g., illustrated newspapers, magazines, posters, handbills).[58] Students can do sequential and comparative studies of catalog covers just as other researchers have used sheet-music covers and long-playing record jackets as material culture evidence.[59] Or they might take David Potter's thesis (claiming advertising to be "the institution of abundance and democracy") and test it against the visual and verbal data of mail-order merchandising.[60]

As catalogs once served multiple educational purposes in nineteenth-century rural school houses, they can now be similarly employed as textbooks for launching twentieth-century students into material culture studies without material objects. I fully recognize, however, that the catalogs can only provide us with images that are but reminders of objects. To appreciate scale, volume, color, and surface, one must eventually turn to the objects themselves, which is where all artifact research must ultimately focus. Yet, as a primer, as a basic text that raises many of the perennial questions of material culture studies, mail-order catalogs prove to be extremely useful in introducing the beginning student to the field.

For example, with the catalogs at hand, one can have students test the various material culture classification systems that have been devised by E. McClung Fleming, Charles Montgomery, and Sidney Browner.[61] Researchers can use catalogs to chart the year-by-year impact of a new energy source, such as electricity, and its expanding influence on, say, the material culture of the American home or farm with the advent of the Rural Electrification Administration. Instances of innovation and invention likewise surface on the catalog's pages where, if the new product is truly a breakthrough, subsequent "Big Books" will chronicle its refinements. The famous 1905 Sears, Roebuck cream separator, for example, is not only a major landmark in catalog and mail-order merchandising history; it is also a significant turning point in the technological history of the American dairy industry.[62] Moreover, preliminary research on other nineteenth-century inventions—the lawnmower, the flush toilet, the phonograph, the stereoscope, the typewriter, the electric iron—can be done in the mail-order catalogs.[63] The wishbooks also contain items that do not sell when they are first introduced but then reappear, sometimes several decades later, and become highly marketable items. The Ward's catalog featured aluminum kitchen utensils as early as 1895, yet such artifacts only began to be used in significant quantities in American households in the 1940s. The catalog-as-question-book prompts the student to ask: Why was this so? Why does Sears begin selling automobiles in 1909, only to discontinue them in 1912? Why didn't the catalogs ever sell liquor? Why tombstones, but never coffins? When do they begin selling birth-control devices? Why do they stop selling patent medicines after 1906, or pistols after 1924?

The dissemination and diffusion of high style, particularly in the decorative arts, is another form of material culture research that can be monitored in the catalogs. Consider the popularization of the arts-and-crafts movement. On one hand, this aesthetic trend symbolized a refutation of the mass-produced, ornate, machine-made goods that the mail-order houses sold by the millions; on the other hand, the mail-order catalogs helped advertise the movement of Morris and Stickley. Sears and Roebuck featured three-piece "Arts and Crafts Library Suites" made of solid oak, as well as "Mission Art Glass Lamps" that burned kerosene. As early as 1902 a version of William Morris's famous reclining chair appeared in a Ward's catalog, and six years later the catalog carried a complete line of mission furniture.[64]

If mail-order catalogs are considered to be two-dimensional paperback museums, it follows that they might prove useful in another aspect of material culture work: museum studies. With a series of reprint catalogs at hand or, better still, an entire run of Sears or Ward's books, students can be assigned the task of simulating the type and arrangement of artifacts in assorted period rooms of residents with various economic, social, religious, and cultural backgrounds in, say, 1887, 1904, 1929, and 1941. In addition to exposing students to many aspects of social, women's, family, architectural, and technological history, such an exercise will dramatize for them both the possibilities and the problems of using period room settings as modes of historical interpretation.[65] Now that several museums (e.g., Minnesota Historical Society, Chicago Historical Society) have used catalogs-as-artifacts in exhibitions, students can be commissioned to write critical reviews of such curatorial publications; their critiques can serve as an excellent basis for a seminar discussion of the theory and practice of museology.[66]

Another experience might be to have students explore the similarities and differences between the mail-order catalogs as gigantic emporiums of what Thorstein Veblen and Lewis Mumford have called "the goods of life"[67] and other nineteenth-century institutions indicative of the Victorian fascination with the material world: institutions such as world's fairs and trade expositions, art and historical museums, as well as department stores.[68] Still another comparative analysis might be attempted between the material culture of the general or country store and its reputed nemesis, the mail-order catalog.[69] Research exercises could compare country-store inventories before and after mail-order catalogs began bringing goods into local communities; again, before and after the beginning of Rural Free Delivery (RFD) in 1893, and again in 1913 with the coming of parcel post.[70]

Such case studies emerge easily, once one begins to ask various questions of the mail-order catalog. Here are two final examples of the catalog as a resource in material-culture studies that grow out of my own American Studies seminars in this field: one originated in a regional studies course concentrating on Chicago's role in midwestern cultural history, 1871–1933; the other in a research seminar in American material culture having a particular focus on the post-Civil War built-environment.[71]

For more than a quarter of a century, mail-order houses sold thousands of pre-cut, mass-produced, balloon frame houses—a domestic structural innovation perfected in Chicago in the 1840s. Such prefabricated buildings left a permanent mark on rural and small town America. Much of this housing stock, especially that built in the early twentieth century, survives throughout the Midwest and deserves careful study as a part of American architectural history.[72] Part of that research can be done in the mail-order catalogs, beginning with the 1908 Sears Spring catalog, where a Modern Homes Department was introduced, selling complete homes and making mortgages on them anywhere east of the Mississippi and north of the Ohio rivers. Sears had to re-acquire a number of these properties during the Depression, and in 1934 the Modern Homes Department was liquidated. But for better than twenty-five years, anyone could buy a complete new house of a standard style from the "Big Book." Letters such as "Dear Sir, For the enclosed check please send me one house number 476" were not uncommon in the Modern Homes division. In different parts of the country, various corporations bought enough mail-order houses, creating entire model company towns or instant subdivisions, as at Carlinville and Wood River in Illinois, at Chester and Plymouth Meeting in Pennsylvania, and at Akron, Ohio.[73]

As the mail-order architecture business expanded, companies such as Ward's and Sears published specialized catalogs—for instance, the *Wardway Home Catalog* of 1925 or the *Sears Modern Home Catalog* of 1926. Such pattern books, complete with floor plans, building specifications, and building elevations were, in many ways, the twentieth-century counterparts to volumes such as George Palliser's *Model Homes for the People* (1876) or A. J. Bickell's *Specimen Book of One Hundred Architectural Designs* (1880). Local contractors planned homes for their customers by resorting to mail-order building books, borrowing from them verbatim or adapting parts of them to fit a particular client's preferences.[74]

The 1926 *Modern Home Catalog*, a book of 144 pages, provides us with a sample of mail-order architecture promotion at its height. Printed almost entirely in color, the text of the catalog promised the reader an easy-installment payment plan and cited every possible advantage of homeownership. Seventy-three "Honor Modern Homes" were listed by their several names, from "The Albany" to "The Woodland." Also listed were eight "Standard-Built" low-priced homes (from "The Estes" to "The Selby"), as well as plans for sunrooms, garages, summer cottages, and outhouses. Homes sold by mail-order companies came complete with hardware, various interior items such as closets, and three coats of exterior paint. Prices ranged from $474 for the "Hanson" (two bedrooms, living room, kitchen, bath, and porch) to $4,319 for "The Lexington" (an elaborate two-story Colonial Revival). Garages started at $82.50; apartment buildings at $2,099; and commercial structures at $2,240.[75]

In Edna Ferber's 1917 novel about mail-order merchandising, the proprietor of a general store in Winnebago, Wisconsin, reflected on the mesmerizing effect the catalog had on many midwestern folk who bought from its pages rather than from her shelves. "I honestly think it's just the craving for excitement that makes them do it," concluded Molly Brandeis. "They want the thrill they get when they receive a box from Chicago."[76] For many Americans, mail-order catalogs symbolized Chicago, and, conversely, Chicago meant mail-order catalogs. Mail-order houses aspired to make that city the country's emporium of "the goods life" and, on occasion, the font of midwest sophistication. Such commercial and cultural imperialism pervades the "Big Books," thereby providing us with semiannual editions of Chicago's famous booster press.

For example, the catalogs offer ample documentation of the railroad's role in Chicago's history. In fact, Chicago's position at the center of the nation's railroad's network influenced Richard Sears to abandon his first headquarters in Minneapolis. Through panoramic maps, alluring illustrations, and enticing prose, mail-order writers continually expounded the economic significance of the Chicago rail nexus. For contemporary American Studies students, this represents a quick lesson in the geography of a major American break-in-bulk depot and its role in the interrelation of nineteenth-century transportation patterns. "Chicago is the commercial center of America," boasts the Ward's catalog of 1895, "and is now recognized as the largest and closest market for manufactured goods."[77] Felix Fay, the hero of Floyd Dell's autobiographical novel *Moon Calf*, recognized it, too. He recalled a small town railroad depot and its "map with a picture of iron roads from all of the Middle West centered in a dark blotch in the corner . . . CHICAGO!" It was a place that many a mail-order reader could also easily imagine, via a mental map often stimulated by actual catalog cartography, an urban landscape containing a panoply of material things.[78]

Mail-order catalogs thus invited their readers to visit Chicago, either as armchair travelers or as actual tourists. For those content to stay down on the farm, the catalogs shaped an image of Chicago for several generations. That was done largely through pictorial depictions of the city's mercantile environment. The catalogs featured several sets of stereographs of Chicago's points of interest and fifty stereograph views that Sears sold of its own plant operations, as well as illustrated brochures such as *A Visit to Sears, Roebuck and Company* (Chicago, 1923).

The catalogs, bulky but engaging travel brochures that they were, enticed readers to travel to the big city, especially to the mail-order merchandising plants where visitors were given guided tours and assorted souvenirs. When Americans were abroad, the Chicago catalogs sometimes followed them. Julius Rosenwald, then president of Sears, Roebuck, even toured the battle lines of the American Expeditionary Forces during World War I, distributing thousands of copies of what the doughboys had requested most often as a memento of home: the current mail-order catalog from Chicago.

Like the Chicago it so well embodies, and like so many of that city's other symbols (e.g., the Water Tower, the Loop, State Street, etc.), the Chicago mail-order catalog is a curious mixture of crudeness and culture, provincialism and cosmopolitanism, vulgarity and aggressiveness, and, of course, abundant Chicago bravado: "World's Cheapest Store!" "World's Largest Supply House!" "The Greatest Price-Maker," "Largest Mail-Order Business in the United States," "Cheapest Cash House in America!" When Sears, "The World's Largest Store," secured its own radio station in 1924, it naturally enough adopted WLS as its call-letters.[79] Such fanfaronade, trumpeted from every nineteenth-century catalog's front and back cover, reiterated on page after page within the "Big Book," is but another example of the postbellum American delight in braggadocio, boldness, and bigness. Especially bigness, a cultural and physical trait that David Burg argues pervades so much of *fin-de-siecle* American material culture, be it monument, landscape plan, furniture, or architecture.[80]

* * * * * *

Mail-order catalogs are thus multifaceted artifacts of late nineteenth- and early twentieth-century America. In Fred Schroeder's estimate, they are laden with American values such as material well-being, middle-class equality, universal literacy, and democratic mutual respect.[81] I agree, and I think they can be viewed as texts with inordinate versatility, helpful in many types of American Studies courses that seek to explore the American experience from many different angles of vision.

For the student of American material culture, mail-order catalogs are equally salutary. From them, we learn not only of the garments of men, women, and children, but also of their undergarments; not only of the vernacular architecture of a people, but also of the tools and building materials used to construct those homes; we can extract specific data about both parlors and privies, toys and turbines. We come to know not only how things were measured and made, but also how they were maintained and repaired—the latter activities being a dimension of artifact study often neglected in much material culture research.

If anyone doubts whether or not mail-order catalogs are authentic American material culture, one should remember that the archivists of the major mail-order firms still receive orders, with payments enclosed, from customers who want products from the original catalogs or from their recent reprints. If that's not wishful thinking generated by a "Wish-book," I don't know what is. Moreover, in addition to the uses that I have proposed for the catalogs as resources for material culture studies (e.g., reference works, graphics libraries, artifact study primers, paperback museums, and data bases for assorted case studies), the catalogs have now also assumed a second life as material culture evidence of our own time's fascination with the collectible and the antique. Vintage mail-order catalogs are becoming increasingly costly and respectable objects of material culture, eagerly sought out by collectors at flea markets, garage sales, and on the antique book market. A 1924 Montgomery Ward's catalog currently brings twenty-four dollars; a 1918 edition is considered a bargain at thirty-five dollars. A 1916 Sears catalog, claiming that its company is the "Cheapest Supply House on Earth," now sells for sixty-five dollars. Not bad prices for artifacts that, after 1905, were usually mailed out free to more than fifteen million Americans each year.[82]

3

Past Cityscapes:
Uses of Cartography in Urban History

SINCE modern historical scholarship began in the European Renaissance, maps have been considered a crucial interpretive tool in deciphering the major economic, political, diplomatic, and military events of the past five centuries. *The Harvard Guide to American History* refers to cartographic data as an invaluable resource for the study of the western world in modern times;[1] it stands to reason, since all previous human activities have occurred in space past as well as in time past, that the historian cannot neglect the factor of physical location in his research and interpretation. As Gustaaf Renier wrote in 1950, "geography is indispensable to history because an event that is not situated in space is as difficult to incorporate in a story as one that is not situated in time. An historian should always have a map at his elbow."[2]

Despite the seemingly obvious usefulness of cartography in historical study, historians have been frequently accused of neglecting maps in their research, in the analysis of their data, and in their communicating with students and colleagues. Historians have been charged with concentrating on the temporal aspects of events, thereby overlooking spatial factors; it is also charged that they have expressed the results of their historical analysis almost exclusively in words and numbers, once again to the exclusion of graphic interpretation by maps.[3]

There are at least three major ways in which scholars can employ cartography in their exploration of the geographical dimensions of history: as a *source of primary information*, whereby extant maps from any previous time period can be studied for the historical data that they contain; as a *method of historical analysis*, whereby the historian explores the spatial ramifications of relevant cartographic data and seeks to correlate it with other documentary, statistical, or artifactual evidence; and as a *means of graphic communication*, whereby diverse historical information can be synthesized, interpreted, and published for a wide audience in an extremely compact format.

In the discussion that follows, emphasis is primarily given to the first of these usages (maps as historical documents), but it should be noted here that the use of mapping as both a research tool and a technique of communicating historical knowledge is, fortunately, gaining support among historians. Social historians, demographers, diplomatic and military historians have become particularly aware of the value of mapping as an analytical method.[4] The recent production of two major historical atlases (*Atlas of Early American History* and the *Atlas of Great Lakes Indian History*)[5] has both brought together new information on these historical topics and has visually interpreted and synthesized it in new ways.

In Anglo-American historical circles, the use of maps as primary historical sources, however, has been pioneered principally by British scholars. In many ways paralleling their innovative work in landscape history,[6] the British have long been interested in examining the visual history encapsulated in maps: they have argued against the viewpoint that maintains that maps are solely to be utilized by historians of cartography or by historical geographers.[7] In several valuable publications (the techniques of which can be easily adapted to the American historical context), these historians have faced squarely the problems of dating maps, the subjectivity of the map-makers, and the possible graphic misrepresentation of the facts on any old map. Moreover, they have introduced their fellow historians to an assortment of methods whereby cartographic interpretation can be done in a historical framework.[8]

For example, J. B. Harley, R. A. Skelton, and K. C. Edwards have each written extremely useful primers[9] in this regard, and Harley's small book *Maps For the Local Historian: A Guide to British Sources* is the most comprehensive of the lot in its aspiration to help historians extract the most insight from the maps they discover in the course of their research.[10] Dealing with maps and plans of towns, estates, and counties as well as with enclosure and tithe maps, marine charts, maps of communication and transportation networks, Harley demonstrates how any historical map has a substantive content and a symbolic language that the historian can learn to analyze in his quest for additional information about life as lived in the past.

Unfortunately, no comparable primer exists for American historians interested in employing cartography in their research and teaching. Periodically, bibliographies have surfaced wherein authors have assayed the "functions of geography in American Studies" or surveyed the "source materials for a history of American cartography."[11] While useful for bibliographical leads, none of these essays specifically attempts to answer questions that intrigue the historian: What is the historical value of a map? How does it affect our knowledge of the past? What does the map prove or establish beyond what is already accepted as historical truth? In other words, what historical evidence can the map be pressed to yield?

In this essay, maps—particularly those depicting an American urban environment—are asked such questions. The data base of this case-study is largely limited to extant maps of the Chicago metropolitan region. Such a focus aspires to make two simple points: first, to show the diversified range of cartographic evidence available for doing the history of a single American city; and second, to suggest the research approaches and classroom techniques that can be tried using urban cartographic resources in concert with other historical data.[12] Furthermore, Chicago has been chosen as the case study because it has long been a center for map production throughout the United States[13]; it has a rich lode of surviving cartographical material—more than 950 separately published maps (not including manuscript maps) of the region prior to 1900; and it is the only city that has been singled out for separate cataloguing in the current National Endowment for the Humanities project for a *Catalog of Maps of the Middle West Printed Before 1900* that will be published by G. K. Hall in 1980.[14]

Geological and Topographical Features

Perhaps the most obvious use of maps is in the locating and defining the spatial relations of places.[15] A historian of American towns and cities understandably needs to locate his subject in space and then attempt to assess what impact geologic, physiographic, and topographic features could have had upon its historical development. Certain types of maps—historical and contemporary—help the urban historian unravel the possible ecological factors that may have influenced urban placement, growth, and—where it occurs—stagnation or decline. Maps of various types demonstrate that simple fact.

The La Hontan map of 1703, despite its scale distortions, aptly shows, for instance, how richly, if subtly, nature had endowed Chicago with a strategic geographical location.[16] Situated astride the extensive water highways of the midcontinent, the site served a vast region stretching eastward through the Great Lakes to the Saint Lawrence River and then to the Atlantic, northward into Canada, westward through the Missouri River system to the Rocky Mountains, and southward to the Gulf of Mexico.

Using Chicago as a primary example, geographer Peirce Lewis has prepared a fascinating map exercise[17] showing geography students how to understand the reason why many American cities are located where they are; also demonstrated is what role factors like streams, rapids, or falls location, portage points, mountain barriers and passes, river bends, peninsulas, marshes, and drastic changes in terrain have played in American urban development. Lewis's four-part analysis (break-in-bulk points, power sources, mineral sources, amenity sites) avoids any claim of strict geo-determinism; his approach is merely a valuable heuristic tool easily adapted by the urban historian to stimulate student inquiry as to how the natural environment can favor the location and the expansion of a city.

In seeking to make connections between extant historical features of a cityscape and its original land forms, a geographer such as Lewis makes extensive use of topographical maps.[18] Since the Chicago region has been mapped topographically four different times, the historian can employ this resource to monitor various changes at four different chronological periods. By comparing the *Metropolitan District of Chicago Report of Drainage and Water Supply Map* (1886–1887) with the Chicago maps in William C. Alden's *Geologic Atlas of the United States* (1902) and then with the twentieth-century U.S. Geological Series maps and revisions for the Chicago area (e.g., in 1929, 1932, 1939, 1963), the urban historian can trace landfill patterns, shifts in spatial relationships, as well as the transformation of open land for changing urban purposes.[19] In the case of Chicago, it is particularly fascinating to watch the changes in the shoreline and debouchment of the Chicago River.[20]

Such urban maps often show how geological history can be a determinant in a city's building material or growth patterns. As demonstrated by various cartographers, as well as by the excellent study by H. B. Wilman,[21] the metropolitan Chicago area is rich in Niagara limestone deposits. Quarry sites documenting this geological past still dot the cityscape (e.g., Stearns Quarry at 28th and Halsted streets) and the city's street maps, as do important buildings such as W. W. Boyington's famous Water Tower constructed of the local limestone. Maps of south Chicago, particularly of the Joliet area, show numerous quarry sites from which "Athens marble" (Chicago braggadocio for Joliet limestone) was extracted for the facades of many southside row-house blocks. Other maps elaborate on the location and content of former barrow pits, pit mines, slag piles, and surface mines, giving a researcher a vivid picture of the way an area's natural resources (sand, crushed rock, gravel, lime, clay, and so on) were used before being covered over with concrete and asphalt.

Philip Hansen of the Education Department in Chicago's Field Museum of Natural History has developed an excellent teaching packet, *Chicago Area Geology*, [22] that comes equipped with maps that depict Chicago in 1821 with mylar overlays showing subsequent land use and transportation patterns. Hansen's modern maps, based as they are on enormous historical research in nineteenth-century documentary and cartographic data, are excellent examples of a historian deploying maps in my proposed third category of usage: that is, using a map as a means of graphic communication whereby diverse historical information can be interpreted and published for a wide audience in an extremely compact format.

Glaciation of an area frequently determined major transportation routes of a city, a fact easily discernible by overlaying a geological map (or a map with geological features) on a historical map depicting early street patterns or natural transport corridors. As the maps of Wilman's summary study show, the accumulated waters of what geologists and some pre-1800 map-makers call Lake Chicago (now Lake Michigan) found their way through the drainage divide via two valleys, or sags, en route westward to the Mississippi. [23] These two routes exist today as the Calumet Sag Channel and Chicago Sanitary and Ship Canal. It is not surprising, therefore, that one can see in these natural valleys the historical modes of urban transportation (Indian trails, canals, plank roads, railroads), side by side on a contemporary road map or paralleling each other as one drives along Interstate 55 in Chicago.

The retreating glacier also bequeathed to the Chicago region a series of physiographic formations that became other Indian trails and, later, highways. [24] As the ice sheet retreated irregularly, it occasionally paused long enough to permit shore currents to create spits, bars, islands (surviving in place-names such as Stoney Island and Blue Island), and beaches, as well as a spokelike pattern of drainage beds radiating out from the mouth of the Chicago River. In later times, these sandy strips were the only well-drained ground, in the spring, and the indigenous peoples used them for overland travel when the surrounding area was waterlogged. In the city plan, some of the major streets that deviate from the general rectangular plan—such as North Clark Street, appropriately named Ridge Avenue, Milwaukee, and Vicennes avenues—are fossils of these old glacial formations and well-traveled Indian pathways. In many other American cities—Boston, San Francisco, Los Angeles, New Orleans, Cincinnati—the urban landscape historian is similarly struck by the impact of natural phenomena on a city's growth. [25]

As mentioned earlier, in order to make interconnections between the landforms of a city, the historian should employ topographical maps. Two guides to this resource are especially helpful: Richard DeBruin and W. Hilton Johnson, *100 Topographic Maps Illustrating Physiographic Features* (Northbrook, Illinois: Hubbard Press, 1970), and John Fraser Hart and Karl Raitz, *Cultural Geography on Topographical Maps* (New York: John Wiley and Sons, 1975). Significantly, modern topographical maps contain more than twice as much cultural data as topographical information (ninety-four cultural symbols, as opposed to thirty-four describing purely physiographic features), but they are a largely neglected data base for most urban historians. The Hart/Raitz volume helps rectify this myopia by providing a first-rate study guide to accompany thirty topographical maps that are reproduced from different areas in North America. This how-to-do-it guide illustrates the importance of environmental influences on human activities, political boundaries, transportation networks, urban growth patterns, land surveys, and place-names.[26]

Settlement Patterns and Paths

In their discussion of land surveys, Hart and Raitz note how maps reveal former land subdivision practices. Since antiquity, societies have divided the land in different ways, according to their own customs and beliefs. Such divisions usually assume certain patterns.[27] These patterns can be part of the evidence for writing the cultural history of a society, since the way in which land is divided influences the road network, the placement of houses, agricultural methods, and the habits of everyday living.

As several excellent studies point out, there have been five principal systems of land subdivision operative in the United States: American Indian, Spanish, French, English, and the Federal Township system.[28] Since American Indians did not generally think in terms of individual land ownership, their influence was usually not a major determinant (other than in place-names) in the shaping of most American cities. The Spanish land-grant system, however, had an impact on urban areas stretching from St. Augustine, Florida, to San Antonio, Texas, to Los Angeles, California. Likewise, the narrow French long lot (usually orthogonal to a watercourse) can be found in New Orleans, Louisiana; Vincennes, Indiana; Detroit, Michigan; and Green Bay, Wisconsin.

The most ubiquitous plat format in the United States, nonetheless, is the gridiron of the American township system.[29] The cadastral grid has an ancestry that goes back at least to the Romans, but Thomas Jefferson gave it a special importance in this country by incorporating it into the Land

Ordinance of 1785, establishing a federal system for the division and sale of public lands, initially for the settlement of the Northwest Territory and eventually for the rest of the public domain that would become the continental United States.[30] The specifications and implementation of the township system have been thoroughly studied, and a copious literature exists for the general historian to consult on this important landscape determinant.[31] Suffice it to say here that if as many American history students were exposed to a landmark (in a dual sense) document such as the U.S. Land Ordinance of 1785 as there are students exposed to the U.S. Constitution written two years later, there would be a much better understanding of how so much of the American life-style—the boundaries of school districts, city street patterns, locations of gas stations and fast-food restaurants, even the spacing of bus stops—has often been strongly influenced by the original gridiron land survey.

The form of a city such as Chicago has been enormously shaped by the geometry of the grid. When, in 1830, James Thompson, who was hired by the Canal Commissioners of the new community, drew the first town plat according to the 1785 Ordinance requirements, predictable patterns of civic space, urban architecture, and transportation networks were set in motion and in place. Later public and private surveyors—Joshua Hathaway, James H. Rees, J. S. Wright, N. P. Inglehart, Samuel E. Gross—replicated the grid system all over the Chicago area because it was a land subdivision pattern that was efficient, relatively orderly, easy to understand, and eminently expandable.

Individual real estate promotion maps and various landownership maps (two of the most abundant types of Chicago cartography) vividly illustrate this multiplication of the grid. So does a current city street map, if the urban historian knows how to dissect it (see fig. 7) for clues to this type of municipal expansion.[32] One of the best guides to the enormous historical information to be found on the ordinary street or road map is Grady Clay's *Close-Up: How to Read the American City.*[33]

Since more than half the American population has taken seriously Will Rogers's quip ("Buy land; they ain't making any more of it!") and now owns land of some description, who owns what land (and who *has* owned what land) is important in any study of an urban community. Nineteenth-century landownership maps (usually done on the large scale of a city ward or a county survey) are therefore vital to the local historian. As Richard Stephenson rightly insists, such maps are especially significant because, in most American urban areas, they predate the more publicized county platbook and the topographic work of the U.S. Geological Survey.[34] Such

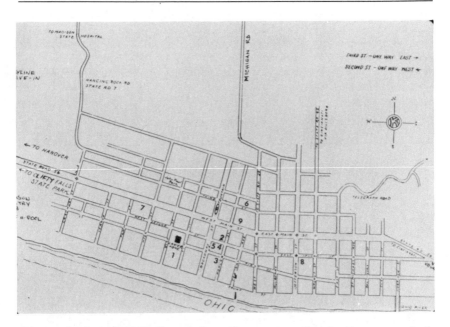

Fig. 7. A detail of a 1978 Madison, Indiana, city street map that provides an example of a typical "break-in-the-grid," a visible switch in the direction or design of urban streets that often helps the observer determine the edges of the city's original settlement and its subsequent real estate history.

landownership maps are invaluable to the social historian interested in tracing family demography; to the economic historian concerned about the shift in land use (especially from agricultural to industrial and commercial); and to the transportation historian intrigued with what roadway patterns initially may have predetermined urban expansion and suburban development.

Historian Gerald Danzer has devised an innovative classroom map exercise using an 1874 "Map of Addison Township, Illinois" (see figs. 8 and 9) from a county atlas to demonstrate how pregnant with historical information is such cartography.[35] In Danzer's inquiry approach, students work with a photoduplicated copy of the township map along with pertinent documentary materials (census data, graphic sources, etc.) in order to locate and interpret influential geographic, economic, transportation, social, and cultural patterns.[36] Since the area covered in this particular township map has historically been a suburban area vis-a-vis Chicago, the

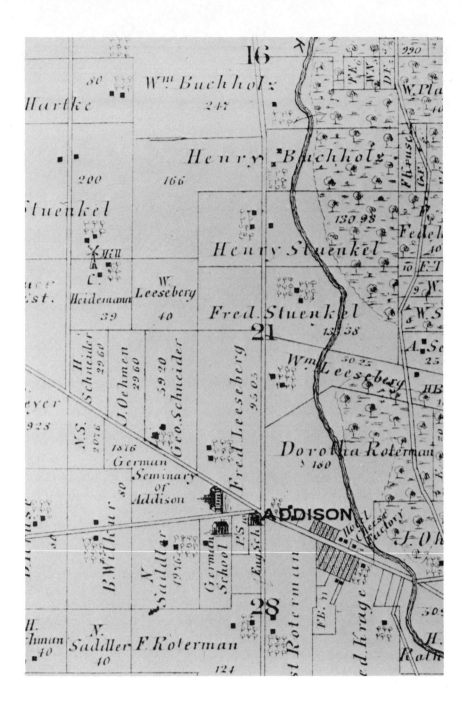

Figs. 8 and 9. Details from a township map and its accompanying engraved illustrations of a Chicago suburb (Addison Township) from the 1874 Atlas of DuPage County, Illinois. Compare the cartographic representations (8) of mill sites, homesteads, and factories with the graphic depictions (9) of similar cultural features found on other parts of the map; the map detail also provides the historian with data on ethnicity, settlement patterns, vegetation cover, and land use.—Courtesy Chicago Historical Society symbiotic relationship of suburb and city political power are explored. Such relationships in any urban environment can be investigated by using several maps in concert; for example, municipal maps delimiting the city's edges at various times can be examined along with detailed maps of local communities in the hinterland just beyond the city's boundaries. Possible mutual influence and interaction can thereby be monitored over a period of time.

Municipal annexation maps immediately demonstrate how a city grew.[37] Other cartographic resources assist the historian in discovering why it grew the way it did. In a city like Chicago, ethnic and racial migrations are one reason. Here, real estate atlases and landownership maps tell an important tale, since they often reflect changing concentrations of ethnicity.[38] When coupled with other graphic evidence—bilingual promotional brochures and maps such as John Gager's 1857 German/ English guide, broadsides, and newspaper advertisements—they enable the historian to reconstruct the changing real estate history of the city.

In this regard, the fire-insurance map becomes a useful tool. Insurance maps were developed in the United States in the late eighteenth century in response to the need for detailed information concerning potential fire risks of individual commercial, residential, and industrial structures. Few buildings in that period were constructed of fire-resistant material. In the early years of the fire-insurance business, underwriters personally inspected properties under construction. As business expanded, in the middle of the nineteenth century, such inspections proved neither feasible nor economical. Hence a practical solution was insurance maps that made available to all underwriters risk information for various American cities and towns.[39] One of the earliest (and eventually the most famous) companies to provide such a service was the D. A. Sanborn National Insurance Diagram Bureau, later incorporated as the Sanborn Map and Publishing Company, a name that has become inseparably associated with American fire-insurance mapping for more than a hundred years.[40]

"Sanborn maps," as they are commonly called, cover all the major urban centers and many lesser cities and towns of the United States. Their potential as source material for studying the history of American cities was pointed out more than eighty years ago by Charles H. Davis and Andrew M. Davis in a paper presented at a meeting of the Colonial Society of Massachusetts.[41] Only recently, however, have historians begun to take up the challenge of using such abundant data in their research.[42] Since fire-insurance maps are color-coded and usually large-scaled (one inch on the map will equal from fifty to four hundred feet on the ground, depending on the scale of the survey), they show the urban built environment in considerable detail. City buildings often are drawn to scale and are usually colored to indicate the type of construction—adobe, stone, brick, cast-iron, wood-frame, or concrete block—with symbols to record particular details such as lofts, skylights, water tanks, as well as window and door construction.[43]

By comparing Chicago fire-insurance maps, for example, one might typically discover a row of sheds along an alley that once housed a machine shop, a stable now being used as a garage or private residence, a public livery converted into a gasoline station. Older maps will show cemeteries that may be now only vacant lots or, as in the case of Lincoln Park in Chicago, a municipal recreation area. Maps from successive surveys, naturally, are another way to plot the growth of city limits and changing land use.[44] Since Sanborn maps were copyrighted, there is an enormous cache of them in the Library of Congress, but they are also available in most city, county, and state offices, as well as in local libraries, historical societies, and from the company.[45]

Working and Selling Places

Even historians who know about fire-insurance maps normally use them only to establish patterns of residentiality. In large urban environments, however, they are also often unique resources for doing cartographic industrial archaeology. Take the Charles Yerkes *Atlas of Chicago Warehouses, Docks, and Freight Depots* published in 1895. Its measured drawings and maps enable the historian to reconstruct the location, size, scale, and relationship of the city's storage facilities, its manufacturing and industrial sites, and its transportation transfer points. An earlier fire-insurance map published (1865) by B. W. Phillips Company offers architectural historians a detailed pictorial representation of a typical Munger and Armour grain elevator (a building type common to nineteenth-century Chicago), complete with accurate exterior and interior structural specifications. In the full-page illustration devoted to this building, the cartographer has also provided the historian of technology with a demonstration of how an elevator was actually loaded and unloaded, via an elaborate set of pulleys and belts, from grain barges anchored on the Chicago River.

Industrial Chicago was mapped frequently throughout the nineteenth century, as upstart businessmen, anxious to get their new company "on the map," often simply printed their own. Hence the city's industrial and manufacturing expansion and accompanying commercial bravado can be easily traced, cartographically, from the W. Phillips Company *Map of Chicago* (1865) to a *Map of Chicago as an Industrial Center* (1901). In the latter wall map, the city is even touted as the "Center of the World's Zone of Commerce."[46]

Business and commercial atlases and maps of all types (e.g., in city directories, broadsides, panoramic maps, etc.) and sizes (e.g., as small as a handbill or as large as a ten-foot-square office wall map) survive to help the student examine the city's economic growth, its architectural "commercial style," and the changing orientation of its central business district (e.g., in Chicago, the central business district has moved from Lake Street to State Street and now to upper Michigan Avenue). Comparing the E. Whitefield *Map of the Business Portion of Chicago* (1862) with the Rand McNally *Guide to Business Districts of Chicago* (1875) shows the historian the location of demolished buildings (especially after the Great Fire of 1871), the beginnings of linear ribbon development outside the city center, the strong orientation of business and commercial houses toward the east bank of the Chicago River, and the process of in-filling that was continually going on as workers' cottages sprouted in the open space behind the large business firms and factories fronting on the downtown's main streets.[47]

Lithograph maps, panoramic-view maps, and letterhead maps augment this historical exploration of the city as an artifact of working and selling places. John Reps, in his introductory essay to *Cities on Stone: Nineteenth-Century Lithographic Images of the Urban West*, suggests the multipurpose nature of these resources:

Their decorative charm and special artistic quality, however primitive in many cases, are obvious. They also provide useful clues to nineteenth-century lithographic techniques. Their utility as valuable sources of information for urban and architectural history is less well appreciated, but is equally important. Their advertising and promotional aspects no longer have any but antiquarian interests, but the identification of leading business and industrial establishments helps us to understand better the shape and structure of our cities a century or so ago.[48]

To trace such change in Chicago, the historian has several lithographic views to consult: D. W. Moody (1853–1854); J. T. Palmatary (1857); E. M. Mendel (1858–1859); A. Rogers (1868); and Currier and Ives (1874 and 1892).[49]

The majority of this urban lithography is executed in the cartographic format of a panoramic map. Known also as bird's-eye views, perspective maps, panoramas, and aero views, panoramic maps are nonphotographic representations of cities, portrayed as if viewed from above at an oblique angle. Although not generally drawn to scale, they show street patterns, individual buildings, and major landscape features in perspective. John Hébert has compiled a checklist, with a valuable introductory essay, in *Panoramic Maps of Anglo-American Cities,* [50] which yields much useful historical information about main street patterns and orientation, buildings no longer extant, and the extent of suburban development. Since panoramic maps combine a ground plan with a perspective drawing, they also suggest the nature of housing stock and the variety of industrial and commercial activities. Many have borders filled with accurate engravings of a town's major structures. Historic Urban Plans of Ithaca, New York, now publishes a catalog describing more than fifty facsimiles of low and high oblique-angle views of American cities that are available for sale.

Lithographs of urban perspectives must, however, be used with caution. As Dana F. White and Howard L. Preston point out, in their study of the largest lithography firm in the South ("Knickerbocker Illustrator of the Old South: John William Orr," in *Olmsted South: Old South Critic/New South Planner,* edited by D. F. White and V. A. Kramer [Wesport, Conn.: Greenwood Press, 1979]), considerable visual manipulation of actual cityscapes occurred, in that artistic values rather than historical knowledge often shaped the lithographer's vision of the real.

Letterhead maps are a final excellent source for writing urban business history. Many Chicago entrepreneurs placed views of their firms and factories at the top of their business stationery and billing forms. Two typical examples are those of the International Harvester Company (located on the north bank of the Chicago River between Pine and Sands streets) and the North Chicago Rolling Mill (located on the west bank of the north branch of the Chicago River). The letterhead maps of these companies were used and reproduced by the historian-geographer team of Wade and Mayer in the researching and writing of their innovative history of the city. [51]

Transportation and Circulation Networks

The two manufacturing sites just noted were located, as were many nineteenth-century industrial sites, in close proximity to a watercourse. As maps of Chicago make abundantly clear, two bodies of water—the broad expanse of Lake Michigan and the placid trickle of the two-forked Chicago River—were crucial transportation routes in the city's history. Nautical and marine charts (e.g., Captain Allen's *Chart and Map of the Improvement to the Harbor of Chicago,* 1837) help the historian plot the changes (even to the point of reversing its direction)[52] of the canalized Chicago River as well as the creation of shore in-fill, harbor facilities, and lakefront park land. The sluggish, narrow, but extremely important Chicago River with its north and south branches has been mapped by canal surveyors (e.g., James Thompson, 1820), by suburban promoters (e.g., N. P. Englehart, *Real Estate Map*, 1858) and enterprising business titans (e.g., *Business Directory and Chart of the Chicago River*, 1883, 1888). The latter map contains, for example, the location, address, and business specialty of every single warehouse, store, or factory crammed along the waterway's slips, turning basins, and minor tributaries. It is a visual redbook of Chicago economic life in the 1880s.[53]

Maps enable the historian to contrast competing urban transportation systems and subsequent shifting land use. Consider how, in the case of Chicago, railroads displaced river and lake transport and conditioned much of the cityscape. Most major trunk lines issued maps of their national systems. Railroads also mapped their major municipal concentrations (e.g., trackage orientation, depot location, and classification yard placement) and various commercial firms often published maps of railroad-related establishments, illustrating their proximity to the rail lines.[54] The R. W. Dobson *Railway Map of Chicago* (1879) is a superb example of such cartography, and it can be compared with a later edition in 1892 to trace railroad and economic expansion.

The evolution of an urban environment like Chicago can be plotted dramatically by placing next to a typical street map of the "walking city" (e.g., W. A. Bushnell, *Map of Chicago*, 1847) a map such as Rufus Blanchard's *Map of Chicago and Its Environs* (1857) that depicts the routes of the city's early omnibus lines, complete with legal cab or hack fares posted in its legend. Once the city grew beyond its walking perimeters and out into "streetcar suburbs," urban dwellers naturally needed maps to get around in that expanded geographical context.[55] Hence street maps—as well as cartography showing horse-car, omnibus, mule-car, street-car, interurban and elevated railroads, and eventually bus and subway lines—proliferated in almost geometric proportion to the rapidly changing transportation technology which, in turn, was influencing suburbanization and municipal annexation.[56] In Chicago, such maps can be complemented by excellent photographic files of the Chicago Surface Lines (e.g., aerial photographs showing changing population densities, commercial ribbon development, etc.) presently housed in the Graphics Department of the Chicago Historical Society.[57]

Civic celebrations such as world's fairs (see fig. 15), industrial expositions, or political conventions naturally spawn maps, particularly those that show visitors the locations of hotels, public buildings, churches, passenger railroad stations, and other municipal facilities.[58] In addition to city guidebooks prepared for special events, there are the excellent WPA urban guides, which, in addition to maps in the text, often include one or more large-scale city maps in the slip case in the back of the guide.[59] John Fondersmith, an urban planner, is currently completing a catalog (*American Urban Guides*) of contemporary guidebooks and guide materials dealing with all aspects of the American urban environment, including urban history and geography.[60]

Finally, the automobile, which changed the cityscape in innumerable ways, gave rise to photographic auto guides and then the ubiquitous oil company road maps. Walter W. Ristow has traced the cartographic origin and influence of American road maps and guides,[61] and elsewhere I have suggested how any contemporary city road map can be a rich historical document.[62]

Suffice it to note here that, if one took a current road map of Chicago and examined the urban space along the south branch of the Chicago River (e.g., from Cermak Road to 95th Street), one could quickly see the historical modes of the city's past transportation types in a horizontal stratigraphy across the map. Within a mile of each other, on either side of Interstate 55, are the old glacial streambed (ca. 13,500 years ago); an Illini Indian foot trail (ca. A.D. 1400–1600); the portage route of the French *coureurs de bois* (ca. 1793); a nineteenth-century drover trail and plank road that became Archer Road (ca. 1840), immortalized by Finley Peter Dunne as the tavern site of "Mr. Dooley"; the path of the Illinois and Michigan Canal (ca. 1848); the road bed of the Chicago and Alton Railroad (ca. 1860). All surround the most recent transportation corridor, I–55, which, as a branch of the Federal Interstate and Defense System, owes part of its origin to the Cold War, being a planned evacuation route in time of nuclear holocaust.

Cultural and Social Geography

Many urban maps illustrate a great variety of cultural features. Toponymy is probably one of the most valuable indicators of cultural history recorded on urban cartography. Place-names reflect a city's character. They often suggest the ethnic or racial identity of a neighborhood's inhabitants as well as the history and routes of settlement. Among the best books on place-names in the United States and Canada are George R. Stewart's *Names on the Land*, published by Houghton Mifflin in 1945, and his *American*

Place-Names, published in 1970 by Oxford University Press. The urban historian should also consult *Names*, a quarterly journal that periodically contains articles of historical interest and geographical significance.

Two general categories of names pervade most maps: names that identify cultural features, such as streets, schools, villages, or subdivisions; and names of natural phenomena. Many cultural features are simply identified by generic terms: cemetery, school, trailer park, playground, hospital. Simple identification, nonetheless, is very valuable to the interpretation of an urban environment, particularly as one watches for concentrations of institutions showing educational, medical, administrative, or recreational activities. If these features are given a specific name, such as St. Procopius High School, DuSable Street, or Concordia Cemetery, then it is possible to progress beyond basic identification and to go on to study the character of urban residents: their religion, nationality, or language, their perception of environmental features, or their sense of humor.[63]

In a polyglot city such as Chicago, many place-names are in languages other than English. As Karl Raitz has shown, it is possible to plot ethnicity on the urban landscape.[64] One technique is based on the fact that many European immigrants were Catholics who often named their churches and parochial schools for the patron saints of their home countries. To be sure, that practice was not always consistent (churches were also named for other saints and various biblical symbols and sites), but the list of patron saints prepared by Raitz and Hart is a useful general index for the identification of ethnic concentrations on urban cartography.[65]

Street names, of course, are literally everywhere on city maps. On a typical Chicago street map, for instance, they can be found to encapsulate former vegetation cover; for example, Ashland Avenue, designated by real estate promoter S. E. Warner, who named his street after the Kentucky homestead ("The Ashland") of his political hero Henry Clay and then lined the thoroughfare with three hundred white ash trees.[66] Obviously, street names recall a community's history in their recording of local heroes (e.g., Anson, Ogden, Damen, Elston); institutions (e.g., Brewery, Depot, Seminary, Church); or simply the people who first lived on the particular street (e.g., Tripp, Kinzie, Hoey, Farrell) or developed its adjoining real estate (e.g., Diversy, Belden, Palmer, Halsted).

Street names are changed for various political, social, and cultural reasons. Maps are essential for monitoring such shifts in nomenclature. Hence the *Blanchard Map of Chicago with New Street Names* (1895) is one bench mark to the urban toponymist, as is any street map brought up to date shortly after the city council instituted a major re-naming of Chicago streets in 1908 and again in the 1930s. To date, only two scholars, Richard Alotta, in *The Street Names of Philadelphia* (Philadelphia: Temple University Press, 1975) and Henry Moscow, *The Street Book: An Encyclopedia of Manhattan's Street Names and Their Origins* (New York: Hagstrom Company, 1978) have accorded a city's place-names the comprehensive historical evaluation they deserve.

In addition to being an index to the names on the land, maps are often drawn to depict the spatial relationships of specific cultural features. Thus, in Chicago, there are maps that can be used to study urban recreational activities: *A Guide to the Parks of Chicago* (1886); the *Bicyclist's Touring Map of Chicago* (1897); *Peltzer's Atlas of Lincoln Park* (1882); and the map of *Graceland Cemetery Grounds* (1876), which, in addition to being a "garden of the dead," was also a private urban park wherein people picnicked and took Sunday carriage drives for their health.[67] Other Chicago maps show boundaries of school districts and the location of public and private schools, while still others illustrate the geographical distribution of the city's places of worship.

Ever since 1857 (when Rufus Blanchard reconstructed a map of the site of Fort Dearborn as of 1812), various Chicago map-makers have been interested in depicting certain historical eras of the city's past. There is obviously a historiography of historical urban maps and that topic would be a productive avenue of research to pursue. In Chicago, the data would include both published re-creations of the city's landscape (e.g., Blanchard's reproductions of the original plot and site of Fort Dearborn and many versions of the extent of the 1871 fire) and unpublished manuscript maps. In the early twentieth century, two local historians, Albert D. Scharf and Charles Dilg, researched and mapped more than two hundred Chicago sites, primarily of the pioneer period. Their cartography, although the avocational work of highly motivated amateurs, is an invaluable resource for the historian of the Chicago region prior to 1840.[68]

Finally, in the category of cultural geography, two Chicago maps have almost a national reputation: the multicolored *Hull House Maps and Papers* (1895) done in co-operation with the U.S. Department of Labor[69] and illustrating a wide range of cultural data (ethnic distribution, family income, location of schools, churches, parks, and theaters) on the scale of the neighborhood block;[70] and W. T. Stead's infamous "Nineteenth Precinct, First Ward, Chicago" map of the blocks between Clark and Dearborn, Harrison and Polk streets, containing details of the location of every brothel, saloon, pawnbroker, and transient house in the "Levee District."

Stead's map was drawn for his muckraking, Social-Gospel tract, *If Christ Came to Chicago* (Chicago: Laird and Lee, 1894).

Town Plans and Civic Design

Both Jane Addams at Hull House and W. T. Stead (his final chapter is an elaborate utopian proposal for a model city) were extremely interested in the revival of comprehensive city planning. Any overall city plan, if one exists, is a final bit of cartographic evidence that the urban historian should use in his research. One might ask, for instance, whether the city's design imitates any of the three highly influential town-plan prototypes of the colonial era. That is, following the research of various historians of town design, does the town plan that one is investigating look like Philadelphia or Savannah, with their square-in-the-grid pattern?[71] Or like Washington or Indianapolis, with their circle-and-diagonal pattern?[72] Or like New York, with its cadastral grid and rationalized numerical street-name-and-avenue pattern?[73]

One might also inquire whether there is any extant evidence of piecemeal planning in the surviving cartography, such as Frederick Law Olmstead's 1869 picturesque Riverside, Illinois, or Nathan F. Barrett's model industrial community at Pullman, both formerly on the outskirts of the nineteenth-century city of Chicago.[74] Several excellent works assist the historian to learn what types of patterns have been imposed on the urban landscape: Norman T. Newton's *Design on the Land* (Cambridge, Mass.: Belknap Press of Harvard University, 1971) and Christopher Tunnard's *American Skyline* (Boston: Houghton Mifflin, 1953) and *The City of Man*, second edition (New York: Charles Scribner's Sons, 1970) are especially useful in identifying cartographic representations of urban residential parks, country club estates, public greens, courthouse squares, riverside promenades, civic centers, railroad plazas, university campuses, garden city developments, zoned suburbs, and land-use plans.

Of course, as Daniel Burnham's master plan for Chicago aptly illustrates (with many maps), no comprehensive master plan for a city can be evaluated without the accompanying cartographic evidence.[75] In Chicago, one can compare, in sequence, types of metropolitan planning, beginning with the 1909 Burnham, *Plan of Chicago*, through the two volumes of the Chicago Land Use Survey, *Residential Chicago* and *Land Use in Chicago* (Chicago: Chicago Plan Commission, 1942–43); to the City of Chicago Department of Development and Planning's *Chicago 21: A Plan for the Central Area Communities* (Chicago, 1973).

* * * * * *

As I hope is evident from this limited survey of the urban cartography extant in Chicago and, by inference, in most American cities, considerable local, community, metropolitan, and regional history can be read off these representations of parts of the earth's curved surface as depicted on flat sheets of paper. Maps are but another vehicle whereby a historian can take a journey into the past—vicariously, to be sure—to distant regions, there to enjoy puzzling over the historical patterns and relations he finds.[76]

The historian must realize, however, that there are limitations to map-reading. Like most other historical evidence, all maps contain distortions of reality, have certain biases of their creators (what the map-maker chooses to put in the center, what is prominently labeled, etc.) and can falsify scale and proportion. The unwary historian must remember that map-publishers have a habit of reissuing maps without bringing them up to date cartographically, merely changing their date of issuance; also one must not forget the penchant of early map-makers to use historical material from earlier sources (documentary and cartographic) without acknowledgment.

The eighteenth-century geographer John Green nicely summarized these caveats of which the historical scholar must be mindful by his suggestion that one "should not take every map that comes out, upon Trust, or conclude that the newest is still the best, but one ought to be at Pains to examine them by Observations of the best Travellers, so he may know their Goodness and Defects."[77] One of the best traveling companions for the historian new to using maps and anxious about establishing their veracity is the work of British historian of cartography J. B. Harley. In a seminal article, "The Evaluation of Early Maps: Towards a Methodology," Harley condenses and codifies the widespread literature on early maps into what he calls "a few skeletal notes on the topic, considering both the evidence of reliability on the maps themselves, and some of the external sources which assist in critical interpretation."[78] Harley's primer, which should be required reading for any course or seminar that uses maps in its historical research, proceeds first to consider physical tests, watermarks, paleography and topographic tests, and comparative cartography; then, the historian is alerted to extant sources that may throw light on early maps—newspapers advertisements, printed prospectuses, map-seller's catalogs, even works of contemporary novelists and pamphleteers. The majority of Harley's examples are drawn from his experience with British maps and map-makers, but his general framework is easily adapted to American cartography. His essay is nicely complemented by a parallel one by Cornelius Koeman that assists the historian in delineating six "levels of historical evidence in early maps," ranging from being the one and only mode of expression of a historical fact to a situation where the cartography merely supplements more important types of evidence.[79]

With these cautions in mind, the historian can venture into the use of urban cartography as a historical resource. One need not be intimidated by provocative statements such as "maps are dangerous types of evidence, too much study of them saps a man's critical faculty."[80] Instead, we need merely to remember the admonition of Marc Bloch: "Maps, like other documents or material remains of the past, are passive objects, and they will speak only when they are properly questioned."[81]

Urban cartography deserves particular inquiry by the historian. Few urban libraries are without a map collection,[82] and the cartographic content of most municipal offices is often as valuable as the statistical and documentary data that historians traditionally consult in such an archive. Maps are also one of the most varied of the major types of a city's historical evidence. In urban environments, cartography had had an application to so many branches of human activity—both practical and intellectual—that a classification of urban maps is likely to have almost as many subdivisions as a classification of books or artifactual data.[83] Insofar as they vary in purpose, in date, in physical form, in detail, and in accuracy, the application of urban maps in the reconstruction of the past is correspondingly wide and hence should be put to much greater use.

Part II
Historic Sites as Artifacts

4

Historic House Museums: Seven Teaching Strategies

THE proliferation of historical societies and historic preservation commissions and organizations in the past two decades has produced a national trend of historic house museums across the United States. A movement that began with New York state's preservation of the Hasbrouck House (Washington's Revolutionary War headquarters in Newburgh) in 1850 now boasts more than five hundred structures. American historic house museums range from tiny seventeenth-century New England farmhouses to elaborate Georgian plantation sites; from trim Gothic Revival cottages to ornate Victorian urban town houses; from log cabins to apartment houses.

The historic house museum, although often memorializing an elite society and thus interpreting primarily its historical associations or architectural novelty, is, nonetheless, a tremendous educational resource for a community's schools and colleges. In fact, the historic house can be used as a cross-disciplinary learning laboratory wherein at least seven approaches to the American past can be explored.

The following are suggestions for ways in which local teachers can employ the house museum as a learning laboratory for the study of American history, if museum staffs are also willing to embark on exploratory ventures. The seven learning strategies can be used by teachers and curators in piecemeal fashion or in any appropriate combination that seems relevant to the educational program of a specific historic house. While our concern here is with techniques and readings for students in senior high school, junior college, or the university, curators can easily adapt the following ideas for a continuing-education study group, a senior citizens' club, or a seminar of interested adults from a local historical society. The recommendations can also be used as a basis for an orientation program for a house museum's new volunteer guides, as a curricular agenda for a regional workshop/seminar of historic house personnel, or simply as a

91

primer for any museum professional who wishes to expand his or her knowledge of the enormous interpretive potential of American historic structures. Finally, curators can extract from the essay ideas for temporary exhibitions and new ways of involving the average visitor in thinking about a historic house from a multifaceted perspective.

Each of the seven approaches proposed here is particularly indebted to a specific disciplinary field of study. In order of discussion, they are cultural anthropology and folklife; environmental and social psychology; decorative arts and social history; cultural and historical geography; American studies and literary history; architectural history; and museum studies. To be of maximum use to the teacher or curator, each approach is presented in three components: *Inquiry Focus* (a capsule description of the purpose, scope, and ramifications of the approach and the questions it seeks to raise about a historic house); *Student Projects* (a summary of suggested class exercises, research ideas, curriculum materials, and field-work techniques that might be explored with students using the approach); and *Bibliographical Resources* (a brief survey of appropriate literature in each discipline that is readily available and easily adaptable for use by curators and teachers). Although this multidisciplinary perspective is presented with a single historic house museum in mind, it can be used comparatively in conjunction with other historic house museums, local residences, and the homes of participating students.

House Forms and Types

Inquiry Focus

Curators of historic houses understandably think of their residences as unique. Cultural anthropologists and material culture folklorists, however, tend to see all human shelter in regional patterns, house forms, or common types. While many American historic house museums were built in a "high" or "academic" architectural style (e.g., a specialized building often designed and constructed by a builder following a pattern book or an architect working within a recognizable style), such structures are often better understood if first compared as to house forms with the extensive vernacular buildings that surround them. House museums were frequently influenced by traditional building forms and, in many cases, have themselves influenced nearby local vernacular house types.

A knowledge of eastern Pennsylvania house types, for instance, will enable a student of that region to realize ways in which the interior floor plans of certain Delaware Valley colonial houses remain distinctly

German, although their exterior facades self-consciously ape English vernacular housing characteristics. An understanding of traditional building practices (and prejudices) helps explain what happened to the eastern urban row houses of Baltimore or Philadelphia when they moved out into the countryside. Row houses, by definition, have no windows in their side walls, but when they appear in the eighteenth-century American hinterland they often continue to be built without side windows. Or, if windows are added, they are of erratic size and spacing. A novice observer might explain the windowless gables on environmental grounds—"to keep the wind out." A student of house types would know the lack of windows is a matter of tradition (not a response to the climate) and a structural fossil that testifies to the house's original urban ancestry.

Students can learn a great deal about historic houses if they know the origins, modifications, and migrations of house forms such as the Georgian I-house, the hall-and-parlor, the dog-trot, the upright-and-wing, the four-over-four, the shot-gun house, or the **H, L**, or **T**-house types. Moreover, having students read in the anthropological and folklife literature of traditional, preindustrial, vernacular shelter types prompts them to grasp the multiple determinants in house form. Such determinants are cogently summarized by Amos Rapoport (*House Form and Culture,* 1969) as physical factors (e.g., climate, character of materials used in the building, and kinds of construction techniques employed in working the materials) and social/cultural factors (defense, territoriality, economic status, kinship patterns, sex roles, child-raising). Rapoport's final chapter, "A Look at the Present," is especially provocative in contrasting American attitudes toward private ownership, single-family dwellings, and room specialization to the domestic residences of other cultures. Whether a simple brush-and-bough affair built by the nomadic Siriono Indians of Bolivia for a single night's use, or an elegant mansion on the beach at Newport, Rhode Island, the cultural anthropology of housing demonstrates to students ways in which the form of a structure can be a strong reflection of the needs and minds of those who built it and, in addition, how it shapes and directs behavior.

In fact, as Peirce Lewis has argued, several major cultural changes are faithfully mirrored in the changing geography and history of American folk housing. In post-Revolutionary American history, he sees at least four major tendencies that every student of American housing should test with extensive field work: "(1) Increased regional diversity in house-types (and culture) between the Revolution and the Civil War; (2) reversal of this divisive trend after the Civil War, and the rapid spread of national, as opposed to regional, house-types; (3) the prolonged isolation of the South as a distinctive architectural region, long after other regions had joined the national stream; (4) an increased tempo of architectural innovation [in the nineteenth century], paradoxically combined with an increased tendency to look backward for architectural reassurance."

Student Projects

Studying historic house museums in terms of house forms and types necessitates that students learn to observe carefully, measure accurately, draw precisely, and study a building in exacting detail. Even if a structure has already been recorded by the Historic American Buildings Survey (HABS) or a local survey, it is important for the students themselves to go over the entire building, calculating and appraising its exterior and interior dimensions. Technical information on how to do this is cited below, and it is a necessary skill for any student of material culture.

The exercise is also valuable because it forces students to examine, describe, and translate three-dimensional artifacts into two-dimensional ones (elevations, isometric perspectives, general-, cross-, and longi-tudinal-sections, decorative and structural views, and floor plans). Finally, it compels one to see the structure as its builder(s) may have perceived its form, materials, and spaces. As Henry Glassie points out (*Pattern in the Material Folk Culture in the Eastern U.S.*, 1968), empathy with the mentality of the builder is a crucial focus of the folklorist approach to housing types; actually, it is an extremely valuable perspective for evaluat-ing any residence. For example, following the lead of the folklorist or the cultural anthropologist, floor plans of the house museum can be plotted, converted to transparencies or slides, and then compared and analyzed with other floor plans of houses in the local area or region, with illustrations and drawings (see figs. 10 and 11) of other house forms found in published scholarship (particularly by folklorists and cultural geographers) on the topic, and with the floor plans of students' own homes. A model to follow in this type of class exercise is H. G. West's "A Change in Plans: Is the Modern House a Victorian Invention?" (*Landscape*, Winter 1952).

Bibliographical Resources

Four sample regional studies of American house forms, the ways they vary geographically, and what these variations mean historically include Fred Kniffen, "Louisiana House Types," *Annals, Association of American*

Geographers (1936); Peirce F. Lewis, "The Geography of Old Houses, *Earth and Mineral Sciences* (1970); Henry Glassie, *Folk Housing in Middle Virginia* (1975); and John E. Rickert, "House Facades of the Northeastern United States; A Tool of Geographic Analysis," *Annals, Association of American Geographers* (1967). Here one should also consult Bernard Rudofsky, *Architecture without Architects* (1965).

Several general surveys of the development of housing as a response to cultural forces are Ettore Camesasca, editor, *The History of the House* (1971); Stephen Gardiner, *The Evolution of the House* (1974); Philip Maguire, *From Tree Dwelling to New Town* (1962); and Christian Norberg-Schultz, *Existence, Space, and Architecture* (1971) and *Intention in Architecture* (1965).

Since most current research in American house forms is being done by geographers, with strong interests in cultural anthropology, and by folklorists, journals such as the American Geographical Association's *Annals* and the American Folklore Society's *Journal*, as well as a relatively new interdisciplinary publication, *Pioneer America,* should be consulted for the latest and most innovative fieldwork and interpretations. Several works outlining recording procedures include Hartley J. McKee, *Recording Historic Buildings: The American Buildings Survey* (1970); Charles E. Peterson, "The Technology of Early American Building," *Newsletter of the Association of Preservation Technology* (1969); Thomas B. Renk, "A Guide to Recording Structural Details of Historic Buildings," *Historical Archaeology* (1969); and Warren E. Roberts, "Fieldwork: Recording Material Culture," in *Folklore and Folklife: An Introduction* (1972), edited by Richard M. Dorson.

Interior Space Concepts

Inquiry Focus

Environmental and social psychologists, as well as historians interested in demography and psycho-history, bring another perspective to the house museum. Their insights can be used to examine the historic home as a container of space, a place wherein real people once ate, slept, argued, recreated, procreated, attended to their sanitary needs, and the like. For instance, two chapters, "The Anthropology of Space" and "Distances in Man," from Edward T. Hall's *The Hidden Dimension* (1969), can stimulate an initial inquiry as to how the original inhabitants (and subsequent generations) most probably experienced and interacted within the structure. One can try to calculate what would be, in Hall's terms, the average intimate distance, personal distance, social distance, and public distance available in and around the home. By having students posit the proximate patterns of

Fig. 10

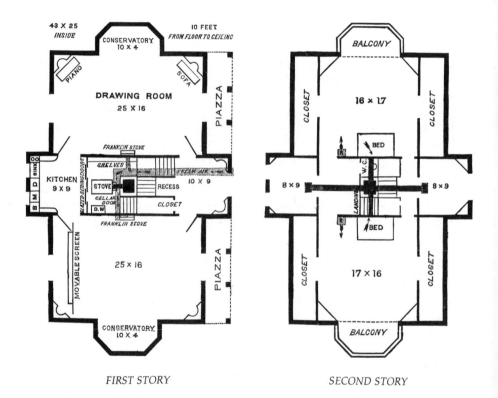

FIRST STORY   SECOND STORY

Figs. 10 and 11. Two different nineteenth-century floor plans show Catherine Beecher's proposals (fig. 10) for a model two-story residence in her influential study on The American Women's Home (New York: J. B. Ford, 1869) and a diagram and inventory (fig. 11) of a Louisville home, ca. 1840, as included in The Letters of Gustavus Wulfing, translated by Carl Hirsch (Fulton, Mo.: Ovid Bell Press, 1941).

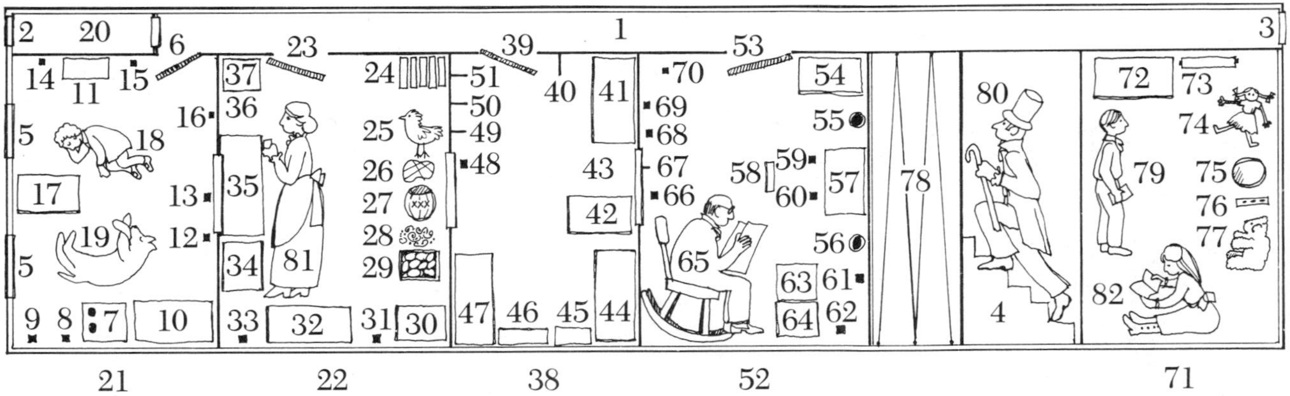

1. Long hallway
2. Window
3. Window
4. Stairway
5. Window
6. Door
7. Stove
8. Chair
9. Chair
10. Bed for Mr. Kayser
11. Linen-chest
12. Chair
13. Chair
14. Chair
15. Chair
16. Chair
17. Table
18. Fritzchen on floor, sleeping
19. Dog (Poppi)
20. Attic
21. Dining-room
22. Kitchen
23. Door
24. Cord-wood
25. Chicken
26. Ham
27. Flour barrel
28. Shavings
29. Potatoes
30. Kitchen cabinet
31. Saucepan
32. Kitchen range
33. Saucepan
34. Case with buckets of water
35. Kitchen table
36. Step
37. Box
38. Bedroom
39. Door
40. Clothes on nail
41. Bed for maid, not in use
42. Cradle
43. Chair
44. Children's bed
45. Chest
46. Fireplace
47. Bed
48. Chair
49. } Nails for clothing
50. }
51. Living room
52. Door
53. Door
54. Desk with book shelves
55. } Window and
56. } flower pot
57. Table with oil cloth where I am writing now
58. Looking glass
59. } Pictures of
60. } parents
61. Chair
62. Chair
63. Dresser
64. Glass cupboard
65. Rocking-chair with Mr. Kayser reading newspaper
66. Chair
67. Window
68. Chair
69. Chair
70. Chair
71. Part of hallway behind the stairs where children play
72. Bench
73. Blackboard
74. Doll
75. Drum
76. Whistle
77. Bear-doll
78. Clothesline over entire hallway for drying clothes
79. Carlchen
80. Lindenheim calling on us
81. Mother
82. Mathilde, spelling

Fig. 11

the historic house, particularly in comparison with others of its own period and of other historical eras, it is possible to raise and test some hypotheses about the residents' perceptual world. Hypotheses, for instance, about the pace, intensity, and civility of domestic life can be considered; so too can the issues of interpersonal relations, sibling rivalry, and the socialization of children.

Many questions are raised by this approach: How do homes reflect changing attitudes toward family, religion, community, and work? To what extent are family roles expressed within a house (men versus women versus children)? What are the expected behaviors of individuals within the various home spaces (the taboos, rituals, social conventions)? Which living spaces are most flexible? Most specialized? How is the house divided into public and private, ceremonial and utilitarian spaces? What role do real, symbolic, or psychological barriers—doors, lower ceilings, front and back hallways, side doors, or changes in wall or floor materials and finishes—tell us about the social history (and stratification) of the residents?

Robert Sommer (*Personal Space: The Behavioral Basis of Design,* 1969) provides an excellent introduction to the techniques of deciphering previous attitudes toward social and economic status, territoriality, conflict resolution, and privacy requirements from residential environments. Erving Goffman (*The Presentation of Self in Everyday Life,* 1959), likewise offers provocative questions about ways in which people express ideals of self within the house, particularly focusing on what Americans have done in the "front" and "back" zones of their living arrangements. In an essay, "Home as an Environmental and Psychological Concept" (*Landscape,* October 1975), D. Geoffrey Hayward provides a five-step method of analyzing the American home as territory, physical structure, locus-in-space, context-for-self-identity, and social and cultural unit.

Student Projects

The various historical "live-in" approaches employed by venturesome historic museum villages are one technique that might be experimented with more extensively in house museums to provide students with an extended spatial, social, and personal experience of the house. Such visits could occur at times when the historic house is closed to the public, particularly in the evening and during winter months when students would encounter a physical environment quite different from the typical sunny afternoon visits of most brief field trips.

In preparation, students should read any surviving descriptions of the house by former occupants (journals, diaries, correspondence, scrapbooks, etc.) or demographic data (genealogies, mortality rates, census data, etc.) and house records (inventories, wills, deeds, account books, etc.) that would expand their insight into the social and psychological import of the environment. They should be encouraged to indulge in the type of social psychology that John Demos (*A Little Commonwealth*, 1970) has done in his experiential and documentary reconstruction of family life as lived in seventeenth-century Plymouth Colony houses. In this context, students might also read J. B. Jackson's suggestive essay, "The Westward-Moving House: Three American Houses and the People Who Lived in Them" (*Landscape*, 1953). Jackson's playful comparison of a seventeenth-century Massachusetts homestead with one in early nineteenth-century Illinois and then one in early twentieth-century Texas gives students a splendid model for attempting imaginative reconstruction of family life in the past.

Photographs, useful in several of the approaches outlined here, provide superb curriculum materials for analyzing previous residential interiors. Using a sufficient sample collection of photos from the historic house and other residences (see fig. 12), students can make various inferences as to how previous occupants of the historic house organized and used space. Did the arrangement of rooms, furniture, and objects influence relationships among family members? Are there common or unique elements in ways that particular socio-economic classes in American society chose to organize their homes? If people are included in the photograph, in what rooms are they shown most often, and in what relationship to the objects around them?

Bibliographical Resources

A survey of the basic research in the psychology of the built environment can be found in the Council of Planning Librarians Exchange Bibliography No. 301, *People and Buildings: A Brief Overview of Research* (1972). Historic house museum curators and teachers will also profit from reading in David Canter, *Psychology and the Built Environment* (1974); J. H. Sims and D. D. Bauman, *Human Behavior and the Environment* (1974); and Kevin Lynch, *What Time Is This Place?* (1972). The provocative work of Herbert J. Gans—*The Urban Villagers* (1962) and *The Levittowners* (1967)—is likewise worth consulting.

Curators with colonial New England or nineteenth-century Victorian houses have particularly rich resources. In the former instance, besides the work of Demos, one might use David Flaherty's *Privacy in Colonial New England* (1967) and the pertinent sections on family life and residential history in the demographic community studies of Sumner Powell, Philip

Fig. 12. Undergraduate student room at Sorin Hall, University of Notre Dame, 1895. Deliberately photographed interiors, while yielding extensive data for social historians, also contain extensive biases in their predetermined arrangements.—Courtesy University of Notre Dame Archives

Greven, Kenneth Lockridge, and Michael Zuckerman. The psycho-history of nineteenth-century domesticity has been charted by Clifford E. Clark, "Domestic Architecture as an Index to Social History: The Romantic Revival and the Cult of Domesticity in America, 1840–1970," *Journal of Interdisciplinary History* (Summer 1976); Kirk Jeffery, "The Family as Utopian Retreat from the City: The Nineteenth-Century Contribution," in *The Family, Communes and Utopian Societies* (1972) edited by Sallie Teselle; and Robert C. Twombley, "Saving the Family: Middle-Class Attraction to Wright's Prairie House, 1901–1909," *American Quarterly* (1975).

Two periodicals, the *Journal of Architectural Education* and *Design and Environment*, often feature articles on residential environments as well as analyses of privacy, personal space needs, and domestic territoriality. Also useful are two surveys of American interiors for comparative study and as a source of slides and transparencies: Meyrie R. Rodgers, *American Interior Design: The Trends and Development of Domestic Design from Colonial Times to the Present* (1947); and Harold L. Peterson, *Americans at Home, from the Colonists to the Late Victorians* (1971).

Perhaps the most comprehensive published collection of interior photography to surface recently is William Seale's *The Tasteful Interlude: American Interiors through the Camera's Eye, 1850–1917* (1975). One should also look at George Talbot, *At Home: Domestic Life in the Post-Centennial Era, 1876–1920* (1976); the Benjamin Blom 1971 reprint of the four volumes of *Artistic Houses: Interior Views of a Number of the Most Beautiful and Celebrated Homes in the United States* (1883); Jeffrey Simpson, *The American Family: A History in Photographs* (1976); and, for a counterculture contrast, Paul Kagan, *New World Utopias: A Photographic History of the Search for Community* (1975). Bernard Mergen and Marsha Peters, "Doing the Rest: The Uses of Photographs in American Studies," *American Quarterly* (Fall 1977), is a bibliographical review essay filled with innovative teaching and research techniques. Curators should know the American Association for State and Local History's *Collections, Use, and Care of Historical Photographs* (1977) by Robert Weinstein and Larry Both, and also keep current with the "Historical Photographs" column in AASLH'S *History News*.

Furnishings and Household Artifacts

Inquiry Focus

For many visitors to a historic house museum, the "things" it exhibits—its furniture, ceramics, silver, glass, wall and floor coverings, and the like—are often only perceived as *objects d'art*, quaint oddities, or as icons to which filial-pietistic homage is due by virtue of their association with a famous owner or user. However, a new breed of historians in the American decorative arts and in cultural history have become increasingly interested in a whole range of common household items (kitchen appliances, hallway stands, mourning pictures, eating utensils, cleaning devices) that are seen to mirror a society's values as accurately as its elite artifacts. This "everyday" material culture—what James Deetz, quoting an anonymous seventeenth-century appraiser, calls "small things forgotten"—deserves equal attention in a house museum, along with its Chippendale chairs or its Tiffany lamps.

Student researchers should investigate and attempt to assess the cultural significance of residential spaces such as kitchens, bathrooms (or external equivalents thereof), bedrooms, stair and hall passages, inglenooks, pantries, nurseries, and the artifacts they contain. Research also needs to be done on servants' quarters, attics, closet spaces, basements, wash-houses and what material culture would be found in each of these areas. Such an approach shows students that, in order to understand the past and the present, it is necessary to study the ordinary and the typical, not just the unique and the luxurious.

To explore the history of the American bathroom, for example, students can work through Siegfried Giedeon's fascinating essay, "The Mechanization of the Bath," in a monumental book (*Mechanization Takes Command: A Contribution to Anonymous History*, 1948, reprinted 1969) that should be required reading for any course using a house museum as a historical laboratory. The material culture of nineteenth-century hallways (hat and clothing stands, mirrors, hall chairs, and card receivers) and dining rooms (table settings and eating utensils) has been imaginatively analyzed by Kenneth Ames in two studies that can serve as models for further research: "Meaning in Artifacts: Hall Furnishings in Victorian America" (*Journal of Interdisciplinary History*, 1978); and "Murderous Propensities: Notes on Dining Iconography of the Mid-Nineteenth Century" in *Three Centuries/ Two Continents* (1977), edited by K. L. Ames.

The changing domestic technologies of heating, lighting, plumbing, food preparation, and garbage removal and the artifacts such changing processes produced likewise merit study. For instance, one might encourage students to speculate on ways in which innovations in heating and lighting technology drastically interrupted the evening orientation of the family toward a shared, communal space and even to the center of that particular room, thereby prompting major implications for parent-child and sibling relationships.

Women's studies can be appropriately integrated into an American history course through the house museum. Here the ideas of William and Deborah Andrews, "Technology and the Housewife in Nineteenth-Century America" (*Women Studies*, 1975), might be contrasted with Ruth Cowan, "The Industrial Revolution in the Home: Household Technology and Social Change in the Twentieth Century" (*Technology and Culture*, 1976). Primary sources, ranging from domestic manuals (such as Catherine Beecher and Harriet Beecher Stowe's *The American Women's Home* to popular home magazines like *Godey's Lady's Book* to etiquette and courtesy books (e.g., Benjamin Wadsworth, *The Well-Ordered Family*), provide a wider cultural context for artifacts associated with "women's work." Trade catalogs, popular advertisements, trade cards, and mail-order catalogs are other avenues into household material culture.

Student Projects

To comprehend artifacts as historical documents in house museums, students require at least two basic skills: the ability to "read" individual objects, and the ability to "read" what archaeologists often call an "assemblage" of artifacts. Beginning exercises for thinking systematically about any single artifact have been developed by E. McClung Fleming, "Artifact Study: A Proposed Model" (*Winterthur Portfolio*, 1975), which recommends a five-fold classification system of the basic properties of any artifact (its history, material, construction, design, and function) and a set of four operations (identification, evaluation, cultural analysis, interpretation) to be performed on these properties. Fred Schroeder's AASLH Technical Leaflet (No. 91), *Designing Your Exhibits: Seven Ways to Look at an Artifact* (1977), is another analytical tool to help beginners study objects, and there are several ideas in the chapter on "Cultural Artifacts" in Stephen Botein et al., *Experiments in History Teaching* (1977).

Once students become conversant with individual artifacts, other exercises can be prepared to help them consider larger assemblages of material culture. Within the house museum, this is often a period room, a floor of rooms, and ultimately all the artifacts contained in the total house environment. Lizabeth Cohen's suggestions for "Reading a Room: A Primer to the Parsonage Parlor," in Old Sturbridge Village's *Rural Visitor* (1975) offers a flexible pedagogy. Scott Swank, at the Education Division of the Winterthur Museum, has devised a four-page "Room-Study Checklist" to guide his students in the probing of five major categories (spatial characteristics, utilitarian purposes, formal characteristics, furnishings, and history of functional concepts) of a historic house room. He divides the class into research teams, charging each to research the room in one of the five categories. After several weeks of independent study, the teams submit their research reports, which, in turn, serve as the "texts" for several seminar discussions on the room and its objects. Katharine H. Rich has done an innovative thesis on "The Use of Nineteenth-Century Wallpapers as a Vehicle for Teaching History" (San Francisco: Lone Mountain College, 1978) that has many applications in historic house educational programs.

One way of demonstrating the technological and consumer revolution in the American home is to provide students with reproductions of inventories for a cross-section of American parlors and kitchens and, if extant, of such rooms in the specific historic house that they are investigating. Prior to discussion and evaluation of that data, each student might be requested also to complete an inventory form listing all the domestic appliances and household accouterments in his or her present home. Provocative historical comparisons can then be reviewed between past and present American attitudes toward personal comfort, material abundance, energy consumption, and even waste disposal. Here it is also useful to have students read chapter five of James M. Fitch's *Architecture and the Esthetics of Plenty* (1961) in conjunction with part two of David M. Potter's *People of Plenty: Economic Abundance and the American Character* (1954).

Bibliographical Resources

American cultural historians have occasionally used household artifacts in their interpretations, and their work can be employed to expand students' knowledge of American residentiality. Pioneer studies by Alan Gowans, *Images of American Living: Four Centuries of Architecture and Furniture as Cultural Expression* (1963), and John Kouwenhoven, *Made in America: Arts in Modern American Civilization* (1948), have been followed by J. C. Furnas, *The Americans: A Social History, 1587–1914* (1969), and Daniel Boorstin's *The Americans: The National Experience* (1965), and *The Americans: The Democratic Experience* (1973). Russell Lynes's *The Domesticated American* (1977) and *The Tastemakers* (1954) are full of helpful ideas on the nineteenth century, while James Deetz's new book, *In Small Things Forgotten: The Archaeology of Early American Life* (1977), is a delightful introduction to seventeenth-century material culture, ranging from kitchen stools to musical instruments, cuts of meat to refuse dumps.

The interaction between technology and culture can be traced in various ways in a house museum. In addition to Giedion and others cited above, see Melvin Rotsch, "The Home Environment" and Anthony Garvan, "Effects of Technology on Modern Life, 1830–1880" in Carroll Pursell and Melvin Kranzberg, *Technology in Western Civilization* (1967); Albert E. Parr, "Heating, Lighting and Human Relations," *Landscape* (1970); and *Technological Innovation and the Decorative Arts* (1973), edited by Ian Quimby and Polly Earl. Two recent essays in *Building In Early America* (1976), edited by Charles E. Petersen, are especially valuable to the historic house currator: Eugene S. Ferguson, "An Historical Sketch of Central Heating: 1800–1860," and Loris S. Russell, "Early Nineteenth-Century Lighting."

Curators and teachers interested in women's studies should look at Alice Kenney's "Women, History, and the Museum" in *The History Teacher* (1974), as well as Elizabeth Baker, *Technology and Women's Work* (1964), and Ruth Schwartz Cohen, "A Case of Technology and Social Change: The Washing Machine and the Working Wife," in *Clio's Consciousness Raised: New Perspectives on the History of Women* (1974), edited by Mary Hartman and Lois Banner.

Scholarship on household material culture is continuing in diverse journals such as *Technology and Culture, Decorative Arts Newsletter, Journal of Interdisciplinary History, New York Folklore Quarterly, Journal of Social History,* and *The Journal of Family History.*

Geographic and Ecological Relationships

Inquiry Focus

In *Sticks and Stones,* one of the earliest studies of the relation of American civilization and architecture, Lewis Mumford insisted on relating "individual structures to their urban site or their setting in the rural landscape." He rightly claimed, "The single building is but an element in a complex civic or landscape design. Except in the abstraction of drawing or photography, no building exists in a void; it functions as part of a greater whole and can be seen and felt only through dynamic participation in that whole."

In the attempt to use the historic house as a comprehensive learning laboratory, a class should therefore evaluate ways in which its original geographical site (see fig. 14) and surrounding topography are maintained. The relationship of the house to past and present ecological features of the area ought to be researched. The position of the house vis-à-vis other residences, as well as to schools, churches, stores, factories, open or farm land, businesses, and other community institutions should be plotted and studied. Here Wilbur Zelinsky's *The Cultural Geography of the United States* (1973) and Philip Wagner's *Environments and Peoples* (1972) are first-rate primers for beginning students.

With a rudimentary background in historical and cultural geography, students of the historic house and its site can probe questions such as: What was the past landscape of which the residence was a part? How did successive generations of inhabitants experience, perceive, and alter this geographical environment? What kinds of behavior (collective and individual) might such a past landscape evoke from the residents? What types of values underlay the creation and management (or mismanagement) of the past landscape? What, if anything, survives to portray or symbolize the past landscape(s) of the home?

Since historic house museums are scattered all over the United States, any investigation of a local site must be guided by the available regional, state, and local geographical research. Two works, however, deserve mention: John Fraser Hart's *The Look of the Land* (1975) is especially valuable for anyone studying a house in a rural environment while Grady Clay's *Close-Up: How to Read the American City* (1970) supplies many visual clues to look for in interpreting the past and present cityscape. For example, Clay's definitions of "turfs" and "beats" are applicable to the environmental, psychological, economic study of any American residence. His work, like that of the historical geographers and landscape historians cited below, forces students to view a historic house in terms of settlement morphology, land usage, zoning ordinances, subdivision practices, land values, and building codes.

Student Projects

To gain a better understanding of the historical evolution of a residence's environmental relationships, students can learn to depict a historic structure in various cartographic presentations. Successive *location maps* relating the house and its property boundaries in reference to transportation networks, the natural topography, and other settlements can be prepared for each of the important historical eras of the home's existence. *Plot plans,* drawn to a more detailed scale, should also be researched and historically significant site features (natural and man-made) represented cartographically. To reconstruct such plans and maps, students will have to consult still another fascinating cache of historical evidence: cadastral surveys, city and county atlases, land-ownership maps, plat books, fire insurance and ward maps, panoramic and bird's-eye-views, and, where available, streetscape, landscape, and aerial photography.

Such exercises require students to think about a home's exterior spatial relationships and how they may have shifted over time; for instance, they can explore the proportions of front yards to back yards to side yards; the position of porches, patios, courtyards, and play areas; the location of outbuildings of all types—carriage houses, servants' quarters, gazebos, privies, root cellars, garages, or spring houses; the role of property lines, fences, and hedges; and, of course, types of lawns, gardens, and landscape plantings.

In addition to mapping all of the residential features by various means (landscape plans, survey drawings, grade levels, topographic features, isometric drawings), students should also be encouraged to construct three-dimensional models of the historic house site at different historical periods. John T. Stewart offers still another possible class project in his suggestions for exploring "Landscape Archaeology: Existing Plant Material on Historic Sites as Evidence of Buried Features and as Survivors of Historic Species" *(APT Bulletin 1977)*.

Bibliographical Resources

Douglas R. McManis, *Historical Geography of the United States: A Bibliography* (1965); G. S. Dunbar, "Illustrations of the American Earth: An Essay in Cultural Geography," *American Studies International* (1973); Alan Kublikoff, "Historical Geography and Social History: A Review Essay," *Historical Methods Newsletter* (1973); and John A. Jakle, *Past Landscapes* (1973) are the bibliographical surveys to consult on the historical and cultural geography of American housing. Ralph Brown, *Historical Geography of the United States* (1948), is the standard reference work (although it only covers the period 1600–1870), and the best historical atlas is still Charles Paullin's *Atlas of the Historical Geography of the United States* (1932).

Of special interest to students of American residential patterns are several articles in *Landscape* magazine: Peirce Lewis, "Common Houses, Cultural Spoor" (January 1975); J. B. Jackson, "The Domestication of the Garage" (Winter 1976); Melvin E. Hecht, "The Decline of the Grass Lawn Tradition in Tucson" (May 1975); Pamela West, "The Rise and Fall of the American Porch" (Spring 1976); and J. B. Jackson, "A New Kind of Space" (Winter 1969). An interesting way of connecting environmental psychology perspectives on the domestic built environment with historical geography is suggested by James S. Duncan's "Landscape Taste as a Symbol of Group Identity," *The Geographical Review* (July 1973).

Since so many historic house museums were originally built in cities, or now, due to urbanization, are located in cities, the work of urban geographers is frequently of special use to the house museum curator. Useful for teaching purposes are Raymond Murphy's *The American City: An Urban Geography* (1966); John R. Borchert, "American Metropolitan Evolution," *Geographical Review* (1967); and Thomas J. Schlereth, "The City as Artifact," *AHA Newsletter* (1977). On student use of rural cartography, see Althea Stoechel's report, *A Study of Delaware County, Indiana* (1971), on her work with students in a laboratory course in American history at Ball State University.

In addition to the leading American geographical journals, valuable articles about domestic building sites can be found in *Environmental History, Landscape Architecture,* the *APT Bulletin,* the Association for Living Historical Farms and Agricultural Museums' *Annual Proceedings,* and the recently revived magazine, *Landscape,* formerly edited by J. B. Jackson.

Literary and Symbolic Interpretations

Inquiry Focus

Grady Clay makes a special point in his study of the built environment that certain structures, monuments, or physical areas "carry huge layers of symbols that have the capacity to break up emotions, energy or history into a small space." The symbolic dimension of cultural experience has been a favorite approach of American studies scholars such as Henry Nash Smith, John William Ward, and Leo Marx. The methodology has also been successfully applied to an artifact by Alan Trachtenberg who, in his influential study, *The Brooklyn Bridge: Fact and Symbol* (1965), demonstrates how this late nineteenth-century monument became both a historical fact and a cultural symbol to the local New York community and to Americans at large. Harold R. Shurtleff's *The Log-Cabin Myth* (1967) is a parallel analysis of a more common and yet equally compelling cultural symbol in the American historical imagination. The cultural symbol approaches can often be applied to the interpretation of historic houses. The symbolic overtones of Mount Vernon, William McGuffey's log cabin, a Van Cortlandt manor, the Hermitage, or San Simeon are obvious; many other house museums have been or are becoming important civic and cultural symbols to past and present local community residents.

The American house has also figured strongly as a symbol in American literature. Washington Irving's *Bracebridge Hall*, Edith Wharton's *The House of Mirth*, William Dean Howells's *The Rise of Silas Lapham*, Nathaniel Hawthorne's *The House of the Seven Gables*, Henry James's *An International Episode*, and William Faulkner's *The Mansion* deliberately employ American architecture to frame a fictive understanding of American life. Short stories like Edgar Allen Poe's "The Fall of the House of Usher," Herman Melville's "I and My Chimney," or George Washington Cable's "Belles Dames Plantation" provide other insights. Poets ranging from James Whitcomb Riley ("Poems Here at Home," 1893) to Adrienne Rich ("From an Old House in America," 1974) also can be used as literary indices of American domesticity.

Jean Mudge, for instance, has done a provocative study on *Emily Dickinson and the Image of Home* (1975). Mudge's interdisciplinary approach draws in part upon insights she gathered while actually living in the Dickinson homestead in Amherst. Her model study, which might be applied to other houses of creative writers such as Mark Twain, Washington Irving, or Henry Longfellow, discusses not only the architectural ambience of the extant house but also various versions of "home" as a central image cluster in Dickinson's poetry and her use of spatial and residential metaphors. To locate other homes of American authors, consult the series of *Literary Tour Guides to the United States* written by Emillie C. Harting (Northeast) and Rita Stein (West/Midwest and South/Southwest) and published by W. W. Morrow (1979). Stephanie Craft has done a more selective but more perceptive cultural history of thirty writers and their houses in a book aptly titled *No Castles on Main Street: American Authors and Their Homes* (Chicago: Rand McNally, 1979).

Student Projects

A seminar can research the symbolic meaning of a historic house from whatever documentary materials may survive: diaries, correspondence, promotional brochures, county and city histories, local biographical dictionaries, and magazine and newspaper accounts. The building may have been a favorite subject for local lithographers, artists, and photographers, and their changing renderings (including distortions) and perspectives (including exaggerations) provide a class with not only clues to local artistic history, but also still other evidence whereby to analyze cultural symbolism.

Occasionally the original owners of the historic house were the deliberate or unconscious promoters of new architectural or social trends for the local community. Their house came to "stand" for something, and everyone knew it. Consequently, the house form or its architectural style is deliberately replicated in the neighborhood by envious peers who wished to make statements about their own cultural, economic, and social status. Of course, a historic house may also inspire architectural progeny that humble the parent. The key point, however, is that the historic house be studied in its cultural and symbolic relations with surrounding structures in order to understand its cultural implications. Such understanding can frequently be gathered by systematic oral history interviewing of older neighborhood residents. Such fieldwork frequently turns up valuable records (most often photographs) of the historic house as well as reminiscences of its communal meaning.

Curtis Dahl has developed a senior seminar, "American Novels/ American Houses," at Wheaton College (Massachusetts) where students do research in literature, biography, local history, photographic collections, and architectural literature in order to explore how literary, pictorial, and artifactual sources can be combined for a larger comprehension and keener appreciation of both fiction and architecture. Dahl notes (*Society of Architectural Historians Newsletter*, October 1977) that, since the great bulk of architecture in fiction is vernacular, this approach to American domestic building emphasizes, as conventional architectural history courses do not always do, the ways that ordinary buildings have a great impact on cultural consciousness.

Bibliographical Resources

Charles Moore and Gerald Allen, *The Place of Houses* (1974), helps students raise the right questions about historic houses as special places laden with cultural implications. So does Clare Cooper in an article, "The House as Symbol" (*Design and Environment*, 1972), and Kenneth Lynch in a book, *The Images of the City* (1960), Theo Crosby, *The Necessary Monument: Its Future in the Civilized City* (1970), and Marvin Tractenberg, *The State of Liberty* (1976), also describe the processes whereby structures become civic and cultural landmarks.

The applicability of the "myth and symbol school" of American studies scholarship to American residential history can be found in portions of Leo Marx, *The Machine in the Garden: Technology and the Pastoral Ideal in America* (1964); John Kouwenhoven, *Made in America: The Arts in Modern Civilization* (1948); Howard Mumford Jones, *O Strange New World: American Culture, the*

Formative Years (1964), *The Age of Energy: Varieties of American Experience, 1965–1915* (1970); and John F. Kasson, *Civilizing the Machine: Technology and Republican Values in America, 1776–1900* (1976).

Other novels that might be used in a course built around the history of the American domestic residence range from Laura Ingalls Wilder's *The Little House on the Prairie* and Washington Irving's *The Sketch Book* to Willa Cather's *The Professor's House* and Arthur Meeker's *Prairie Avenue*. Sections of Booth Tarkington's *The Magnificent Ambersons,* Henry James's *Washington Square,* William Faulkner's *The Sound and the Fury,* Theodore Dreiser's *Sister Carrie,* and William Dean Howells's *A Modern Instance* are also appropriate. Autobiographies as diverse as Henry Adams's *The Education of Henry Adams* and Alfred Kazin's *A Walker in the City* contain moving evocations of American homes and their symbolic meaning to their residents.

Several literary scholars have demonstrated how architectural metaphors have been cardinal images of value for important American writers; see Vicki Halper Litman, "The Cottage and the Temple: Melville's Symbolic Use of Architecture," *American Quarterly* (1969); William E. Bridges, "Warm Hearth, Cold World: Social Perspectives on the Household Poets," *American Quarterly* (1969); and three essays by Allen Guttmann: "Images of Value and the Sense of the Past," *New England Quarterly* (1962); "Washington Irving and the Conservative Imagination," *American Literature* (1964); and chapter II of *The Conservative Tradition in America* (1967).

Architectural Features and Styles

Inquiry Focus

The first question often raised about a historic house is its architectural style. Another approach would be to postpone such study until a detailed investigation has been conducted on the building as an artifact of demographic, technological, environic, social, and cultural history. Inferences drawn from this cross-disciplinary analysis can then be compared and contrasted with the aesthetic ambience and the architectural style of the structure.

Building terminology, stylistic nomenclature, and structural principles must be mastered before any in-depth architectural analysis can proceed. John J.-G. Blumenson's slide/tape kit, *Architectural Description: Domestic* (AASLH, 1976) is a useful program (cassette, slides, script, and bibliography) that defines the basic architectural vocabulary of American residential structures. Beginners find Blumenson's approach especially valuable since he moves from general characteristics (over-all design types, story arrangements, materials, roofs, etc.) to specific features (porches, chimneys, windows, doors, etc.).

Students should be shown how stylistic designations aid in relating buildings—particularly of different chronological periods surrounding a historic house—to one another. But more than that a seminar should come to realize that stylistic classifications acknowledge building as not just a craft but an art form that reflects the philosophy, intellectual currents, cultural aspirations, and historical associations of its time. Careful stylistic analysis, forcing as it does a consideration of early, middle, late, neo- and proto-styles quickly convinces students that stylistic periods, like most other manifestations of social change in the past, do not have sharp chronological demarcations.

Investigation of architectural designs, motifs, and features must go beyond mere "facadism," a common fault that John Maass ("Where Architectural Historians Fear to Tread," *Journal of the Society of Architectural Historians*, March 1969) rightly sees in much American architectural scholarship. Structural aspects of a residence must not be slighted: how technical developments affected architecture as a visual art should be explored; what problems may have arisen in the construction of the building should be speculated upon; the relation of the style chosen and the structural principles demanded by climate and available materials should likewise be evaluated. Where architectural drawings survive, students should try to calculate what happened between the architect's plan on paper and the actual completion of the building. Where the historic house appears in debt to pattern-book literature, these influences should be carefully traced. Where the homestead is the work of an anonymous builder, an attempt should be made to recreate the stylistic template of the individual or individuals who designed and erected the structure. More research also needs to be done on aesthetic and design proclivities of local contractors, subcontractors, and craftsmen who may have been involved in creating the total aesthetic ambience of the building.

Student Projects

Individual research projects can be assigned to trace, via drawings and chronological charts, various stylistic components and iconographic features of the historic house. For example, a detailed art history of cornice forms, arch types, brick patterns, chimney crowns, dormers, fascia details, stairway newels, mullion arrangements, or quoin styles can become the basis for an extended class exploration of the entire several-thousand-year history of Western design and decoration. Another exercise would be to divide a class into two research teams: one to investigate the stylistic features of the exterior of the building; the other to probe the origins, development, and forms of such features within the home's interior. After the research is completed, extended seminar discussions should explore the relation between the two.

The historical associations that many American architectural styles sought to evoke can be another fascinating technique of connecting later phases of American history with earlier periods (e.g., Georgian, Dutch-Colonial, Mission, English-Colonial, Pueblo, Spanish-Colonial) and of American history with European history (e.g., Renaissance Revival, Romanesque, Egyptian, Second Empire, Gothic, Greek Revival). As Laurence Lafore suggests in his study of the domestic architecture of Iowa City, Iowa (*American Classic*, 1975), "a single dwelling may instruct us in the history of mankind: in the glories and sometimes the depravities of past generations; in discoveries of engineers and chemists; in sociology and economics and taste; in the genius and folly of nations and individuals." The Victorians were particularly enamored of historical associationism in their structures, and any curator of a nineteenth-century historic house museum should consult Peter Conrad's *The Victorian Treasure-House* (1973). From it, curricular exercises can be extracted to show students how to take apart a Victorian home for its multiple parts, many of which are, of course, much older than America itself.

As has been proposed in several previous teaching strategies for the historic house museum, such historical study should be again linked to students' own domestic environments. Florence Ladd has developed a class assignment for her students in architecture and planning that can be easily adapted to an American history course based in a historic house. As outlined in an essay, "Doing Residential History: You Can Go Home Again," *Landscape* (Winter 1976), Miss Ladd demonstrates how having students explore the personal living environments that they and their parents have experienced expands their sensitivity to the history of American domestic space. Her work can be supplemented by a study like Edward O. Laumann and James S. Morris, "Living Room Styles and Social Attributes: The Patterning of Material Artifacts in a Modern Urban Community," *Sociology and Social Research* (April 1970), as well as by Sim Van Ryn and Murray Silverstein's *Dorms at Berkeley: An Environmental Analysis* (Berkeley, Cal.: Privately printed, 1967).

Bibliographical Resources

The American Technical Society's *Architectural and Building Trade Dictionary* (1974) defines building terminology from Aaron's rod to zonolite concrete. Henry Russell-Hitchcock, *American Architectural Books* (1946), is the best catalog of pattern books and nineteenth-century design manuals. Many pattern books by important American architects (Asher Benjamin, Minard Lafever, Richard Upjohn, etc.) are currently being reprinted in facsimile editions by Dover Press and the American Life Foundation.

Guides to the American historical styles have proliferated with the advent of the historic preservation movement. Among the most useful for the student of American domestic architecture are John J.-G. Blumenson, *Identifying American Architecture: A Pictorial Guide to Styles and Terms, 1600–1945* (1977); John Poppeliers, et al., *What Style Is It?* (1977); and Marcus Whiffen, *American Architecture Since 1780: A Guide to the Styles* (1969).

Various techniques for deploying architecture in the teaching of American history can be adapted from articles in the *Journal of Architectural Education.* One should also consult Richard Rabinowitz, "The Crisis of the Classroom: Architecture and Education," *History of Education Quarterly* 14 (Spring 1974). Periodicals that often deal with American domestic architecture include *American Architect, Historic Preservation, Architectural Forum, The Old House Journal, Architecture and Building, Journal of the Society of Architectural Historians,* and the *Journal of the American Institute of Architects.*

A selection of the best local studies of American residential architecture include Roger Kennedy, *Minnesota Houses* (1967); Wilbur D. Peat, *Indiana Houses of the Nineteenth Century* (1962); Bainbridge Bunting, *Houses of Boston's Back Bay: An Architectural History* (1967); Charles Lockwood, *Bricks and Brownstone: The New York Row House, 1783–1929* (1972); I. T. Frary, *Early Homes of Ohio* (1936); Antoinette F. Downing and Vincent Scully, Jr., *The Architectural Heritage of Newport, Rhode Island, 1640–1915* (1952); Bernard Foerster, *Architecture Worth Saving in Rensselaer County, New York* (1965); D. B. Alexander, *Texas Homes of the Nineteenth Century* (1966); Victor Steinbrueck, *Seattle Cityscape* (1962).

Architectural history can also be combined with humor as the delightful parodies and spoofs by Osbert Lancaster (*A Cartoon History of Architecture,*

1975) and Terence Harold Robsjohn-Gibbons (*Homes of the Brave,* 1954) aptly demonstrate.

Museum Interpretation Analysis

Inquiry Focus

A historic house possesses at least two histories: its past existence as an actual residence and its past and present life as a house museum. The history of the changing interpretations of a historic house museum (see fig. 13) is a final method of showing students both the problems and the possibilities in researching the past and of communicating that knowledge primarily through physical history.

A class can start by reviewing how the particular arrangement and display of artifacts, the conducting of visitor tours, the types of audiovisual programs, and the nature of available published materials are used in the current interpretation of the historic house. In this comprehensive perspective, the class evaluates the house museum as a curatorial publication, analyzing the form and content of the historical interpretation with much the same critical rigor as they might review a historical monograph.

Using all the skills that they have developed in the previous six approaches, students can be encouraged to try to decipher the epistemological assumptions and possible historical biases of the curators, exhibit designers, or architectural historians who have restored and refurnished the historic house. An attempt should be made to identify any evidential gaps that a curator might have faced in preparing the historical interpretation. The nature of documentation for the historical generalizations conveyed in the interpretation should be critiqued. How well the historic house works as an educational environment for various learners (e.g., from school children to adults) should be reviewed and discussed.

Historical museums, while devoted to the cause of expanding the public's historical consciousness, are often curiously myopic about their own histories as institutions. Little attention is paid to the origins and development of most house museums as part of both the history of American museums and of American cultural history. James S. Smith's "The Museum as Historian" (*San Jose Studies,* 1976) is one of the few essays that attempts to comment on ways in which the organization of present day museums reveal attitudes that Americans have held and continue to hold toward the past. History students are inevitably interested in and can be instructed by probing such a historical topic.

Fig. 13. In the kitchen of Old World Wisconsin's Ketola House (b. 1894–1900), a site interpreter begins preparations for a family meal. Many of the artifacts used to furnish and to interpret the Finnish log-construction homestead in its 1915 restoration were authenticated through mail-order catalogues of the period.—Courtesy Old World Wisconsin

Previous site plans, models of earlier building arrangements, photography of earlier period rooms, and the like provide an intriguing entry into local and national history. Moreover, this component of the historic house can be a marvelous introduction for students to museum studies and the workaday work of museum professionals. The curatorial and educational staff of the Camron-Stanford House in Oakland, California, are currently developing such an approach. For example, they are using period rooms such as a "colonial kitchen" (once a part of their house but now installed nearby in the Oakland Public Museum) as a teaching exhibition space devoted to involving visitors in their building's history as a museum. They plan to interpret and display permanently the techniques and artifactual remains of the first curators of their house: items such as traveling teaching kits, circa 1910; early exhibit cases and object taxonomies; and an extensive photographic collection. Documentary materials such as collection policies, project plans for the museum's physical expansion, staff reports, and memoranda on educational policies may also be exhibited.

Student Projects

Teaching students the techniques for evaluating house museums as interpreters of the American past can be done by acquainting them with the critical appraisals of David Lowenthal, Richard Rabinowitz, Peirce Lewis, and Irwin Richman, each of whom has been particularly concerned with what Lowenthal calls "the American way of history" and how it is presented by museums. A comprehensive outline of evaluative criteria for a class project to evaluate a historic house's interpretation can be adapted from Thomas Leavitt's proposals (*Technology and Culture,* 1968) and those for systematic exhibit review of museums. With such criteria as guidelines, students can be required to prepare written evaluations of a house museum's interpretation for a seminar discussion in which the museum curatorial and educational staff should also be involved. Students should be pressed to offer specific recommendations for improving an interpretation if they find it deficient.

Surprisingly little serious scholarship, outside the work of Alma Wittlin and Whitfield Bell, has been done on the cultural history of American museums. There is still less on the history of historical museums, except Laurence Coleman's pioneering compendium of the 1930s. Such reading can be assigned for class discussion, since it will provide students with an introductory context for another long-term class project: the writing of a history of the house museum that they have been using as a learning laboratory. As a team of cultural historians, the students should be encouraged to study their historic house museum in the context of the United States historic preservation movement, general trends in American historiography, and the cultural history of nineteenth- and twentieth-century America. Such a comparative analysis might turn up intriguing parallels and paradoxes, as well as suggest a different angle of vision on the American past. In any event, students would quickly learn that there is a changing historiography in museum interpretation just as there is in historical monograph literature.

Bibliographical Resources

To initiate students into the history of museums, one should consult standard references such as Alma S. Wittlin, *Museums: In Search of a Usable Future* (1970); Whitfield J. Bell, Jr., et al., *A Cabinet of Curiosities: Five Episodes in the Evolution of American Museums* (1967); Laurence V. Coleman, *The Museum in America* (1939); and Herbert and Marjorie Katz, *Museums, U.S.A.* (1965); Edward Alexander, *Museums in Motion* (1979).

Critical perspectives can be found in essays by David Lowenthal on "The American Way of History" (*Columbia University Forum*, Summer 1966) and "Past Time, Present Spaces, Landscape and Memory" (*The Geographical Review*, January 1975). Other critiques can be extracted from Peirce F. Lewis, "The Future of the Past: Our Clouded Vision of Historic Preservation," *Pioneer America* (July 1975); Richard Rabinowitz, "Learning in Public Places: The Museum," (paper delivered at American Educational Research Association, New Orleans, La., 1973); and Frank Barnes, "Viewpoint: Living History—Clio or Cliopatria," *History News* (September 1974).

Charles F. Montgomery's short essay, "The Historic House—A Definition" (*Museum News*, 1959), offers students a four-part classification of historic house types, while A. E. Parr provides a good overview in "History and the Historical Museum," *Curator* (March 1972). On interpretive techniques, see Freeman J. Tilden, *Interpreting Our Heritage* (1967); and William T. Alderson and Shirley Payne Low, *Interpretation of Historic Sites* (1976). To acquaint a class with the development of the period room and its role in museum interpretation, consult E. P. Alexander, "Artistic and Historical Period Rooms" (1964); and A. E. Parr, "Habitat Group and Period Room" (1963), both published in *Curator*.

Techniques for helping students develop a house museum's interpretation can be borrowed from chapter 5 of this book, "The Historic Museum Village as a Cross-Disciplinary Learning Laboratory" and the author's "It

Wasn't that Simple" (*Museum News,* February 1978). Excellent suggestions can also be found in Lizabeth A. Cohen, "How to Teach Family History by Using an Historic House" (*Social Education,* December 1975) and a primer, "Field Study at Historic Houses" in the winter (1975) edition of *Almanac* published by the Museum Education Center, Old Sturbridge Village.

History News, Curator, Museum News, and the *Museologist* are the principal journals of the American museum profession where articles on interpretation and museum history can be found. *The History Teacher,* the *Society of History Education News Exchange, Social Education,* and *Teaching History: A Journal of Methods* are other journals that often contain how-to-do-it essays on using museums in history teaching. See also Linda F. Place, et al., "The Object as Subject: The Role of Museums and Material Culture Collections in American Studies," *American Quarterly* (August 1974), and Mary Lohmann, *A New Look at History* (1975).

5

The Historic Museum Village
As a Cross-Disciplinary
Learning Laboratory

UNIVERSITY and college teachers of history have been tardy in recognizing the immense pedagogical potential of historical museums and of the artifacts that such institutions usually house. In fact, the late William Hesseltine urged his colleagues that "the artifact, in contrast to the literary remain, gives no answers to the historian's queries."[1] Fortunately, other scholars researching and teaching in museum education, historical archaeology, and American Studies have invalidated Hesseltine's dismissal of the museum and its material culture evidence as illustrative, rather than instructive.[2] In the past decade the educational services divisions of many museums have expanded the assistance they offer to history teachers; concurrently, scholars in cross-disciplinary fields such as American Studies have ventured into museums and into the use of various artifacts to interpret the American past.

Despite this increased interest and research on several fronts, the historic museum village still remains a largely unexploited resource by American historians. The educational potential of the more than one hundred and twenty museum villages in the United States continues to be a pedagogical tool to which museum personnel and academic historians should devote considerably more energy.[3] In my own teaching and research in American Studies, particularly in the seminars that I teach in American material culture, I have endeavored to employ the multifaceted resources of historic museum villages in the Middle West. Greenfield Village in Dearborn, Michigan, has been such a valuable data base and educational laboratory over the past several years that I would like to use it here as a case-study for suggesting a series of simple techniques whereby a historic museum village can be used by a teaching historian as a cross-disciplinary, comparative, experimental learning environment. In creating this case-study, I have profited greatly from my collaboration with several members of the Greenfield Village professional staff.[4]

I can best explain what we try to do with the historic museum village at Greenfield by dividing my remarks into the three major ways in which we explore the village. We try to perceive the historic museum village as:

A total living environment
A repository of cultural artifacts
An above-ground archaeological site

In brief, students study the museum village as a macrocosm and in microcosm. Through our three categories, we attempt to break down the village into increasingly smaller components for historical analysis.

The Museum Village as a Total Living Environment

In approaching the museum village as a total living environment, we explore the museum's origins, development and philosophy through published histories and guidebooks, by researching its library resources,[5] archival holdings, and, of course, by carefully examining its actual physical site as an interrelated environment system.

The provenance of a historic museum village—be it an actual indigenous historical site, such as Colonial Williamsburg (Virginia) and Deerfield Village (Massachusetts), or a latter-day reconstruction of a historical context, such as Old Sturbridge Village (Massachusetts) and Greenfield Village (Michigan)—always provokes fascinating questions of historical interpretation. For example, Greenfield Village initially was an artifactual projection of Henry Ford's recollection of his nineteenth-century agrarian boyhood in the Middle West. Beginning in 1926, the man who helped create the modern auto age embarked on an elaborate physical re-creation of small-town rural America. It seems ironic to us that the genius of the assembly line would engage individual glass-blowers, blacksmiths, and cobblers to practice their crafts. Greenfield Village was (and, in numerous ways, still is) Henry Ford's personal perspective on American history. As cultural historian Roderick Nash has argued, in a convincing essay,[6] Ford's was a view of the American past held by a majority of middle-class Americans throughout much of the early twentieth century.

In studying the collecting, curatorial, and interpretive policies of a historic museum village, I have my students evaluate such policies and the ways they have changed in the context of the history of American museums and the United States historic preservation movement, as well as the general (professional and popular) literature of American historiography.[7] In addition to comparing Greenfield's founding purpose to the historiography of the 1920s, we probe the background of similar historic museum villages—Old Deerfield Village (Massachusetts); Monticello (Virginia); and, of course, Colonial Williamsburg (Virginia)—created in that same decade of unprecedented American historic preservation. Such comparative analysis turns up some intriguing problems, parallels, and paradoxes in the cycles of both American museum practice and American historical scholarship.

In looking at the historic museum village of Greenfield as a total living environment, we are guided by several studies that afford different techniques for "reading" an entire community as something of a huge material document with much historical data embedded in its physical form. We become familiar with the extended artifactual analyses of a total urban environment, a typical midwestern nineteenth-century town, a large university campus, and another historic museum village.[8] From the insights extracted from these cross-disciplinary studies, we subject Greenfield to the following inquiries:

What was its original design and what has been its actual growth pattern to date? (Here we use slides of aerial photographs of the village taken at various periods since 1926, as well as extant cartography of the area in the same fifty-year period.)

What changes have occurred in the village's basic town plan (see fig. 14) site layouts, and arrangement of historic and nonhistoric structures? (Here we examine copies of the plans, blueprints, and measured drawings of Edward J. Culter (1883–1961), museum architect, 1926–1955, who prepared the original site drawings of many buildings relocated to Greenfield and supervised their placement and reconstruction in the museum village.)

What focal points or distinctive communal districts exist in the village and what is their historic import? (Here, for example, we analyze Greenfield's recreation of a New England town green in light of the analysis of Paul Zucker, *Town and Square: From the Agora to the Village Green* [Cambridge, Mass.: MIT Press, 1970].)

What types of geographical, ecological, and topographical features (natural or man-made) are present, and what type of historical ambience do they create? (Here we modify several studies from John Jakle's *Past Landscapes* (Monticello, Ill.: Council of Planning Librarians, 1974), as well as May T. Watts's playful *Reading the Landscape of America*, rev. ed. (N.Y.: Macmillan, 1975), in order to execute a historical geographer's analysis of the museum village.)

This type of comprehensive site analysis teaches students to identify anomalies in a museum village, such as a series of nineteenth-century residences originally located on level terrain, but relocated in the reconstructed village along a high, natural ridge. Failure to site the houses on topography similar to their original location in southern Michigan necessitated adding to them historically inaccurate rear brick foundations, portico exits, and superfluous back porches. A similar misrepresentation in siting that can be useful for heuristic purposes in a row of slave quarters originally situated in a deliberately regimented line in their Georgia context, but relocated as a rather scattered, informal, relaxed site in Greenfield. Practically all historic museum villages have such distortions. The point is not to single out the historical anachronisms of Greenfield so much as it is to illustrate how even interpretive mistakes can be converted into valuable teaching exercises.

The Museum Village as a Repository of Cultural Artifacts

Once we have an introductory overview of the museum village, we begin to dissect it under a second category—that is, as a collection of artifacts that can be studied separately and/or comparatively. Here there are several factors worth identifying and researching. For example, given the architectural diversity of Greenfield, we are able to perform certain regional[9] comparisons of building types, such as those found in New England (the Secretary House of 1760, Exeter, New Hampshire, or the Noah Webster House of 1822, New Haven, Connecticut); in the South (the Susquehanna House of 1652, Chesapeake Bay, Maryland); and in the Middle West (the Greek revival Ann Arbor House 1830, Ann Arbor, Michigan, or the Orville Wright balloon frame, pre-1870 residence from Dayton, Ohio).

It is also possible in a historic museum village of any antiquity, or, as in the case of Greenfield one of any similar ecleticism, to teach students how to recognize and how to sequence structures chronologically by style, building technology, or facade features.[10] At Greenfield, for example, a historian can conduct his or her students along an architectural time-corridor, beginning with late medieval British building (the Cotswold group) to seventeenth-century American cottages such as the Plymouth House, eighteenth-century structures like the Georgian Secretary's House, to a whole range of classic, folk, vernacular, and revival nineteenth-century buildings (e.g., Henry Ford House, George Matthew Adams House, Mattox House, the Chapman House, Sarah Jordan Boarding House). Along this three-hundred-year time-line of the built environment, we can

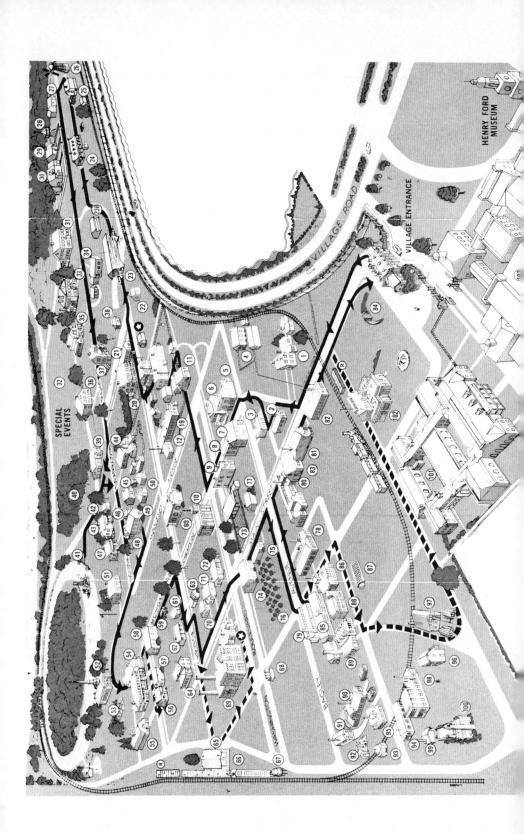

HENRY FORD MUSEUM

VILLAGE ENTRANCE

VILLAGE ROAD

SPECIAL EVENTS

1. Henry Ford Birthplace
2. Edsel Ford Workshop
3. 58 Bagley Avenue Shop
4. Miller School
5. Wright Cycle Shop
6. Wright Birthplace
7. Magill Jewelry Store
8. Heinz House
9. Grimm Jewelry Store
10. Sir John Bennett Jewelry Shop
11. Edison West Orange Laboratory
12-19. Edison Menlo Park Compound
12. Carbon Shed
13. Electric Train
14. Carpenter Shed
15. Machine Shop
16. Glass House
17. Edison Laboratory
18. Laboratory Dump
19. Office and Library
20. Sarah Jordan Boarding House
21. Fort Myers Laboratory
22. Whittier Tollhouse-Shoeshop
23. Ackley Covered Bridge
23B. Covered Bridge Lunch Stand
24. Susquehanna House
25. Plympton House
26. Cape Cod Windmill
27. Cotswold Forge
28. Cotswold Dovecote
29. Cotswold Stable
30. Cotswold "Rose Cottage"
31. Secretary Pearson House
32. Special Events Field
33. Noah Webster House
34. Edison Homestead
35. Ann Arbor House
36. Watchmaker's Chalet
37. Luthur Burbank Birthplace
38. Burbank Garden Office
39. Stephen Foster Birthplace
40. Village Picnic Grove
41. Edison Steamboat "Suwanee"
42. Charles Steinmetz Cabin
43. George Matthew Adams Birthplace
44. McGuffey School
45. McGuffey Birthplace
46. Mattox House
47. John Chapman House
48. George Washington Carver Memorial
49. Abe Lincoln Courthouse
50. Slave Quarters
51. Scotch Settlement School
52. Martha-Mary Chapel
53. Garden of the Leavened Heart
54. Clinton Inn
55. Addison Ford Barn
56. Pioneer Log Cabin
57. Richard Gardner House
58. Waterford General Store
59. "Owl" Night-Lunch Wagon
60. The Town Hall
61. Dr. Howard's Office
62. Phoenixville Post Office
63. Tintype Studio

64. Plymouth House
65. Smiths Creek Depot
66. Steam-Powered Sawmill
67. Railroad Water Tower
68. Electric Generating Unit
69. Edison Illuminating Company
70. Currier Shoe Shop
71. Kingston Cooper Shop
72. Village Blacksmith Shop
73. Village Lunch Stand
74. Plymouth Carding Mill
75. Hanks Silk Mill
76. Mulberry Grove
77. Deluge Fire House
78. Lapeer Machine Shop
79. Sandwich Glass Plant
80. Armington & Sims Machine Shop
81. Loranger Gristmill
82. Village Print Shop
83. William Ford Barn
84. Detroit Floral Clock
85. Village Planing Mill
86. Harahan Sugar Mill
87. Village Greenhouse
88. Cotton Gin Mill
89. Fairfield Rice Mill
90. Stony Creek Sawmill
91. Spofford Up-and-Down Sawmill
92. Walking Beam Engine
93. Haycock Boiler
94. Village Boiler Shop
95. Martinsville Cider Mill
96. Richart Carriage Shop
97. Tripp Up-and-Down Sawmill
98. Mack Avenue Ford Plant

99. Macon Brick Works
100. Haggerty Power House
101. Education Building and Lovett Hall
102. Soybean Laboratory
103. Henry Ford Museum
(R) Railroad Platforms
★ Rest rooms may be found adjacent to buildings 69 and 20, and in the rear lower level of buildings 33 and 35. There are also rest rooms in the Village Gate House.

Fig. 14. Bird's-eye view visitor's map and legend of contemporary Greenfield Village outdoor history museum in Dearborn, Michigan.— Courtesy Greenfield Village and Henry Ford Museum

monitor any architectural element (design template, materials used, construction technology, spatial concepts, ornamentation, etc.) of these structures in a variety of exercises designed to hone the students' abilities to analyze any building for historical information and insight.

Since we are interested in the historic museum village as a learning laboratory in which to develop our skills in historical and cultural geography as well as the newly emerging field of environics, we naturally examine sites and structures as to their proper placement in diverse physical environments.[11] In the siting of residential structures alone, Greenfield offers a wealth of potential data for observation, investigation, and comparative analysis: wilderness locations, rural environments, agricultural sites, small villages, town or semiurban locations, and principally urban settlements.[12]

A historic museum village can also be taken apart as to the different functions that its principal and ancillary structures have served or may now serve. We compare the function of a building chronologically, regionally, and even its technological efficiency and adaptability as a habitat. In such an investigation we are interested, in addition to its historical interpretation of residentiality,[13] in how the historic museum village portrays civic life, education, business, industry, and religion.[14] In addition to a structure's historical function, the seminar reflects on it as a potential agent or indicator of social change. We ask whether it, as an artifact (e.g., an electrical power plant), principally *affected* or *reflected* the culture of which it was a part.

We also inquire whether certain structures in a museum village can be interpreted as being or having been important cultural symbols. The symbolic dimension of cultural experience has been a favorite approach of American Studies scholars such as Henry Nash Smith, John William Ward, and Leo Marx.[15] The methodology has also been applied by Alan Trachtenberg to artifacts such as the *Brooklyn Bridge* (New York: Oxford University Press, 1965). We, in turn, have adapted Trachtenberg's techniques to Greenfield Village symbols like the McGuffey School, the Martha-Mary Chapel, or the Greek Revival Town Hall.

The Museum Village as an Above-Ground Archaeological Site

In the previous discussion of the museum village as a collection of artifacts, I have limited my remarks to some teaching devices that can be primarily applied to buildings. The general techniques outlined above, however, are also quite applicable to other evidences of material culture that abound in most historic village museums: interior furnishings, gardens, industrial sites, street furniture, and the like.

There is also a third and final general way in which I seek to use a historic museum village like Greenfield: it is an excellent outdoor laboratory in which I can instruct and test my students in "above-ground archaeology." Like the traditional archaeologist who usually extracts his historical data from subterranean excavations, the above-ground archaeologist also concentrates on the extant physical evidence of past human activity, but he probes above-ground. "Observation, description, and explanation comprise the three levels of archaeological study," writes James Deetz, in a work *(Invitation to Archaeology)* that is one of the seminar's primary reading assignments, "and the archaeologist proceeds through these levels in a certain way so that he might finally be able to say many things about past cultures based upon their scanty and imperfect remains." The above-ground archaeologist does the same with what remains above ground. With the historic museum village as our site, we try to implement the archaeologist's objectives in our attempt to "read" its artifacts. The ultimate objective of our efforts in the museum village is to alert ourselves to the visual clues in any environment that can be "read" in order to decipher part of its history—be it a college campus, a neighborhood, or a city street.[16]

Even a cursory review of the inordinate amount and variety of physical history that is literally lying all around them in a historic museum village never fails to amaze students. One can extract a great deal of historical knowledge and understanding from material culture evidence such as place-names, public sculpture, building iconography, funerary art, fence rails, geological configurations, field patterns, roof lines, man-hole covers, farmstead arrangements, street lights, carriage blocks, bridges, trade signs, geographical features, refreshment stands, power-supply sources, murals, barn types, street lay-outs, and historical markers and monuments.

A historic museum village can even have its own unplanned archaeological fragments, such as Greenfield's abandoned water wheel, once operative, but now overgrown with rushes, or formerly used millstones now lying relict behind a village building. To the trained above-ground archaeologist, a historical anachronism in an artifact is also usually quickly apparent. For instance, such a person will be aware that there is an appreciable difference in the way the Greenfield Cape Cod Windmill originally stood and how it now appears, with its added stone foundation (ostensibly to keep museum visitors from being decapitated by its giant vanes) as reconstructed on a site in the Village. For any museum village, one can construct all types of exercises to drill students in the grammar and syntax of visual historical literacy. I endeavor to have them develop the eye of the above-ground archaeologist so that they can become more conscious of and knowledgeable about the ample artifactual evidence of the past in their own home towns, countrysides, and cityscapes. Many of the heuristic tools that I have outlined here, of course, have been employed individually by scholars in various disciplines. Few, to my knowledge, have sought to apply them directly and collectively to the historic museum village.

There are, quite naturally, limitations to a museum village as a learning environment. I have already noted that a museum village can often be a highly subjective projection of a single individual's view of the past—be he founder or curator. There are also numerous potential interpretive problems involved in a reconstructed village such as Greenfield, where the relocation, restoration, or reconstruction of buildings has often been done quite far away from the original sites of the structures. Finally, there is always an inevitable degree of what David Lowenthal calls "museumization" or the "truncation of historical landscapes," wherein all "American historical areas tend toward a highly selective display of the past—selective as to epochs, contents, events, and personalities."[17]

An adaptive teacher or museum curator, however, can turn interpretive dilemmas into pedagogical possibilities. Students are prompted to evaluate how successfully the historic museum village "works" as a learning environment in each of the three categories outlined above. For instance, I require students to submit critiques of the museum staff's interpretations of the village as a whole, of individual artifacts contained therein, and as an above-ground archaeological site. Students are required to offer specific recommendations for improving such interpretations if they find them deficient. In this last process, students are alerted to the multiple interpretive problems that each museum village curatorial staff constantly faces.[18] Examination of the historic museum village as a total environment and as an archaeological site also enables students in their study of its history, art, and architecture to bring to bear the other work they are pursuing in the social and behaviorial sciences. It has been my experience that readings in cultural anthropology, historical archaeology, sociology, environics, and cultural geography force a student to confront the historic museum village with a broader series of questions and insights than if they were only exposed to reading the traditional architectural surveys or the literature of museum interpretation.

Finally, I find that students take away a type of visual historical literacy from this multidisciplinary approach to a historic museum village that is applicable in interpreting many other forms of past man-made environments. The seminar's combination of readings, discussions, archival and library research, and extensive on-site physical investigations provides them with a critical and perceptive sensitivity to the history that survives among us in material form.

6

The 1876 Centennial: A Model
for Comparative American Studies

THE celebration of America's bicentennial in 1976 produced a plethora of cultural phenomena for interpretation by cultural historians and social critics. Activities ranged widely from genuine efforts to explain the nation's purpose and identity to all forms of hucksterism and bad taste. One of the worst examples of the latter was the Jackwill Casket Company of Knightstown, Indiana, which offered for sale special bicentennial caskets featuring red tops, blue sides, and white interiors with two American flags.

A far better by-product of the bicentennial has been a renewed interest in the Philadelphia Centennial celebration of 1876, and, in fact, in the entire decade of the 1870s and in Victorian America generally. A half-dozen new books, a best-selling historical novel, and a whole spate of journal and magazine articles have sought to interpret "the way we were" in 1876.[1] The trend of much of this writing, whether academic or popular, has been to demonstrate that Americans of the bicentennial era share a much closer affinity to the men and women of the centennial age than to the generation that founded the Republic.[2]

There does seem to be merit in such a claim. Unusual events crowded the centennial year, events that historians now recognize as significant in the emergence of modern America. A detailed, concentrated study of these developments is an excellent framework for an undergraduate American Studies course in the Gilded Age period.[3]

For example, a political historian examining the year 1876 can focus on such events as the impeachment proceedings against Secretary of War William W. Belknap; the first national convention of the Greenback party; the furor over the defeat of General George A. Custer by Sitting Bull's Sioux; or the extradition of "Boss" Tweed back to New York from Spain to serve a prison sentence. The year 1876 also saw President Grant apologize to Congress and attribute the scandals of his second administration to his own "errors of judgment, not intent." Also in 1876, prohibition was first proposed as a constitutional amendment. Most of all, the controversial Hayes-Tilden campaign and disputed election took place.

Social historians have discovered that the centennial year provides ample evidence of trends destined to characterize America down to World War I. Examples include a growing disparity between enormous new wealth, personified by such families as the Astors, Belmonts, and Vanderbilts, on one side, and the plight of the laboring poor on the other side, a contrast symbolized by the execution of twenty "Molly Maguires" in the anthracite coal fields of Pennsylvania during the summer of 1876.

To the intellectual historian, 1876 is important for other reasons: the beginning of the Johns Hopkins University and German-inspired graduate education and research; the introduction of the Dewey decimal system of library classification; Josiah Willard Gibbs's publication of the theory of thermodynamics (that so influenced Henry Adams); Charles Sanders Peirce's mathematical formulations; and Felix Adler's founding of the New York Society for Ethical Culture.

Students of American art recall 1876 as the date of Winslow Homer's *Breezing Up;* John La Farge's mural decoration of Boston's Trinity Church; Erastus D. Palmer's sculpture of *Chancellor Robert R. Livingston;* and the initial completion of Central Park by Frederick Law Olmstead and Calvert Vaux. Popular culture enthusiasts can point to professional baseball's elevation to the status of national pastime through the formation of the National League; to a shift in undergraduate student lifestyles by the opening of the first fraternity house in the United States (Kappa Alpha at Williams College); or to the persistence of best-seller pulp publications such as John Habberton's *Helen's Babies: Some Account of their Ways, Innocent, Crafty, Angelic, Impish, Witching, and Repulsive, Also a Partial Record of Their Actions During Ten Days of Their Existence, by Their Latest Victim.*

Finally, the scholar of literature also has considerable material to study for the year 1876. Henry James published *Roderick Hudson;* Herman Melville wrote the two-volume narrative poem *Clarel;* William Cullen Bryant composed *A Lifetime* and *The Flood of Years,* while William Dean Howells published *A Day's Pleasure and Other Essays.* In the same year, Mark Twain brought out *The Adventures of Tom Sawyer,* his elegy to American boyhood and pre-Civil War rural life, a work, incidentally, that was promptly excluded from the children's room of the Brooklyn Public Library and banned completely from the Denver Public Library.

* * * * *

Much more evidence could be marshaled to demonstrate how teachers in American Studies or other cross-disciplinary programs might use 1876 to interrelate many different facets of American cultural history. One can also conveniently consolidate this approach by selecting a single cultural phenomenon—"The International Exhibition of Arts, Manufactures, and Products of the Soil and Mine, in the city of Philadelphia"[4] (see fig. 15) held May 10 to November 10, 1876—as a prime example of the state of literature, politics, art, economics, science, popular culture, intellectual life, and technology in Victorian America.

The idea of the Centennial Exhibition was first conceived, interestingly enough, by an academic. John L. Campbell, a little-known college professor of mathematics, natural philosophy, and astronomy at Wabash College in Indiana, proposed the event as early as 1864. The exhibition that gradually evolved a decade later could hardly have been better designed to provide future teachers with an excellent cross-disciplinary model for studying late nineteenth-century American life.

Merle Curti once suggested, in a brief essay on "America at the World Fairs, 1851–1893," that the involvement of the United States in the major international exhibitions of the nineteenth century could serve as an extremely useful framework for organizing a course in cultural history.[5] The United States International Exhibition of 1876, known then, as now, more simply as "the Centennial," is ideally suited for that purpose. It can be used to achieve several pedagogical objectives traditionally important to teachers of American Studies. Three of these goals are:

1. To create a viable cross-disciplinary learning environment that serves as a model course wherein students can identify, compare, and, where possible, interrelate and integrate diverse cultural evidence from various fields of study;

2. To show students how to employ both verbal and documentary sources and various types of visual or artifactual data such as technology, art, photography, cartography, and architecture in their study of cultural history;

3. To illustrate how an informed cultural perspective on part of the past (e.g., knowing how Americans observed their centenary in 1876) can assist students in analyzing events in their own time and culture (e.g., the 1976 bicentennial as a cultural index of twentieth-century American society).

The five-year quest for official United States government endorsement of the 1876 exhibition offers an excellent case study of congressional infighting, lobbying techniques, sectional antagonisms, and logrolling in both the House and the Senate. Gore Vidal's recent historical novel, *1876,* dramatizes that aspect of the Gilded Age for students.[6] The eventual participation of fifty-six countries and colonies in what became a kind of cultural Olympics provides a fascinating chapter in American diplomatic history. America's position *vis-a-vis* the ruling powers (Britain, France) and the emerging powers (Germany, Japan) can be noted by where their pavilions were placed on the fairgrounds, what objects they exhibited in them, and what they in turn said about the American exhibits.[7] Finally, techniques for financing the fair can be studied as a way of understanding the economic history of the United States during the late nineteenth century. Eighteen seventy-six also happens to be the year in which the United States first moved from a negative to a positive balance of trade.[8]

Documentary and statistical data for students to do this type of analysis is abundant and readily available. No less than six major histories[9] of the centennial were written in the 1870s; gazetteers, catalogues, historical registers, portfolios, and numerous guidebooks also abound.[10] Primary research can be conducted through the fifteen volumes of official catalogs and by analysis of the proclamations and reports about the centennial published by the Government Printing Office.[11]

An initial foray into this surfeit of data quickly teaches the student the validity of Daniel Boorstin's claim that late nineteenth-century Americans were mesmerized by the new science of statistics.[12] For example, in addition to keeping accurate attendance records (8,004,274 paid admissions, 1,906,692 free, for a total of 9,910,966 when the total United States population was roughly 46,000,000), many other facts were carefully recorded at the centennial: a meterological record for each hour; the number of telegrams sent and received (151,428); the number of children lost (504) and how long it took to return them to their parents or guardians (499 the same day, 5 the next day); and how many people died at the fair (4). One can also ascertain the number of arrests (675) made by the Centennial Guards for offenses ranging from larceny (160) to fornication and bastardy(1).

Although several literary works were written especially for the centennial observance by authors such as Bayard Taylor, John Greenleaf Whittier, and Sidney Lanier, the exhibition inspired no really memorable imaginative literature. It did, however, prompt several insightful prose essays by the era's leading literary giants. In the *Atlantic Monthly* (July 1876), William Dean Howells wrote "A Sennight of the Centennial," a perceptive account of his seven-day visit to the exhibition and what he thought it augured for

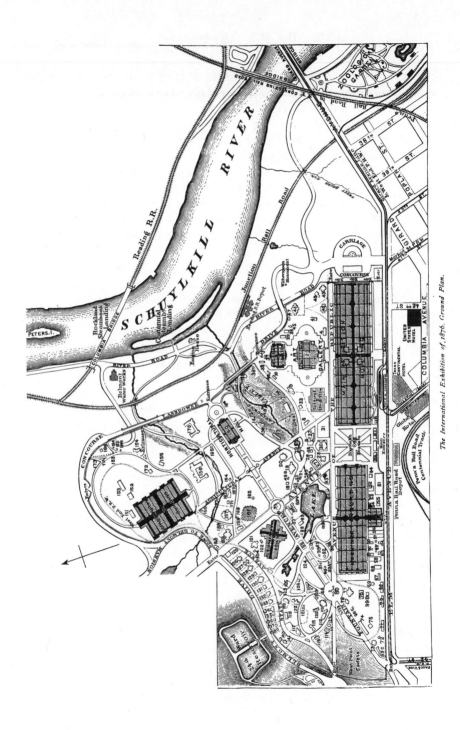

The International Exhibition of 1876. Ground Plan.

KEY TO ABOVE GROUND PLAN.

South-east Section.

1. Main Exhibition Building.
2. Memorial Hall (Art Gallery).
3. Annex to Art Gallery.
4. Photographic Gallery.
5. Carriage Building.
6. Centennial National Bank.
7. Public Comfort (clothes room).
8. Swedish School-house.
9. Penna. Educational Departm't.
10. Singer's Sewing Mach. Build'g.
11. Lafayette Restaurant.
12. Hunters' Camp.
13. Milk Dairy Association.
13A. Extension to Milk Dairy.
14. Bible Society.
15. Public Comfort.
16. Phila. Municipal Headquarters.
17. Soda Water.
18. Moorish Villa.
19. German Government Building.
20. Brazilian Government Build'g.
21. Kittredge & Co.
22. Soda Water.
23. Philadelphia "Times" Build'g.
24. Glass Factory.
25. Cigar Stand.
26. American Fusee Company.
27. Centennial Photographic Association.
28. Penna. R. R. Ticket Office.
29. Centennial Medical Departm't.
30. Judges' Hall.
31. Department of Public Comfort.
32. Japanese Government.
33. Kindergarten.
34. Soda Water.
35. Public Comfort Station.
36. Cigar Stand.
37. Stand Pipe.
38. French Government Building.
39. Stained Glass.
40. Vienna Bakery.
41. Bankers' Exhibit.
42. Empire Transportation Co.
43. Centennial Fire Patrol No. 2.
44. Portuguese Governm't Build'g.
45. Pavilion of French Art.
46. Burial Casket Building.
47. Public Comfort (clothes room).
48. Police Station.
49. Police Station.
49A. Music Stand.
49B. French Ceramic Pavilion.

South-west Section.

50. Machinery Hall.
51. Shoe and Leather Building.
52. British Boiler House.
53. Boiler House.
54. Corliss Boiler House.
55. Weimer's Furnace.
56. Boiler House.
57. Stokes & Parrish MachineShop.
58. Boiler House.
59. Nevada Quartz Mill.
60. Gas Machine.
61. Yale Lock Company.
62. Brick Working Machine.
63. Storehouse.
64. Artesian Well.
65. Rock Drilling Machinery.
66. Jesse Starr & Son.
67. Gunpowder Pile Driver.
68. Automatic Railway.
69. Tiffany's Gas Machine.
70. Pennsylvania Railroad.
71. Engine House.
72. Emil Ross Saw Mill.
73. Gillinder & Son Glass Factory.
74. Annex (Saw Mill).
75. Saw Mill Boiler House.
76. Campbell Printing House.
77. Fuller, Warren & Co.
78. Liberty Stove Works.
79. Boston "Herald" and "Advertiser."
80. Catholic Total Abstinence Fountain.
81. Kiosque.
82. Turkish Cafe.
83. Pennsylvania State Building.
84. Pop Corn.
85. Rowell's Newspaper Build'g.
86. Lienard's Relief Plans.
87. Public Comfort Station.
88. Soda Water.
89. New York "Tribune."
90. French Restaurant.
91. Sons of Temperance Fount'n.
92. Colossal Arm of Liberty.
93. World's Ticket Office.
94. Catalogue Office.
95. Loiseau's Prepared Fuel Co.
96. Office Board of Finance.
97. Office U. S. Centennial Com.
98. Bartholdi's Fountain.
99. Jerusalem Bazaar.
99A. Vermont State Building.
99B. Chilian Machine Building.
99C. Police Station.
99D. Statue of Elias Howe.
99E. Columbus Monument.
99F. Averill Paint Company.

North-west Section.

100. U. S. Government Building.
101. United States Hospital.
102. United States Laboratory.
103. Cigar Stand.
104. Tent.
105. U. S. Signal Service.
106. Bishop Allen's Monument.
107. Soda Water.
108. Cigar Stand.
108. Canada Log House.
110. Arkansas State Building.
111. Spanish Building.
112. West Virginia State Building.
113. Spanish Government Build'g.
114. Spanish Government Build'g.
115. Japanese Building.
116. Mississippi State Building.
117. George's Hill Restaurant.
118. California State Building.
119. New York State Building.
120. }
121. } British Government Build'gs.
122. }
123. Public Comfort Station.
124. Tunisian Camp.
125. Centennial Fire Patrol No. 1.
126. Ohio State Building.
127. Indiana State Building.
128. Illinois State Building.
129. Wisconsin State Building.
130. Michigan State Building.
131. New Hampshire State Build'g.
132. Connecticut State Building.
133. Massachusetts State Building.
134. Delaware State Building.
135. Maryland State Building.
136. Tennessee State Building.
137. Iowa State Building.
138. Missouri State Building.
139. Block House.
140. Fire Patrol.
141. Rhode Island

North-east Section.

150. Agricultural Building.
151. Agricult'al Annex (Wagons).
152. "   " (Pomology).
153. Brewers' Building.
154. Butter and Cheese Factory.
155. Tea and Coffee Press Build'g.
156. American Restaurant.
157. Kansas State Building.
158. Southern Restaurant.
159. New Jersey State Building.
160. Horticultural Hall.
161. Women's Pavilion.
162. Gliddon Guano Building.
163. New England Log House.
164. Pop-Corn.
165. Cigar Stand.
166. Cigar Stand.
167. Soda Water.
168. Bee Hives.
169. School House.
170. German Restaurant.
171. Virginia Building.
172. Boiler House.
173 to 183. Wind Mills.
184. Police Station.
185. Hay Packing.
186. Practical Farmers' Office.
187. Public Comfort Station.
188. Centennial Guards.
189. Public Comf'ort (cl. room).

Fig. 15. *Ground plan and key to the 1876 "International Exhibition of Arts, Manufactures, and Products of the Soil and Mine, in the City of Philadelphia," reproduced from Joseph M. Wilson's* The Masterpieces of the Centennial Exposition, *vol. III (Philadelphia: U.S. Centennial Commission, 1876).*

American civilization. Other American men of letters wrote similar prose pieces on the centennial's cultural significance: E. L. Godkin in *The Nation;* Walt Whitman in his privately printed *Two Rivulets,* and in his *Specimen Days;* as well as Mark Twain in his *Notebooks.* These essays provide students with contemporary appraisals of the role that technology, industrial might, and new sources of energy were expected to play in American and world history.[13]

In addition to such domestic commentaries, the centennial also stimulated an outpouring of studies and travelogues by foreign visitors to the United States. Although it would be another decade before James Bryce would publish one of the classics of the genre (*The American Commonwealth* [1888]), a multitude of foreign travelers churned out articles, pamphlets, and books about their experiences in Philadelphia and Centennial America. Students can compare these foreign appraisals with similar travelogues written by Americans from various parts of the United States. For instance, D. Bailey's *"Eastward Ho!" or, Leaves from the Diary of a Centennial Pilgrim* (a privately printed account of one Ohioan who went to the fair) is a marvelous document that gives a typical midwesterner's view of America in 1876.

Over the past two decades, scholars and teachers in American Studies have become increasingly interested in using artifacts to interpret American civilization. John Kouwenhoven and Harold Skramstad have issued provocative manifestoes and bibliographic exhortations on how the study of "American things"—be they bridges or beer cans, works of art or buildings—can expand our understanding of the American past.[14] Obviously, the Centennial, a mammoth artifact containing millions of physical objects, is itself a natural laboratory that can be used to acquaint students with the study of material culture as historical evidence.

To prepare students to "read" artifacts as they do books, it is helpful to know some of the newer techniques developed by such scholars as Richard Latham, Henry Glassie, and E. McClung Fleming.[15]

In using the Philadelphia exhibition as a teaching laboratory for analyzing cultural artifacts, one can rely upon a variety of resources. Numerous maps and design plans of the site are extant, as well as some of the actual objects exhibited at the Centennial. Some may be in local museums nearby or in private collections. Nineteenth-century tradebooks, manufacturers' catalogues, a recent paperback reprint of *Frank Leslie's Historical Register of the Philadelphia Exposition* (New York: Paddington Press, 1974), and various illustrated histories such as the three-volume *Masterpieces of the Centennial International Exhibition-Illustrated* (Philadelphia: Gebbie & Barrie, 1876) provide comprehensive inventories of Centennial artifacts. Excellent slides and other graphic materials can be prepared from these sources for classroom use.

On May 10, 1976, the National Museum of History and Technology of the Smithsonian Institution in Washington, D. C., opened an exhibit of more than 30,000 objects, a display intended to recapture, with as much historical accuracy as possible, "the total ambience of the International Exhibition staged in celebration of the Centennial of the Declaration of Independence."[16] The exhibit is both a milestone in museological interpretation and a novel laboratory for material culture study. Its philosophy has been "to return to the Centennial, not to show the Centennial from a perspective of one hundred years later." As one of its chief designers accurately claims, "this is not an exhibit *about* the Centennial, it *is* the Centennial—rather drastically diminished in size, to be sure, but the Centennial nonetheless."[17]

The Smithsonian reproduced the milieu of the 1876 fair by a series of ingenious display techniques planned and designed with reference to old photographs and engravings. Since Centennial exhibitors naturally showed only their finest and newest products, the Smithsonian staff, for greater authenticity, restored or refurbished many of the machines and other exhibits to like-new appearance.

To document their extensive and painstaking recreation of the Centennial, the Smithsonian staff issued a 224-page, oversize paperback catalogue, *1876: A Centennial Exhibition.* The catalogue, which also includes an important supplement *(List of Objects Exhibited)*, is profusely illustrated and contains an excellent series of brief, interpretive essays on the cultural history of Centennial objects. This reference material can be further supplemented by several other works, also extensively illustrated, thereby providing students with visual approximations (and often the physical dimensions) of the original artifacts. These volumes include: C. B. Norton, *Treasures of Art, Industry and Manufacture Represented in the American Centennial Exhibition at Philadelphia, 1876* (Philadelphia: S. T. Souder and Co., 1877–1878); *Album of the International Exhibition at Philadelphia to Commemorate the Centennial of the United States of America* (New York: J. Bein Co., 1876); and Frank Leslie's previously mentioned *Historical Register.*

The majority of the artifacts displayed at Philadelphia in 1876 can be quickly categorized by the titles of the buildings[18] that housed them: Machinery, Manufactures, Art, Horticulture, Government, Foreign Nations, and State Exhibits. Manufactured objects dominated the multimillion-dollar display. It resembled a giant trade exposition, a four-hundred-acre shopping mall, and a P. T. Barnum carnival, all rolled into one event.

Study of the centennial's material culture helps students to understand the many labels that historians have given to this period. Appropriate readings to accompany study of the artifacts would include Howard Mumford Jones, *The Age of Energy* (1971); Ray Ginger, *The Age of Excess* (1965); and Thomas Cochran and William Miller, *The Age of Enterprise* (1942).

Howard Mumford Jones makes particular use of the Philadelphia Centennial and its greatest artifact, the Corliss steam engine. To this day, the mighty Corliss engine, acclaimed as a major manifestation of American technological prowess in the nineteenth century, remains the prime symbol of the Centennial. It deserves a full-length treatment along the lines of two other recent studies of symbolic artifacts belonging to the centennial era: Alan Trachtenberg's *The Brooklyn Bridge, Fact and Symbol* and Marvin Trachtenberg's *The Statue of Liberty*. [19]

Since examination of the material culture of the centennial reveals a society that felt no ambivalence regarding the machine, nor any qualms about an infinite multiplication of machine-made products, it is also important to have students read Siegfried Giedion's *Mechanization Takes Command, A Contribution to Anonymous History*. Giedion illustrates very well the multiple ways in which machinery has altered American culture.

The Centennial was not just objects, events and ideas; it was also a place. John Maass has analyzed its architectural styles, its site plan, and the philosophy of its chief designer Hermann J. Schwarzmann.[20] In less than two years, Schwarzmann moved 500,000 cubic yards of earth, planted 153 acres of lawns and flower beds, and transplanted more than 20,000 trees and shrubs, thereby transforming 284 acres of fields and ravines into a lovely sylvan park. Amid this pastoral setting were erected the buildings for Machinery and Manufactures, thus creating a marvelous example of America's paradoxical fascination with "the machine in the garden."[21] The Centennial's individual buildings and their architectural history can be studied in Maass's monograph as well as in other journal literature and contemporary publications.[22]

The fair's environic legacy (e.g., a picturesque layout of large pavilions in a park, multiple transportation systems, efficient public facilities and services) can be traced through subsequent world expositions. It can also be viewed as a prototype for an emerging menality that was to remake the national environment. "Here in Fairmount Park, within topographically defined limits, was a characteristically American organization of space," argues J. B. Jackson, the interaction between landscape and architecture, the areas with specialized functions, the emphasis on the linear process; here also was displayed the principle of regulated flow—of energy, of materials, of people. The whole world could see and wonder at the qualities of Americans: their indifference to history, their delight in organizing space and time and labor, their eagerness to acquire new ideas, their abundant creativity. It is from this event, all but forgotten by most of us, that we can well date the birth of a new relationship between the American people and their landscape.[23]

A variety of special topics in American cultural history of the 1870s can be explored through the medium of the Centennial and its material culture. Three examples will suggest the possibilities.

The Woman's Pavilion was an important innovation in the history of world fairs, as well as an excellent index to the temper of the woman's movement in Victorian America. Organized, financed, and operated entirely by women, the building exhibited steam engines run by women alongside fine needlework executed by them; it also contained a printing press from which women issued a daily journal *(The New Century For Women)*. Immediately next to the press were rows of homemade preserves prepared by American homemakers.

Participation in the Centennial, on their own terms, looms large in the autobiographies of several nineteenth-century feminists.[24] Susan B. Anthony's reading of the Declaration of Independence for Women at the Fourth of July ceremonies in Independence Square likewise ranks as an early example of "confrontation politics" by a reformer. The document is an important testament in the history of women's liberation.

The Centennial also pointed out the plight of the native American people, another economically disadvantaged and politically disfranchised segment of American society. Although George Catlin published his sympathetic two-volume *Illustrations of the Manners, Customs, and Condition of the North American Indians* in 1876, it was the cry of revenge for Custer's defeat and the total disdain for Indian culture that characterized the attitudes of most Americans that year. Nowhere is that better demonstrated than in the ways in which Indian artifacts were displayed at Philadelphia. Robert A. Trennert has studied that aspect of the exhibition in depth and it is worthwhile to acquaint students with his essay.[25] It is also valuable to have them read and compare General George A. Custer's *Life on the Plains and Horrors of Indian Warfare* (1883) with Helen Hunt Jackson's *A Century of Dishonor* (1881).

A strange perspective on the American past is revealed in the Centennial's artifacts. The Philadelphia fair ostensibly commemorated 1776, yet very few relics of the revolutionary era were exhibited: only a pair of false teeth once used by George Washington, a few Revolutionary War army uniforms, and the contents of a "New England Kitchen of 1776."[26] More in keeping with George Bancroft's progressive, optimistic, providential interpretation of American history was the future-oriented perspective of the Centennial designers. In fact, as the published addresses delivered at the Centennial reveal (particularly those given on July 4), the generation of 1876 viewed their 1776 ancestors more as provincial bumpkins than Founding Fathers. The poster for Philadelphia's Fourth of July celebration was graphic evidence of that tendency. On the left was depicted a ragged band in front of dismal log cabins, with the caption "1776—THREE MILLION OF COLONISTS ON A STRIP BY THE SEA." On the right stood a stalwart, prosperous group in a new town, with the legend "1876—FORTY MILLIONS OF FREEMEN RULING FROM OCEAN TO OCEAN." A strangely myopic view of the past, coupled with an ebullient pride in the present, and an absolute confidence in an even greater future characterized Americans' historical sense of themselves in 1876.

*   *   *   *   *

No such historical perspective dominated Bicentennial America. The nation celebrated its two-hundredth anniversary of freedom in ways quite different from that of the centennial. Yet the vantage point of 1876 is quite helpful in interpreting 1976. The manner in which Americans assessed 1976 is a cultural index to the understanding of twentieth-century America. The bicentennial was both different from and similar to the centennial.

Unlike a century ago, Congress decided not to center the bicentennial celebration in any one geographic location, or on any one major event. In fact, 1976 was much more oriented toward local and state activities than toward national or international events.[27] Moreover, unlike the political uniformity of the centennial's national administration, at least two groups vied for control of the bicentennial: the government's official bureaucracy (the American Revolution Bicentennial Administration)[28] and a nonprofit, private foundation (the People's Bicentennial Commission) that inclined more toward social and economic reform and an aspiration to provide "revolutionary alternatives for the Bicentennial."[29]

In addition to these two ideologically opposed organizations, the bicentennial spawned numerous other groups according to the degree of cultural pluralism present in the United States; for instance, such groups as the Bicentennial Ethnic-Racial Council and Alliance, the Study of Black-Heritage Project, and the Council of Christians and Jews Bicentennial Commission. Also, contrary to the 1876 celebration, when all manner of technology to exploit the continent's natural and man-made resources was emphasized, the cultural mood of 1976 showed a pronounced interest in ecological conservation, environmental protection, and historic preservation. Finally, despite all the myths, romantic sentimentality, and half-truths it generated, the bicentennial also produced a large amount of solid historical research and writing in American history. The output appears to be even more extensive than the Civil War publications of the 1960s. This is in marked contrast to 1876.

Historians, of course, are always struck by the sameness and the strangeness of the past. With the added perspective of what happened in 1876, students quickly recognize this. While there was no single artifactual focal point to the bicentennial, the event by no means was without its material culture; witness the twelve carloads of Americana transported by the Freedom Train; the cross-country trek of fifty different covered wagons on the Bicentennial Wagon Pilgrimage; Operation Sail; and the Smithsonian Institution's Folklife Festival of the crafts of thirty-four nations; not to mention thousands of courthouses, railroad stations, residences, churches, log cabins, and school houses that were restored as bicentennial projects.[30] Finally, as during the centennial, the American addiction to consumerism and the exploitive nature of corporate business were made manifest in the millions of items manufactured for souvenir sale during the year-long "Buy-Centennial."

Other parallels between the two eras abound. A "Women's Coalition for a Third Century" lobbied for the passage of an Equal Rights Amendment as a fitting bicentennial implementation to the still unachieved goals of Susan B. Anthony, Elizabeth Cady Stanton, and other nineteenth-century leaders of the women's movement. Native Americans continue to decry their second-class citizenship and the denial of access to social, political, and economic equality. The federal government, despite its claims to sponsor a grass-roots, loosely structured bicentennial program, continued the centennial era's fascination with bureaucracy and statistics by underwriting such agencies as BINET, the Bicentennial Information Network, or the computerized *Official Master Register of Bicentennial Activities.*

Naturally, the bicentennial generated much national introspection—some critical, a great deal narcissistic, and some of it insightful—from a variety of viewpoints. As a finale to a course using the 1876 centennial as a paradigm, it is valuable to introduce students to this contemporary writing. Perhaps an entire seminar might be devoted to analyzing the common cultural themes, paradoxes, anxieties and hopes that appear in the large numbers of books, essays, symposia, conference reports, and articles inspired by the nation's two-hundredth anniversary.

Several excellent anthologies and collections of essays have already been published. Three good items for promoting discussion among under-graduates from a cross-disciplinary vantage point are the American Enterprise Institute pamphlet series, *America's Continuing Revolution;* the National Endowment for the Humanities' *American Issues Forum;* and *An Almost Chosen People: The Moral Aspirations of the Americans,* edited by Ronald Weber and Walter Nicgorski (Notre Dame, Indiana: University of Notre Dame Press, 1976).

Other materials continue to become available, providing the cultural historian and teacher of American Studies with a surfeit of social and historical commentary. Once students have read, discussed, and evaluated these studies, they should be encouraged to do their own reflection on the meaning of American culture as we enter the last quarter of the twentieth century. Of course, it is a difficult task to appraise the status of a contemporary civilization, particularly one's own. Nonetheless, interpreters of American civilization have delighted in doing that ever since the first colonists arrived.

Part III
Landscapes as Artifacts

7

Vegetation as Historical Data:
A Historian's Use of Plants and Natural
Material Culture Evidence

HISTORIANS have been tardy in recognizing that the environment, natural and man-made, is an amazing historical document. In our teaching, we have not adequately explored the ways in which, rightly seen, a landscape reveals as much of a society's culture as does a novel, a newspaper, or a Fourth of July oration. In our research, we have not sufficiently probed urban, suburban, and rural terrains as palimpsests of linguistic, ecclesiastical, economic, technological, and social history; we have not investigated the ways place-names reveal inter- and intra-urban migration and forgotten resources; road systems hint at military policies and former religious alliances; boundaries and courthouse styles recall former political antagonisms; tree plantings document former landowner-ship patterns; or how the vegetation in public parks can reveal nineteenth-century attitudes toward aesthetics, sanitation, or recreation.

Fortunately, a historical interest in landscapes and the plants found on them, while neglected by most of my colleagues, has been nurtured by scholars in other countries and in other disciplines. For instance, the importance of plants in historical research has long been acknowledged by the German *Volksbotanik* tradition of scholarship.[1] British local historians, preservationists, and antiquarians have also investigated their countryside from Land's End to John o'Groat's for what one of their number calls the "history on the ground." Community historians like Penelope Lively, medievalists such as Maurice Beresford, and W. G. Hoskins, dean of English landscape observers, have developed excellent models and techniques for historical analysis of the environment.[2]

My interest in using extant material culture *in situ* to understand the past is greatly indebted to these scholars. My work with plants as historical evidence has also been heavily influenced by a number of Americans in

147

various disciplines. Ecologists and forest historians have dramatized the importance of previous forest covers, vanished natural resources, and climatic conditions.[3] Agricultural historians and folklorists have deciphered the enormous significance of plants and soils in the situation of houses and farms.[4] Cultural and historical geographers such as Carl Sauer, John Fraser Hart, and Fred Kniffen have explored the multiple ways that Americans have arranged their landscapes and the vegetation upon them.[5] Maverick investigators like J. B. Jackson and Grady Clay have provided us all with numerous insights[6] to the history that survives on the land.

* * * * *

In my own work as a cultural historian within the cross-disciplinary field of American Studies, I am working toward compiling "a series of techniques for identifying, interrogating, and interpreting the natural and built environment in order to gain an increased sensitivity to and an understanding of life as lived in the past."[7] Like the traditional archaeologist who usually works "below ground," I concentrate on using material objects and physical sites as primary evidence; employing extensive field work as a research technique; adapting anthropological explanatory concepts, such as typology or diffusion, to the approach where feasible; and having historical knowledge about humankind as the principal learning objective.[8]

Naturally, such an investigator encounters an extensive array of vegetation on whatever landscape he traverses. More often than not, if the researcher knows what to look for and how to interpret it, he can gain significant historical insight from such data. Let me illustrate this claim with a few examples of what one type of plant life—trees—can tell the cultural historian. I admit that there is a slight bias in this choice of data, for trees are a highly visible natural shard, easily identifiable to the average traveler along a back road or to a walker in the city. Trees, for the most part, are also rather permanently located and not terribly difficult to estimate as to age. For that reason, they have long been a tool of climatologists and archaeologists concerned with dendrochronology.[9] Finally, they possess a durability to survive (barring natural and man-made wrath) as historical markers of various sorts. Indeed, in Texas state parks, they even have something of a "life-after-death," where the acclaimed "first," although now quite dead, tree of the Texas high plains is memorialized in the smallest state park in the country.[10]

Trees have played an intriguing role in American history. Among the first products sought from this continent were ship masts for the Royal

Navy. In fact, ship-mast locusts planted in the nineteenth century still survive in Branch, Smithtown, Long Island. One of the first ordinances of the Plymouth colony regulated the cutting of timber, and the Broad Arrow policy of reserving trees was initiated even when more than two-thirds of the continent was tree-covered. Consequently, an initial question that the above-ground archaeologist asks of any stand of trees (as of any vegetation), is, simply, is it virgin? Or, more likely, is it second or third, or fourth growth? If the investigator is able to ascertain that the tree cover is virgin, he naturally raises questions, such as how extensive was it? How might it have conditioned settlement patterns or farming practices? What influence might it have had on house-building types or even industrial development? The hardwood forests of neighboring Michigan, for example, sustained the cabinet-making component of the Singer Sewing Machine Works in South Bend, Indiana, as well as the carriage and wagon manufacturing plants of the Studebaker Brothers. In northern Illinois, where a prairie-and-grove vegetation pattern prevailed, nineteenth-century cartography reveals how settlers resorted to tract timber lots in order to conserve their wood supplies and insure an allotment for all landowners.

The landscape historian also remembers that early immigrants to North America used plants as indicators of environmental potential. Settlers often selected their land according to the kinds of trees that grew upon it. For instance, differences in the natural drainage of two glacial tills in Rush County, Indiana, produced differences in vegetation that were well-known and clearly understood by early immigrants.[11] The better-drained areas, which were dominated by sugar maple and oak, were known as "sugar-tree lands," whereas the wet, swampy ground was referred to as "beech land." "We cannot be certain that every purchaser used forest cover as an index of land quality," concludes Wayne Kiefer, "but there is good reason to believe that many of them did so and even better reason to believe that they were justified in doing so."[12]

Trees survive an ample documentation of rural history in their delineation of earlier boundaries, borders, and benchmarks. The careful observer can still locate metes and bounds markers by the black oaks and white oaks used in 1850 to orient Newbold Road in McHenry County, Illinois, or the huge catalpa at the corner of North and West streets in Blooming Grove, Indiana. On the University of Notre Dame campus, a string of Osage orange, paralleling Douglas Road, is all that remains of a long hedgerow (see fig. 16) that once divided one of the many fields of the 2400-acre University Farms. Throughout the nineteenth century, such vegetation (e.g., benchmark beeches, county-line cottonwoods) were used to mark range boundaries and cadastral surveys, as well as individual farmers' fields.[13]

Routes of explorers or immigrants can be retraced by following extant trail trees along the "49er Road" in El Dorado County, California. "Summit trees" still beckon the observant traveler as he crosses nineteenth-century mountain passes, and "snub-trees" signal a previous transportation technology to the highway driver.[14] Indian trail trees (see fig. 17) abound in northern Illinois, where the Pottawatomies bent or buried young tree spouts or saplings to indicate the direction of their travel routes east and west, to designate sources of fresh water, as well as to mark the path to the Chicago portage. To the above-ground archaeologist, identifying a trail tree is not difficult. These man-formed, natural road signs are inevitably found on ridges along glacial tills. In the upper Midwest they are usually white oak and generally smaller than other trees of similar age, due to having been buried early, as in the case of the tree at 630 Lincoln Street in Wilmette, Illinois.[15] Examples of bent or tied trail trees survive in Missouri's Clark National Forest and in Southport, North Carolina.

Political, diplomatic, and military historians often fail to remember how frequently significant war-making, council-talking, or peace-making conferences have taken place in American history beneath the branches of a mammoth oak, elm, or sycamore. Pennsylvania's Treaty Elm of 1681, for instance, now survives as depicted by painters Benjamin West (*William Penn's Treaty with the Indians*, 1771) and Edward Hicks (*Peaceable Kingdom*, ca. 1830), as well as in numerous scions still living in eastern Pennsylvania. Not more than four miles from the University of Notre Dame campus, the Miami Indians met in council among themselves, as well as with Robert Sieur de La Salle in 1681 at St. Joseph County's famous Council Oak. Similar council sites exist throughout the United States, recalling parallel deliberations from the sixteenth to the end of the nineteenth centuries. Least we think this a thing of the past, there is a "Council Elm" in front of Eckhart Hall at the University of Chicago, where, in April 1942, the world's leading atomic scientists held a highly secret discussion (outdoors, for fear of being bugged) that was an important conference in their quest for the first self-sustained nuclear chain-reaction. Moreover, it should not be forgotten that the tentative charter for the United Nations was drawn up at Bretton Woods and Dumbarton Oaks.

Plans for war were made during the Revolutionary war under Daniel Byrnes's sycamore, (Stanton, Delaware); in the War of 1812, under the St. Michael's box elder (Talbot County, Maryland); and in the Civil War, among the Union beeches (Holly Springs, Mississippi). In fact, if the extant natural evidence is to be believed, the strategy for practically every military campaign that Andrew Jackson ever fought in the southeastern United States seemed to have been first outlined at the base of a live oak or a loblolly pine.[16] American battlefields like those of Fallen Timbers or The Wilderness were fought with tactics imposed, in part, by the landscape's vegetation. Finally, treaties suing for peace are symbolized by natural artifacts such as the Medicine Creek Treaty (1854) Fir in the Nisqually Valley of Washington or the Cherokee Indian Treaty (1785) Oak at Lake Hartwell, South Carolina.

Most of these tree sites are now historical monuments. They have been designated as sacred groves commemorating and communicating a view of the past in the same way that public statuary and other civic memorials serve as communal totems. The above-ground archaeologist identifies, documents, and interprets such artifacts for insights into a community's sense of history. W. Lloyd Warner's interrogation of the "ritualization of the past" in a New England town's monuments (including its historical vegetation) provides a useful technique to apply to any environment's communal symbols and shrines. Warner's analysis[17] recommends that the landscape analyst of "historic" vegetation (see fig. 17) take careful note of where and when historical markers were placed (would you believe a large-tooth aspen serving as century-old historical monument in the bell tower of the county courthouse in Greensburg, Indiana?);[18] what historical events or personalities are consistently noticed or neglected in a town's monuments; who in the community designated and funded such landmarks; whether the events memorialized are spread evenly across a town's history or whether they tend to cluster at one or more historical periods (i.e., the Revolutionary or Civil wars).

Cultural historians and geographers have already begun raising such questions about the placement of bicentennial parks and plantings that have sprouted all over the American landscape since 1976.[19] The historian knows this to be a tradition that goes back to colonial "Liberty Trees" (symbolic artifacts that the British promptly chopped down whenever they captured an American town) as well as to the commemorative plantings that mark every major anniversary in U.S. history. The careful observer of any American urban environment can also find extant plantings by famous people memorializing what they and their age judged prosperity would deem historic: John Kinzie's four Lombardy populars in front of his Chicago River homestead; the Cassius Clay Kentucky coffee-trees; Andrew Jackson ("Old Hickory") and his shag-bark hickories (what else?) in Tennessee; the John Hancock elms on the Boston Commons; Brigham

Fig. 16. A relict Osage orange fencerow on the University of Notre Dame campus survives as historical evidence of the migration of a type of natural material culture and stands perpendicular to another artifact, a barbed-wire fence, that displaced Osage orange as a midwestern fencing material in the 1870s.—Photograph by T. J. Schlereth

Fig. 17. Indian trail tree along a residential street in Wilmette, Illinois, in 1979. Originally a natural marker bent to indicate travel direction or water supply, the trail tree now has its own metal marker (at left of tree) placed by a local historical society to denote the area's early Indian presence.—Photograph by John V. Smith

Young's walnuts in Utah; and, of course, the ornamental Japanese cherry trees planted in 1909 and 1912 in the city whose namesake will be forever associated in American mythology with a fruit tree to which he supposedly gave the ax.

The landscape historian also seeks to extract insight about the past from the relict vegetation left by previous, but usually anonymous, generations. Consequently, he is ever on the lookout for "wedding" or "bride and groom" conifers (usually in pairs of two or four trees) that nineteenth-century midwestern rural folk planted religiously to mark major turning points in their own lives—a new home and a new spouse. In southern Illinois, some extant tree plantings in front of farm houses reveal the demographic patterns of the population, since parents planted a conifer or a hardwood for every child that lived past infancy. An excellent illustration of this folk custom survives on the lawn of the Israel and Martha Washburn homestead in Livermore, Maine, where seven sugar maples were supposedly planted in the 1800s, one for each of seven Washburn sons. Changes in the rural countryside can also be ascertained when one sees the persistence of the "wedding" or "children" conifers still towering, much like natural porticos to the Greek Revival houses they often fronted, despite the fact that the homesteads are now gone or have been replaced by twentieth-century building types such as mobile homes.

Trees have also always been important to pioneer Americans at time of death, as well. When southern Illinois was first settled, in the early nineteenth century, many of the inhabitants came from the Carolinas. In their new homes, they noticed that the forests of the area were mainly of oak, hickory, and maple, woods not easily worked. One of their concerns was to have pine coffins to be buried in, when death came. Hence, they got relatives and friends who were to come later to bring some pine trees from their native Carolinas. These trees they planted in their front yards, usually two white pines, one for each spouse. Many of the "white coffin pines" have outlived their planters, and can be found throughout southern Illinois, a number in Union County.[20]

Vestiges of early settlement patterns survive, as well, in double rows of sixty-foot Balm of Gilead trees that still line both sides of the miners' ghost-town of Vicksburg, Colorado; former land use can be discovered by the parallel rows of Red Rome apple trees (the fragments of a nineteenth-century orchard) that now grace the backyards of the fashionable suburb of Bloomfield Hills, Michigan; and May T. Watts, in her marvelous book, *Reading the Landscape of America*, has shown us how to recognize extant clumps of arborvitae, daffodils, and daylilies as natural fossils of former homesteads.[21] Watts has also provided us with a superb primer for dating and interpreting a typical American house and garden as of 1856, as of 1906, and as of 1963.

The vegetation of cemeteries, parks, forest preserves, town commons, malls, public gardens, and market squares and private gardens all tell the explorer of the landscape an immense amount about the history of a place and its people. At Notre Dame, for example, the University Arboretum laid out by Brother Philip Kunze in the late nineteenth century, survives as a testament to the German professor's aspiration to plant the campus with every tree species indigenous to the United States that would grow in the northern Indiana climate.[22]

From the afforestation attempts of Father Ioann Veriaminov in the Alaskan Aleutian Islands, as early as 1803, to the conservation and forestry work of Gifford Pinchot and John Muir in the 1880s and 1900s, to the shelter-belt and reforestation of Franklin D. Roosevelt's Civilian Conservation Corps in the 1930s, there is an important physical record of personal, local, state, and federal involvement in the preservation and re-establishment of the natural environment of the continent.[23] Following the lead of Phoebe Cutter, the above-ground archaeologist becomes adroit at "recognizing a WPA rose garden or a CCC Privy."[24] In every American city there is abundant material cultural evidence of the impact of the New Deal on the landscape:

In many highly urbanized areas of the United States, however, the vegetation of the past and its influence on the local history survives only in the region's place-names. George Stewart, the dean of American toponymists, correctly insists that "the history of any region can be read in terms of its nomenclature."[25] For instance, those who fly into O'Hare field in Chicago have baggage tags labeled "ORD." That abbreviation recalls, not the name of the person for whom the airport is named, but its former land use as a productive fruit growing region known as Old Orchard—a place name, incidentally, still extant as a nearby shopping center and a suburb.

Plant place-names are usually categorized by onomastic scholars as objectively descriptive names. Inevitably, such names tell a history. When Chicago real estate promoter S. E. Warner decided to name the main street of his development in honor of his political hero, Henry Clay, he called it Ashland, in reminiscence of the Whig party leader's home, "The Ashland," in Kentucky. Warner left still another marking on the land when he planted both sides of his residential avenue with rows of white ash.

In Indiana place names, the local flora has been extremely influential:

Beechwood, Cloverdale, Maple Valley, Hemlock, Burr Oak, Pine, Quercus Grove, Plum Tree, and Sycamore are towns scattered throughout the state.[26] The sixteenth-century French presence survives in *La Porte*, "the door," which recalls a natural opening in the primeval forest cover that served as a portal through which trade passed between southern and northern Indiana.

In addition to being fossils of past vegetation patterns, the plant place-names that now grace our cities and suburbs are often the result of political, religious, economic, or aesthetic decisions made centuries ago. Take the example of Philadelphia. William Penn, with typical Quaker humility and love of equality, decided that his model town plan would have no streets named after special persons. Hence, beginning at the eastern boundary of his plat, he simply called the first street by that name. To distinguish the cross streets, however, he succumbed to the Quaker love of botany and applied "the names of the things that spontaneously grow in the county." Some of these names were later changed, but enough of them are extant to make the famous rhyme for remembering the order:

> "Market, Arch, Race and Vine;
> Chestnut, Walnut, Spruce and Pine."[27]

The above-ground archaeologist, ever attentive to place-names as evidence, recognizes this "most far-reaching and typical habit of American naming" when it consistently reappears in cities and towns across the country, even in the street patterns of arid western communities where such tree species have never grown.[28]

Whenever an individual is confronted with giving a large number of names to a landscape, he usually resorts to some discernible systematic method. The landscape investigator watches for such patterns. Those driving to South Bend, Indiana, for example, from the east, along the Indiana Toll Road, cannot help but be struck by the botanical logic of the nineteenth-century St. Joseph County surveyor who identified the sectional division roads, east to west, in alphabetical sequence, as Ash, Beech, Currant, Dogwood, Elder, Fir, Gumwood, Hickory, Ironwood, Juniper, and on to Oak, Pine, and Quince. Three Oaks, Michigan, and San Diego, California, have a similar pattern of tree place-names for a section of streets, with San Diego using "Upas" as a quiet joke on the unsuspecting residents of that particular block.

Twentieth-century real estate developers all over the United States are equally enamored of flora place-names. They use them to elicit in prospective buyers' minds the image of English country estates, British and

American history, as well as the social pretensions and economic status of living in a feudal deer park or imperial forest preserve.[29] Such Anglophilia, historical associationism, and reverie for the pastoral, intrigue the above-ground archaeologist who finds, with almost monotonous regularity the same binominal place-names formed by a collective noun (e.g., Forest, Green, Hurst, Wood) and often a deliberately horticultural modifying adjective (e.g., Locust, Pine, Oak, Poplar).

*　*　*　*　*

There are at least four other groups of historians of whom I am aware who use vegetation in their work. Let me conclude by quickly summarizing the nature of their current research interests.

Lately, historic preservationists have become more extensively involved in the restoration or reconstruction of botanical and pleasure gardens, parks, and the preservation of natural forest preserves, wilderness areas, and landscapes of outstanding historical and ecological significance.[30] Recently, an entire conference devoted to historic gardens and landscapes discussed the importance of historical landscape architecture and preservation.[31] John T. Stewart and others have developed techniques of what they call "landscape archaeology" in their research into existing plant material on historic sites as evidence of buried features and as survivors of historic species.[32]

In the area of historical ethnobotany, John R. Stilgoe has students do research using plants, particularly herbs and herbals, in his investigations of American folk medicine and folklore. (Stilgoe is also an avid and insightful reader of the landscape, and his publications are a must for anyone interested in environmental history).[33] Folklorists with geographical interests and geographers with folklore proclivities are also studying the social and communicative functions of the visual folk art of private gardens, suburban front-lawn plantings, and the personal landscape habits of residential neighborhoods of varying economic, ethnic, and social backgrounds.[34]

Art historians likewise are turning to the American landscape and its vegetation, not only to re-analyze the familiar American school of landscape painters such as Thomas Cole, Asher Durand, and Thomas Moran, but also to explore the historical information depicted in other pictorial forms (engravings, lithographs, photographs), to discover what such sources can tell the field biologist, the agricultural historian, the student of landscape change, and the cultural historian. Two intriguing studies, both of which were originally museum exhibitions, reflect this trend: William C.

Lipke and Philip Grime, editors, *Vermont Landscape Images, 1776–1976* (1976) and Jay E. Cantor, *The Landscape of Change: Views of Rural New England, 1790–1865* (1976).

Old Sturbridge Village in Massachusetts, publisher of *The Landscape of Change* catalogue, also includes the Pliny Freeman living-history farm, an outdoor museum that seeks to recreate southern Massachusetts farming methods around the year 1840. This farm site is but one of more than forty living historical farms now in existence throughout North America. This form of historical museum interpretation, by definition, requires extensive research into the historical relationship between human beings and plants. The curators and historians within the Association for Living Historical Farms and Agricultural Museums (ALHFAM) are presently investigating some of the most fascinating topics in current material culture research: the recreation of genetic diversity in seed banks and the documentation of all aspects of the American farm's cultural ecology, particularly its transformation and use of a region's natural resources. While the primary aim of such museums is to communicate a sense of the reality of farm life in the past, they have become also involved in contemporary political and economic goals. Several curators envision their living-history farms as bases for what Jay Anderson calls "experimental archaeology." In their exploration of the historical relationship between man, plants, and the environment, these historians see the potential of their museums as experimental stations preserving and rediscovering traditional foodways that may be drawn upon in the future if a need for alternative means of food procurement and processing is forced upon us by a breakdown in our present technological systems.[35] In their attempt to reproduce for the people of today ways in which individuals once lived and farmed at some specific time and place in the past, this innovative cadre of historians and curators is also grappling with many of the major interpretive challenges of modern museology.[36]

Hence, despite initial neglect, a number of American historians have realized the immense potential of plants as a resource in their teaching and research. Those of us interested in what John Stilgoe calls "the ghostly interface of inter-mingled landscapes," the natural and man-made shards that still exist in space past as well as in time past, are hopeful about the new directions of what some have called "environmental history." Like Francis Parkman, who tramped over every inch of a battlefield, a village, or a town site while writing his eleven-volume series on *France and England in America*, we are anxious to connect what we learn in archives and libraries with what material culture evidence we discover on the rural countryside or still extant in the urban cityscape. Vegetation, as new books[37] by Eugene

Kinkead and Neil Jorgenson clearly show, is assuredly a vital element of this abundant artifactual record. Knowledge of its historical significance, like all knowledge of the past, remains crucial to both collective and personal identity.

8

Regional Studies in America: The Chicago Model

REGIONAL studies have been a useful way of comprehending American culture ever since Edward Johnson wrote his *Wonder-Working Providence of Zion's Saviour in New England* in 1654. More recent scholarship and teaching, particularly in American Studies, has continued this tradition by focusing on the culture of the South, New England, the West, and the Middle West.[1] The objective in such investigations has usually been to explore the possible existence and dimensions of a regional culture as well as its relationship to the national culture.

In such a context, the cultural history of Chicago from the 1870s to the 1920s provides a striking microcosm of the political, economic, literary, and artistic developments in the nation at large. It offers a fertile area of study for the social scientist interested in urban history, the literary scholar working in regional literature, and the art historian intrigued by the rise of modern architecture. Ray Ginger and Hugh D. Duncan[2] have tried, with varying degrees of success, to explore the interrelations between the city's politics, economic growth, literary achievement, and architectural innovation. What I am suggesting here is a bibliographical framework that expands the Ginger-Duncan perspective by a comprehensive survey of the primary sources and secondary literature available for a systematic study of Chicago's regional culture and its relation to American history from 1871 to 1919.

Naturally, this Chicago model is most accessible to American Studies scholars who are researching and teaching in the Middle West, but the published sources on the city are now so plentiful that one can easily do much research, or an American Studies course, on the topic in Oslo, Tokyo, or Berlin. Recently, British scholars developing course materials for the Open University in the United Kingdom concurred in what social scientists have long maintained: Chicago is probably the best researched, and perhaps the best example, of a typical urban complex in the modern world.

160

Moreover, what I also mean to suggest by this essay is the feasibility of scholars developing other interpretive frameworks using other American cities as the foci of regional inquiries: seventeenth-century Boston; eighteenth-century Baltimore or Philadelphia; early nineteenth-century Cincinnati or New Orleans; late nineteenth-century San Francisco or St. Louis; twentieth-century New York or Los Angeles.

To gain a general perspective of Chicago's development, 1871 to 1919, there are numerous, often highly personal, accounts of its history done by Joseph Kirkland, Lloyd Lewis and Henry Smith, Edgar Lee Masters, Wayne Andrews, Emmett Dedmon, Bessie Pierce, and, more recently, Edward Wagenknecht, Finis Farr, and Stephen Longstreet.[3] Pierce's three volumes comprise the most detailed scholarly study of the period to 1893, but it has now been superseded somewhat by Harold Mayer and Richard Wade's well-written single volume, *Chicago: Growth of a Metropolis**.[4] Mayer, a geographer, and Wade, a historian, collaborated with Glen Holt, a historian of photography. Holt integrated their research with numerous photographs in an excellent example (see figs. 1 and 2) of how to employ visual material to document as well as illustrate a historical narrative. Holt has explained his methodology in "Chicago through a Camera Lens: An Essay on Photography as History," published in the spring of 1971 in the Chicago Historical Society's quarterly, *Chicago History,* a publication that should be consulted for articles on music, art, economics, literature, and theater, in addition to history. As should be evident from the sources I cite below, I maintain that in its general outlines, as well as in many of its specific dimensions, the Chicago story, 1871 to 1919, is the national story. This position is also held by such scholars as Arthur M. Schlesinger, Sr., Constance Green, Daniel Boorstin, and Howard Mumford Jones.[5]

In order to review the highlights of American politics from the late nineteenth through the early twentieth century, one finds excellent sources offered in Chicago. Vernon Simpson and David Scott have collected many of them in *Chicago's Politics and Society: A Selected Bibliography**[6] which they augment with annual supplements. The rise of city bosses, ethnic politics, and the protests for social reform can be nicely studied using Chicago data. *Machine Politics, The Chicago Model,** by Harold Gosnell,[7] is the best general introduction and Joel A. Tarr, Claudius O. Johnson, Alex Gottfried, and Mike Royko provide good biographical commentaries.[8] A lively study of the picturesque "Lords of the Levee," principally John "The Bath" Coughlin and Hinky Dink Kenna by Lloyd Wendt and Herman Kogan[9] captures the exploits of the city's most notorious alderman and the machinations of the infamous city council.

Mayor Carter Harrison's two-volume autobiography[10] offers one personal account of the city's political life, while Charles E. Merriam, University of Chicago political scientist and reform councilman, offers another in his memoirs.[11]

William T. Stead's prediction *If Christ Came to Chicago,* published by Laird and Lee in 1894, was but one prognosis of the need for reform in *fin de siecle* America. Chicago's Municipal Voters' League, the Civic Federation, and the Union League Club[12] were various Midwest Mugwump counterparts to the National Civil Service Reform League. Individual reformers such as Jane Addams, Francis Willard, Clarence Darrow, Louise deKoven Bowen, Eugene Debs, Alice Hamilton, and Graham Taylor[13] left descriptive reminiscences of their efforts and of the city they sought to improve. Women were particularly involved in Chicago reform and cultural uplift, and Allen Davis's new biography of Jane Addams, published by Oxford in 1973, recreates the atmosphere in which they worked and the obstacles they had to overcome. The Arno Press has published a new edition of the 1895 *Hull House Maps and Papers,* [14] which, along with data gathered in Edith Abbott's *Tenements of Chicago, 1908–1935,* published in 1936 by the University of Chicago Press, Florence Kelley's various writings, and Louise deKoven Bowen's speeches,[15] offers the social scientist superb primary sources for the study of urban problems. Harvey Zorbaugh, Louis Wirth, Nels Anderson, and Homer Hoyt have also provided classic models[16] of such social analysis done at the University of Chicago. *Division Street, America,* * published by Pantheon in 1967, by Louis ("Studs") Terkel is a more recent and more popular example of urban sociology using Chicago as a laboratory.

As in other American cities, the boss system and its cult of ethnicity thrived, in part, because it manipulated the diverse neighborhoods of Chicago's inner city—the Irish, Germans, and Scandinavians who came in the mid-nineteenth century, and the immigrants who traveled later from Italy, Russia, Austria-Hungary, the Balkans, Greece, and the black Americans from the South. John Allswang has surveyed the immigrant history of the city in *A House for All Peoples: Ethnic Politics in Chicago, 1890–1936,* published by the University of Kentucky Press in 1971, but practically every major ethnic minority is represented in the specific monograph literature.[17] To do Chicago ethnic studies, one should also visit the Polish Museum at 984 Milwaukee Avenue; the Ling Long Chinese Museum, 4012 South Archer; the Maurice Spertus Museum, 72 East 11th Street; and the DuSable Museum of African-American History, 3806 South Michigan.

An important chapter of the black man's American history is likewise dramatized in Chicago, especially during and after World War I, when European migration declined and Southern blacks, encouraged by newspapers like the *Chicago Defender*, began moving up the Mississippi Valley. St. Clair Drake and Horace R. Clayton first studied this significant development[18] and more recently Harold F. Gosnell, in *Negro Politicians: The Rise of Negro Politics in Chicago,* and Allan H. Spear, in *Black Chicago: The Making of a Negro Ghetto, 1890–1920,** both published by the University of Chicago Press in 1935 and 1967, respectively, have examined its political and social consequences. William Tuttle on a scholarly level, Carl Sandburg from a newsman's viewpoint, and the Chicago Race Relations Commission from a documentary perspective have each[19] provided insight into the causes and consequences of the bloody Chicago race riot of 1919.

Chicago has always been one of the nation's more violent cities, from the Fort Dearborn ambush in 1812 to the Haymarket riots of 1886 to the St. Valentine's Massacre in 1929. The Pullman strike of 1894 provides a superb case study in which are woven important strands of economic, labor, social, constitutional, business, and political history. Pullman has been examined in detail[20] from Richard T. Ely's excellent contemporary account, "Pullman, A Social Study," which appeared in the February 1885 *Harper's New Monthly Magazine,* to Stanley Buder's *Pullman: An Experiment in Industrial Order and Community Planning, 1880–1930,** published in 1967 by Oxford University Press. For students in geographical proximity to Pullman, now a part of the city of Chicago, William Adelman of the Illinois Labor History Society has prepared an illustrated walking guide[21] to the planned company town. The Pullman Civic Organization, intent on preserving S. S. Beman's architecture, also offers guided tours of the Historic Landmark District.

Of course, Chicago's demographic, industrial, and commercial growth in the late nineteenth century is the American economic paradigm par excellence. In the hundred years from 1830 to 1930, the city grew from a settlement of fifty people to one of three-and-a-third million. In the half-century between 1840 and 1890, the rapidity of Chicago's economic development outstripped that of every other city in the world, so that by 1920 only London, New York, and Berlin exceeded her in size and commercial importance. Pierce[22] has traced this expansion up to 1893, while Mayer and Wade and Dorsha Hayes's chauvinistic *Chicago, Crossroads of American Enterprise,* published by Julian Messner in 1944, give the sweep of the city's economic history. The story is better told in assorted biographical monographs: Harper Leech and John Carroll on Armour, Morris Werner on Rosenwald, John Tebbel on the Fields as well as the

McCormicks, the Medills, and the Pattersons. Forest MacDonald had done a good book on Insull; Siegfried Giedion's playful *Mechanization Takes Command: A Contribution to Anonymous History** has stimulating chapters on the Pullmans, the Armours, and the McCormicks and their role in the history of American technology.[23]

For work in economic, political, and business history, the Municipal Reference Library of the City of Chicago, on the tenth floor of City Hall, and the Chicago Historical Society, on Clark at North Street, are excellent resources. Much documentary material on political and economic developments has been collected by Ernest W. Burgess and Charles Newcomb (census data), Homer Hoyt (land values), and Evelyn Kitagawa and Philip M. Hauser (local community sources).[24]

A number of scholars, particularly Bernard Duffey, Hugh Duncan, Dale Kramer, and Henry May,[25] have argued that roughly from Hamlin Garland's publication of *Crumbling Idols* in 1893[26] to Sherwood Anderson's departure for New York in 1920, Chicago had a significant share of the nation's literary inspiration, production, and consumption. The literary awakening has also been described by the participants in a diverse crop of autobiographies: multivolume personal accounts by Garland,[27] Dreiser,[28] and Anderson;[29] Sandburg's nostalgic *Always the Young Strangers;* Eunice Tietjens's *The World at My Shoulder;* Edgar Lee Masters's *Across Spoon River;* Harriet Monroe's *A Poet's Life;* and Floyd Dell's amusing *Homecoming, An Autobiography.*[30]

The Chicago press, equally well remembered in the reminiscences of Ben Hecht, Melville Stone, Burton Rascoe, and Arthur Meeker,[31] was perhaps the liveliest Fourth Estate in the nation between 1875 and 1925. More than a dozen dailies flourished, and newspaper offices and city rooms were once a source of genuine literary talent. Eugene Field's column, "Sharps and Flats," in *The News* has been studied by Slason Thompson;[32] Jean Shepherd has anthologized George Ade's "Stories of the Streets and Town,"[33] and James Farrell has brought out a modern edition of *Artie and Pink Marsh, Two Novels* (1963) in the University of Chicago Press series on Chicago in Fiction. Of course, Finley Peter Dunne's creation of "Mr. Dooley" of Archer Road (his original was a barkeep on Dearborn Street) offers insight into the local color movement as well as American political satire. Dunne's pieces have been collected by Louis Filler and Robert Hutchinson.[34] Ring Lardner[35] and his fellow raconteur Ben Hecht were also members of the Chicago press corps. Nelson Algren has written an introduction for a modern edition of Hecht's *Erik Dorn,* published in 1963 by the University of Chicago Press; and *The Front Page,* a delightful play Hecht did in collaboration with Charles McArthur in 1928, has recently enjoyed a successful revival on the London and Chicago stage.

In addition to Hecht, writers like Theodore Dreiser, Carl Sandburg, Sherwood Anderson, and Floyd Dell cut their literary teeth on Chicago journalism. Before this cadre of authors came into its own, an older generation had been exploring a variety of new literary topics, even if they were uncertain in experimenting with new literary forms. Edmund Wilson and Guy Szuberla have sparked new interest in Henry Blake Fuller,[36] whose *With the Procession,* * *The Cliff-Dwellers,* and *Under the Skylights* have all been reprinted.[37] Clara and Rudolf Kirk have revived Edith Wyatt, while David Henry's biography of William Vaughan Moody remains the best survey of the poet-playwright's limited achievement.[38]

Blake Nevius and Kenneth Jackson have worked with the numerous novels of Robert Herrick,[39] who, in his *Web of Life,* published by Macmillan in 1900, saw Chicago as a representative emblem of the American industrial age, a prototype of "all the sharp discords of the nineteenth century." In his more famous novel of 1905, *The Memoirs of an American Citizen* (Daniel Aaron has written a perceptive introduction to a Harvard University Press 1963 edition), Herrick used a fictional character, Van Harrington, not only as a typical Chicagoan, but, as the book's title suggests, a representative American of the 1890s. Herrick, like Fuller, explored all the concerns that later Chicago writers would make their stock in trade: the impact of the dominant business ethos upon cultural values; the nature of urban life and its ramifications for literary art; and the migrant experience of Americans from the country to the city.

Naturally, the literature of the better-known Chicago giants is the most accessible way of examining these themes as well as other representative trends in the American literature of the period.[40] In paperback have been available Dreiser's *Sister Carrie* and his trilogy on the city's traction magnate Charles Yerkes *(The Titan, The Financier, The Stoic)*; Upton Sinclair's *The Jungle*; Frank Norris's *The Pit*; Sherwood Anderson's *Marching Men.* Dell's *Moon Calf* (1920) and *Briary Bush* (1921), both published by Knopf, are a bit harder to find but still useful for the ambience of the city's literary movement. Depending on how far one wishes to extend a study of the Chicago "school" of fiction, there is also the work of James Farrell, Richard Wright, Nelson Algren, and Saul Bellow. The point, argues Bernard Duffey, the historian of *The Chicago Renaissance in American Letters,*[41] is that "the group reality of twentieth-century American literature began in Chicago because in Chicago a chief strain which has favored our modern writing was first recognized."

Many of the Chicago writers were also poets, and for a while the city was America's poetic center. *Poetry, A Magazine of Verse* was the movement's chief organ and remains its best primary source. The journal's success was largely the work of Harriet Monroe, a bad poet but a formidable entrepreneuse who knew how to combine philanthropy and the arts. Her career deserved the thorough re-evaluation given it by Ellen Williams (see supplement below), done from the Harriet Monroe Papers at the University of Chicago. (The Newberry Library in Chicago, particularly because of its extensive Middle West Authors Collection, is the best research center for manuscript study of other Chicago authors.) Carl Sandburg and Vachel Lindsay were among Miss Monroe's proteges, the best editions of their works being Sandburg's *Complete Poems,* published by Harcourt, Brace in 1970, and Lindsay's *Collected Poems,* published by Macmillan in 1925. The standard biographies of Sandburg and Lindsay, respectively, are by Karl Detzer and Ann Massa.[42] Miss Massa's essay is a fine example of American Studies scholarship, but it does not totally supplant Edgar Lee Masters's tribute to *Vachel Lindsay, A Poet in America* (Scribner's, 1935), which says as much about Masters as it does about his fellow Illinoian. Masters was a man of really only one literary achievement, *The Spoon River Anthology;* published by Macmillan in 1915, the book has been recorded, as has the poetry of Lindsay and Sandburg, on the Caedmon Spoken Arts Series of Columbia Records.

In addition to *Poetry,* Francis Browne's Emersonian *Dial,*[43] and Stone and Kimball's innovative *Chapbook,*[44] the later being the first of the American "little magazines," Chicago was also the birthplace of Margaret Anderson's iconoclastic *Little Review.*[45] Margaret, as was her way, told her story as *My Thirty Years' War* and also edited an anthology of what she considered the *Review's* best works.[46]

Thus, for anyone willing to look closely, Chicago's literary and poetic achievements not only paralleled currents in other parts of the country, but in several instances stimulated them. For many years, the East had dismissed Chicago as a muddy grain pit, a Porkopolis devoted only to "cash, cussing, and cuspidors." Between 1871 and 1919, however, the city became self-conscious and self-corrective about its cultural life in various forms. Its history during these years furnishes the American Studies scholar with an abundance of cultural evidence useful for investigating important developments in late nineteenth- and early twentieth-century art, music, and education.

Much of the city's cultural awakening revolved around preparing and executing the World's Columbian Exposition of 1893, a cultural event highly symbolic of late nineteenth-century American achievements and aspirations.[47] The fair can be used as a point of reference and a point of departure to trace trends in art, music, and popular taste. Alson J. Smith's breezy survey of *Chicago's Left Bank*, published by Regnery in 1953, does this to a certain extent in his attempt to portray Chicago as a Florence to New York's Rome.[48]

Smith devoted a chapter to Chicago as "The Jazz Capital" and reviewed the way in which black talents such as Louis Armstrong, Joe "King" Oliver, "Jelly Roll" Morton, and singer Bessie Smith made significant contributions to what historians[49] of music identify as the "Chicago style," a subspecies of jazz predominant in the nation from 1917 to 1929. The cultural and social ramifications that jazz has had on American popular music and popular taste can be examined in the Chicago context, and Chadwick Hansen[50] has used the locale, in turn, to trace a reverse influence of the dominant white society upon jazz as a musical expression of the black subculture.

From the beginning, the city's jazz was located on Chicago's South Side, and not far from that musical creativity arose another, albeit quite different, cultural asset—the University of Chicago, a school founded practically overnight in 1892 with John D. Rockefeller's money, land from Marshall Field, and guidance from the presidential entrepreneurship of Hebraist William Rainey Harper. Richard Storr's first volume on *Harper's University, The Beginnings*, published by the University of Chicago Press in 1966, surveys the institution's history to 1905; other monographs can be consulted to see the university as a case history of the important trends of late nineteenth-century American higher education: the rise of graduate and professional schools;[51] the new emphasis of the social and behavioral sciences;[52] and the increased concern to involve the university in social issues.[53]

Harper recruited a faculty with such vigor and largesse that some claimed the highest degree an educator could get was a C.T.C. (Called To Chicago). Many of the giants of American intellectual history got the call, responded, and each provides an excellent biographical approach by which to study American thought at the turn of the century. Jacques Loeb has been placed in the development of American behavior psychology by Donald Flemming;[54] Lloyd J. Averill[55] has argued for Shailer Mathews's place in liberal theology; R. M. Barry[56] for the role of George Herbert Mead in philosophy, and L. L. and J. Bernard[57] for Albion Small's impact on American sociology. Thorstein Veblen, of course, used his Chicago environment to write his classic *The Higher Learning in America*,* as John Dewey used the university's Laboratory School[58] (see fig. 18) to gather data for his equally famous *The School and Society*, published by the University of Chicago Press in 1899 and reissued in 1954. Joseph Dorfman relates Veblen's career to general economic theory in America, and Laurence Cremin has nicely placed Dewey's work in the history of progressive education.[59]

In literature, journalism, and jazz, the acclaimed Chicago Renaissance was a temporary though significant phenomenon, restricted largely from the 1880s to the 1920s. In architecture, the city's achievement has been constantly creative since William Jenney discovered the true skyscraper principle by using a skeleton-type of construction on the ten-story Home Insurance Building in 1884–1885. "The Developments in Chicago in the late nineteenth century," writes Hugh C. Miller, "were as consequential in world cultural history as the developments in twelfth-century France that produced Gothic architecture and in fifteenth-century Italy that produced Renaissance architecture. Of these three equally significant nodal points in

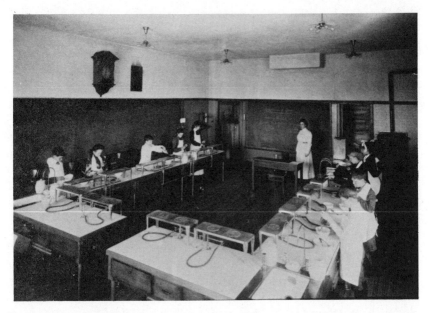

Fig. 18. A typical hands-on, inquiry-centered, student-involved, progressive-education classroom in 1904 in the University of Chicago's Laboratory School, inspired by the philosophy and pedagogy of John Dewey.—Courtesy the Laboratory School of Chicago

the history of western man, only the consequences of the Chicago School were truly global in scope."[60]

Even if this estimate approaches hyperbole, there still can be little doubt that a radical shift in urban architectural forms occurred in Chicago following the 1871 fire through a confluence of changing economic and social circumstances, technological innovations, and imaginative talent. Carl Condit has long been the dean of Chicago architectural historians surveying this amazing development. His numerous studies[61] should be supplemented by the general estimates of Siegfried Giedion, Lewis Mumford, Mark Peisch, William Jordy, and articles in the recent anthology edited by Edgar J. Kaufman.[62] Naturally, individual architects have been evaluated: John Wellborn Root by his sister-in-law Harriet Monroe and now by Donald Hoffman; Daniel Burnham by Charles Moore; Frederick Law Olmsted by Julius Fabos and others; and Henry Hobson Richardson by Henry Russell Hitchcock.[63]

Understandably, a considerable amount of scholarship has been devoted to Louis Sullivan and his brash protege Frank Lloyd Wright. The works of Sullivan and Wright, both buildings and writings, are excellent sources for American Studies students interested in exploring the interrelations between material and verbal culture. Sullivan's extant architecture is documented in Ira Bach and Arthur Siegel's walking guides[64] and in the slide collection of the Carnegie Study of the Arts of the United States;[65] his prose writings have been collected in a fine edition by Maurice English, *The Testament of Stone: Themes of Idealism and Indignation from the Writings of Louis Sullivan,* published in 1963 by Northwestern University Press. Sullivan's *Kindergarten Chats** and *The Autobiography of an Idea** have also been reprinted.[66] Hugh Morrison's biography[67] can be supplemented by Wright's own testimony to his hero (*Genius and the Mobocracy,** published by Duell, Sloan, and Pearce in 1949) and especially by Sherman Paul's classic *Louis Sullivan, An Architect in American Thought,** brought out by Prentice-Hall in 1962.

The literature on and by Wright forms a bibliographical essay in itself with many titles now being reprinted by the Horizon Press. Edgar Kaufman and Ben Raeburn have combined the *Writings and Buildings of Frank Lloyd Wright,* published by Horizon in 1960, in a useful source book. Frederick Gutheim has been concerned principally with Wright's writings,[68] while Martin Pawley and Yukio Futagawa and Edgar Kaufman have emphasized his buildings.[69] For photographic and slide resources on Wright, also see Bach, Siegal, the Carnegie Arts study, and the collections of the Frank Lloyd Wright Association in Oak Park, Illinois. Of course,

Wright's influence extended far beyond Chicago, and the research on his prolific work of later years is deliberately excluded in this essay. Two works that should be mentioned, however, are H. Allen Brooks, *The Prairie School: Frank Lloyd Wright and His Midwest Contemporaries*, published by the University of Toronto Press in 1972, and Grant C. Manson, *Frank Lloyd Wright to 1910: The First Golden Age*, published by Reinhold Publishers in 1958. One should also note here three superb Chicago facilities for doing research in the city's architectural history: the Burnham Library in the Art Institute (Adams and Michigan); the photograph and print collection at the Chicago Architectural Foundation, now housed in the former residence (at 18th and Prairie) that H. H. Richardson built for J. J. Glessner in 1886–1887; and the Commission on Chicago Historical and Architectural Landmarks.

As one becomes familiar with Chicago's architectural creativity, one sees, as have Hugh Duncan and Guy Szuberla,[70] certain interconnections between the literature and the architecture of the period, 1871–1919. Diverse cultural ramifications can also be explored, say, in the community planning of S. S. Beman's industrial Pullman, F. L. Olmsted's residential Riverside, or D. H. Burnham's metropolitan Plan of Chicago in 1909.[71] Victoria Ranney has made *Olmsted in Chicago*, published by R. R. Donnelly in 1972, her special province and provides an excellent bibliography at the conclusion of her essay. W. R. Hasbruck has written a new introduction to Burnham's grandiose Plan, recently reissued—in 1972—by the Prairie School Press. Carl Condit devotes a thorough chapter to the Burnham concept in his *Chicago, 1910–1929: Building, Planning, and Urban Technology*, published by the University of Chicago Press in 1973.

The Chicago architects determined to emphasize their innovations in their founding of the Western Association of Architects. Their publication, *The Inland Architect and Builder*—not unlike Garland's hopes for his region's contribution to literature—spoke of a West trying to assert its artistic modernity in steel and glass, those supremely modern industrial materials. The reality of that modernity is more evident in the inspiration that the original "Chicago School" continues to provide for architectural practice, both in Chicago and in the nation. A third generation of the city's architects represented by Ludwig Mies van der Rohe and many of his Chicago followers openly acknowledge their indebtedness to the early masters of the period, 1871–1919.

Further inquiry into Chicago's history, 1871 to 1919, would yield many other cultural trends with significance for the national culture. Suffice it to say that none of the national struggles, problems, and achievements during these fifty years were missing in the region that James Bryce once called "the most American part of America." Chicago was archetypal, a representative place wherein the "Age of Energy," the sobriquet Howard Mumford Jones[72] aptly uses to describe the "varieties of American experience, 1865–1915," came to something of an apex. Chicago, in this period, was not just middle America; it was America.

Recent Trends: Chicago Studies, 1975–1980

In the five-year period since the publication of the foregoing essay, so much excellent scholarship on Chicago's cultural history has surfaced that a brief sequel seemed apropos. As in the preceding essay, here I have confined my review of the recent literature[73] to research dealing with topics from the 1870s to the 1920s, the time frame wherein I think the most convincing case can be made for studying Chicago as a striking microcosm of the political, economic, literary, social, cultural, and artistic developments in the nation at large.

I have argued the validity of that thesis in "America, 1871–1919: A View of Chicago" (*American Studies* 17, no. 2, Fall 1976). My insistence in that essay, as in this one, on a cross-disciplinary perspective to the study of Chicago received support from Perry Duis's survey, *Chicago: Creating New Traditions**, a profusely illustrated exhibition catalogue written to accompany the Chicago Historical Society's bicentennial exhibit of the same name.[74] Duis and I agree that the principal areas of Chicago's cultural history spanning the years between the Great Fire and the Great War are politics and reform: industrial, transportation, and merchandising activity, literary realism, and innovations in architecture and city planning.

In Chicago political history, neighborhoods and ethnicity have always been critical ingredients. Following the national trend among urban historians who are examining the city in microcosm, recent research in Chicago has particularly focused on several south- and west-side neighborhoods. Glen Holt and Dominic Pacyga have provided us with the best introductory overview, a 175-page paperback titled *Chicago: A Historical Guide to the Neighborhoods: The Loop and the South Side**, that analyzes fourteen communities,[75] using the 1909 edition of the *Rand McNally New Standard Map of Chicago* as a base map. The primer also includes a perceptive use of historical photography (Holt was the historian who researched the photography used in the Mayer and Wade volume *Chicago: Growth of a Metropolis*, cited in the previous essay) and detailed economic and social statistics. One interesting use that can be made of the Holt/Pacyga volume is to have students compare it to Albert Hunter's *Symbolic Communities: The Persistence and Change of Chicago's Local Communities* (Chicago, 1974), a work that re-examines most of the neighborhoods originally defined by Edward L. Burchand (*District Fact Book For Seventy-five Chicago Local Communities*, 1935) and others of the Chicago School of Urban Sociology. In a general fashion, Hunter attempts to identify those things that have remained constant in the Chicago neighborhoods and those that have changed, such as the trend toward less segregation by ethnic groups and more by race.

While the detailed, interpretive histories of many Chicago individual neighborhoods are still lodged largely in the primary sources as suggested in Frank Jewell's section on "Neighborhoods" (pp. 195–212 in the *Annotated Bibliography of Chicago History* published by the Chicago Historical Society in 1979), portents of a "new" local history have already appeared. Two of southside Chicago's famous neighborhoods—Prairie Avenue and Hyde Park—have been examined with painstaking research. Victor Dyer has compiled a model bibliographical guide to the city's most fashionable millionaire's row of the 1880s, and Jean Block has attempted to read the communal history of Hyde Park from 1856 to 1910 through its extent housing stock.[76] Recent research into the city's west-side communities runs the gamut of the economic and social status prevalent in the nineteenth-century city. Here a seminar interested in social mobility and ethnic and racial identity could read, in concert, sociologist Richard Sennett's *Families Against the City: Middle-Class Homes of Industrial Chicago, 1872–1890**,[77] comparing it to Ira Berkow's oral history of Jewish immigrant life around an open-air market—*Maxwell Street: Survival in a Bazaar*, published by Doubleday in 1979—and labor historian William Adelman's on-site explorations of the working-class ghettos in the Pilsen area and the police and labor violence in the Haymarket.[78]

A future area of local history study into which enterprising students might venture, I anticipate, will be the processes of suburbanization. To date, that complex phenomenon has not been studied on a community-by-community level since the initial research by the Park-Burgress school in the 1920s. One tentative model worthy of further testing has been proposed by Barbara M. Posadas:[79] "A Home in the Country: Suburbanization in Jefferson Township, 1870–1889," *Chicago History* 7, no. 3 (Fall 1978).

As in most American cities, ethnicity was often a component in the Chicago suburbanization process. The flight of the southside Irish still farther south and west is a migration still to be carefully chronicled and interpreted. At present, most students of Chicago ethnicity (see fig. 19) continue to study their subjects *in situ*. For similar classroom analysis, we now have several excellent documentary collections of social scientific data, an anthology of first-rate essays on most of the major ethnic communities, and a handful of new monographic studies on what might be called "the Catholic ethnics."

The city of Chicago's Department of Development and Planning provide the two documentary sourcebooks *(The People of Chicago* and Historic City*)*, each of which can be adapted to an assortment of exercises introducing students to basic concepts in quantitative history, particularly demography. *The People of Chicago: Who We Are and Who We Have Been: Census Data on Foreign Stock and Race, 1837–1970* is basically a census-by-census analysis of the city's population by country of origin, with a helpful Mother Tongue Addendum. The detailed footnotes, offering the necessary qualifications that must be made about the demographic data, are, in themselves, a valuable teaching tool. If *The People of Chicago's* principal value is in its statistical data, then the major use of *Historic City: The Settlement of Chicago* is its cartographic materials. Using a series of fold-out, color-coded maps that accompany the paperback, one can chart the internal migrations of twenty-one ethnic populations in 1870, 1900, and 1920. Imposed on a 1970 street pattern of Chicago, the maps also show changes in built-up areas, shorelines, railroad networks, and rivers and harbors.[80]

In *The Ethnic Frontier: Essays in the History of Group Survival in Chicago and the Midwest** (Grand Rapids, Mich.: William B. Eerdmans, 1977), Melvin G. Holli and Peter d'A Jones have assembled the best current scholarly introduction to a wide range of issues dealing with Chicago ethnicity: the role of ethnic leaders, race and housing, and the inner dynamics of specific ethnic communities. Two of the anthology's authors—Edward R. Kantowicz and Edward H. Mazur—have also done new monographic studies on the city's Poles and Jews, respectively.[81] Inasmuch as many of Chicago's "meltable" and "unmeltable" ethnics were Catholics, a recent study by James M. Sanders, *The Education of an Urban Minority: Catholics in Chicago, 1833–1965* (New York: Oxford University Press, 1977), fills a significant gap in the story.[82] So does the work of civil servant Barbara C. Schaaf and literary historian Charles Fanning, on one of the city's most highly visible of Catholic subcultures, the Chicago Irish.[83]

Both Schaaf and Fanning propose an interpretation (deploying the Dunne/Dooley persona as primary evidence) of Irish urban ward politics in the nineteenth century. Political scientist Michael McCarthy, in "On Bosses, Reformers and Urban Growth: Some Suggestions for a Political Typology of American Cities" *(Journal of Urban History* 4, no. 1 [1977]: 29–38), offers other explanations, using comparative data from Chicago

Fig. 19. Front entrance to Casa Aztlán, a local community center at 1831 S. Racine in Chicago's Pilsen district, formerly a Czech neighborhood now inhabited by Spanish-speaking Americans. Wall murals such as these created by Arelio Diáz, Marcos Raya, and others serve as both visual histories and above-ground archaeological evidence.— Photograph by T. J. Schlereth

and New York. McCarthy argues that the reason some cities have had political machines and others have not depends on whether or not suburbanization resettled the middle class outside the political boundaries of the city or within city limits. When the middle class becomes overwhelmingly suburban, as he believes it did in Chicago (e.g., another instance of a research hypothesis on suburbs waiting to be validated or disproven), then the nucleus for a reform movement is missing and bossism and machine politics prevails.

In the past five years, however, students of Chicago politics have been less interested in bosses than in reformers. Two new emphases emerge from the recent literature: women as urban reformers and slum clearance as urban reform. In the first instance, John P. Rousmaniere's short summary essay, "Cultural Hybrid in the Slums: The College Woman and the Settlement House, 1889–1894" (*College Settlement Association* 22 [1970]: 45–66) is the place to begin, followed by new studies by Kenneth L. Kusmer, Kristin S. McGrath, and Thomas Philpott.[84] With Philpott's careful cross-disciplinary analyses of the reformers' social and political philosophy as well as the physical structures they built to implement that policy of social control, we have an excellent model on which to conduct similar studies of the urban built environment. Guy Szuberla has also demonstrated that approach in his argument that settlement-house architecture such as the Hull House of Irving and Allen Pond reflected a strong desire to "Americanize" the immigrant.[85] A parallel theme echoes through Devereux Bowly's *The Poorhouse: Subsidized Housing in Chicago, 1895–1976* (Carbondale, Ill.: Southern Illinois University, 1978).

Another mainstay of cross-disciplinary research, particularly in the field of American studies, has been the exploration of the reciprocal interrelationship between history and literature. In the context of specific courses[86] on Chicago, that has meant using Chicago authors and their works as perspectives on the city's cultural history and, in turn, when studying the creative corpus of Chicago writers, to examine the historical milieu in which their literary achievement took place. Recent research continues to validate the approach when using the fiction, poetry, and prose writing of the era from 1871 to 1919.

Although no new major syntheses have appeared to displace the major literary interpretations (e.g., Duffey, Kramer, Duncan) of the period, four short articles by Ann Douglas, Charles Fanning, Anthony Grosch, and Carl Smith, on the city's social novels, merit addition to the basic bibliography on Chicago fiction.[87]

Also of value is a new bibliography of fictive writing about Illinois, describing works by author and title, subject and place name. Prepared by Thomas L. Kilpatrick and Patsy-Rose Hoshiko, *Illinois! Illinois! An Annotated Bibliography of Fiction* (Metuchen, N.J.: Scarecrow Press, 1979) contains more than twelve hundred annotated entries on novels dealing with Chicago. On the important interrelation between Chicago journalism, literature, and social reform, we now have John Erickson's dissertation, "Newspapers and Social Values: Chicago Journalism, 1890–1910" (University of Illinois at Urbana, 1973); and on the interconnection between the first of Chicago's and the nation's little literary magazines and the intellectual history of *fin-de-siecle* America, we can learn from Wendy L. Clauson Schlereth's history of ideas contained in *"The Chapbook: A Journal of American Intellectual Life, 1894–1898"* (Ph. D. dissertation, University of Iowa, 1980). Finally, in the past five years, important reassessments of four major participants in the so-called Chicago Renaissance have been published: Jonathan Yardley has done the now-standard biography of Ring Lardner, while Robert Conrow has brought up to date information about fellow newspaperman/poet Eugene Field.[88] In *Henry B. Fuller of Chicago: The Ordeal of a Genteel Realist in Ungenteel America,* Bernard Bowron establishes the literary and historical context for that much misunderstood novelist, editorialist, and editorial staff member of *Poetry* magazine—which, in turn, has been given a thoroughly researched, intensive study by Ellen Williams in her analysis of *Harriet Monroe and the Poetry Renaissance: The First Ten Years of Poetry, 1912–1922.*[89]

Williams notes how Monroe, through family connections and personal tenacity, gained access to the city board rooms and corporate offices. Seeking to combine philanthrophy and poetry, young Harriet persuaded a hundred fellow Chicagoans (mostly businessmen) to subscribe fifty dollars a year for five years to support her magazine. A Philadelphia paper sneered at Chicago for using "the proceeds of pork for the promotion of poetry" but that mode of cultural underwriting was more the rule than the exception during the period from 1871 to 1919, when most of the city's major cultural institutions were founded.

The individuals who were movers and shakers in both worlds—business and art—have received some attention in the past half-decade. Perhaps the best overview strictly in terms of business history is a careful statistical and demographic study[90] by Jocelyn Maynard Ghent and Frederic Cople Jaher, of 1,186 members of the Chicago business elite, two-thirds of whom made their own fortunes in manufacturing, meatpacking, and merchandising. An important area of Chicago business history that I almost totally neglected in my initial review of the literature was merchandising, particularly mail-order selling. I now use reprint catalogues from Sears, Roebuck and Montgomery Ward in my Chicago course; and elsewhere,[91] I have proposed the range of American studies teaching techniques that can be developed from these rich, versatile, primary sources that once were the arbiters of taste, culture, and life style of much of rural and small-town America. Although the Montgomery Ward firm lacks a substantial historical treatment, there is a detailed study of Sears, Roebuck by Boris Emmet and John Jeuck, *Catalogues and Counters: A History of Sears, Roebuck & Company* (Chicago: University of Chicago Press, 1950).

Lawrence P. Bachman's perceptive reassessment[92] of Julius Rosenwald (probably the most astute Sears executive, 1862–1922) illustrates, however, that the current interpretive trend in the historical study of Chicago businessmen is decidedly less on their corporate acumen than on the purpose, scope, and impact of their cultural philanthropy. I have explored this intriguing problem in American cultural history through the career of a single Chicagoan, Charles Hutchinson, then through one cultural activity (music) over a single generation, whereas Helen Lefkowitz Horowitz has surveyed the entire generation from the 1880s to 1917 in several arenas of cultural life.[93] Several of the Chicago institutions analyzed by Horowitz have also been the subject of specific studies:[94] the Newberry Library, the Fine Arts Building, and the Art Institute. In its centennial year, the Art Institute[95] received both internal and external re-evaluation. Finally, we now have an excellent interpretive digest of "The Chicago Little Theatre, 1912–1917," by Homer N. Abegglen (*The Old Northwest* 3 no. 2 [June 1977]: 153–172), as well as a bit of pioneering spade work by James S. Newell on "The Development and Growth of the Kenneth Sawyer Goodman Memorial Theatre and School of Drama, Chicago, Illinois, 1925–1971" (Ph.D. dissertation, Wayne State University, 1973).

Chicago is currently home for fifty-eight colleges and universities, many of whom have their origins in the nineteenth century. Inasmuch as educational history can be an excellent entry point into the history of ideas, the University of Chicago serves as an intellectual history laboratory for the exploration of American research and scholarly publishing in sociology,[96] law,[97] education,[98] religion,[99] political science,[100] physics,[101] and history.[102] Also now available is an anthology of selections from the papers of the university's first eight chief executives[103] as well as a photographic interpretation of the university's architectural environment.[104]

Architecture in Chicago, the urban environment that the British *Architectural Review* recently called "the New World's most architectural city," continues to be a source of enormous historical interest to scholars, preservationists, and building enthusiasts of every sort. The *AR* devoted its entire October 1977 issue to both a historical ("How Chicago Happened") and a contemporary ("Change of Heart in Process City") appraisal of the city's built environment. A particularly valuable exercise that teachers can initiate, dissecting the streetscape as a historical landscape, is the perceptive block-by-block analysis these British architects give to "Halsted Street: A Journal Through Average Chicago." William T. Brown's *Architecture Evolving: An Illinois Sage** (Chicago: Teach'em Inc., 1976) offers similar teaching strategies using the Chicago context. Brown's primer was especially prepared for "those who are not conversant with sophisticated architectural issues but who wish to gain an introduction to a new body of knowledge and who may or may not live daily among the architectural monuments." The book, which covers the three basic Chicago architectural schools—Commercial, Prairie, and Miesan—is intended, in Brown's estimate, "as much for those in the rural suburbs as for those in the metropolis."

In the first and last of the three major Chicago architectural movements—Commercial and Miesan, or as they are also sometimes labeled, Chicago School I (1880–1920) and Chicago School II (1938 to the present)—the majority of recent research has been on the modern era (see fig. 20). With the exception of a brief essay[105] by Jack Tager, exploring the interrelationship of business entrepreneurs, real estate speculators, and architectural firms, and two delightful, nostalgic picture books of "lost Chicago" assembled by David Lowe,[106] the major historiographical focus—Nory Miller called it "a war of ideas"—has been by the modernists about the modernists.

The "war" Miller refers to is a "battle of the books." Two books, to be exact, that grew out of two major architectural exhibitions mounted in 1977: one by Miesan Oswald W. Grube, *100 Years of Architecture in Chicago**; another by revisionist Stuart E. Cohen, entitled *Chicago Architects**.[107] While the nuances of this major divide in Chicago architectural historiography are too numerous and complicated to narrate here,[108] the basic positions of the two exhibitions can be summarized by noting where they opened in Chicago. The functionalist, rationalist, technologically-minded *100 Years of Architecture* was housed in Chicago's Museum of Contemporary Art; the *Chicago Architects'* paean to the eclectic, the romantic, and the historic appeared in the city's art moderne Diana Court Building.

Grube and associates survey the triumph of a rational aesthetic, particularly as revealed in the evolution of the Chicago skyscraper. This aesthetic insists that the logical facade of a building should be a visual expression of

Fig. 20. Modern Chicago with three of its most historically formative artifacts: railroads and their bridges, the Chicago River, and the skyscraper skyline viewed from the northwest. The 1974 Sears Tower, designed in Chicago's Miesan architectural tradition by Bruce Graham, currently reigns as the tallest office building in the world.— Photograph by T. J. Schlereth

the way it is held up and that the logical plan of a building should be uninterrupted, generic space. That is to say, Chicago, and hence modern, architecture should be viewed primarily as an expression of modern technology. *100 Years* also claims to delineate that historical development over a century, thereby showing the "continuity of structure and form" between two architectural schools—1871 to 1893, and 1938 to the present.

Stuart Cohen, however, is primarily interested in rescuing from oblivion the "city's unknown and forgotten architecture." Thus *Chicago Architects* is a useful review of those midwestern builders (George Frederick Keck, Andrew Rebori, Emery Stanford Hall, Howard Van Doren Shaw) whom the historical surveyors often merely mention. Moreover, Cohen's appreciation of those whom John Entgenza has called "the minor poets" (men such as Hugh Garden, Irving Pond, Dwight Perkins, Henry Ives Cobb) is a definite contribution to our historical knowledge and a fine example of detailed archival research.

Within that framework, Cohen's sixteen-page essay (the remainder of the book contains superb illustrations) sets out to document that work of Chicago architects "which is most unknown today because it represents a diversity of formal, spatial, symbolic and technological ideas which cannot be discussed as the work of a school." Rather it is, claims Cohen, "the architecture of a private experience, mostly houses, schools, and churches, rather than large corporate or government commissions." Although Cohen insists that his argument "does not relate either in ideology or chronological sequence to the cleansed history of Chicago architecture," he certainly deploys the structural-functional tradition as his polemical foil. Thus the two paperbacks are useful battle reports in Chicago's escalating, architectural cold war; as such they can be pitted against each other in the classroom, dramatizing for students the fact that architectural history is not always the tranquil, noncontroversial discipline that its critics sometimes claim.

Of course, one Chicago architect about whom there has always been abundant controversy is Frank Lloyd Wright; understandably, abundant materials continue to pour forth from a cadre of investigators who probe the master's writings and buildings. For Wright's Chicago years, there is now a paperback reprint of Grant Manson's *Frank Lloyd Wright to 1910** (New York: Van Nostrand Reinhold, 1958); Robert C. Twombly has rewritten and expanded his earlier biography, *Frank Lloyd Wright: An Interpretive Biography** (New York: Harper and Row, 1973) and issued it under a new title, *Frank Lloyd Wright: His Life and His Architecture* (New York: John Wiley and Sons, 1979); and a detailed *Plan for Restoration and Adaptive Use of the Frank Lloyd Wright Home and Studio** (Chicago: University of Chicago Press,

1979). The *Plan*, in addition to being a significant contribution to the study of the early years of the Prairie School, is an exceptional example of the painstaking techniques of restoration archaeology. It reveals the exceedingly complex series of changes (most made by Wright himself) in the fabric of the house and studio between 1889 and 1957. With regard to Wright and the Prairie School, three new finding aids make the teacher-scholar's task a bit easier. William Allin Storrer traveled over 78,000 miles in search of Wright's total *oeuvre* and now, in a newly revised second edition, thinks he has finally compiled it.[109] On a more local level, Paul E. Sprague has prepared a new *Guide to Frank Lloyd Wright and Prairie School Architecture in Oak Park** (Oak Park, Ill.: Landmarks Commission, 1976), while out of Oak Park, Thomas A. Heinz edits the *Frank Lloyd Wright Newsletter*. Robert L. Sweeney's *Frank Lloyd Wright: An Annotated Bibliography* (Los Angeles: Hennessey and Ingalls, 1978) now supersedes Kenneth Starosciak's compendium mentioned in the previous essay.

If one wishes to teach Chicago architectural development through arch-individualists like Wright, there is a parallel approach that uses archtypal buildings. Recent scholarship on single structures includes John Vinci on Sullivan's Stock Exchange Trading Room, James O'Gorman on H. H. Richardson's warehouse for Marshall Field, and Harry Price on Sullivan's Auditorium Building.[110] Another superb source of background information (e.g., architect, client, real estate history, etc.) along with elevation drawings, floor plans, and photographs are the brochures prepared by the Commission on Chicago Historical and Architectural Landmarks[111] on individual Chicago sites, structures, and districts. The commission has also taken the lead in pointing out a direction in urban architectural history that I would predict will dominate the energies of many researchers in the 1980s: nineteenth- and twentieth-century vernacular housing. Chapter 2, "Chicago Houses and Styles," of a new commission publication[112] by Linda Legner is a fine, introductory field-guide to simple row houses and store-fronts, ordinary greystones, and Beaux-Arts apartments, unpretentious bungalows, and balloon-frames.

Such ubiquitous, prefabricated housing stock erected block-by-block by real estate developers and contractors now makes up the bulk of Chicago's seventy-five neighborhoods. To begin any comprehensive analysis of this extensive laboratory of urban material culture, I urge students to read "Chicago," an essay[113] by J. B. Jackson, dean of American landscape historians, followed up by Irving Culter's fine geography, *Chicago: Metropolis of the Mid-Continent**, and then Brian Berry's social, economic, and demographic portrait, *Chicago: Transformation of Urban System*.[114]

Planners, of course, develop urban systems. In turn, planners and their plans are important indices to urban history. Daniel Burnham's comprehensive 1909 plan for the city of Chicago continues to attract the most attention from scholars. In what is now called the definitive biography of Burnham, Thomas S. Hines has assessed Burnham the planner (finding him a perfect example of David Noble's "paradox of progressive thought"), while Cynthia Field has concentrated primarily on Burnham's plan.[115] Others have explored the relation of Chicago businessmen and the plan, of Burnham and Fredrick Law Olmsted, the other nationally known planner working in Chicago (e.g., Riverside, Illinois; Jackson Park), and of the deficiencies of the 1909 plan, particularly its shortsightedness concerning the future impact of the automobile.[116] In addition to the historians of city planning, geographers and social historicans have also begun interpreting the significance of the placement, type, and size of parks,[117] a key hallmark of the Burnham Plan.

As part of a seventieth anniversary of the publication of the plan, the Art Institute of Chicago (where, in the Burnham Library, the bulk of the manuscript, graphic, and documentary data on the plan is housed) published, in 1979, an excellent exhibition catalogue, *The Plan of Chicago, 1909–1979**, edited by John Zukowsky. The catalogue contains, in addition to two interpretive essays, a valuable provenance and checklist of the plan drawings. In conjunction with the plan exhibition, a symposium on "The Plan of Chicago: Its Past and Future" took place in the spring of 1980, the results of which are published in the special April 1980 issue of the *Inland Architect*.

Burnham openly acknowledged his debt in the 1909 Plan to the 1893 plan of the World's Columbian Exposition, where he served as director of works. Hence the Chicago World Fairs are a final teaching technique to be employed in an interdisciplinary course in American urban studies. With the monographs by David Burg and R. Reid Badger[118] and new articles by other researchers,[119] we have almost total coverage of the 1893 extravaganza. The Century of Progress, while on scale similar to the Columbian Exposition, has, however, generated far fewer publications. The best of the lot are all articles: a general introduction by Cathy and Richard Cahan, an account of discrimination against blacks and the resulting protest, and a brief assessment of the 1933 fair's art moderne architecture.[120]

In the past half-decade, Chicago studies on the 1871–1919 period continued to exhibit many of the characteristics of that particular historical era—rapid growth, exuberant vitality, and genuine diversity. Contemporary research, teaching, and writing about Chicago during this period has broadened and sophisticated our understanding of the way in which numerous innovations and reforms in social and communal life, literature, and architecture pioneered in Chicago had an impact and a significance that went far beyond the city's limits. Recent scholarship, in my judgment, thus upholds a thesis that Frank Lloyd Wright argued in 1918, when he referred to Chicago as "the national capital of the essentially American spirit." For a brief sixty-year interlude in the city's history, that was certainly true; in the later half of the nineteenth century and the first quarter of the twentieth, Chicago's role in the transformation of America from a rural, agrarian society into an urban technological one remains unprecedented in prior American urban history.

9

Above-Ground Archaeology: Discovering a Community's History through Local Artifacts

IN 1893, a young historian from Wisconsin addressed the World's Congress of Historians and Historical Students sponsored in conjunction with the World's Columbian Exposition held in Chicago that year. His topic: "The Significance of the Frontier in American History." His name: Frederick Jackson Turner. A few years later, also in Chicago, but in an Irish neighborhood tavern along Archer Avenue, another historian delivered another assessment of the American past. His claim: "I know histry isn't true, Hinnissy, because it ain't what I see ivryday in Halsted Street." His name: Martin Dooley, fictional persona of Chicago journalist Finley Peter Dunne.[1]

Although both the Turner and the Dooley theses have been prone to hyperbole, each in their own way recalls for us an important axiom that many historians neglect to consider in their historical research: that the landscape, whether at the scale of the western frontier or the local streetscape, whether natural or man-made, is an amazing historical document. In fact, in his classic study of *The Making of the English Landscape*, W. G. Hoskins has gone so far as to insist that the land and its artifacts are "the richest historical record we possess."[2] The landscape offers the historian engaging, challenging reading from an ever lively, often unfinished, occasionally undecipherable, but always significant manuscript. The landscape as historical document is filled with hurried erasures, encoded messages, delightful facetiae, different languages, strange symbols, expert forgeries, smudged signatures, garbled testimonies, and subtle anachronisms that await the best (and most curious) philologists, cryptographers, epigraphers, sillographers, and paleographers. To be sure, the language of any landscape is so dense with evidence and so complex and cryptic at times that we can never be certain we have read it all or that we have read it all right. Yet it is "a rich and beautiful book always open before us," argues J. B. Jackson. "We have but to learn to read it."[3]

The American landscape—despite all our celebration of it in language ranging from prose to poetry and in visual expression, from painting to photography—remains largely unresearched by professional historians. We all have seen but few have truly read. Ironically, this landscape lies all around us, ever accessible and inexhaustible. We need to realize that this historical landscape is at once "a panorama, a composition, a palimpsest, a microcosm; that in every respect there can be more and more than meets the eye."[4] In short, I propose we investigate this landscape as a mammoth, open-air historical archive, library, and museum, wherein local and community history can be discovered, identified, classified, and interpreted in a personal and novel way. In such a context, the rural agrarian countryside, the suburban tract development, or the central city core can be examined as a gigantic material culture collection, an assemblage of artifacts that includes every tangible, physical object of human ingenuity found extant on the land.

How might such diverse historical evidence be examined? What shall we call this type of historical study? I have used the neologism *above-ground archaeology* to identify my method,[5] and I have called its study that of "the history on the land."

The concept of above-ground archaeology is simple. Like the below-ground, prehistorical, postmedieval, or historical archaeologist,[6] the above-ground archaeologist concentrates on using material objects and physical sites as primary evidence; on employing extensive field work as a fundamental research technique; on adapting anthropological explanatory concepts (e.g., typology, diffusion, templates, space-time slope patterns)[7] where feasible; and the above-ground archaeologist, too, concentrates on acquiring historical knowledge and understanding about humankind as the principal objective of any research investigation. The above-ground archaeologist simply does his or her "digging" into the past "above-ground."

In the past decades, archaeologists themselves have endorsed such an approach in studying the American landscape. "Archaeological methods can profitably be applied to any phase or aspect of history," argues Grahame Clark. "A coherent and unified body of subject matter entirely appropriate to the archaeologist," writes James Deetz, "is the study of all the material aspects of culture in their behavioral context, regardless of provenance."[8] Applying the archaeological methodology that Clark suggests to the range of material data Deetz wishes to survey, archaeologists like James Dalibard, Bert Salwen, and Cary Carson have shown how important information and insight about human behavior, past and present, can be extracted from material culture data without necessarily having to dig it up in the usual mode of archaeological excavation.[9] Historical and cultural geographers concur with this assumption. "The student of the cultural landscape is a kind of contemporary archaeologist," suggests Peirce Lewis, "with somewhat different materials, similar methods, and nearly identical motives, we are all trying to understand the human condition—nothing less."[10]

In addition to its obvious debts to archaeology as traditionally conceived (see fig. 21), above-ground archaeology borrows much of its theory and practice from related fields such as art history, geography, architectural history, toponymy, history of urban and town planning, folkways research, and the history of technology.

Above-ground archaeology also goes by various synonyms—*environmental history, material culture studies, urban archaeology, history under foot, nearby history, landscape archaeology.*[11] In Great Britain, the undertaking is often called *landscape history* or *history on the ground.* In fact, the British have been the pioneers of such an approach to local history in the world's English-speaking countries. Penelope Lively, Maurice Beresford, and W. G. Hoskins have explored their countryside from Land's End to John O'Groat's, providing us with excellent models for historical analysis of the American environment, particularly on the small town and the country level.[12]

Above-ground archaeology has, likewise, been heavily influenced by American scholarship. The ideas of landscape historians such as Grady Clay and J. B. Jackson are invaluable to any environment interpreter; cultural geographers such as John Fraser Hart and Fred Kniffen, along with historical geographers like Peirce Lewis and John Stilgoe are required reading for anyone anxious to pick up clues for reading the landscape.[13] Folkways scholars such as Don Yoder, urban naturalists like Eugene Kinkead, or midwest botanists such as the late May T. Watts help us decipher city backyard gardens, suburban front-yard plantings, and the planned vegetation of residential neighborhoods of varying ethnic, economic, and social backgrounds.[14]

A common denominator uniting these assorted above-ground archaeologists is their identical recognition that this diverse American material culture survives in our everyday environment and usually not within the confines of our historical museums or historical societies. Hence, above-ground archaeology might also be considered, as I have argued elsewhere, as "the history outside the history museum."[15] Here, largely using midwest examples as illustrations, I would like to propose several

Fig. 21. The Cliff Palace at Mesa Verde, Colorado, testifies both to the historical archaeological research (below and above-ground) conducted there and to the genius of American vernacular architecture.—Courtesy National Park Service

ways in which this approach to using local artifacts as indices to local history can be applied to any community's natural and built environment.

Geological/Geographical Features

The configurations of many American above-ground archaeology sites are the *way* they are because of *where* they are. The history of places such as Baltimore and Buffalo, Richmond and Louisville, Chicago and Cincinnati, offers us ample evidence of that simple but often forgotten fact.[16] Fort Wayne, for example, in the northeast corner of Indiana, owes its existence largely to the fact that it was a military garrison commanding the portage between the Maumee and the Wabash river systems and the Great Black Swamp. Early travelers wisely journeyed around the swamp (part of an enlarged Lake Erie, in glacial times) rather than attempt to cut straight through it. A settlement eventually grew up around the military post located at the southernmost tip of the swamp, where traffic turned north and west.

To be sure, geography has by no means predetermined American history, but it has played a significant role up through the nation's nineteenth- and early-twentieth-century regional and urban development. Geologic forces, set in motion thousands of years ago, have often influenced a city's building materials. The brownstones of Boston, the greystones of Chicago, the cobblestones of upstate New York, all provide above-ground architectural evidence of what anonymous builders shaped out of the below-ground geological past. Both human artistry and the earth's chemistry have been at work in the history of these residences.

The rock strata of what geologists call the Cincinnati Arch or Dome, extending east and west from approximately Peebles, Ohio, to Madison, Indiana, is another instance of physical geography influencing historical settlement. Driving into Madison (see fig. 7) down State Route 62 or away from the town on State Route 7 (aptly named Hanging Rock Road), one encounters this physical evidence. Such severe topography required the 1835 railroad track bed (the first in Indiana, running from Madison to Columbus) to climb an incline of four hundred feet in little more than a mile and necessitated the gouging of two gigantic railroad cuts into the natural ravine. The observant town-watcher is impressed by both that engineering feat and its surviving artifact evidence, as well as by the fact that the building stone used in St. Michael's Catholic Church (1837–1839) in Madison, Indiana, is the same as that found in the railroad and highway cuts.

Stone fresh from the quarry is "live," full of quarry sap (moisture) that must be allowed to rise to the surface and form a protective skin to the stone. When this has not been done, the stone—especially any moldings and carvings—may crumble and weather badly. And, again, limestone and sandstone, being sedimentary rock, must be laid with the grain of the layers of which they are composed in the same horizontal position as they lay in their natural bed in the quarry. Occasionally the wall of the building will show individual blocks of stone that are more worn and weathered than others, and we have tangible evidence of an unknown mason's poor artisanry or past carelessness.

In midtown Manhattan, Sidney Horenstein, an invertebrate paleontologist at New York's American Museum of Natural History, leads field trips of above-ground archaeologists in pursuit of fossils, those traces of former life preserved in stone. Believe it or not, these relics of past geological ages stare out at us from the walls of bank lobbies, from hotel elevator doors, and from stone-clad buildings of all types.[17] Horenstein notes that we can find all kinds of faces in the facades of stone along city streets. In the cavernous lobby of the RCA Building, for instance, there is the physical history of the way a limestone vein was formed when cross-sections of a prehistoric reef built up in a shallow tropical sea that covered what is now northern Vermont, some 475 million years ago. In a Bun-n'-Burger restaurant on West 48th Street, more recent history is evident on a beige balcony, where two mollusks (a clam and a snail), 120 million years ago, helped build up a shell bank, near what now is Austin, Texas. Horenstein, as he explores the wealth of natural and civil history within New York's confines, also suggests places where the reader of the landscape can find Indian caves in Manhattan and notes that a mastodon skeleton, left over from the Ice Age, is buried beneath an apartment house.

In addition to the paleontological history that we can discover in the marble and stone canyons of our cities, there is the imprint of geology upon the road maps and in the place-names of our regions. In Philadelphia, the Limekiln Turnpike assumed its name from the lime quarries of Montgomery County, the road's first terminus in 1693. The famous "Rock of Ages" quarries that line State Road 14, en route to Graniteville, Vermont, have provided funeral monuments and public sculpture for American cemeteries and parks since the Civil War.

Landscape Vegetation

From the creation of the first New England commons and the earliest design of a city square in Philadelphia, Americans have been creating and planting all sorts of public landscapes that are significant historical data to the above-ground archaeologist. The placement, size, design, and vegetation of city parts, market malls, arboretums, public gardens, and other deliberately planned civic open spaces reveal to the landscape historian an amazing amount of information about a town's social, political, cultural, recreational, and even medical history.

Each of these artifacts has been studied separately by naturalists, botanists, and a new breed of historians calling themselves environmental or ecological historians.[18] It is possible, as Galen Cranz has demonstrated in researching the history of American parks, to construct a typology by which to interpret this material culture form in a particular locale. For instance, in Chicago, Cranz traces the evolution of the Pleasure Garden park (e.g., Jackson park) of the 1850–1900 period, the Reform park (e.g., Pulaski Park) first appearing on the landscape about 1900 to 1930, followed by the Recreational Facility park (e.g., Seward Park) developed in the Depression Thirties.[19] Phoebe Cutler has done the same careful research for the extant natural historical evidence of numerous WPA projects that were planted in the 1930s and 1940s.[20]

To cite still another instance, consider what history we might extract from a single, familiar form of plant life: trees, frequently overlooked elements in the cultural landscape, but as important in interpreting settlement history as houses, crops, barns, or fences. Richard Francaviglia has convincingly shown how the specific placement of rows of lombardy poplars around homesteads and along town streets are as important indices for measuring the Mormon landscape as cattle and sheep in the same pasture, "inside-out" granaries, hay derricks, and central-hall-plan houses.[21]

While one must be alert to the impact of imported tree species (and other plants) on historical landscape, attention should also be paid to those trees indigenous to any one area that may have been carried beyond their original habitats for various historical purposes. One such American tree (see fig. 16) is the Osage orange (Maclura pomifera), originally having a native range limited to the south-central United States (eastern Texas, southeastern Oklahoma, southwestern Arkansas, and the northwestern corner of Louisiana), but eventually playing an important role in the nineteenth-century settlement of the prairies and plains. This tree, known to the Indians who bear its name (Osage) and to the French traders who called it the bois d'arc (because the Indians used the durable wood for making their bows), now can be found from Maryland to Kansas, and from Illinois to Mississippi in a variety of cultural configurations.

Because of the popularity of the Osage orange as fencing material (i.e., popular names for the species are "the hedge Osage" or "hedge apple") in the mid-nineteenth century,[22] the above-ground archaeologist most frequently finds it so used throughout the Middle West. Across eastern North America for some three hundred miles, the pioneers had dealt with forests, but on the prairies of the Midwest, they faced a different natural feature—grasslands. Since the early settlement of the Atlantic coast, they had relied primarily upon stone walls and wooden fences, either the zig-zag, post-and-rail, or board fence; but on the prairies they needed a new fencing material. Wood was still available from forests, since, even into the western grasslands, stream channels provided some timber for building. If extensive land was to be enclosed, however, thousands of miles of fencing would be necessary. Wooden posts and wire constituted one possibility; but in the mid-nineteenth century, midwesterners began turning to an English practice: the use of hedges to form a "living fence."

As John J. Winberry points out, in a model natural material culture analysis,[23] the popular acceptance of Osage fencing came about through the efforts of Professor J. W. Turner of Illinois College, Jacksonville, beginning in 1845. Until the 1870s, when barbed wire began to be mass-produced in small factories and soon became the predominant western fence,[24] the Osage spread profusely. Even when displaced as fencing material by barbed-wire, the Osage orange was so prized as wood for fence posts that many barbed-wire fences were strung on Osage orange posts, an appropriate recognition of the useful small tree no longer employed as hedge fencing. The hard, durable wood of the Osage also survives on the landscape as railroad ties, wheel spokes, soil conservation service shelter-belts and windbreaks, and even policemen's clubs. The Osage orange has obviously undergone major changes of role through the two hundred years since its botanical classification. To an observer of the history of the land, however, whether planted in a line or standing alone in a field, "the Osage orange is a landscape relic, a silent reminder of an America long past."[25]

Place and Street Names

In many urbanized areas of the United States, the vegetation of the past and its influence on the local history survives primarily in the region's place-names. In fact, as George Stewart, dean of American toponymists, rightly insists, "the history of any region can be read in terms of its nomenclature."[26] Consequently, the alert above-ground archaeologist must also be a recorder and interpreter of place and street names. More often than not, such names are time-capsules containing fascinating histor-ical, linguistic, geographic, and folkloristic data that expand our sense of local history.

Consider what we might learn if we were to travel about a random dozen Indiana counties, simply paying close attention to the place-names of the counties and their major settlements. Natural locational names are frequent and constitute a mini-geography/history lesson on any local road map, be they *Butler Center, Liberty Center, South Whitley, South Milford,* or simply, the town of *Southwest.* Indian peoples who once inhabited our landscape and from whom our state derives its name still speak to us when we come upon *Lagro, Elkhart, Winona Lake, Oswego, Aboite, La Fontaine* (a Miami chief who sent his sons to my university in the 1840s), *Topeka,* and *Oesse.*

Early transportation patterns and stream crossings (e.g., *Rockford, Milford*), milling sites (*Liberty Mills, Waterford Mills, Pleasant Mills*), and railroad junctions, terminal points, and founding railroad agents are remembered in the town names of *Toledo, Andrews, Bippius, Larwill, Collins*. As with many regions of the United States, the majority of northeastern Indiana place-names tells us something of the area's original settlers: who they were (e.g., *Spencerville, Huntertown, Peterson, Decatur, Craigsville, Hoagland, Fort Wayne*); where they came from (*Middlebury*, Vermont; *Syracuse*, New York; *Bristol*, England; *Berne*, Switzerland; *Zanesville*, Ohio; *Waterloo*, Belgium; *Metz*, France); whom they admired (*Plato, Cromwell*, Samuel *Huntington*, John *Fremont*, Amos *Kendall*, Joseph *Warren*, Franklin *Pierce*, James *Monroe*, Pope *Leo* XII, and even Shakespeare's ghost *Banquo*).

Sometimes a place-name helps us establish the approximate date of a town's founding, as in the case of *Vera Cruz* and *Churubusco*, named for two American victories in the war with Mexico. Of course, some town names tell of historical incidents (e.g., the town of *Treaty* in Wabash County), of early natural resources *(Petroleum)*, of the high hopes of the city founders *(Urbana, Domestic)*, of a certain prescience of northern Indiana winters *(Artic)* or a simple acknowledgment of reality *(Farmer's Retreat, Needmore, Home Place)*. The Indiana town of *Auburn* has an equally intriguing bit of historical nomenclature. Laid out in 1836, it was named by early settlers who came from Auburn, New York, whose ancestors, in turn, had come from the English village of Auburn. However, the local history of this Indiana community also has a marvelous anecdote connected with its name. Ronald Baker and Marvin Carmody, in their work on *Indiana Place-Names*, report that, supposedly, a group of local Indians were sitting about a fire in this vicinity when one of them stuck his hand in the fire. With understandable quickness, he removed it, shouting, "Ah, burn!" The natives, indigenous and imported, have called it such ever since.[27]

Indiana place-names and street-names are now being carefully researched. In addition to the Baker-Carmody guide, there is the journal *Indiana Names*, with which every Indiana landscape researcher should be familiar. I also recommend George Stewart's two classics, *Names on the Land* for one's home bookshelf—and his reference text, *American Place-Names*, for what I would call a basic, do-it-yourself, above-ground archaeologist's field kit.[28] In that kit, I might also suggest including the previously cited works of John Fraser Hart *(The Look of the Land)* for one's meandering over the rural countryside, and Grady Clay's superb primer *(Close-Up: How to Read the American City)* for one's tramping through the urban built environment.

Street Histories

An indefatigable walker of city streets, Clay prompts us to ferret out the historical information implicit in the assorted street names and street types—be they boulevards or parkways, avenues or roads, simple lanes or byways—found in most American urban environments. Clay has made a special study of alleys,[29] but acknowledges, as do street historians Anthony Vidler and Bernard Rudofsky,[30] that, to be able to understand city streets as historical markers, the above-ground archaeologist should classify them by a simple typology; for just as there are ceramic types and house types, so there are street types: trader trails and turnpike/toll roads; main streets of central business districts; linear ribbon developments; commercial/ highway strips; and limited access and interstate systems.

The Indianapolis Historic Preservation Commission has prepared a model analysis (in the form of a wall map) denoting the survival of these various street types in Marion County.[31] Here are depicted some twenty-five major and minor routes, including some whose historic name is extant as a current street name that, more often than not, tells where the original road went or came from: hence, *Millersville Road, Allisonville Road, Pendleton Pike, Shelbyville Road, Madison Road, Crawfordsville Road, Zionsville Road,* and the *North Michigan* (Northwestern) *Road.* In Madison, Indiana, one sees the origin of the Michigan Road duly marked, and traveling north along State Route 421, one reaches a picturesque 1866 tollhouse that was once one of that early turnpike's way-stations. Occasionally a street sign or road sign tells the landscape historian of a city's influence far beyond its boundaries, as happens when one comes upon the Little Chicago Road just outside of Indianapolis or the boulevard to Indianapolis just outside of Chicago.

Where possible, the above-ground archaeologist tries to locate the streets of the original inner city, which, prior to transportation innovations such as the horse-car and the electric trolley, constituted what urban historians call the "walking city."[32] In much of the United States settled after the Federal Land Ordinance of 1785, a gridiron street pattern affords a clue toward determining the edges of the first settlement or the original city plan. Clay offers valuable advice on how to find the grid of first surveyor or town planner, as well as subsequent grids and their "breaks" that can be guides to the city's growth.[33]

To cite an Indiana example, consider the river town of Madison (see fig. 7) in Jefferson County. If one were to start walking west, say, beginning at the original plat's co-ordinates (e.g., Jefferson Street and East Main Street), one would come to West Street. There the above-ground archaeologist notices that all the east-west streets make a discernible jog to the northwest. A "break" has occurred. Suddenly, one realizes, at West Street, that one is actually at the "east" boundary of a new town plat, with its co-ordinates formed by West Main Street and Broadway.

In Madison, as in most river or port towns—such as New Orleans, to choose a city farther downriver—the original plat was largely determined by the orientation of the major watercourse, which was the geographical rationale for the town's economic base in the first place. Such a fact is invariably recorded in street names such as *Dock, Front, Water, Levee, Wharf, Embarcadero, Hydraulic,* or *Ferry Street.* Where cities have back-filled their earlier shoreline or river banks, as in Boston, such street names, although now considerably inland, survive to help the above-ground archaeologist document the original water boundary of a city.

Routes of the original railroad tracks offer another fix on a town's origins and growth. In addition to revealing which towns grew (e.g., Fort Wayne, Indiana) and which were frozen in time (e.g., Madison, Indiana) because the railroads went in another direction, the railroad track pattern strongly determined many a city plan. For example, in Hays, Kansas, since the first rails were laid northwest-southwest, the town plat followed suit. So, too, in Norman, Oklahoma; Fresno, California; and Atlanta, Georgia, which began as a railroad grid town originally called *Terminus.*

As Sam Bass Warner has demonstrated in Boston, many American cities grew along streetcar streets that lead to "streetcar suburbs." In some suburban communities (eventually to become urban as cities continually annexed villages on their perimeters), the farther your house was from the transportation stop, the less grand was your residence. In other streetcar suburbs, the reverse was true, as in parts of Chicago's Hyde Park, where the large number of surviving carriage houses provides above-ground archaeological evidence that one needed an earlier mode of transport to get to and from the commuter station.

Along trolley lines grew neighborhoods and lengthy commercial shopping ribbons. The development of College Avenue in Indianapolis typifies that growth. Every fourth block sports a small community shopping center with drug store, barbershop, cleaners, grocery, and doctor's office, all within easy walking distance. When Henry Ford put an autonomous power source in everyone's stable, however, he began the severing of the public-transit umbilical cord.

With the advent of the automotive age, the above-ground archaeologist encounters a plethora of evidence. In addition to the development of highways, expressways, and freeways, there emerged a new type of special street—the automobile showroom row—to take its place with the many other special-function corridors (e.g., market, financial, civic, printing, entertainment streets) found within American cities. Early automobile rows or streets often replaced great family mansions along former nineteenth-century "avenues of affluence." Along South Michigan Avenue in Chicago, North Meridian in Indianapolis, and Van Ness Avenue in San Francisco, the palaces of Packard, Cadillac, and Chrysler fronted on streets once lined with private castles, pavilions, and chateaux.

When the above-ground archaeologist walks the city's streets, I suggest watching for what I call "time collages" (see fig. 22) and what below-ground archaeologists call a "tell."[34] Often one will find, lined up along a single streetscape or clustered about a civic space, a series of artifacts from different chronological eras of a community's history. As an above-ground researcher, one can discover architectural styles layered horizontally just as the below-ground archaeologist searches for potsherds in a vertical stratigraphy. Such "time collages" also reveal changes in land use, economic and social status, and shifts in population densities. Occasionally, what appears to be a single artifact is, in fact, a complex time collage by itself; for instance, the Bates/Hendricks/Coburn/Hagedorn house of 1851, 1856, and 1865, in Indianapolis. The original south portion, built by Harvey Bates, the first sheriff of Marion County, was done in the Greek Revival mode, with its main door opening onto Madison Avenue. The 1856 addition, a lovely Second Empire Mansard, fronts on South New Jersey Street.

Vernacular Building

In doing landscape history field work, consider every building as a historic site. For example, whatever has been added is important; whatever has been removed tells a tale; whatever was never completed—such as the second half of Chicago's Newberry Library, halted in construction by the panic of 1893—raises historical questions for the explorer of urban artifacts. When "reading" a house,[35] the smallest details can yield ideas: an archway in Philadelphia, or pairs of meathooks on an Alexandria, Virginia, facade are clues to the building's former use as a stable or a slaughterhouse now transformed into a residence and an apartment building. Such conversions abound on the landscape: one-room Indiana schoolhouses and interurban stations made over into private homes; breweries turned into shopping centers; public liveries in Chicago converted into gas stations.

Above-ground archaeology takes a particular interest in American vernacular building (see fig. 21) in its multiplicity of forms: the hall-and-parlor, the shotgun, the bungalow, the four-over-four, the row house, the Georgian I-house, the dog-trot. These are crucial primary evidence for identifying and interpreting the local history of a community through its surviving residential environment. Vernacular building is, in fact, the material culture of the American Everyman.

Fig. 22. Standing in Boston's Government Center, the landscape researcher confronts a "time collage" spanning three centuries: the 1740–1742 Faneuil Hall (center), the nineteenth-century Crescent Office Building (right), and the Brutalist architecture of the 1969 Boston City Hall.—Photograph by T. J. Schlereth

Inasmuch as architectural historians have tended to concern themselves only with the so-called high or academic styles (e.g., a specialized building type designed and constructed by a builder following a pattern book or an architect working within a recognizable artistic vocabulary), the other 95 percent of surviving American domestic buildings has gone largely uninvestigated and unappreciated. Fortunately, settlement geographers, folkways experts, popular-culture enthusiasts, and private citizens have become intrigued with the ways and locations in which average Americans live.[36] The above-ground archaeologist freely borrows from their pioneering field study and archival research in order to construct working definitions and tentative typologies.

Vernacular building—be it Mormon central-hall housing in the West; dog-trot homes of the South; cobblestone structures of the country's heavily glaciated regions; the upright-and-wing buildings of the Midwest; or the ubiquitous, prefabricated, catalogue architecture of mail-order houses such as Sears, Roebuck—remains a vital artifactual relic of a large majority of Americans. "When fully interpreted," argues Wilbur Zelinsky, "these houses tell as much, not only about the physical locale and the technology of the place and era, but also about the source and dates of the builder or renovator, the contacts and influences he experienced, his ethnic affiliation, and possibly also class, occupation, and religion. In a very real sense, the house is the family's universe in microcosm, the distillation of past experience and a miniature model of the way it perceives the outer world as it is or, perhaps even more, as it should be."[37]

Thinking in terms of such commonplace, statistically representative housing prompts us to be cognizant of a community's neighborhoods: who has lived where, when, and why. Local material culture evidence often identifies the ethnicity of a place through its churches, place-names, types of businesses, and communal institutions. For instance, numerous artifacts immediately impress a visitor as to how heavily Germanic was the nineteenth-century "Over-the-Rhine" district in Cincinnati, the *Nord Seite* of Chicago, or any number of Teutonic enclaves in Indianapolis. In 1893, when the Germans built their cultural activities center at 401 East Michigan Street in Indianapolis, they called it *Das Deutsche Haus*, a fact that the structure's iconography makes very clear. However, one is puzzled by the imposing, out-of-scale, classical marquee that appears to have been added later and proclaims the building to be "The Athenaeum." A bit of further research clears up the mystery first raised by the artifactual evidence: the name change is the result of strong anti-German prejudice during World War I, when many Germans altered their surnames and those of their institutions to avoid ethnic discrimination. Population shifts in ethnic neighborhoods, as in the Pilsen area of Chicago (originally Czech, now Latino) can also be spotted in changes in the names of parishes, businesses, and the presence of distinctive street art (see fig. 19).

Working Places

Working-class neighborhoods in most American towns and cities exist in close proximity to working places. This is true in Indiana, a state that ranks ninth in manufacturing in the United States. The extant physical remains of American technology, business enterprise, civil engineering, and industrial achievement range from the early steel mills at Gary to the American Car and Foundry at New Albany; from the Singer Sewing Machine works in South Bend to the glass factories at Gas City; from the cotton mills at Cannelton to the over-shot stone mill at Spring Mill.

Appropriately enough, the field of industrial archaeology had its origins in the cities of Great Britain, the mother country of the Industrial Revolution. Now the movement has spread to the United States, where the landscape is littered with thousands of artifacts (see figs. 23, 24) that physically document this enormous change in western civilization.

The best general introductions to this relatively new way of exploring the history outside the history museum are by the British. Handbooks and field guides by Kenneth Hudson and J. P. M. Pannell are the place to begin.[38] American industrial archaeology, largely because of its neglect by historians, remains practically a virgin research field for the professional and the amateur alike. Railroad cuts, mine shafts, canal segments, relic trolley and streetcar lines, abandoned factories, previous sewer systems, water towers, quarries, workers' housing, and numerous other artifacts lie about on the land waiting for identification, classification, and interpretation to help us better understand local community history and the history of technology, labor, business, and government.

John D. Tyler has argued the case for a profitable alliance of industrial archaeology and the museum curator, while Robert Vogel has made a similar proposal to American historic preservationists.[39] In any event, we are now getting a number of good typologies of industrial artifacts that make field identification easier for both the beginner and the advanced student. For example, T. A. Comp and D. Jackson have done an excellent guide to "dating and identifying bridge truss types"; Fred Schroeder provides us with a detailed analysis on Victorian breweries; Larry Lankton has done the same for water-supply systems, as have Ross Holland for lighthouses and Terry Jordan for windmills.[40] For the above-ground archaeologist's basic reference shelf, there is also Robert Vogel's comprehensive local community study of the Mohawk-Hudson river valley, Theodore A. Sande's pictorial survey, *Industrial Archaeology: A New Look at the American Heritage*, and Donald Sackheim's *Historic American Engineering Record Catalog*.[41]

Commercial Archaeology

American technology and industry have produced all forms of material culture evidence, but few of the progeny have had such widespread impact as has the automobile. This moveable artifact has practically reoriented the nation's countryside and cityscape. The horseless carriage has, in short, nurtured what historian James Flink calls "the American car culture." Or, as Marshall McLuhan puts it, "The car, in a word, has quite refashioned all

Figs. 23 and 24. In Minneapolis, Minnesota, industrial archaeological evidence (above) includes J. J. Hill's stone railroad bridge, framing the city's past, and present flour-milling and storage sites. Relict lock apparatus (below) from the Chesapeake and Maryland Canal survives in northern Maryland.—Photographs by T. J. Schlereth of the spaces that unite and separate men."[42] Indiana car makers alone turned out 375 different makes and models, in a half-dozen cities, between 1894 and 1963.[43]

Part of this story is being told in the expanding number of historic car museums, transportation museums, private collections of vintage vehicles, and antique-car clubs that have proliferated since World War II. Soon, of course, there must follow museums of customized cars, psychedelic-painted vans, as well as those mechanical/sculptural/mobile hybrids that Southern Californians call "truckitecture." (In a state such as Indiana, where the mobile home and recreational-vehicle industry comprise the second-largest sector of the private economy, it seems inevitable that soon some museum attention will be paid to these artifacts).

Some historians, preservationists, and museum curators may scoff at the American highway and its artifacts as a source of historical study and museum exhibitions, but to anyone interested in probing the attitudes of the typical contemporary American who now changes his address every five years, drives more than 10,000 miles annually, and eats every third meal outside his home, the omnipresence of gasoline stations, motels, and drive-ins of all types looms as a significant cultural phenomenon. Should we not, therefore, give serious attention to the identifying and interpreting (perhaps even collecting?) of the pluralistic, eclectic, vernacular, regional—sometimes tediously similar but other times refreshing idiosyncratic—manifestations of the "neon culture" that has been with us since George Claude's invention was first installed on a theater in New York in 1923?[44] On the commercial strip, where buildings are diminutive, neon or electric signs are gigantic and expensive. Has not the huge graphic sign in space become the monumental architecture of the American highway landscape? Is it not possible, as Robert Venturi has argued, "to learn from Las Vegas?"[45]

For the above-ground archaeologist seeking interpretive guides to the surfeit of artifacts that clamor for notice along the highway strip, Bruce Lohof and John A. Jackle have studied the American "service station as the evolution of a vernacular form"[46] while John Baeder and Richard Gutman have surveyed diners.[47] On tourist camps and motels, the work of Reyner Banham and Warren Belasco is useful,[48] as is that of Neil Harris and William Kowinski on shopping centers and malls.[49]

The highway restaurant, be it a White Tower or a White Turkey, a Howard Johnson or a Frank-n-Stein, has its origins in American culinary and transportation history stretching back to the tavern and inn of the colonial period. Again, the coming of the automobile heavily influenced its further evolution and diversification. Physical evidence of this historical development survives all over the back roads, state routes, and major U.S. highways built prior to the advent of the interstate system. As Marshall Fishwick rightly claims, "The impact of fast foods, not only on our stomachs but on our psyches, has only begun to be realized and reported."[50] The impact of the fast-food industry on the American landscape, likewise, has yet to be interpreted fully. Nonetheless, it is a veritable museum of popular culture, a fact recently demonstrated by some eighteen scholars who contributed essays about *The World of Ronald McDonald*,[51] an empire that has expanded from a single store in 1955 in Des Plaines, Illinois (now on the National Register of Historic Places), to 4,500 stores that gross an annual four-million-dollar business.

Service stations, diners, motels, and drive-ins have all become a ubiquitous fact of most city perimeters—a historical development now being documented and studied by an assortment of academic historians, museum curators, preservationists, and local history buffs who have banded together in the Society for Commercial Archaeology.[52] These local historians, in addition to studying all the artifacts named above, also recognize that many of today's commercial interiors, particularly those located along the neon strip, aspire to be minihistory museums and are done in a "mood," "theme," or "period" architecture of the past. Redwood and Ross is an eighteenth-century English clothier; Victoria Station is a reflection of the great train days. The Jolly Ox, Win Schuler's, and the Steak and Ale hark back to Tudor England. Howard Johnson's Williamsburg colonial exteriors are now matched by McDonald's local history interiors. In Saginaw, Michigan, the McDonald chain's drive-in exploits the city's "one-time-lumber-capital-of-the-world" theme; in Kokomo, Indiana, the restaurant draws its identity from the early days of the local automobile industry; in South Bend, Indiana, within a mile of the University of Notre Dame campus, is a McDonald's interior with more than five hundred photographs of former Saturday-afternoon fever.

* * * * *

As is probably apparent by now, these suggestions for greater recognition of the history that is outside the history museum have a strong populist flavor. Such is the avowed objective of above-ground archaeology, for this approach considers the entire "city as a museum," the "city as an artifact." As my fellow urban historian Sam Bass Warner wrote:

Every city and town is a living museum of the past. . . . Given the nature of urban growth, somewhat in the manner of rings of a tree, the artifacts of the past are all around us. Moreover, these artifacts reflect some of the most important forces governing the development of the future city: the successive laying down of lines of transportation by old roads and canals which were followed by railroads and highways, the outward-spreading industrial sectors of every city, the core city survivals of warehouses, offices, and stores.[53]

I, like Warner, would like to see us value "people's history" as a primary agenda for history teachers and historical society curators: that is, to show average citizens various ways of knowing themselves and their communities through an understanding of their own pasts and past of others.

Many of those pasts remain unrecognized and unstudied. To find them, we need to look up—to discover a moment of time past in an 1835 sundial ensconced on a Cincinnati commercial building, as well as to look down, to find stone railroad ties still embedded in the streets of New Castle, Delaware. In short, local and community history can be read in asphalt and cast-iron, in house of worship and in just plain houses; in diners and equestrian statues, in inner city neighborhoods and in suburban tracts, in city plans and city streets (see fig. 7).

To be sure, above-ground archaeology cannot be done without the data we normally find in libraries, archives, municipal record offices, and museums. As with the below-ground archaeologist, the researcher who works primarily above ground does not solve every historical riddle in the field. The available textual sources for the identification and interpretation of those men and women whom Marwyn S. Samuels calls a "landscape's authors" should always be consulted.[54] In addition to the physical evidence of authors who wrote on the landscape and filled it with designs— street patterns, railway lines, water conduits—there is a documentary record of their intentions often available to those who care to look. City and county archives are filled with the data of landscape authorship (see fig. 8). It is available in surveyors' notes, city and county council minutes, municipal ordinances, newspaper editorials and columns, city directories, fire-insurance maps, corporate stockholders' meetings, promotional literature, and in various public and not-so-public archives. Here, as well as in a locale's built environment, those who shaped the landscape have left traces of their ideas and intentions about where things ought to be and how they ought to look.

Most historians know and use these documentary or verbal sources. We have been slow, however, in equipping ourselves with a visual literacy to accompany our almost exclusive lexical literacy. I think we need to acknowledge that the past is visual, as well as verbal. The modern student who aspires to be an above-ground archaeologist is constantly striving to acquire a visual historical literacy with which to read an environment encountered.

There are many untold stories in the artifacts that still exist in space past as well as time past. I think that history teachers and historical museums and societies in particular should seek out ways to assist their students and patrons in acquiring such a visual historical literacy with which to decipher the American landscape. "Reading the landscape is a humane art," D. W. Meinig reminds us, "unrestricted to any profession, unbounded by any field, unlimited in its challenges and its pleasures."[55] Employing the techniques of above-ground archaeology to read the history on the land, I am persuaded, helps us to recognize and interpret the past as it survives in the present with a vividness and an intimacy that enables any of us to discover the delight of "doing history" on our own.

Part IV
Coda

10

Collecting Ideas and Artifacts:
Common Problems of History Museums and
History Texts

M OST Americans consider their major contacts with "the past" to be
twofold: the history texts that they labored over in various courses
during their classroom schooling; and the historical museums, monuments, and sites that they occasionally visit on a weekend outing or an
extended vacation. Both history texts and history museums reinforce that
perception by subtly suggesting that historical reality is found only between the covers of a book or within the glass cases of an exhibition.

History museums, like history textbooks, have proliferated in almost
geometric progression in the past three decades. Outdoor museum villages
alone number more than 120 complexes of many sizes and descriptions in
forty-two states.[1] Despite competition from numerous other forms of
popular history (historical novels, like *Ragtime*; films, like *Gone with the
Wind*; or television specials, such as *Roots*), historical texts and historical
villages exert an inordinate influence on the average American's views of
the national past and on his understanding of history as a way of knowing.

Recently, it has happened that several constituencies (museum
curators, history teachers, interested citizens) have been "collected," on
occasion, to exchange ideas and techniques for improving and expanding
our mutual sense of the past.[2] The opportunity to come together in a
sustained way and share perspectives about and approaches to a humanistic study that intrigues us all has been most helpful and encouraging.

With that in mind, I take this opportunity to raise some questions about
common problems of history museums and history texts. In the process I
hope to be something of a deliberate gadfly, an agent provocateur, and a
devil's advocate, prompting all of us to evaluate our attitudes toward, our
distortions about, and our uses of the American past. Thus, I would first
like to offer a critical assessment of six "historical fallacies" that we all face in

the researching, interpreting, and communicating of the past.[3] Then, having fired my verbal salvos, I'd like to make a few suggestions as to how we might work to mitigate these problems.

Fallacy 1: History Is Progressive

The assumption that American history is singularly progressive pervades history texts and museums alike. Since their origins in the nationalistic fervor of the early nineteenth century, American textbooks have been the histories of winners, of individuals who succeeded in *The March of America, The Victory of Freedom,* or *The Triumph of Democracy,* all current contemporary text titles. Given their beginnings in the isolationist post-world war eras, the 1920s and the 1950s, it is not surprising that historical museum villages have been equally addicted to promulgating a view that the American past has been one success story after another. Such a fallacy is bolstered in various ways. For example, authors of history texts usually follow a chronology of political or military history. Despite an excess of artifactual survivals that should force an extensive study of social, economic, and cultural history, historical museums are prone to similar time-line interpretations that define all their activities as being either before or after the Revolutionary or the Civil War.

The tendency to organize American history around the watershed "dates" of warfare and politics is further reinforced and distorted by many of the battle re-enactments of which we are so fond. We may have eventually won the Revolution, but we tend to forget how many battles we lost along the way or, at best, how many prudent retreats we beat. But in Bicentennial America, defeats became draws, routs were hailed as steadfastness. Thus Germantown officials explained, "We're not celebrating a defeat; we're talking about George Washington and history." American forces fled Long Island after suffering casualties twenty times that of the British, but Brooklyn's official historian pointed out that Washington was able to extricate his men, so "it was not the spectacular British victory it might have been."

When Baltimore's mayor was reminded that a bicentennial staging of a mythical battle of the War of 1812, in which British soldiers supposedly arrested the city fathers, had no basis whatsoever in historical fact, he replied, "So what? Just because it never happened doesn't detract from it." And its's not just Baltimore: of the modern version of Lafayette's desperate flight from Conshohoken, Pennsylvania, town officials confessed, "It was a re-enactment of sorts, but we didn't run like Lafayette's men did." And in White Plains, New York, city fathers similarly admitted, "Yes, we got thrown off the hill, but," they added, "we stood our ground."[4]

Museum villages, perhaps biased by the associational aura of the houses of "Great White Men" that often form the nucleus of their sites, tend to champion an inevitable and triumphal evolution of democratic principles, a glorious series of technological advancements, and a continual rise in the American standard of living and material progress. In the reconstructed landscapes of most living history farms, for instance, one hardly ever sees an abandoned farmstead, dilapidated, rusty machinery, unmended fence rows, or an uncultivated field. Likewise, museum villages are not highly populated with Loyalists or Luddites, Anti-Federalists or Knights of Labor, Molly Maguires or Copperheads.

Fallacy 2: History Is Patriotic

Various observers accuse textbooks and museums of being over patriotic. Ruth Miller Elson, for example, has written an excellent history *(Guardians of Tradition)* of the rampant regional hagiography—the New Englanders wrote all the books!—and filial pietism in American history texts. Frances Fitzgerald's *America Revised* documents similar oversimplification and chauvinism throughout twentieth-century history school texts.[5]

In the same way, sophisticated curators and museum visitors are aware that cultural nationalism in some form or other is probably inevitable in most historical museums. Many historical sites are shrines to which visitors are beckoned to make pilgrimages, particularly on the national holy days—Memorial Day, July Fourth, Thanksgiving—when the American democratic faith is reiterated in numerous secular homilies. Historical villages often inculcate, in ritual and symbol, a worship of the national scriptures—the Declaration of Independence, the Constitution—as well as the republic's civic saints, prophets, and martyrs, particularly Revolutionary and Civil War heroes. The log cabin where Lincoln was born is enclosed in a Greek temple that the worshiper of the common man's president must approach by way of an imperial, baroque staircase that would do credit to the autocracy of Louis XIV's Versailles. Plymouth Rock is similarly encased in a ciborium of classicism.

We need to be cognizant of how much we use the past to reinforce what Robert Bellah and other sociologists define as the "American civil religion."[6] Such civic piety dominates many museum exhibits and much interpretation. In fact, one theoretician of museology has openly admitted that his colleagues often "borrowed the techniques of early religious instruction" in designing their exhibitions.[7] Hence, we all need to identify the subtle as well as the obvious chauvinism to which museum installations, like textbooks, are invariably subject.

Perhaps one small way to reduce such idolatry would be a simple change in terminology: that is, to begin referring to houses, sites, and villages as simply *historical* rather than *historic*. The latter label, as applied to most sites, is pretentious, overemphasizing an area's uniqueness in the *past* as well as distorting its distance, in terms of common human experience, from the *present*.

We might also distribute brochures, such as was done at the Sun Oil Company's exhibition in 1976 to test the political and social attitudes of visitors to Revolutionary Boston of 1776. From a multiple-choice question ballot relating to the Stamp Act, the Boston Massacre, and the Tea Party, the vast majority of the nation's bicentennial visitors emerged ideologically and temperamentally much more Tory than Patriot.[8] Such devices should be more extensively used by teachers of history, curators of historical societies, and professional historians to expose instances of history distorted by an overzealous or naive patriotism. We might even consider mounting more museum counter-exhibitions such as Jesse Lemisch's collection of "Bicentennial Schlock."[9]

Fallacy 3: History Is Nostalgia

The myths and icons that Americans have often made of their history are usually rooted in a nostalgic wish for a previous golden age that in reality never existed. Yet the compulsion to invest historical landscapes with such intense emotional freight is so strong that one observer in Denmark has even concocted a "Nostalgia Index" to help residents and tourists to enjoy all phases of that nation's past.[10] Antique dealers have recognized, with obvious capitalistic delight since the end of the Second World War, that nostalgia has become a growth industry. Moreover, we all convert our contemporary environments into "historical" ones by the incorporation or fabrication of assorted memorabilia. Hence, modern fireplaces, heated electrically if at all, simulate true warmth with Victorian coal or rustic birch-log effects. Fake diamond-shaped "medieval" sashes are pasted on windows with nonfunctional shutters; electric fixtures resemble candles and kerosene lamps. Modern plastic, stainless steel, and reinforced concrete may have their advocates, but for every contemporary tubular chair or curtain-walled building, two traditionals are manufactured.[11]

Most of us, nonetheless, recognize such anachronisms for what they are. History texts and historical museums, however, we take much more seriously. Too seriously, in fact, when, in the case of outdoor museum villages, we are beguiled into believing that every landscape was always mowed and tidy; that all products were lovingly handicrafted; that no one's calico or gingham was ever soiled; and that life proceeded in an orderly, eternally happy, blissfully secure environment. If this were historically accurate, who would not be nostalgic about the loss of such a utopia?

In fact, the past is otherwise. The title of Otto Bettmann's most recent book—*The Good Old Days: They Were Terrible!*—sums up another, if equally exaggerated, side of American history that is only slowly creeping into the interpretive framework of textbooks and exhibitions. To counter the rose-colored-glasses view of our over-romanticized perception of the past, we need something like what I call—for want of a better term—an "anxiety/ insecurity quotient."

In the sanitized environment of most living history farms, for instance, we need artifacts, exhibitions, and simulations that help us experience something of the isolation, the monotony, the scarcities, the high mortality rate of a frontier prairie existence. How does one convey, to a museum visitor, the overwhelming dread of drought or mortgage foreclosure? The anxiety of frequent childbirth? The uncertainty of fluctuating grain prices? The haunting seizures of depression and chronic loneliness? The instances of insanity and suicide that also characterized nineteenth-century American rural life? Might there be a *Wisconsin Death Trip* for every *Little House on the Prairie?* [12] We need to ask how hardscrabble an existence is actually portrayed within the settlement confines and how sensitive it is, in historical verisimilitude, to life as lived in the past.

Fallacy 4: History Is Consensus

Walking through many outdoor museums or living history farms, the casual observer would conclude that America in the 1800s was a relatively tranquil, even idyllic, place. Few artifacts or interpretations suggest the need for any legal or civil authorities to adjudicate, much less punish domestic or criminal disorder. In fact, there is little significant material culture evidence of conflict or dissent.

I make this point to call to our attention our common failing as historians in homogenizing and bowdlerizing the past. In Chicago, for instance, much attention is lavished on the few remaining mansions of Prairie Avenue's merchant princes, while forty blocks away, the 75th Street

Viaduct, scene of one of the most major American labor conflicts, the 1877 national railroad strikes, goes totally unnoticed.

Textbooks and museums have remained lodged too long in the consensus historiography of Louis Hartz, Daniel Boorstin, and David Potter of the 1950s.[13] Historical museums are still, with a few exceptions, remarkably peaceable kingdoms: planned communities with overmanicured landscapes that, in the words of geographer David Lowenthal, have "the flavor of a well-kept suburb," or picturesque small towns (see fig. 25) wherein the entire populace lives in tranquil harmony. Since the visitor to such sites usually does not see the artifacts of convict laborers, domestic servants, hired hands, or slaves in the statistical proportion in which such material culture would have cluttered most communities, he or she comes away from the museum village with an oversentimentalized, even utopian perspective.

Fig. 25. Unfortunately, many recreated historical "villages," because of inadequate research into the accurate placement and interpretation of structures, perpetuate the view of the small town in American history as one of an immaculate, well-ordered, tranquil community, an idyllic neighborhood uncluttered by poverty, crime, or social conflict.— Photograph by T. J. Schlereth

Deliberate utopian ventures constitute an inordinately large proportion of American outdoor museums. There are more Shaker villages in the United States presently than there are Shakers. Unfortunately, the acute social and religious radicalism of these dissenters and their consequent ostracism by society at large is never adequately portrayed in the twentieth-century restorations of their life styles, which are now, ironically, organized into a National Historic Communal Societies Association. In fact, more often than not, the once bitterly maligned "counter-cultures" of earlier eras have been homogenized into respectable middle-class cultural establishments.

Russell Handsman, based upon his experiences in Litchfield, Connecticut, and elsewhere, has noted that the historical-consensus mentality is also influencing the historic preservation movement. Instead of looking to their own past as an indication of uniqueness, regional identity, ethnicity, and even eccentricity, "towns involved in preservation actions are predominantly opting for homogenization," more often than not of a Colonial or Victorian style.[14]

Homogeneity pervades American history textbooks, in part because of pressure from local school boards, in part because the authors tend to plagiarize from one another, but particularly because they have traditionally omitted from their historical surveys the large components of the population who tend to be documentarily inarticulate. The same holds true for museum villages. Despite the increased scholarship and availability of materials on racial and ethnic minorities, historical texts and historical villages alike are still largely populated by white, Anglo-Saxon, nondenominational, Protestant male historical figures.

In the museum context, Old World Wisconsin (see fig. 13) is aspiring to be multinational, multiethnic, and multicultural, and the black experience is slowly being integrated in some plantation site interpretations, but a great deal remains to be done. Likewise, trends in American religious history have not been translated into museum village installations which, while they invariably have a single Georgian or Federal white clapboard church, are hardly suggestive of the extensive religious pluralism (and conflict) that existed in most American communities. To be sure, women's work has been depicted, but only that centering around the home and hearth, particularly in kitchens furnished with more equipment than any cook could ever have used. Although a few museum exhibits, such as the Corcoran Gallery's *Remember the Ladies*, have aspired to show that colonial women, for example, were shopkeepers, fur-traders, printers, farmers, artisans, and medical practioners,[15] most villages project colonial America as primarily a man's world. If it is any comfort to museum curators, textbooks have been even more resistant to women's studies; the typical U. S. history text devotes only about one or two of its five hundred to eight hundred pages to women's lives and contributions in all historical periods of the American past.

Fallacy 5: History Is Simple

To embalm *any* single version of the past, however, would be the opposite danger of redressing these heretofore neglected dimensions of American history. As teachers of history, whether in a classroom or in a museum gallery, we realize that we are constantly perched on the proverbial horns of a pedagogical dilemma. On one hand, we all search for attention-getting lecture titles or exhibit scripts, for relevant time-lines and interpretive themes, even for mnemonic devices where possible, in order to communicate our knowledge and understanding of the past to others. Perforce, we resort to generalizations, abstractions, simplifications. Yet we all know that we are doing the past a grave injustice, and we realize that, on the other hand, we must somehow simultaneously revive for students and museum visitors the enormous complexity and interrelatedness of past human activity.

American history was not so simple as portrayed by most history texts and outdoor villages.[16] Most colonial outdoor museums subtly nurture the assumption that their sites depict, *in situ,* the totality of more than two centuries of colonial America, despite the similar claims of every other colonial village. Ubiquitous pioneer settlements do the same for the post-eighteenth-century era. Yet the United Empire Loyalist Farms (Upper Canada) or Plimoth Plantation (Massachusetts) are obviously not the same colonial environments as Historic Saint Augustine (Florida) or Williamsburg (Virginia). Nor are Old Sturbridge Village (Massachusetts) or Greenfield Village (Michigan) the same early nineteenth-century rural settlements as New Salem (Illinois), Connor Prairie (Indiana), or the Living History Farms (Iowa). I would venture that much could be learned by having visitors compare and contrast these sites. Such a museological perspective would encourage more interinstitutional staff co-operation, more interinstitutional team research, more meaningful collective visitor experiences, and, hopefully, less provincial, simplistic, interpretation concepts and exhibit designs.

For, as Kevin Lynch reminds us, the major "danger in the preservation of [a historical] environment lies in its power to encapsulate some image of the past, an image that may in time prove to be mythical. . . . We should expect to see conflicting views of the past, based on conflicting views of the present."[17] Otherwise we create the false impression that the past was one simple, singular story. Thus Newburyport, Massachusetts, and Alexandria, Virginia, appear to have had only one past, and that for a brief moment in the eighteenth century. Similar distortions could be cited from towns that, in Walter Muir Whitehall's words, "celebrate rather than cerebrate" their history[18] as solely that of the misnamed "Gay Nineties"—a decade of the Populist revolt, the violent Pullman and other labor strikes, and Coxey's army protest march on Washington, D.C.

Selective preservation, restoration, and reconstruction in a museum village, like selective arrangement of chapters and the number of pages allotted in a textbook, promotes a discontinuous perspective on the past. Moreover, that practice often deliberately denigrates the excluded historical periods as inferior and unworthy of study and understanding. Consider, for instance, how little attention is given, either in textbooks or in historical museums, to the era between 1660 and 1730, the so-called glacial age of American history.

To enshrine any one version of the American past violates historical truth. Instead, city museums might show divergent Yankee, Irish, Negro, and Chinese views of what, say, Boston or San Francisco was like in the 1870s; rural museums, likewise, should not merely demonstrate assorted pioneer crafts—rug pulling, butter-churning, goose plucking, candledipping, etc.—but also show visitors the complex interrelationships of land law, crop choice, farm-making costs, tenancy, changes in agricultural technology, and the vicissitudes of money markets and stock exchanges. Living history farms need to give more attention to the role of women, children, and hired hands in agricultural endeavors, to the physical health of the rural population, as well as to the symbiotic relationship of farm and small town.[19]

Fallacy 6: History Is Money

My final historical fallacy, that history is money, is actually very much a reality in our consumer-oriented society. As has been pointed out by many observers, clever entrepreneurs have constantly found an abundance of ideas and materials in American history.[20] Best-selling novels, popular films, and television series adapt historical themes constantly. Commercials use historical motifs as well: old Quakers sell oatmeal, log cabins sell syrup, "great American homes" such as Monticello sell paint.

The search for a marketable past understandably was the motive of the investors who transplanted the London Bridge to the Arizona desert at Havasu—only to discover that they now must use chemical agents to keep the landmark looking suitably "ancient" because the clean, arid air strips the bridge's stones of their centuries of accumulated grime and soot. Similar pecuniary objectives motivate commercial promoters who have developed "History-Lands" and "Frontier-Towns," not to mention Walt Disney, the creator of two of America's greatest make-believe landscapes, Disneyland and Walt Disney World.

God must have loved the historical souvenir, since He made so many of them. I have often wondered why the popular-culture enthusiasts have not turned their attention to this omnipresent material culture evidence of our attitudes toward the past. Each of us can recall a more outlandish example: the lucrative market for the wood chips and sawdust that came from repairs to Independence Hall in 1975—fragments of the true cross? or Walter Knott's "authentically cracked"—*i.e.*, frozen in dry ice and a heli-arc torch applied to a built-in fracture line instead of being drilled out like most replicas—Liberty Bell; or the plastic toy "Minutepeople," "Uncle Samwiches," "Patriot Pink" lipstick. The list is endless.

Historical replicas fill the public landscape, hawking goods and services and celebrating civic pride. Ersatz Independence Halls and Mount Vernons of every size and material have sprung up all over the country, serving as banks, schools, libraries, courthouses, shopping centers, prisons, and even, as at the Henry Ford Museum in Dearborn, Michigan, as exhibition halls.[21] One of my favorite reproductions is Emilio Capaldi's 1955 creation of Independence Mall on the Concord Pike outside of Wilmington, Delaware, which attempts to replicate all of historic Philadelphia in a U-shaped shopping center. My own home city of South Bend claims credit for originating the idea of painting its fireplugs in the likenesses of Revolutionary War soldiers and other American heroes—all males, despite the project's originator being a woman—and other cities such as Niles, Michigan, and Columbus, Ohio, have followed suit. The fireplug troops now outnumber the combined forces of Washington's several ragtag, eighteenth-century armies, although they lack their prototypes' capacity for strategic withdrawals.

As Peirce Lewis rightly points out, it is easy to scoff at the historical merchandising of the "buy-centennial," at the Disneyland gaucheries, to excoriate them as fantasies for escapists, garish frauds sold by itinerant peddlers of historic snake-oil.[22] I think, however, it is the responsibility of museum curators, historian-teachers, and anyone with a serious interest in the past to expose and analyze what such artifacts reveal about our communal attitudes toward tradition, leisure, consumerism, social interaction, and, of course, American history.

One place to start is to show that the commercialization of the past is hardly new. Thomas H. Pauley's recent essay tracing the hundred-year history of the most overused symbol of the bicentennial, the trio of revolutionary musicians from the picture known as "The Spirit of '76," demonstrates this point. By following the work, first known as "Yankee Doodle," from its beginnings as a chromolithograph sold at the Centennial Exposition in 1876, Pauley finds modern usage to be an appropriate tribute to a work that immortalizes the spirit of the industrial revolution of the nineteenth century more than the political upheaval of the eighteenth. This icon has become so familiar that the American public recognizes it even when the revolutionaries are played by three salesgirls renting cars, puppets promoting children's television, costumed cows selling milk, or three comic characters (Mickey Mouse, Donald Duck and Goofy) at the head of "America on Parade" in Main Street, U.S.A., Disneyland.[23]

Such a historiography of usage of a popular historical artifact points up the longstanding tendency of Americans to look upon history not as a dimension, not as a context, not as a continuum along which we live and, in the words of the psalmist, have our being, but instead as a thing, a commodity to be bought and sold in the public market place like a piece of real estate.

What should we do about all of this? Is Clio to be a muse or just to be amusing? How might we work toward mitigating some of the common problems that beset all of us who care about history both as the community's collective autobiography and as a personal means of self-identity and understanding? Like most self-appointed gadflies, I am long on critique but will be mercifully short on correctives. I have three tentative suggestions that I hope will be useful.

Reflection 1: History Should Be Inquiry

We all can benefit from continually assuming a critical, self-evaluative stance in our historical work and our view of the ways that history is depicted all about us. My list of fallacies is but a starting point to which others could—and should—add their own special concerns about what David Lowenthal calls "the museumization of history."[24] To help develop this analytical perspective, I can endorse several other readings that have sharpened my own critical eye as a historian and as a frequenter of history museums. They would be my required reading in any course in American museology and history teaching. In addition to the marvelous essays of geographers like Peirce F. Lewis and David Lowenthal,[25] I would recommend that we all reread Thorstein Veblen's collected works, particularly his classic on *The Theory of the Leisure Class*. Equally worthy of our attention are Erving Goffman's *The Presentation of Self in Everyday Life*; Roland Barthes, *Mythologies*; Daniel Boorstin, *The Image: A Guide to Pseudo-Events in America*; Edward T. Hall, *The Hidden Dimension* and *The Silent Language*; *Icons of America*, edited by Ray Browne and Marshall Fishwick; Russell E. Richey and Donald G. Jones, *American Civil Religion*; W. Lloyd Warner, *The Living and the Dead: A Study of the Symbolic Life of Americans*; *Recycling the Past: Popular Uses of American History*, edited by Leila Zenderland; Dean Mac-Cannell, *The Tourist: A New Theory of the Leisure Class*; and, finally, two works by historians on the doing of history: Gene Wise, *American Historical Explanations*, and J. P. Hexter, *The History Primer*.[26]

Reflection 2: History Should Be Communal

My second suggestion is equally painless. I would strongly urge that we do much more of the "collecting" of ourselves—museum professionals, teaching historians, the general populace, volunteer historians—in order to improve the quality of individual and institutional historical study. As a person who has long been interested in bridging the world of the museum and the academy, I have been struck by two opposite deficiencies that the two guilds appear to share in the tripartite enterprise (research, analysis, communication) that I take to be history. Historians tend to be big on research, whereas curators like to emphasize communication.

C. R. Elton nicely summarizes the typical historian's myopia in claiming that "too many supposedly 'real' historians seem to think that their work is done when they have completed the finding-out part of it."[27] On the other hand, many of the past technical leaflets of the American Association for State and Local History tended to overemphasize the sheer how-to-do-it aspects of museology and consequently do not give detailed research its just due. Obviously, both groups would benefit from working the other side of the fencerow and learning more about each other's turf.

I know, for instance, that the staff of the Conner Prairie Pioneer Settlement at Noblesville, Indiana—which works in concert with the historians at Earlham College, who, in turn, employ the skills of the curators in their history teaching—fully recognize the abundant research time, energy, and patience involved in ferreting out just the basic facts about rural life in a southern Indiana hamlet in the 1830s. The department of research in many history museums, however, often regards the research process as its special prerogative. I would argue that historical research is everyone's responsibility—docents, volunteers, interns, even visitors.

Why, then, shouldn't interpreters at a historic site be encouraged to keep a research diary or log, wherein they might record and later research whatever questions they are struck by or were asked by visitors as they husk corn, dye yarn, repair a harness, or explain a settlement pattern? Why shouldn't volunteers be prompted to post interpretive problems or research topics—e.g., the price of flax in 1837, or the variants in barn types in northern Indiana—on the staff-room bulletin board, where colleagues could see what they are studying and hence share information and insights about bibliography, research design, or other approaches to the problem?

For that matter, why shouldn't a seriously motivated visitor to a historical site be given the opportunity to research a question that the museum's exhibitions or artifacts raised for him or for her in the institution's library of books, staff research reports, laboratory analyses of artifacts, minutes of curator/designer meetings, or the registrar's records that are the documentation on which the interpretation of a historical environment is based?[28] Might there not be a marquee somewhere in the museum or a listing in the official guidebook where a visitor could see posted the entire staff and their research specialties and where and when these individuals might be located for consultation? Why not have monthly seminars at which volunteers and interns as well as members of the research staff make presentations on work in progress and receive communal critique and suggestions? Assuredly, one of the delights of historical scholarship, it should not be forgotten, is that it *is* social as well as solitary.

The academic historical profession has, unfortunately, only slowly begun to move outside our traditional classrooms, with our supposedly prerequisite textbooks, and into the world of films, slides, and educational media.[29] We have entered the museum world even more reluctantly, despite various manifestos by historians and curators alike.[30] Once we do use museums more extensively, we will quickly realize that the creative process of exhibition—a museum's most fundamental means of communication—is one of the best contexts for exploring the intersection of material culture and its larger constellations of meaning in the American experience. We will also recognize that the exhibition process (fig. 6) offers the teaching historian an amazingly diversified range of pedagogical approaches to understanding the past. Lastly, since museum exhibitions are primarily collaborative ventures—more analogous to architecture or film production than to personal forms of art, such as writing a historical monograph, that usually require only a solitary artist for their execution—we historians will hardly be able to escape more exposure to multidisciplinary scholarly teaching endeavors.[31]

As a cultural historian within the cross-disciplinary field of American Studies, I cannot help but endorse such a perspective. It implies a diversified mental style, a mode of discovery, a way of understanding that encourages us to think about the interrelations between literature, folklore, music, painting, and history.

Reflection 3: History Should Be Personal

Indeed, such an interdisciplinary perspective is also a major part of my third and last recommendation. It is one that grows out of my current teaching and writing interests as well as my collaboration with several museums and historical societies.[32] For several years I have been extremely interested in exploring the history outside as well as inside the history classroom and history museum. I have been trying to teach myself and my students what I have described in the previous essay as "the history on the land," through the techniques of what John Cotter and I call "above-ground archaeology."[33]

I end on a populist note, not only because my own technique of "above-ground archaeology" strives to enable anyone literally to do history on his or her own, but also because I would like to see "people's history" as the primary agenda for history teachers and museum curators: to show average citizens various ways of knowing themselves and their communities through an understanding of their own past and the pasts of others. Of course, outside history classrooms and history museums, many Americans are already doing this: they are discovering their heritage in family albums, Bibles, and genealogies; in the built-environment of their own homes and localities; and in the oral histories of childhood and parental memories.

We all need such tangible reminders of the people we have known, the places where we have traveled, the experiences that we have had, in order to remember who we are. So strong is this fundamental human need that, in East Africa, when the Masai were moved, they took with them, in addition to their personal artifacts, "the names of their hills, plains and rivers in the new country . . . carrying their cut roots with them as a medicine." Such portable symbols of the past, like the permanent artifacts of any landscape, aid in maintaining human continuity.[34]

Loading their jalopies for the trek to California, the uprooted Okies in John Steinbeck's *The Grapes of Wrath* are told there is no room for their personal letters, for a religious icon, a china dog from the 1904 St. Louis Fair, or a copy of *Pilgrim's Progress*—the physical remnants of their arduous lives in the Depression dustbowl. But they knew, as should we, that "the past would cry to them in the coming days." For, as Tom Joad, one of the novel's characters, poignantly reminded them, and us: "How can we live without our lives? How will they know it's us without our past?"[35]

Appendix 1

Chronology to the History
of Photographic Processes

I. DIRECT POSITIVE PROCESSES

Metal:

Copper, silver-plated	Daguerreotype	1839–c. 1855	Silver tone, before 1842; brown tone, after 1841
Iron, japanned black	Tintype (Ferrotype, Melainotype)	1854–c. 1900	Chocolate-colored, after 1870
Glass	Ambrotype	1854–c. 1870	Earliest have black velvet backing. Later, colored glass.
Leather and Oilcloth	Pannotype	1854(?)1860	Extremely rare

II. NEGATIVE PRINT PROCESSES

(A) **Negatives**

Paper:

Uncoated, often waxed or oiled.	Calotype	1841–c. 1895	Rare, usually of America
With gelatin surface	Eastman paper negative	1884–c. 1895	Rare, usually of poor quality

Glass:

Thick, edges often ground, coating grayish, uneven	Collodion	1851–c. 1880	Not used to any extent in America until c.1855. By c.1860, universal.
Thin, edges sharply cut, coating black, very smooth and even	Gelatin dry plate.	c.1880–c.1920	Occasionally used today.

SOURCE: Based upon a reference chart prepared by the International Museum of Photography at the George Eastman House, Rochester, New York. Reproduced with permission.

Gelatin: Looks like "film," but completely gelatin; brittle; edges uneven	Eastman American Film	1884–c.1890	Used in Kodak No. 1 (1888): circular image 2½″, Kodak No. 2(1889), circular image 3½″.
Clear plastic (nitro-cellulose): Extremely thin, curls up and wrinkles easily	Roll film	1889–1903	CAUTION: INFLAMMABLE.
N.C. (non-curl). Somewhat thicker, coated on both sides with gelatin to prevent curling.	Roll film	1903–1939	Test by cutting small piece from corner, put in ash tray, touch with lighted match. If it flares, base is nitrate.
Machine-cut sheets, exactly rectangular, edges stamped with name of manufacturer.	Sheet film or Cut film	1913–1939	
Clear plastic (cellulose acetate): Marked *SAFETY* on edge.	Roll film Sheet film	1939 to present.	

(B) Prints

Paper: Uncoated, brown to yellow-brown tone	Silver print.	1839–c.1860	Also called salted paper.
Coated paper, extremely thin, brown image, high gloss, usually on mount	Albumen print.	1850–c.1895	"Printing upon albumenised paper seems to be dying a slow but natural death." *Amateur Photographer*, August 3, 1894.

Sizes of Mounts: Carte de visite, 4¼ x 2½		Introduced to U.S. c. 1859.
Cabinet, 4½ x 6½		Introduced to U.S. 1866.
Victoria, 3¼ x 5		Introduced, 1870.
Promenade, 4 x 7		Introduced 1875.
Boudoir, 5¼ x 8½		Date introduced unknown.

Imperial 6⅞ x 9⅞	Date introduced unknown.	
Panel 8¼ x 4	Date introduced unknown.	
Stereo approx. 3 x 7	Introduced to U.S. 1859.	(Rounded comers.)
"Artiste," "Cabinet," "Deluxe" Stereo, approx. 4½ x 7 or 5 x 7	Introduced to U.S. 1873.	

Appendix 2

An Exercise in Urban Map Analysis: Metropolitan Chicago

Orientation: Before attempting to answer the more detailed questions below, establish the following facts in reading any urban road/street map:

What is the date of the map?_____

What is the date of the cartographic data on which the map is based?

_____

What type of map is it? _____

Where was it made? _____

Are there any discernible cultural values expressed by the way the map was drawn or made? _____

Where is the cardinal point orientation located on the map? _____

_____

What types of features are delineated in the map's legend(s)? _____

_____

Trace, with a pencil, the city boundaries as they existed on the map:

What is the northern boundary? _____

What is the eastern boundary? _____

What is the southern boundary? _____

What is the western boundary? _____

Identify and mark the co-ordinates of city's center as to its street- and house-numbering system:

_____ Street and _____Street

Do you note any intriguing variations in the city's perimeters?

Any major annexations? Any gerrymandering? If so, identify:

_____

_____

_____

1. *Topographical Features*

Identify and give examples of any geological features (e.g., quarries, etc.) that the map may reveal: _____

_____

Evaluate their possible historical significance. _____

Identify, classify, and give examples of any major land forms (prairies, hills, etc.) _____

_____

Evaluate their possible historical significance. _____

Identify, classify, and give examples of the major types of vegetation that are noted on the map: _____

Evaluate their possible historical significance. _____

Identify, classify, and give examples of the major types of water configurations (e.g., rivers, marshes, etc.) on the map: _____

Which watercourses appear to be largely natural? _____

Which watercourses appear to be drastically man-altered or entirely man-made? _____

What is the geographical orientation of the map area's major drainage system(s)? _____

2. *Surveyor/Cartographer Patterns*

Does the map reveal any possible evidence of where the original or subsequent land-survey lines were drawn? If so, identify them: _____

What type of land-survey pattern (English, French, U.S., etc.) predominates on the map? _____

What type of land-survey patterns appear to be exceptions from the predominant pattern? _____

If the predominant land-survey pattern follows the 1785 U.S. Land Ordinance Survey, where on the map does one find major "breaks-in-the-grid?"* _____

What evidence does the map contain that might help explain the direction in which the city expanded or failed to expand? _____

3. *Transportation*

Identify and give examples of every type of transportation mode that exists or has existed in the area covered by the map: _____

Rank these transportation modes as to the order of importance as of:
a) Date of the map _____

---

*See Grady Clay, *Close-Up: How to Read the American City,* pp. 42–50.

b) 1871 _____

c) 1929 _____

How many multiple-transportation corridors (i.e., railroads, highways, etc., close to each other) can you find on the map? _____

_____

In what geographical direction(s) are the multiple-transportation corridors? Why? _____

Does the map indicate street and road classifications? If so, what are they?

Does the map offer any clues to their date of origin or historical significance?

Are many streets diagonal? List: _____

Radial? List: _____

Circular? List: _____

Any other geometrical form? List: _____

Any highly irregular form? List: _____

4. *Economic Features*

What does the map suggest about the location of past or present industrial or manufacturing sites? _____

_____

Is there any cartographic evidence of past or present wholesaling or retailing activities on the map? _____

_____

Where is "downtown?" Does the map reveal any other "towns?" "Uptown," "Chinatown," "New Town," "Old Town," "Cross Town?" _____

_____

5. *Settlement Patterns*

Does the map provide any clues as to past or present settlement patterns?

Is there any evidence of housing stock type in any of the areas of the map?

Can one identify, by using the map, the process of suburbanization of the city or the urbanization of the suburbs? If so, how? _____

_____

Can the suburbs depicted on the map be classified into northern, eastern, southern, and western suburbs? If so, classify and attempt to decide, on the basis of cartographic data which suburbs are probably the most prestigious

and wealthy and which are the least prestigious and economically deprived. _____
_____
_____
_____

6. *Open Spaces*

How many parks can be located on the map? _____
Are they concentrated in any particular area? _____
   If so, attempt to explain why this might be so: _____
_____

Is it possible to classify the parks as to types (i.e., field-house parks, vest-pocket parks, etc.)? _____
_____

Can any historical information be extracted from a comparison of the place-names of the parks? _____
_____
_____

How many cemeteries are on the map? _____
Are they concentrated in any particular area? If so, attempt to explain why this is so? _____
_____

How many cemeteries are inside and how many are located outside the city limits on the map? _____

Can the map be used to establish the oldest cemetery in the area? _____

Can any historical information about the city be extracted from a comparison of the place-names of the cemeteries? _____

What other types of open urban spaces (e.g., golf courses, playgrounds, etc.) does the map illustrate? _____
_____

7. *Place-Names*

Does the map reveal any obvious patterns of place-naming?. If so, identify:
_____

What appears to be the most repetitious place-name, besides the city's name?
_____

Of the following typology of place-names, how many can be found on the map? If possible, give at least one example for each place-name type:

Names for a person _____

Names for other places _____

Locational names _____

Descriptive names _____

Inspiration names _____

Humorous names _____

Indian and pseudo-Indian names _____

Names from languages other than English _____

Incident names _____

Folk etymology _____

Coined names _____

Mistake names _____

Legends and anecdote names _____

Note: What additional question(s) might you suggest that could be asked of this map (and answered by a careful reading of it) that would also expand our understanding of Chicago's urban history?

Question(s): _____

_____

_____

Answer(s): _____

_____

_____

Appendix 3

American Material Culture Technique: Historical Museum Exhibit Review

Preliminary Guidelines

Task:

To visit and write a critical review of a major historical museum exhibition, considering it as a scholarly organization of historical evidence and therefore a type of historical publication that should accomplish the following basic objectives: (1) stimulate historical interest; (2) promote historical thought; (3) furnish a sense of historical development and continuity; and (4) establish the relationship of the subject matter in a historical context larger than the specific topic of the exhibition itself.[1]

In completing this task, the student should remember that historical museum exhibition reviews should serve the same purpose as book reviews; accordingly, the review should attempt to follow these guidelines: (1) say what the exhibit is about, in general; (2) explain its relationship to other exhibits on the subject; (3) judge its worth, according to the quality of the artifacts, the manner in which the artifacts are interpreted, and the way in which the artifacts are displayed. The reviewer should also say what the exhibit was planned to do, whether it accomplishes what it had been planned to accomplish, and, if not, why it falls short of its aim.[2]

Review Questions

Purpose:

What does the exhibition intend to accomplish? What clues as to purpose are found in the exhibition or its ancillary components?

What has determined the nature and scope of this particular historical investigation? Are there any clues (as there are in a book's preface or a movie's credits) as to the intellectual debts of the author or authors of the exhibition?

Did those who created this historical exhibition encounter any major difficulties in achieving what they set out to accomplish? Are such methodological or evidential problems (consciously or unconsciously) admitted in any way in the exhibition?

Organization:

Can you detect any separate components of the exhibition (e.g., period rooms, cluster exhibits, etc.)? Why are they arranged as they are? Is there a sense of order and logic? Whose?

How does the visitor enter and leave the exhibition? Does it make a difference?

Is the exhibition purely a historical narrative? Biographical? Thematic? Topical? A combination of such organizational techniques? Might it have communicated more historical understanding if another pattern had been used? What would you suggest?

What allotment of physical space and number of objects is given to different subjects in the exhibition? Why? Is the proportion correct, given what you know of this historical period?

Does the arrangement of the exhibition engage and maintain your historical interest throughout?

Method:

Is the exhibition constructed in a format appropriate to the historical topic under discussion? Or does the medium of communication clash with the historical message conveyed? How could this have been avoided?

Which objects in the exhibition are really quite useless as historical evidence in studying the past? With what type of material culture would you replace them?

Do you find what Wilcomb Washburn calls the proper historical "respect for the object"[3] in the method of display?

What objects are missing from the exhibition? What other material culture, while appropriate to the topic, could not be included?

Do you think that a sufficient number of objects and other sources have been consulted to present honestly the topic under consideration? Does the exhibition depend on what historians call *primary* or *secondary* sources?

How is one of the historian's most frequently used explanatory methods—chronology—utilized in the exhibition? Can we truly sense change, over time?

What techniques are employed in the exhibition to demonstrate causality and motivation in human history?[4]

Pedagogy:

How effective is the exhibition in raising important historical questions for various audiences (e.g., different age levels and educational backgrounds) about its content and format?

How well does the exhibition serve the casual visitor? In your estimate, how well does the exhibit serve the scholar, the expert, or the close student of history?

What parts of the exhibition do you find you had to "read" again in order to understand? Hence, what components were confusing? What parts did you delight in "re-reading" a second or third time?

How effective is the exhibit in making you want to return to visit the museum again for another "read," as you would return to a good novel or to see an engaging movie a second time?

Scholarship:

In what ways could you search out and prove the historical authenticity of the exhibition?[5] That is to say, how would you follow up on its footnote citations or its bibliographical clues? Where do you find such citations and leads?

How would you document the exhibition for a fellow historian who, say, in the year 2040, might be researching the ways in which history was depicted in its major museums some sixty years previously?

With what types of scholarly research do you think the exhibition has been prepared? On what do you base your judgment? What part of the research appears most inadequate? Why? What strikes you as most accurate, or even unique, in the research that underlies the exhibition?

Does the exhibition communicate the present state of research knowledge in its subject area?

Does the exhibition illustrate current efforts to expand research knowledge in its subject area?

Fabrication:

What types of technology, construction, design techniques, aesthetic moods are deployed in the exhibition?[6] To what purpose? Do they transmit or distort historical information and insight?

Who played the major role in the collective creation of the exhibition— Museum curators? Academic historians? Technical designers? Museum administrators? Others? How could you tell? Can you tell by the exhibit alone, or must you consult other sources?

How effective are the following aspects of the exhibition—if they are present at all—in conveying accurate historical information and insight about the subject of the exhibition:

Textural materials, labels, etc.
Artifact placement
Display cases
Use of audio/visual

Cartography and photography
Use of allied supportive techniques (specify)

Institution:

What does the exhibition suggest about the historical museum in which it is housed?

How does the exhibition under review and its institutional context relate to other history museums in the area (that you may know) or to other historical museums in the exhibition topic area (e.g., American history) that you may have visited elsewhere?

In what ways does the exhibition relate to other elements of the historical museum in which you have found it? As a way of understanding the past, how do you think the museum administration ranks the exhibition in comparison with their other modes of historical presentation (e.g., library, publication program, lecture series, and the like)?

Summary:

Is the content of the exhibition expressed in a way easily understandable to contemporary visitors?

Does the exhibition make full and effective use of the museum's resources on the subject area of the museum?

In what ways does the exhibition's content provide useful links to current knowledge in allied subject areas?

How might this exhibition be improved? How does it compare with any or all of the other types of historical evidence on the topic you have consulted?

Does the exhibition do what an effective historical museum exhibition should accomplish? That is, to repeat from above, does it—

(1) stimulate historical interest; (2) promote historical thought; (3) furnish a sense of historical development and continuity; and (4) establish the relationship of the historical subject matter in a historical context larger than the specific topic of the exhibition itself?

Sources:

For additional scholarship on the subject of historical museum exhibition reviews, consult the following sources, several of which serve as documentation for this exercise.

1. Robert Vogel, "Assembling a New Hall of Civil Engineering," *Technology and Culture* 6, no. 1 (Winter 1965): 61–62.

2. Thomas W. Leavitt, "Toward a Standard of Excellence: The Nature and Purpose of Exhibit Reviews," *Technology and Culture* 9 (January 1968): 70–75; and

his "The Need for Critical Standards in History Museum Exhibits: A Case in Point," *Curator* 10, no. 2 (June 1967): 91–94.

3. Wilcomb Washburn and Gordon Gibson, Letter, *Museum News* 42, no. 6 (February 1964): 7; and Wilcomb Washburn, "The Dramatization of American Museums," *Curator* 6, no. 2 (1963): 109–124.

4. Thomas J. Schlereth, "It Wasn't That Simple," *Museum News* 56, no. 3 (January 1978): 36–44.

5. E. McClung Fleming, "The Period Room as a Curatorial Publication," *Museum News* 50, no. 10 (June 1972): 39–43.

6. Harold K. Skramstad, "Interpreting Material Culture: A View from the Other Side of the Glass," in *Material Culture and the Study of American Life*, edited by I. M. Quimby (New York: W. W. Norton & Company, Inc., 1978), pp. 175–200.

7. H. H. Shettel, "Exhibits: Art Form or Educational Medium?" *Museum News* 52 (September 1973): 32–41.

8. Royal Ontario Museum, "Evaluating Existing Galleries," in *Communicating with the Museum Visitor: Guidelines for Planning* (Toronto, Canada: Royal Ontario Museum, 1976), pp. 203–209.

Notes

Introduction

1. Stephen Botein, et al., *Experiments in History Teaching* (Cambridge, Mass.: Harvard-Danforth Center for Teaching and Learning, 1977), pp. 5–6. The best sources for tracing the history of the "new history" are the articles to be found in two of the movement's unofficial journals, *The History Teacher* and *Teaching History: A Journal of Methods.*

2. Quoted in David F. Kellum, *The Social Studies: Myths and Realities* (New York: Sheed and Ward, 1969), p. 27.

3. Peter Martorella, "John Dewey, Problem Solving, and History Teaching," *Social Studies* 69, no. 5 (1978): 190–194.

4. Clyde Kluckhohn and W. H. Kelly, "The Concept of Culture," in *The Science of Man in the World Crisis*, edited by Ralph Linton (New York: Columbia University Press, 1945), pp. 78–106. Also see A. L. Kroeber and Clyde Kluckhohn, *Culture: A Critical Review of Concepts and Definitions* (New York: Vintage Books, 1963).

5. Melville Herskovits, *Cultural Anthropology* (New York: A. A. Knopf, 1963), p. 119.

6. James Deetz, *In Small Things Forgotten: The Archaeology of Early American Life* (New York: Doubleday, 1977), pp. 24–25.

7. Quoted by Kenneth Clark, *Civilization: A Personal View* (London: British Broadcasting Corporation, 1969), p. 1.

8. Leslie A. White, *The Science of Culture* (New York: Farrar, Straus and Giroux, 1969), pp. 364–365.

9. Quoted by Brooke Hindle in *Technology in Early America: Needs and Opportunities for Study* (Chapel Hill, N.C.: Institute of Early American History and Culture, 1966), p. 15.

10. Ralph Waldo Emerson, "The American Scholar," in *Great American Essays*, edited by Norman Cousins (New York: Dell, 1967), p. 121.

11. Siegfried Giedeon, *Mechanization Takes Command* (New York: Oxford University Press, 1948).

12. Historians who have sought evidence to counter the elitism in traditional literary sources have often turned to demographic and artifactual data. Here consult Lynn White, "History: The Changing Past," in *Frontiers of Knowledge in the Study of Man* (New York: Harper, 1956), pp. 71–72; and Richard Dorson, *American Folklore and the Historian* (Chicago: University of Chicago Press, 1971), pp. 142, 148–150.

13. *Henry IV*, part II, act 3, sc. 1, line 80 ff.

14. Two of Glassie's major works are *Pattern in the Material Folk Culture of the Eastern United States* (Philadelphia: University of Pennsylvania, 1963), and *Folk Housing in Middle Virginia: A Structural Analysis of Historic Artifacts* (Knoxville, Tenn.: University of Tennessee Press, 1975).

15. Henry Glassie, "The Nature of the New World Artifact: The Instance of the Dugout

Canoe," in Theodore Gautner and Walter Escher, *Festschrift fur Robert Wildhaber* (Basel, 1973), p. 168.

16. Mark Schorer, quoting T. S. Eliot in an essay, "Technique as Discovery," in *Critiques and Essays on Modern Fiction, 1920–1951*, edited by John W. Aldridge (New York: Ronald Press, 1952), pp. 68–69.

Chapter 1

1. Helmut and Alison Gernsheim, *L. J. M. Daguerre: The History of the Diorama and the Daguerreotype* (New York: Dover, 1968); L. J. M. Daguerre, *An Historical and Descriptive Account of the Various Processes of the Daguerreotype and Diorama* (1839; facsimile reprint, New York: Arno, 1971).

2. Lady Elizabeth Eastlake, "Photography," *London Quarterly Review* (American edition) 101 (1857): 241–255, as quoted in *On Photography: A Source Book of Photo History in Facsimile*, edited by Beaumont Newhall (Watkins Glen, N.Y.: Century House, 1965), pp. 96–103, 108–118.

3. Holmes did not actually invent the stereoscope, as has often supposed; however, he did popularize it. The principle of the stereograph had actually been put forth by Charles Wheatstone as early as 1838.

4. See chapter 9, "Above-Ground Archaeology." The Boston survey was not, however, the first American urban photographic survey. The earliest work appears to have been done in Philadelphia, beginning in 1853. The Library Company of Philadelphia owns a number of images of seventeenth-, eighteenth-, and nineteenth-century structures by James McClees and Frederick DeBourg Richards from the 1850s and by John Moran from the 1860s. Unfortunately, there is no documentation as to why they were done, but there is a consistency to them that suggests they were motivated by a coherent antiquarian concern. Moreover, it is known that Richards was commissioned to photograph historic Germantown in 1859 (see Kenneth Finkel, *Nineteenth-Century Photography in Philadelphia* [New York: Dover, 1980]). I am indebted to William Stapp for this information.

5. George E. Francis, "Photography as an Aid to Local History," *Proceedings of the American Antiquarian Society*, April 1888, p. 274.

6. For example, see Edward B. Watson and Edmund V. Gillon, Jr., *New York: Then and Now* (New York: Dover, 1975).

7. H. D. Gower, L. Stanley Jast, and W. W. Topley, *The Camera as Historian* (London: Sampson Low, Manston and Co., 1916), pp. 9 and 29.

8. *History Study Pictures* (Chicago: The Art Study Company, 1900).

9. Order from *Documentary Photo Aids*, P.O. Box 956, Mount Dora, Florida 32757; *The American Experience*, Scholastic Book Services, 906 Sylvan Avenue, Englewood Cliffs, N.J. 07632.

10. Ralph Henry Gabriel, editor, *The Pageant of America*, 15 volumes (New Haven: Yale University Press, 1926–1929).

11. F. Jack Hurley, *Portrait of a Decade: Roy Stryker and the Development of Documentary Photography in the Thirties* (Baton Rouge: University of Louisiana Press, 1972), p. 10, as quoted by Bernard Mergen, " 'Doing the Rest': The Uses of Photographs in American Studies," *American Quarterly* 29, no. 3 (1977): 281.

12. Roy E. Stryker and Paul H. Johnstone, "Sources and Materials for the Study of Cultural History: Documentary Photographs," in *The Cultural Approach to History*, edited by Caroline F. Ware (New York: Columbia University Press, 1940), pp. 324–330.

13. Mergen, "Doing the Rest," pp. 280–303; Glen Holt, "Chicago through a Camera Lens: An Essay on Photography as History," *Chicago History* 1, no. 3 (Spring 1971): 158–169; Walter Rundell, "Photographs as Historical Evidence," *The American Archivist* 41, no. 4 (October 1978): 379–398; Michael Thomason, "The Magic Image Revisited: The Photograph as a Historical Source," *Alabama Review* 30 (April 1978): 83–91.

14. Frances FitzGerald, *America Revisited: History Schoolbooks in the Twentieth Century* (Boston: Little, Brown, 1979).

15. A photograph is technically defined as a chemically fixed image holding a lens-produced pattern of light, an aggregate of space, and a finite amount of time.

16. Robert A. Weinstein and Larry Booth, *Collection, Use, and Care of Historical Photographs* (Nashville: American Association for State and Local History, 1977), pp. 4–5.

17. For the appropriate technical nomenclature and definitions that archivists use regarding still photography and the "arrangement and description of pictorial records," see chapter 22 of T. R. Schellenberg, *The Management of Archives* (New York: Columbia University Press; 1965), pp. 322–343.

18. Paul Smith, editor, *The Historian and Film* (New York: Cambridge University Press, 1976); John O'Connor and Martin Jackson, *Teaching History with Film* (Washington, D.C.: American Historical Association, 1974); *Film and History* (Newark, N.J.: Historians Film Committee, 1971–); Steven Schoenherr, *Multimedia and History*, 3rd edition (Newark: History Media Center, University of Delaware, 1976).

19. G. M. Martin and David Francis, "The Camera's Eye," in *The Victorian City: Images and Realities*, edited by H. J. Dyos and Michael Wolff (London and Boston: Routledge and Kegan Paul, 1973), p. 228.

20. Adams has written a five-volume introductory compendium on photographic processes that includes, in addition to *Basic Photo: Camera and Lens* (1948), volumes on *The Negative; Exposure and Development* (1948, 1957) *The Print; Contact Printing and Enlarging* (1950, 1961); *Natural-Light Photography* (1952, 1965) and *Artificial-Light Photography* (1956), published by Morgan and Morgan in New York.

21. *The Focal Encyclopedia of Photography* (New York: McGraw Hill, 1972); Richard L. Williams, series editor, *Life Library of Photography* (New York: Time-Life Books, 1972).

22. On technical history, consult C. N. Mees, *From Dry Plates to Ektachrome Film* (New York: Ziff and Davis, 1961), and Beaumont Newhall, *Latent Image* (Garden City, N.J. Doubleday, 1967); on photographic science, see George Eaton, *Photographic Chemistry* (New York: Morgan and Morgan, 1957), and H. Baines, *The Science of Photography* (New York: John Wiley and Sons, 1970).

23. Eaton S. Lathrop, Jr., *A Century of Cameras: From the Collection of the International Museum of Photography at George Eastman House* (Dobbs Ferry, New York: Morgan and Morgan, 1973). Also consult George Gilbert's *Collecting Photographica: The Images and Equipment of the First Hundred Years of Photography* (New York: Hawthorne Books, 1976); Michael Auer, *The Illustrated History of the Camera from 1839 to the Present* (Boston: David and Charles, 1976); K. C. Lahue and J. A. Bailey, *Glass, Brass, and Chrome: The American 35mm Miniature Camera* (Norman: University of Oklahoma Press, 1972). For a review of these works, see Reese V. Jenkins, "Photographica: The Artifacts of Photography," *Technology and Culture* 18, no. 2 (1977): 231–236.

24. For a version of a reference chronology to the history of photographic processes, see a chart prepared by the George Eastman House in Rochester, New York, Appendix I.

25. Other useful guides to dating and identifying photographs are Arthur T. Gill, *Photographic Processes: A Glossary and a Chart for Recognition* (London: Museum Association,

1978), and Albert R. Baragwanath, "Dating Photographs," *Curator* 20 (March 1977): 42–47.

26. William E. Parker's "Everett A. Scholfield (1843–1930): A General Research Report," *Afterimage*, May/June 1976, pp. 22–33; William Peterson, "Early Mystic Photograph Identification," *Log of Mystic Seaport* 25 (Winter 1973): 129–139.

27. N. G. Burgess, *The Photograph and Ambrotype Manual* (1858; reprint ed., New York: Arno Press, 1973); J. Towler, *The Silver Sunbeam* (1864; reprint ed., Hastings-on-Hudson, N.Y.: Morgan and Morgan, 1969); Edward M. Eastabrooke, *The Ferrotype* (New York: Anthony, 1883); Paul L. Anderson, *Pictorial Photography: Its Principles and Practice* (Philadelphia: Lippincott, 1917).

28. Floyd and Marion Rinhart, *American Daguerrean Art* (New York: Clarkson N. Potter, 1967); Beaumont Newhall, *The Daguerreotype in America*, 3rd rev. ed. (New York: Dover Publications, 1976).

29. The design and workmanship of cases and frames for nineteenth-century photographs deserves careful study by researchers for American material culture. Such work should be placed in a broad context of popular-culture history.

30. Richard C. Rudisill, *Mirror Image: The Influence of the Daguerreotype on American Society* (Albuquerque: University of New Mexico Press, 1971); Harold Francis Pfister, *Facing the Light: Historic American Portrait Daguerreotypes* (Washington, D.C.: Smithsonian Institution Press, 1978).

31. The collodion process came to be known as a "wet-plate" process because collodion was a gluey liquid that was spread on glass plates and coated with light-sensitive chemicals. The plates had to be exposed while moist and developed immediately because the coating's sensitivity to light diminished as it dried.

32. Considerable research on the *carte de viste* remains to be done, but places to begin include Helmut and Alison Gernsheim, *The History of Photographs*, and William Welling, *Collectors' Guide to Nineteenth-Century Photography* (New York: Collier Books, 1976).

33. Edward W. Earle, editor, *Points of View: The Stereograph in America—A Cultural History* (Rochester, N.Y.: Visual Studies Workshop Press, 1979).

34. George E. Hamilton, *The Stereograph and Lantern Slide in Education* (Meadville, Pa.: Keystone View Co., 1939), and *Oliver Wendell Holmes: His Pioneer Stereoscope and Later Industry* (New York: Newcomen Society of America, 1949); Harold Jenkins, *Two Points of View: A History of the Parlor Stereoscope* (Elmira, N.Y.: World Color Production, 1957); William Culp Darrah, *Stereo Views: A History of Stereographs in America and Their Collection* (Gettysburg, Pa.: Darrah, 1964).

35. Earle, *Points of View*, p. 6.

36. Jack Pollack, "Tantalizing Glimpses of the World's Biggest Stereograph Collection at the University of California at Riverside," *Smithsonian Magazine* 9 (February 1979): 88–95.

37. O. W. Holmes, "The Stereoscope and the Stereograph," *Atlantic Monthly* 3 (1857): 241–255.

38. Richard L. Maddox, a London physician, used gelatin (which dried) instead of wet collodion on his photographic plates—a technique that liberated the photographer from his darkroom, since dry plates could be developed at any reasonable time after they were taken. Moreover, dry plates had quicker exposures, so cameras could now be hand-held rather than mounted on tripods. Finally, since the manufacture and the development of the dry plate could take place at times other than actual exposure, these two components of photography could be turned over to others—plate (later film) manufacturers and plate (later film) developers. With the advent of dry-plate photography, the photo-finishing industry was born.

39. Carl W. Ackerman's *George Eastman* (1938), now more than forty years old, is the only complete biography. For Boorstin's interpretation of Eastman, see his *The Americans: The Democratic Experience* (New York: Random House, 1973), pp. 373–376.

40. Originally a shooting term, the "snapshot," taken with little or no delay in aiming, began to acquire a photographic meaning in the late 1850s, when the first instantaneous photographs were made. A writer in 1859 talked of "snapping" the camera shutter at a subject, and in 1860 Sir John Herschel, a pioneer in photography and the inventor of its name, used the term "snap shot" in discussing the possibility of a rapid sequence of instantaneous photographs for motion analysis. The phrase did not come into more general use until the 1880s, when instantaneous photography became more feasible and widespread through the hand-held camera.

41. Brian Coe and Paul Gates, *The Snapshot Photograph: The Rise of Popular Photography, 1888–1939* (London: Ash and Grant, 1977); Jonathan Green, editors, *The Snapshot* (New York: Aperture, 1974); Ken Graves and Mitchell Payne, *American Snapshots* (Oakland, Cal: Scrimshaw Press, 1977).

42. Roy Meredith, *Mr. Lincoln's Camera Man: Matthew B. Brady* (New York: Dover, 1974); Glen Holt, "Chicago through a Camera Lens: An Essay on Photography as History," *Chicago History* 1, no. 3 (Spring 1971): 158–169; Alexander Gardner, *Gardner's Photographic Sketchbook of the Civil War*, edited by E. F. Bleiler (New York, 1959); *The Depression Years as Photographed by Arthur Rothstein* (New York, 1978); *Jacob A. Riis; Photographer and Citizen*, edited by Alexander Alland, Sr. (Millerton, N.Y.: Aperture, 1974).

43. Compare, for example, "Souvenirs of Experience: The Victorian Studio Portrait and the Twentieth-Century Snapshot," in *Snapshot*, pp. 64–67; *A Victorian Album: Julia Margaret Cameron and Her Circle*, edited by Graham Overden (New York, 1975), with Jennifer Harper, *City Work at Country Prices: The Portrait Photographs of Duncan Donovan* (Toronto: Oxford University Press, 1977), and E. J. Bellocq; *Storyville Portraits: Photographs from the New Orleans Red-Light District, Circa 1912* (New York: Museum of Modern Art, 1970, 1978).

44. George N. Bernard, *Photographic Views of Sherman's Campaign War* (New York: Dover, 1977); David Douglas Duncan, *Yankee Nomad: A Photographic Essay* (New York: Holt, Rinehart, 1951, 1966).

45. Compare Jacob Riis, *How the Other Half Lives* (New York: Dover, 1971), and *Battle with the Slums* (New York: Macmillan, 1902), with Alexander Alland, *Jacob Riis: Photographer and Citizen*; F. M. Szasz and Ralph S. Bogardus, "The Camera and the American Social Conscience: The Documentary Photography of Jacob A. Riis," *New York History* 55 (October 1974): 409–436; Louise Ware, *Jacob A. Riis, Police Reporter, Reformer, Useful Citizen* (New York: D. Appleton Century Company, 1938); Roy Lubove, *The Progressive and the Slums: Tenement-House Reform in New York City, 1890–1917* (Pittsburgh: University of Pittsburgh Press, 1962), and Francesco Cordasco, editor, *Jacob Riis Revisited: Poverty and the Slum in Another Era* (Garden City, N.Y.: Anchor, 1968).

46. Judith M. Gutman, *Lewis W. Hine and the American Social Conscience* (New York: Walker and Company, 1967); the Brooklyn Museum, *America and Lewis Hine* (New York: Aperture, 1977), and Judith Gutman, *Lewis Hine, 1874–1940, Two Perspectives* (New York: Grossman Publishers, 1974).

47. As valuable introductory texts, see Dorothy M. and Philip B. Kunhardt on *Matthew Brady and His World* (New York: Time-Life Books, 1977), and Victor Boesen and Florence Curtis Graybill on *Edward S. Curtis: Photographer of the North American Indian* (New York: Dodd, Mead, 1977).

48. National Archives and Records Service, *The American Image: Photographs from the National Archives, 1860–1960* (New York: Pantheon Books, 1979).

49. A short discussion of OEO historical photographs, especially in comparison with the visual documentary evidence of the FSA is found in Sandler, *The Story of American Photographs*, pp. 228–243. On the EPA, see Mergen, pp. 292–293.

50. Neal Slavin, *When Two or More Are Gathered Together* (New York: Farrar, Straus and Giroux; 1976), p. 6. Merger, following the Slavin technique, extrapolates a set of questions (p. 295) for the historian to raise when studying group portraits: "Are the people in the photograph aware of a group identity or cohesiveness? Does the photograph communicate this identity? Does the act of being photographed bring cohesiveness to the group? Does the photograph create stereotypes or capture already existing ones? What is happening in the photograph that defines the identity of the group?"

51. John Faber, *Great News Photos and the Stories behind Them* (New York: Dover, 1960, 1978); *Great Photographic Essays from Life* (Boston: Little, Brown, 1978); Sheryle and John Leekley, *Moments: The Pulitzer Prize Photographs* (New York: Crown Publishers, 1978). A general overview can be found in Time-Life, *Photojournalism* (New York: Time-Life Books, 1971), and Wilson Hicks, *Words and Pictures* (New York: Aron, 1973).

52. E. H. Gombrich, "The Visual Image," *Scientific American* 227 (September 1972): 82–96; Erwin Panofsky, *Studies in Iconology* (New York: Harper and Row, 1962); Jonathan Bayer, *Reading Photographs: Understanding the Aesthetics of Photography* (New York: Pantheon, 1977).

53. Howard S. Becker, "Art as Collective Action," *American Sociological Review* 39, no. 6 (1974): 767–776; Allan Sekula, "On the Invention of Photographic Meaning," *ArtForum* 13, no. 5 (1975): 36–45; Peter Robertson, "More Than Meets the Eye," *Archivaria* 2 (Summer 1976): 33–43; Time-Life, *Photojournalism*, "Techniques of Persuasion," pp. 98–117.

54. G. D. Freeman, *Midnight and Noonday, or the Incidental History of Southern Kansas and the Indian Territory* (Caldwell, Kans.: G. D. Freeman, 1892), pp. 199–200; C. Francis Jenkins, "How To Secure Expression in Photography," *Cosmopolitan*, June 1899, p. 131.

55. Mergen, "Doing the Rest," p. 283. In this context, a crucial interpretation is Alan Thomas's *Time in a Frame: Photography and the Nineteenth-Century Mind* (New York: Schocken, 1979).

56. Neil Harris, "Iconography and Intellectual History: The Half-Tone Effect," in *New Directions in American Intellectual History*, edited by John Higham and Paul Conkin (Baltimore: The Johns Hopkins Press, 1979), p. 196.

57. Here see Helmut Gernsheim, *Creative Photography, Aesthetics, Trends, 1939–1960* (London: Faber and Faber, 1962); Aaron Schart, *Art and Photography* (London: Penguin Press, 1968); Robert M. Doty, *Photo-Secession: Photography as a Fine Art* (Rochester: George Eastman, 1960); Max Kozloff, *Rendering* (New York: Simon and Schuster, 1968); Charles H. Chaffin, *Photography as a Fine Art* (New York: Morgan and Morgan, 1971); Susan Sontag, *On Photography* (New York: Dell, 1978); Weston Naef, *The Collections of Alfred Stieglitz: Fifty Pioneers of Modern Photography* (New York: Metropolitan Museum of Art, 1978).

58. Lilly Koltun, "The Photograph: Annotated Bibliography for the Archivist," *Archivaria* 5 (Winter 1977/78): 125; Koltun also recommends Michel F. Braive, *The Photograph: A Social History* (Toronto: McGraw-Hill, 1966) as another valuable reference text.

59. Catalogued collections such as these can be compared with John Wall's *Directory of British Photographic Collections* (New York: Camera/Graphic Press, 1977) for purposes of cross-cultural interpretation of American photographic subject matter.

60. Weinstein and Booth, *Collection, Use, and Care of Historical Photographs*, pp. 73–86;

Steven Schoenherr, "Teaching With Audio-Visual Documents: Resources in the National Archives," *The History Teacher* 10, no. 3 (May 1977): 381–394.

61. All of these paperback titles are currently published by Dover Publications, Inc., 180 Varick Street, New York, New York 10014), a major reprint house specializing in historical photography. Those firms whose current catalogues the historian should also consult for reproductions of collections of nineteenth and early twentieth-century photography are: New York Graphic Society, George Eastman House, Light Impressions, Morgan and Morgan, and Aperture.

62. Light Impressions Corporation offers slide sets on the daguerreotype, photography in the nineteenth century, the Farm Security Administration photographs, Lewis Hine, and others. Their address is P. O. Box 3012, Photo Slide and AV Department, Rochester, New York.

63. In addition to *The American Image,* consult Mayfield S. Bray, *Still Pictures in the Audiovisual Archives Division of the National Archives* (Washington, D.C.: National Archives, 1972), and selected pamphlets published by the National Archives Trust Fund Board: *Pictures of the American West, 1848–1912; Indians in the United States;* and *Pictures of the Civil War.*

64. See, for example, Instructional Resources Corporation, *The American History Slide Collections* and *America in the Depression Years* (12121 Dove Circle, Laurel, Maryland 20811) and compare to National Museum of Man, *Canada's Visual History* (Scholar's Choice, Ltd., 1150 Homon Street, Vancouver, B.C. V6B 2X8).

65. Also consult William Welling's chapter on "Photographic Archives," in *Guide to Nineteenth-Century Photographs,* pp. 131–140.

66. David Phillips, *The Taming of the West: A Photographic Perspective* (Chicago: H. Regnery Co.: 1974).

67. Otto Bettmann, *The Good Old Days, They Were Terrible!* (New York: Random House, 1974).

68. On current trends in the precise archival documentation of historical photography, see Klaus B. Hendriks, "The Preservation of Photographic Records," *Archivaria* 5 (Winter 1977–78): 92–100; ISBD (NBM): *International Standard Bibliographic Description for Non-Book Materials* (London: IFLA International Office for UBC, 1977); Ron D'Altroy, "An Effective Photographic Archives," *Canadian Archivist* 1 (1969): 18–21; Camilla P. Luecke, "Photographic Library Procedures," *Special Libraries* 47 (December 1956): 455–461; Renata V. Shaw, "Picture Organization: Practices and Procedures, Part I," *Special Libraries* 63 (October 1972): 448–456; "Part II," *Special Libraries* 63 (November 1972): 502–506; Paul Vanderbilt, "Filing Your Photographs," *History News* 21 (June 1966): 117–124.

69. Marie Czach, "At Home: Reconstructing Everyday Life through Photographs and Artifacts," *Afterimage* 5 (September 1977): 10–12.

70. Renata Shaw, "Picture Searching," "Picture Organization," and "Picture Professionalism," in *Special Libraries* 62, no. 12 (December 1971): 524–528; 63, no. 1 (January 1972): 13–24; 63, no. 10 (October 1972): 448–456; 63, no. 11 (November 1972): 502–506; 65, no. 10/11 (October/November 1974): 421–429; 65, no. 12 (December 1974): 505–511; Paul Vanderbilt, "On Photographic Archives," *Afterimage* 4 (September 1976): 8–15. A slightly different finding aid, one useful to the historian seeking assistance in various types of research projects, is Linda Moser, *Grants in Photography: How To Get Them* (New York: American Photographic Book Publishing Company, 1978).

71. Beaumont Newhall, editor, *On Photography: A Source Book on Photo History in Facsimile* (Watkins Glen, N.Y.: Century House; 1956); and Nathan Lyons, *Photographers on*

Photography (Englewood Cliffs, N.J.: Prentice Hall, 1966); here also see *The Valiant Knights of Daguerre: Selected Critical Essays on Photography and Profiles of Photographs Pioneers*, by Sadakichi Hartmann (Berkeley, Cal.: University of California Press, 1978).

72. Rudolf Arnheim, *Visual Thinking* (Berkeley, Cal.: University of California Press, 1969); Estelle Jussim, "The Research Uses of Visual Information," *Library Trend* 25 (April 1977): 763–777; Jergen Rensch and Weldon Kees, *Non-Verbal Communication* (Berkeley, Cal.: University of California Press, 1972); Bram Dijkstra, *The Hieroglyphics of a New Speech* (Princeton, N.J.: Princeton University Press, 1978); R. L. Gregory, *The Intelligent Eye* (New York: McGraw-Hill, 1970).

73. Howard Becker, "Photography and Sociology," *Studies in the Anthropology of Visual Communication*, Fall 1974, p. 7.

74. John Collier, Jr., *Visual Anthropology: Photography as a Research Method* (New York: Holt, Rinehart, and Winston, 1967); Karin Becker Ohrn, "Re-Viewing Photographs: Unexplored Resources for Communications Research," *Journal of Communication Inquiry*, Winter 1977, pp. 31–39; also consult Wright Morris, "Photographs, Images and Words," *The American Scholar*, Autumn 1979, pp. 457–469.

75. Thomas J. Schlereth, *The University of Notre Dame: A Portrait of Its History and Campus* (Notre Dame, Ind.: University of Notre Dame Press, 1976), pp. xv–xix.

76. Cameo examples of such research would include William E. Parker, "Everett A. Scholfield (1843–1930): A General Research Report," *Afterimage*, May/June 1976, pp. 22–33; Paul Byers, "Still Photography in the Systematic Recording and Analysis of Behavioral Data," *Human Organization* 23 (1964): 78–84.

77. *Afterimage* (Visual Studies Workshop: 1972—   ) *History of Photography: An International Journal* (London: Taylor and Francis, 1976—   ); *Exposure* (New York: Society for Photographic Education, 1963—   ); *Image* (Rochester, N.Y.: George Eastman Associates, 1952—   ); *Aperture* (Millerton, N.Y.: 1952—   ). Also refer to Albert Boni, editor, *Photographic Literature: An International Guide* (New York: Morgan and Morgan, 1962, 1970).

78. Bonnie Barrett Stretch, "The Golden Age of Landscape Photography: How the West Was Framed," *American Art and Antiques* 2, no. 2 (March/April 1979): 62–69. On individual landscape photographers, see Helen S. Griffin, "Carleton E. Watkins: California's Expeditionary Photographer," *Eye To Eye* 6 (September 1954): 26–32; M. V. Hood and R. B. Haas, "Eadweard Muybridge's Yosemite Valley Photographs, 1867–1872," *California Historical Society Quarterly* 1 (March 1963): 5–26; Beaumont Newhall and Diana Edwins, *William H. Jackson* (Dobbs Ferry, N.Y.: Morgan and Morgan, 1974); J. D. Horan, *Timothy O'Sullivan: America's Forgotten Photographer* (New York: Bonanza Books, 1966).

79. David Phillips, *The Taming of the West: A Photographic Perspective* (Chicago: Henry Regnery, 1974); Karen and William Current, *Photography and the Old West* (New York: H. N. Abrams, 1978); Robert A. Weinstein, "Silver on Glass: The Unknown Frontier Photographers," *Record* 39 (1978): 28–47.

80. Elizabeth Lindguist-Cock, *The Influence of Photography on American Landscape Painting, 1839–1880* (New York: Garland, 1979); Van Deren Coke, *The Painter and the Photograph* (Albuquerque: University of New Mexico Press, 1964); and Thomas Eakins, *The Photographs of Thomas Eakins* (New York, 1972).

81. Compare Richard Rudisill's *Photographers of the New Mexico Territory, 1854–1912* (Sante Fe: Museum of New Mexico, 1973); Masie and Richard Conrat, *The American Farm: A Photographic History* (Boston: Houghton Mifflin, 1977); Weston Naef and James N. Wood, *Era of Exploration: The Rise of Landscape Photography in the American West, 1860–1885* (Boston:

New York Graphic Society, 1975) with Walter Prescott Webb, *The Great Plains* (New York: Grossett and Dunlap, 1931); Henry Nash Smith, *Virgin Land: The American West as Symbol and Myth* (New York: Random House, 1950); William H. Goetzmann, *Exploration and Empire: The Explorer and the Scientist in the Winning of the American West* (New York: Random House, 1966), and Richard S. Bartlett, *The New Country: A Social History of the American Frontier, 1776–1890* (New York: Oxford University Press, 1966).

82. A sample of current work would include Walter Rundell, Jr., *Early Texas Oil: A Photographic History, 1866–1936* (College Station, Tex.: Texas A & M University Press, 1977); and Ralph Andrews, *Picture Gallery Pioneers: 1850–1875* (Seattle: Superior Publishing Co., 1964).

83. Mergen, "Doing the Rest," pp. 292–293.

84. Phyllis Lambert, "Photographic Documentation and Building Relationships Past and Present," *Archivaria* 5 (Winter 1977–78): 62–65.

85. In *American Architectural Books* (1946; reprint ed., New York: Da Capo, 1976), Henry-Russell Hitchcock notes that apparently the first photographic documentation of colonial architecture in book form is to be found in Corner's *Examples of Domestic Colonial Architecture* (1891).

86. Eric Arthur and Dudley Witney, *The Barn: A Vanishing Landmark in North America* (Ontario, Canada: Galahad Books, 1972); Paul Hirshorn and Steven Izenour, *White Towers* (Cambridge, Mass.: MIT Press, 1979); Henry-Russell Hitchcock and William Seale, *Temples of Democracy: The State Capitols of the U.S.A.* (New York: Harcourt, Brace, 1976).

87. Three institutions possessing extensive photographic holdings pertinent to American architecture are the Historic American Buildings Survey (HABS), the Historic American Engineering Record (HAER), and the U.S. Department of the Interior National Register of Historic Places. Somerset House (Teaneck, N.J.) now sells the fifty thousand photographs of the Library of Congress's Historic American Buildings Survey, arranged by state, and published on sixty-frame monochrome microfiche.

88. For reference use here, see Julius Shulman, *Photographing Architecture and Interiors* (New York: Whitney Library of Design/Hill and Wang, 1962) and John Veltri, *Architectural Photography* (Garden City, N.Y.: American Photographic Book Publishers, 1974).

89. Richard Pare, "Creating the Photographic Record: The United States Court House Project," *Archivaria* 5 (Winter 1977–78): 82.

90. Glen E. Holt, "Chicago through a Camera Lens: An Essay on Photography as History," *Chicago History* 1, no. 3 (Spring 1971): 158–169; Arthur J. Krim, "Photographic Imagery of the American City, 1840–1860," *The Professional Geographer* 25, no. 2 (May 1973): 136–139; Michael Thomason, "The Magic Image Revisited: The Photograph as a Historical Source," *The Alabama Review*, April 1978, pp. 83–91; Thomas J. Schlereth, "A Chicago Scrapbook: Five Portraits of a City's Past," *The Old Northwest* 3, no. 4 (December 1977): 429–436.

91. E. H. Chapman, *Cleveland: Village to Metropolis* (Cleveland: Press of Case Western Reserve University, 1964); J. H. Cady, *The Civic and Architectural Development of Providence* (Providence, R.I.: The Book Shop, 1957); J. A. Kouwenhoven, *The Columbia Portrait of New York* (New York: Doubleday, 1953).

92. Other anthologies of historical photography on New York published by Dover are Bernice Abbott, *New York in the Thirties*; Andreas Feininger, *New York in the Forties*; Joseph Byron, *Photographs of New York Interiors at the Turn of the Century*; Alfred Stieglitz, *Camera Work: A Pictorial Guide*; Victor Laredo and Henry Hope Reed, *Central Park: A Photographic Guide*; Richard Wurts, et al., *The New York World's Fair 1939/40*; Edward B. Watson and

Edmund V. Gillon, Jr., *New York Then and Now;* Mark Feldstein, *Unseen New York;* Victor Laredo and Thomas Reilly, *New York City: A Photographic Portrait.*

93. George Stewart, in his book on *U.S. 40: Cross-Section of the United States of America* (Boston: Houghton Mifflin, 1953), shows in a detailed two-page analysis (pp. 158–159) how a single photograph—in this case one taken northward from the tower of the Liberty Memorial in Kansas City—"may be permitted to stand for the portrait of the typical American city as traversed by U.S. 40."

94. Simon Baker and Henry W. Dill, Jr., *The Book of Our Land—An Airphoto Atlas of the Rural United States* (Washington: U.S. Department of Agriculture, 1970).

95. Here consult T. Eugene Avery, *Interpretation of Aerial Photographs* (Minneapolis: Burgess Publishing Co., 1962); Roger M. Minshull, *Human Geography from the Air* (New York: St. Martin's Press, 1968); and Nathaniel A. Ownings, *The American Aesthetic* (New York: Harper and Row, 1969).

96. Thomas H. Garver, editor, *Just before the War: Urban America from 1935 to 1941 as Seen by the Photographers of the Farm Security Administration* (Los Angeles: Rapid Lithograph Co., 1968). A useful film, *Photography and the City* (1969), tracing the influence of photography on the shaping of cities and/or proposals for solving urban problems, is distributed by the University of California Film Distribution Office, University Park, Los Angeles, Cal. 90007.

97. Sam Walker, "Documentary Photography in America: The Political Dimensions of an Art Form," *Radical America* 11, no. 1 (1977): 53–66; Victor Greene, "Old Ethnic Stereotypes and the New Ethnic Studies," *Ethnicity* 5 (1978): 398–350.

98. Steven E. Schoenherr, "Hull House through Photographs: A Curriculum Unit in Photohistory," no. 5, *The Newberry Library Papers in Family and Community History* (Chicago: Newberry Library, 1978).

99. Compare Edward S. Curtis, *The North American Indians,* edited by Joseph E. Brown (Millerton, N.Y.: Aperture, 1972), *In the Land of the Head-Hunters* (Yonkers-on-the-Hudson, N.Y.: World Book Co., 1915), and *Indian Days of Long Ago* (Yonkers-on-the-Hudson, N.Y.: World Book Co., 1914) with *Dwellers at the Source: Southern Indian Photographs of A. C. Vroman, 1895–1904* (New York: Grossman, 1973). A biography of Curtis by Victor Boesen and Florence Curtis Graybill (Curtis's daughter) called *Edward S. Curtis, Photographer of the North American Indian* (1977) is available from Dodd and Mead.

100. Gregory Bateson and Margaret Mead, *Balinese Character: A Photographic Analysis* (New York: New York Academy of Sciences, 1942); John Collier, *Visual Anthropology: Photography as a Research Method* (New York: Holt, Rinehart and Winston, 1967); Margaret Mead, "Some Uses of Still Photography in Culture and Personality," in *Personal Character and Cultural Milieu,* edited by D. G. Haring (Syracuse: Syracuse University Press, 1956), pp. 79–105.

101. Greene, "Old Ethnic Stereotypes and the New Ethnic Studies," pp. 334–336. Another quite different visual analysis of American workers can be found in Martin Sandler's *The Way We Lived: A Photographic Record of Work in a Vanished America* (Boston: Little, Brown, 1977).

102. Visual histories of Jews in America (e.g., Catherine Noren, *The Camera of My Family* [New York: A. A. Knopf, 1973]) can be compared with studies using photographic data to investigate ethnic life prior to immigration: Lucian Dobroszycki and Barbara Kirschenblatt-Gimblett, *Image before My Eyes: A Photographic History of Jewish Life in Poland, 1864–1939* (New York: Schocken, 1977) and Mendel Grossman, *With a Camera in the Ghetto,* edited by Zvi Szner and Alexander Sened (New York: Schocken, 1977).

103. The exhibition "Six Generations Here: Ethnicity and Change on a Wisconsin

Family Farm, 1951–1978" will be temporarily housed at Old World Wisconsin, Eagle, Wisconsin.

104. See essays "The Modern World and Taste" (pp. iv–vi) and "Photography, Society, and Taste" (pp. 65–66) in *At Home: Domestic Life in the Post-Centennial Era, 1876–1920*.

105. William Seale, *The Tasteful Interlude: American Interiors through the Camera's Eye, 1860–1917* (New York: Praeger, 1975); Merger, "Doing the Rest," p. 288.

106. Jeffrey Simpson, *The American Family: A History in Photographs* (New York: Viking Press; 1976); Oliver Jensen, *et al.*, *American Album* (New York: Simon and Schuster, 1968); Stephen Sears, *et al.*, *Home Town, U.S.A.* (New York: Simon and Schuster, 1975). *The Family Album*, assembled by Mark Silber, with a foreword by Weston Naef (Boston: David R. Godine, 1973), deals with pictures taken by two amateurs, Gilbert ("Burt") Tilton and Fred W. Record in the 1890s and 1900s. An attempt to use visual evidence to write a history of an assortment of nineteenth- and twentieth-century extended families (e.g., California utopian experiments) can be found in Paul Kagan's *New World Utopias: A Photography History of the Search for Community* (Baltimore: Penguin Books, 1975).

107. On "The Studio of Smith and Telfer," see Gerard F. Reese's essay of that title in the New York State Historical Association's *The Smith and Telfer Photographic Collection* (Cooperstown, N.Y.: New York State Historical Association, 1978), pp. 9–11; on Koopman, consult Paul W. Petraits, "Henry Ralph Koopman II: The Life and Times of a Neighborhood Photographer," *Chicago History* 7, no. 3 (Fall 1978): 161–177; and on E. A. Scholfield, refer to William Parker's previously cited essay in *Afterimage*, May/June 1976, pp. 22–33.

108. Quoted in Beaumont Newhall, *The History of Photography* (New York: Metropolitan Museum of Modern Art, 1949), p. 167.

109. Richard Chalfen, "Introduction to the Study of Non-professional Photography as Visual Communication," *Folklore Forum* 13, Bibliographic and Special Series (1975): 4–14.

110. Karin Becker Ohrn, "The Photoflow of Family Life: A Family's Photograph Collection," and Steven Ohrn, "I've Been Duped: Reducing the Home-Made to Data," in *Folklore Forum* 13, Bibliographic and Special Series (1975): 27–36 and 37–44.

111. Judith Mara Gutman, "Family Photo Interpretation," in *Kin and Communities: Families in America*, edited by Allan J. Lichtman and Joan R. Challinor (Washington, D.C.: Smithsonian Institution Press, 1979), pp. 241–243.

112. Barbara Norfleet, *Weddings* (Cambridge, Mass.: Carpenter Center for the Visual Arts/Harvard University Press, 1976).

113. "Family Photo Interpretation," in *Kin and Communities*, pp. 256–260.

114. "Family Photo Interpretation," in *Kin and Communities*, pp. 262–263.

115. Stanley Milgram, "The Image-Freezing Machine," *Psychology Today*, January 1977, p. 48.

116. "Family Photo Interpretation," in *Kin and Communities*, p. 261.

117. Paul Byers, "Cameras Don't Take Pictures," *Columbia University Forum* 9 (Winter 1966): 28–32.

118. On this point, see Peter Robertson, "More Than Meets the Eye," *Archivaria* 2 (Summer 1976): 33–43, and a reply by R. Scott James, "The Historical Photograph," *Archivaria* 3 (Winter 1976–77); 118–120.

119. "Visual Sources for Material Culture Research," *Material History Bulletin* 8, Special Issue (1979): 59–64; Trachtenberg, "Photographs as Symbolic History," in *American Image*, p. xix.

120. Huyda, "Photographs and Archives in Canada," *Archivaria*, p. 12.

121. John Kouwenhoven notes one of the most shocking examples of the alteration of a photograph. During the Warren Commission's investigation of the assassination of President John F. Kennedy, it was uncovered that some time in March or April 1963, Lee Harvey Oswald's wife took a snapshot of him holding a rifle and pistol. As published by *Life* (and also by *Newsweek* and the *New York Times*) it showed a rifle that was not the kind used in shooting the president—giving rise to speculation that Oswald was not the killer. When the commission investigated, they found that Mrs. Oswald's snapshot had been retouched prior to publication in ways that "inadvertently altered details of the rifle"—thus destroying its value as accurate information. (Kouwenhoven, "Historical Photographs as Documents," p. 15.)

122. Howard Becker's section (pp. 14–24) on "Some Common Problems" in his essay "Photography and Sociology" is excellent in its attempt to answer each of these methodological conundrums.

123. An experimental effort to grapple with this major issue would be Warren Susman's "Toward an Iconography of the Period, 1929–1947," in *Culture and Commitment, 1929–1945* (New York: Braziller, 1973) pp. 327–369.

124. Robert U. Akeret, *Photoanalysis: How To Interpret the Hidden Psychological Meaning of Personal and Public Photographs* (New York: Peter Wydem, 1973); Arlene Eakle, *Photograph Analysis* (Salt Lake City: Utah Family History World, 1976).

125. Tractenberg, "Historical Photographs as Symbolic History," p. xxv.

126. J. A. Kouwenhoven, "Photographs as Documents," p. 15; K. B. Ohrn, "Re-Viewing Photographs: Unexplored Resources for Communication Research," p. 34.

127. Two instances of such projects are the "Chicagoland-in-Pictures" Project for Historical Photography housed in the Chicago Historical Society, North Avenue and Clark Street, Chicago, Illinois 60614; and the "Indiana Historical Society Photography Contest," Indiana Historical Society, 315 W. Ohio Street, Indianapolis, Indiana 46202.

128. As quoted in Weinstein and Booth, *Collection, Use, and Care of Historical Photographs*, pp. 15–16.

Chapter 2

1. Edna Ferber, *Fanny Herself* (New York: Frederick A. Stokes Co., 1917), p. 115.

2. Harry Crews, *A Childhood: The Biography of a Place* (New York: Harper and Row, 1978), p. 54.

3. Boris Emmet and John E. Jeuck, *Catalogues and Counters: A History of Sears, Roebuck and Company* (Chicago: University of Chicago Press, 1950), p. 9. A basic mail-order industry bibliography would also include Frank B. Latham, *A Century of Serving Customers: The Story of Montgomery Ward* (Chicago: Montgomery Ward Co., 1972); Nina Baker, *Big Catalogue: The Life of Aaron Montgomery* (New York: Harcourt, Brace, 1956); and *Our Silver Anniversary: Being a Brief and Concise History of the Mail-Order or Catalog Business Which Was Invented By Us a Quarter of a Century Ago* (Chicago: A. Montgomery Ward Co, 1897); on Sears, consult David L. Cohn, *The Good Old Days: A History of American Morals and Manners as Seen through the Sears, Roebuck Catalogs, 1905 to the Present* (New York: Simon & Schuster, 1940); Louis Asher and Edith Neal, *Send No Money*, (Chicago: Argus Books, 1942), and Gordon L. Weil, *Sears, Roebuck, U.S.A.: The Great American Catalog Store and How It Grew* (New York: Stein & Day, 1977).

4. Daniel Boorstin, *The Americans, The Democratic Experience* (New York: Random House, 1973), pp. 128–129.

5. See Maria Elena De La Iglesia's *The Catalog of American Catalogs* (New York: Random House, 1973) and her *The Complete Guide To World-Wide Shopping by Mail* (New York: Random House, 1972); Cecil C. Hoge, *Mail Order Moonlighting* (New York: 1975).

6. Viola I. Paradise, "By Mail," *Scribner's* (April 1921), p. 480.

7. Rae Elizabeth Rips, "An Introductory Study of the Role of the Mail-Order Business in American History, 1872–1914" (Master's Thesis, University of Chicago, 1938), pp. 2–3.

8. For the cover of the *1926 Spring/Summer Catalog*, Montgomery Ward reproduced John Trumbull's painting of Franklin, John Adams, and Thomas Jefferson drafting the Declaration of Independence as the store's tribute to the American sesquicentennial. Inside the catalog (p. 3), the company claimed its own founder, not Franklin, as the mail-order catalog's originator: "Selling goods by mail was unknown in 1872. A. Montgomery Ward, the pioneer, was the young man with vision who foresaw a new merchandising method—who laid down his principles, and so won a niche in the 'World's Hall of Business Fame.' "

9. Lawrence B. Romaine, "Benjamin Franklin: The Father of the Mail-Order Catalog and Not Montgomery Ward," *The American Book Collector* 11, no. 4 (December 1960): 25–28. For a still earlier claim for a mail-order prototype, see Gerald L. Alexander, "Widlldey's Enterprising Map of North America," *Antiques* (July 1962), pp. 76–77.

10. *Publishers Central Catalog* (Summer 1979), p. 26; *Marboro Books Catalog* (Spring 1979), p. 14.

11. For ordering and pricing information on Sears catalog reproductions, write to Book Digest, Inc., 540 Frontage Road, Northfield, Illinois, 60093, for the 1897, 1900, 1908, and 1923 editions; Castle Books, 110 Enterprise Avenue, Secaucus, New Jersey, 07094, for the 1906 edition; and Crown Publishers, 34 Engelhard Avenue, Avenel, New Jersey, 07001, for the 1902 and 1927 editions and the anthology, *Sears Catalogs of the 1930s*.

12. *Montgomery Ward and Company Catalogue and Buyers Guide No. 57* (Spring and Summer 1895), with an introduction by Boris Emmet (New York: Dover Publications, 1969).

13. See, for example, Robert D. Watt, editor, *The Shopping Guide of the West: Woodward's Catalogue, 1883–1953* (Forest Grove, Vancouver, B.C.: Douglas and McIntyre, 1978).

14. For the location of Sears catalogs on microfilm in the libraries and research centers in any state, write to Lenore Swioskin, Archivist, Sears, Roebuck and Company, Fortieth Floor, Sears Tower, Chicago, Illinois.

15. Published accounts of this pedagogy include Minnesota Historical Society Education Division, *The Wishbook: Mail Order in Minnesota—A Study Guide for Teachers* (St. Paul, Minn.: Minnesota Historical Society, 1979); William R. Smith, "Social Studies: Making Comparisons With Mail-Order Catalogs," *The Instructor, A Journal of the New York State Educational Association* (September 1976), pp. 71–72; and James Kavanaugh, "The Artifact in American Culture: The Development of an Undergraduate Program in American Studies," in *Material Culture and the Study of American Life*, edited by Ian M. G. Quimby (New York: W. W. Norton & Company, Inc., 1978), pp. 69–71.

16. Nicholas Westbrook, "The Wishbook as History Book," unpublished paper delivered at the Seventh Biennial National Meeting of the American Studies Association, Minneapolis, Minnesota, September 28, 1979; Fred E. H. Schroeder, "Semi-Annual Installment on the American Dream: The Wishbook as Popular Icon," in *Icons of Popular Culture*, by M. Fishwick and R. B. Browne, (Bowling Green, Ohio: Bowling Green University Popular Press, 1970), pp. 73–86; Fred E. H. Schroeder, "The Wishbook as Popular Icon," in *Outlaw Aesthetics: Arts and the Public Mind* (Bowling Green, Ohio: Bowling Green University Popular Press, 1977), pp. 50–61; Joan Siedl and Nicholas Westbook, "The

Wishbook: Mail Order in Minnesota," Exhibition at the Minnesota Historical Society, St. Paul Minnesota (November 1978–   ).

17. For an application of the inquiry approach to another historical topic, see my "A Question is an Answer: An Experimental Inquiry in American Cultural History," *The History Teacher* 6, no. 1 (November 1972): 97–106.

18. To date, no scholar has done a systematic, definitive study of either mail-order catalogs or mail-order goods. The best work on catalogs has already been cited in note 16; mail-order goods, as a type of material culture evidence, however, still await their cultural historian. Mail-order merchandising, although discussed in several individual corporate histories (cited above in footnote 3), still suffers from a lack of a broad, interpretive, historical overview of the entire industry.

19. Lovell Thompson, "Eden in Easy Payments," *Saturday Review of Literature* (April 3, 1937), pp. 15–16; Ralph Andrist, *American Century; One Hundred Years of Changing Life Styles in America* (New York: American Heritage Press, 1972), p. 8.

20. *Rears and Robust Mail-Order Catalog for Spring/Summer/Fall/Winter* (Wheeling West Virginia: *The Morning Call*, 1940). Copy available in Research Library of the Chicago Historical Society. In his 1970 article ("Semi-Annual Installments on the American Dream"), Fred Schroeder suggests (p. 76) that little folklore about mail-order catalogs has been collected or indexed in standard sources such as *The Journal of American Folklore* or B. A. Botkin's *Treasury of American Anecdotes*. I am persuaded that the *Rears and Robust* compendium would qualify as an excellent example of catalog folklore and fantasy.

21. Schroeder, "The Wishbook as Popular Icon," p. 56; *Sears, Roebuck Catalog* (Spring/ Summer 1969), p. 1079.

22. Crews, *A Childhood*, pp. 54–55, 57. In similar fashion, nine-year-old R. Waldo Ledbetter, Jr., a character in George Milburn's novel about the impact of the mail-order catalog on an Oklahoma town in the 1920s, kept both a Ward's and a Sears catalog "in a big pasteboard box in his room under his bed." "His father [who later organizes the town's anticatalog campaign] didn't understand about catalogues. His father never would know how much fun a person could have with mail-order catalogs, making believe he is a rancher fitting himself out with everything from branding irons to angora chaps; or a farmer equipping a model farm; or simply a father ordering toys for his son. The toy list was the most fun of all" (*Catalogue*, pp. 83–84).

23. In 1918, Sears offered, via its mail-order catalogs, a series of "useful knowledge" almanacs on farm life. These volumes are superb documents for studying the agrarian material culture of that particular period. The books were titled *Farm Knowledge: A Manual of Successful Farming; Written by Recognized Authorities in all Parts of the Country. . . . The Farmers' Own Cyclopedia*, edited by E. H. D. Seymour (New York: Doubleday/Sears, Roebuck, 1918). The four volumes were *Farm Animals* (I); *Soils, Crops, Fertilizers, and Methods* (II); *Farm Implements, Vehicles, and Buildings* (III); and *Business Management and the Farm Home* (IV).

24. See, for example, Rips, "Role of the Catalog in American History," pp. 17–34; Emmet and Jeuck, *Catalogues and Counters*, p. 718.

25. Robert Heilbroner, *The Economic Transformation of America* (New York: Harcourt, Brace, 1977). Also useful on this point is Herbert Casson, "Marvelous Development of the Mail-Order Business," *Munsey's Magazine* 38 (January 1908): 513–515.

26. For a good contemporary summary of the various positions in the antimail-order campaign, see the 1908 (December) issue of *The Outlook*, which provides an overview of the conflict; likewise, see Lewis Atherton, *Mjin Street on the Middle Border* (New York: Quadrangle Books, 1966), pp. 231–233.

27. Milburn, *Catalogue*, Chapter 18; also see Cohn, Chapter 28, "The Burning of The Books," *Good Old Days*, pp. 510–517.

28. Harold Wentworth and Stuart Berg, *The Dictionary of American Slang* (New York: Simon and Schuster, 1967), p. 221.

29. Ida M. Tarbell, *The Nationalizing of Business, 1878–1898* (New York: Macmillan, 1936), and Robert Wiebe, *The Search for Order, 1877–1920* (New York: Hill and Wang, 1967). The view of corporate growth as an economic system that demanded disciplined patterns of rational and objective order is also the theme of two books by Samuel P. Hays, *The Response to Industrialism* (Chicago: University of Chicago Press, 1957), and *Conservation and the Gospel of Efficiency* (Cambridge: Harvard University Press, 1959).

30. *Sears, Roebuck Catalog* (Spring/Summer 1908), p. 309. The stereo views were later called "Trip Through Sears, Roebuck and Company."

31. On Taylorism, see Samuel Haber, *Efficiency and Uplift: Scientific Management in the Progressive Era, 1890–1920* (Chicago: University of Chicago, 1964), and David Noble, "Harmony Through Technological Order: Taylor, Ford, and Veblen," in his *The Progressive Mind, 1890–1917* (Chicago: Rand McNally, 1969), pp. 37–52.

32. See, for instance, Bruce Daniels, "Probate Inventories as a Source for Economic History," *Connecticut Historical Society Bulletin* 37, no. 3 (January 1972): 1–9; Abbott Cummings, *Rural Household Inventories* (Boston: SPNEA, 1964); Monroe Fabian, "An Immigrant's Inventory," *Pennsylvania Folklife* 25, no. 4 (Summer 1976): 47–48.

33. Deborah C. Andrews and William D. Andrews, "Technology and the Housewife in Nineteenth-Century America," *Women Studies* 2, no. 3 (1974): 309–328; Susan May Strasser, "Never Done: The Ideology and Technology of Household Work, 1850–1930" (Ph.D. diss. University of New York at Stony Brook, 1977); Elizabeth Faulkner Baker, *Technology and Woman's Work* (New York: Columbia University Press, 1964); Gwendolyn Wright, "Sweet and Clean: The Domestic Landscape in The Progressive Era," *Landscape* 20, no. 1 (October 1975): 38–43; Ruth Schwartz Cowan, "The 'Industrial Revolution,' in the Home: Household Technology and Social Change in the Twentieth Century," *Technology and Culture* 17, no. 1 (January 1976): 1–23.

34. Here, see Siegfried Giedion, *Mechanization Takes Command: A Contribution to Anonymous History* (New York: Oxford University Press, 1975); Anthony Garvan, "Effects of Technology on Modern Life, 1830–1880," and Melvin Rotsch, "The Home Environment," in Carroll Pursell and Melvin Kranzberg, editors, Volumes I and II of *Technology in Western Civilization* (New York: Oxford University Press, 1967), pp. 546–562 (Volume I) and pp. 217–236 (Volume II); Joann Vanek, "Time Spent in Housework," *Scientific American* 231 (November 1974): 116–120, and "Household Technology and Social Status—Residence Differences in Housework," *Technology and Culture* 19 (July 1978): 361–375.

35. Cohn, *Good Old Days*, pp. 285–316.

36. See Arthur M. Schlesinger, *Learning How To Behave: A Historical Study of American Etiquette Books* (New York: Macmillan, 1946); R. Gordon Kelly, *Mother Was a Lady: Strategy and Order in Selected American Children's Periodicals, 1865–1890* (Westport, Conn.: Greenwood Press, 1974); Gerald Carson, *The Polite Americans: A Wide-Angle View of Our More or Less Good Manners Over 300 Years* (New York: William Morrow and Co, Inc., 1966); and Stow Persons, *The Decline of American Gentility* (New York: Columbia University Press, 1973).

37. Ward's assessment of "The Meaning of Lindbergh's Flight" can be found in *American Quarterly* 10 (1958): 3–16.

38. Schroeder, "The Wishbook as Popular Icon," pp. 51–53, 60.

39. Thomas J. Schlereth, "Material Culture Studies in America: Notes Toward a Histor-

ical Perspective," *Proceedings of the First International Conference on Material History* (Ottawa, Canada: National Museum of Man, 1979, pp. 89–98.

40. Kenneth Ames, "Meaning in Artifacts: Hall Furnishings in Victorian America," *Journal of Interdisciplinary History* 9, no. 1 (Summer 1978): 26.

41. Lawrence B. Romaine, *A Guide to American Trade Catalogs, 1744–1900* (New York: Arno, 1976). The Pyne Press American Historical Catalog Collection includes seventeen reprint catalogs that are extremely useful in comparative material culture exercises. The subjects of the catalogs range from glassware to ornamental ironwork, architectural elements to sporting goods, carriages to cameras. For a catalog of the reprint catalogs available, write the Pyne Press, 92 Nassau Street, Princeton, New Jersey 08540.

42. Correspondence with Emilie Tari, Curator of Collections, Old World Wisconsin, August 27, 1979; likewise, Robert G. Chenhall's *Nomenclature for Museum Cataloging: A System for Classifying Man-Made Objects* (Nashville: American Association for State and Local History, 1978) uses several Sears and Ward's catalogs as key reference texts; see pages 501, 504.

43. Interview with Ms. Lenore Swioskin, Archivist, Sears, Roebuck and Company, Chicago, Illinois, June 1, 1979.

44. Tari, describing her work at Old World Wisconsin, notes: "The catalogs are without question a basic research tool in any fully conceived interior restoration that dates after approximately 1890. . . . Taken in combination with photographic evidence and oral history material, it [is] possible to pull together quite a broad and comprehensive picture of the material culture of a social/economic group that has rarely been methodically studied or researched."

45. Claudia Kidwell, *Suiting Everyone: The Democratization of Clothing in America* (Washington, D.C.: Smithsonian Institution Press, 1977), pp. 160–164; author's correspondence with Claudia Kidwell, Curator of Costume, Smithsonian Institution, August 20, 1979.

46. Correspondence with Rodris Roth, Curator, Division of Domestic Life, Smithsonian Institution, September 10, 1979.

47. See "Chicago History Galleries," Chicago History Society and "The History of Chicago Exhibit," Chicago Museum of Science and Industry. A temporary bicentennial exhibition, "Creating New Traditions," at the Chicago Historical Society also paid considerable attention to mail-order catalogs, as did its accompanying publication, *Creating New Traditions*, by Perry Duis, (Chicago: Chicago Historical Society, 1976), particularly chapter 5 on "Merchandising."

48. Craig Gilborn, "Pop Pedagogy: Looking at the Coke Bottle," *Museum News* (December 1966), pp. 12–18.

49. Exhibit Panel, "The Wishbook: Direct From the Factory To You," in "The Wishbook: Mail Order in Minnesota" Exhibition, Minnesota Historical Society, St. Paul, Minnesota (November 1978–   ).

50. William Seale, *The Tasteful Interlude: American Interiors Through the Camera's Eye, 1850–1917* (New York: Praeger, 1975); George Talbot, *At Home: Domestic Life in the Post-Centennial Era, 1876–1920* (Madison, Wis.: State Historical Society of Wisconsin, 1976); and Clay Lancaster, *New York Interiors at the Turn of the Century* (New York: Dover, 1977).

51. See this photograph, reproduced from the collections of the Nebraska Historical Society in Andrist, *American Century*, p. 3; for parallel uses of historical photographs in American Studies, see Barnard Mergen and Marsha Peters, "Doing the Rest: The Uses of Photographs in American Studies," *American Quarterly* 29, no. 3 (Summer 1977), and chapter 1 of this book.

52. Milburn, *Catalogue*, p. 167.

53. Andrist, *American Century*, p. 7; also see Daniel Boorstin, "A. Montgomery Ward's Mail Order Business," *Chicago History*, new series, 2 (Spring–Summer 1973): 147.

54. Boorstin, *The Americans*, p. 128.

55. David Potter, *People of Plenty; Economic Abundance and the American Character* (Chicago: University of Chicago Press, 1954); Daniel Boorstin, *The Image: A Guide to Pseudo-Events in America* (New York: Atheneum, 1961); Marshall McLuhan, *Understanding Media: The Extensions of Man* (New York: McGraw-Hill, 1964).

56. Erving Goffman, *Gender Advertisements* (New York: Harper Colophon, 1979). This monograph first appeared as volume 3, number 2 of *Studies in the Anthropology of Visual Communications* (Fall 1976); also see Betty Friedan's analysis of the "sexual sell" in *The Feminine Mystique* (1963; reprint edition, New York: Dell, 1970).

57. Robert Atwan, Donald McQuade and John W. Wright, *Edsels, Luckies, and Frigidaires: Advertising the American Way* (New York: Dell, 1979), pp. 111–246.

58. Edgar R. Jones, *Those Were the Good Old Days* (New York: Simon and Schuster, 1979) and Victor Margolin, Ira Brichta, and Vivan Brichta, *The Promise and the Product: 200 Years of American Advertising Posters* (New York: Macmillan, 1979); also useful in this context is Clarence P. Hornung's *Handbook of Early Advertising Art*, 3rd edition (New York: Dover Pictorial Archives Series, 1956), particularly the introduction (pp. ix–xiv) and the bibliography.

59. Lester S. Levy, *Picture the Songs: Lithographs from the Sheet Music of the Nineteenth Century* (Baltimore: The Johns Hopkins Press, 1976).

60. Potter, *People of Plenty*, pp. 166–208; likewise, consult Ivan L. Preston, *The Great American Blow-up: Puffery in Advertising and Selling* (Madison: University of Wisconsin Press, 1975).

61. E. McClung Fleming, "Artifact Study, A Proposed Model," *Winterthur Portfolio* 9 (June 1974): 161–173; Charles Montgomery, "Some Remarks on the Practice and Science of Connoisseurship," *American Walpole Society Notebook* (1961), pp. 7–20; Sidney Browner, "Tools, Toys, Masterpieces, Mediums," *Landscape* 19, no. 2 (January 1975): 28–32.

62. Kenan Heise, "Mail Order Democracy," *Chicago Magazine* 25, no. 11 (November 1976): 106–107; Eric M. Lampard, *Rise of the Dairy Industry in Wisconsin, 1820–1920*, (Madison: University of Wisconsin Press, 1963).

63. Cohn, *Good Old Days*, pp. xi–xix.

64. Russell Lynes, *The Tastemakers* (New York: Harper, 1949), p. 190; Perry Duis, *Chicago: Creating New Traditions* (Chicago: Chicago Historical Society, 1976), p. 116.

65. Edward P. Alexander, "Artistic and Historical Period Rooms," *Curator* 7, no. 4 (1964): 263–281; E. McClung Fleming, "The Period Room as a Curatorial Publication," *Museum News* 50, no. 10 (June 1972): 39–42.

66. Thomas W. Leavitt, "Toward a Standard of Excellence: The Nature and Purpose of Exhibit Reviews," *Technology and Culture* 9 (1968): 70–75.

67. Lewis Mumford, *Technics and Civilization* (New York: Harcourt, Brace, 1934), p. 105.

68. On the relationship between world fairs, department stores, and museums, see Neil Harris, "Museums, Merchandising, and Popular Taste: The Struggle for Influence," in *Material Culture and the Study of American Life*, edited by Ian M. G. Quimby, (New York: W. W. Norton & Company, Inc., 1978), pp. 140–174. A case study of this relationship in Chicago can be done by comparing either the Sears or Ward's catalogs with the information found in Helen Lefkowitz Horowitz, *Culture and the City: Cultural Philanthropy from the 1880s to 1917* (Lexington, Ky.: University of Kentucky Press, 1976), David F. Burg, *Chicago's White City of 1893* (Lexington, Ky.: University of Kentucky Press, 1976), and Lloyd Wendt

and Herman Kogan, *Give the Lady What She Wants* (Chicago: Rand McNally, 1952). For additional department-store history, consult Boorstin, *The Americans,* pp. 101–109 and his bibliographical notes (pp. 629–630), along with Robert Hendrickson, *The Grand Emporiums; The Illustrated History of America's Great Department Stores* (New York: Stein and Day, 1978).

69. The country store has been studied by Lewis Atherton (e.g., his *Pioneer Merchant in Mid-America* [Columbia, Mo.: University of Missouri Press, 1939] and *The Southern Country Store, 1800–1860* [Baton Rouge: Louisiana State University Press, 1949]), as well as by Gerald Carson (*The Old Country Store* [New York: Oxfrd University Press, 1954]) and Thomas D. Clark (*Pills, Petticoats and Plows: The Southern Country Store* [Indianapolis: The Bobbs-Merrill Co., 1944).

70. For additional information on rural free delivery and parcel post, see Wayne E. Fuller, *RFD, The Changing Face of Rural America* (Chicago: University of Chicago Press, 1964), as well as his *The American Mail: Enlarger of the Common Life* (Chicago: University of Chicago Press, 1972).

71. American Studies 486: *Chicago: Studies in a Regional Cuture, 1871–1933* (Spring 1979); American Studies 484: *American Material Culture—The History on the Land* (Fall 1979), Department of American Studies, University of Notre Dame) filed with the National American Studies Faculty, from which copies are available at ASA headquarters, College Hall, University of Pennsylvania, Philadelphia, Pennsylvania.

72. Arthur A. Hart, "M. A. Disbrow and Company: Catalog Architecture," *Palimpsest* 56, no. 4 (1975): 98–119.

73. John F. Hart, *The Look of the Land* (Englewood Cliffs, N.J.: Prentice Hall, 1975), pp. 155–156; *Sears Midwest* (June 1969), p. 8.

74. In its Book Department, Sears also published its own builders' manuals, such as William A. Radford's two-volume *Practical Carpentry* (Chicago: Radford Architectural Company/Sears, Roebuck and Company, 1907), which purported to contain "a complete, up-to-date explanation of modern carpentry and an encyclopedia on the modern methods used in the erection of buildings from the laying out of the foundation to the deliver of the building to the painter." This pattern book of twentieth-century vernacular architecture contained fifty perspective views and floor plans of low- and medium-priced houses. A local builder could buy all fifty plans and illustrated views for only five dollars. Sears also sold another book of plans *(Twentieth-Century Practical Barn Plans),* likewise edited by Radford (who also published the journal *The American Carpenter and Builder*), containing fifty building plans of farm structures.

75. *Sears, Roebuck Modern Homes Catalog* (Chicago: Sears, Roebuck and Company, 1926); also see Emmet and Jeuck, *Catalogues and Counters,* pp. 522–524.

76. Ferber, *Fanny Herself,* p. 115.

77. Montgomery Ward and Company, *Catalog and Buyers Guide* (Spring/Summer 1895), p. 108.

78. Floyd Dell, *Moon Calf, A Novel* (New York, 1920), p. 2.

79. Gary Deeb, "Radio: What It Was, What It Is, and What It Is Most Likely to Become," and Clifford Terry, "The Glory Days of Radio," in *Chicago Tribune Magazine,* March 4, 1979, pp. 22–34, 28–33.

80. David F. Burg, "The Aesthetics of Bigness in Late Nineteenth-Century American Architecture," in *Popular Architecture,* by Marshall Fishwick and J. Meredith Neil (Bowling Green, Ohio: Bowling Green University Press, 1976), pp. 106–114.

81. Schroeder, "Semi-Annual Installment on the American Dream," pp. 82–83.

82. C. W. Fishbaugh, "Collectible Catalogues," *Collector Editions* (New York, 1979),

p. 6; see also Leslie Parr, Andrea Hicks, and Marie Storeck, *The Best of Sears Collectibles, 1905–1910* (New York: Arno Press, 1976).

Chapter 3

1. Frank Friedel, *et al.*, editors, *Harvard Guide to American History*, 2 vols. (Cambridge, Mass.: Belknap Press of Harvard University, 1974), 1:44.

2. Gustaaf J. Renier, *History: Its Purpose and Method* (Boston: Beacon Press, 1950), p. 116. In order to nurture such frequent usage of maps by historians, John H. Long and C. James Haug have organized an information network for Cartographical Analysis in History sponsored by the Newberry Library and the Social Science History Association. To joint the network, write Cartographical Analysis in History, the Newberry Library, 60 West Walton Street, Chicago, Illinois, 60610.

3. Adele Hast, "Data in Search of Maps," paper presented at the American Historical Association Annual Meeting, Dallas, Texas, December 30, 1977, and Louis DeVorsey, Jr., "The Neglect of Cartographic Sources," paper presented at the Organization of American Historians Annual Meeting, Chicago, Illinois, May 2, 1973. I am particularly indebted to Ms. Hast, along with her colleagues John H. Long and Robert W. Karrow, Jr., for sharing many insights with me during my work at the Hermon Dunlap Smith Center for Study of the History of Cartography, The Newberry Library, Chicago, Illinois.

4. As a sampler of current research in these fields, consult Theodore Hershberg, "The Historical Study of Urban Space: Introduction," *Historical Methods Newsletter* 9 (1976): 99–104; Alan Kulikoff, "Historical Geographers and Social History: A Revised Essay," *Historical Methods Newsletter* 6 (1973): 14–21; John H. Long, "The Case for Historical Cartographic Data Files," paper presented at the American Historical Association Annual Meeting, Dallas, Texas, December 30, 1977, and his "Studying George Rogers Clark's Campaign With Maps," in *The French, the Indians, and George Rogers Clark in the Illinois Country: Proceedings of the Indiana American Revolution Bicentennial Symposium* (Indianapolis: Indiana Historical Society, 1977), pp. 67–91; Alan K. Henrickson, "Maps as an Idea; the Role of Cartographic Imagery During the Second World War," *American Cartographer* (1975).

5. Lester J. Cappon, editors, *Atlas of Early American History: The Revolutionary Era, 1760–1790* (Princeton, N.J.: Princeton University Press and the Newberry Library, 1976) and "Research Prospectus," *Atlas of Great Lakes Indian History*, available from the Newberry Library, Chicago, Illinois. Also see Hast, "Data in Search of Maps," pp. 3–9.

6. W. G. Hoskins, *The Making of the English Landscape* (London: Hodder and Stoughton, 1955, 1963); Maurice Beresford, *History on the Ground: Six Studies in Maps and Landscapes*, revised edition (London: Methuen, 1971); and Penelope Lively, *The Presence of the Past: An Introduction to Landscape History* (London: William Collins and Sons, 1976).

7. J. H. Parry, "Old Maps Are Slippery Witnesses," *Harvard Magazine* 78 (April 1976): 38.

8. W. Gordon East, *The Geography behind History* (New York: W. W. Norton & Company, Inc., 1967); J. B. Harley, "The Evolution of Early Maps: Towards a Methodology," *Imago Mundi* 21 (1967): 62–74; C. R. Crone, *Maps and Their Makers: An Introduction to the History of Cartography*, fourth edition (London: Hutchinson, 1968).

9. J. Brian Harley, *Maps for the Local Historian: A Guide to British Sources* (London: National Council of Social Science for the Standing Conference for Local History, 1972); R. A. Skelton, *Looking at an Early Map* (Lawrence, Kansas: University of Kansas Libraries,

1965), and K. C. Edwards, editor, *British Landscapes Through Maps* (London: Geographical Association, 1970).

10. In addition to the collected essays published in 1967 (see note no. 9) there is an earlier edition of Harley's guide: J. B. Harley and C. W. Phillips *The Historian's Guide to Ordinance Survey Maps* (London: Standing Council for Local History—National Council of Social Service, 1964).

11. Roger Minshull, "The Functions of Geography in American Studies," *Journal of American Studies* 7, no. 3 (December 1973): 267–278; John A. Wolter, "Source Materials for the History of American Cartography," *American Studies International* 12, no. 3 (Spring 1973): 12–27; G. S. Dunbar, "Illustrations of the American Earth: An Essay in Cultural Geography," *American Studies International*, 12, no. 1 (Autumn 1973): 3–15; and John A. Jakle, *Past Landscapes: A Bibliography for Historic Preservationists Selected from the Literature of Historic Geography* (Monticello, Illinois: Council of Planning Librarians Exchange Bibliography, 1974).

12. The various uses of Chicago maps as data for urban history can be inserted in a curricular approach that employs Chicago, 1871–1919, as a focus for a course in regional studies. See chapter 8, "Regional Studies in America: The Chicago Model."

13. Chicago is also the home of the Chicago Map Society, founded in 1976 for the purpose of supporting and encouraging the study and preservation of maps and related materials. *A Guide to Nineteenth-Century Mapmakers of Chicago* is currently being compiled by the society. The work will contain vignettes of all individuals and firms involved in various phases of map-making activities, ranging from surveying, printing, map coloring, and mounting to map selling. The guide is scheduled for publication in 1980; also to be published is a comprehensive *Chicagoland Atlas* by Rand, McNally Company that purports to be more extensive in coverage than the City of Chicago, Department of Plats, Bureau of Public Works city atlas.

14. At present, Daniel C. Haskell, *Manhattan Maps: A Cooperative List* (New York: New York Public Library, 1931), and the City of Boston Engineering Department's *List of Maps of Boston* (Boston: Municipal Printing Office, 1903; Supplement, 1904), appear to be the only other comprehensive bibliographical surveys (i.e., in the specialized library usage of the term) of an American urban environment. For additional information on the Midwest Map Project, which is housed at the Newberry Library, Chicago, Illinois, write to the Hermon Dunlap Smith Center, The Newberry Library, 60 W. Walton, Chicago, Illinois 60610.

15. Barbara Vimri Aziz, "Maps and the Mind," *Human Nature* (August 1978), pp. 50–59; Nancy Green and Michael Donovan, "Maps: One Kind and Another," *Print* (March/April 1979), pp. 37–49; Roger M. Downs and David Stea, *Maps in Minds: Reflections on Cognitive Mapping* (New York: Harper and Row, 1977).

16. Louis Armand de Lom d'Arce, Baron de La Hontan, *Nouveaux voyages de M. le baron de La honton dans l'Amerique septentrionale* (1703) as reproduced in Alfred T. Andreas, *History of Chicago*, 3 vols. (Chicago: A. T. Andreas, 1884–1886), 1:9; also see Irving Cutler, *Chicago: Metropolis of the Mid-Continent*, second edition (Dubuque, Iowa: Kendall/Hunt Publishers, 1976).

17. Peirce F. Lewis, "Physical Geography and the Location of Cities," Class Handout, Department of Geography, Pennsylvania State University (1970). A slightly modified version of this essay appears in published form in the Association of American Geographers, *The Local Community: A Handbook for Teachers* (New York: Macmillan, 1971).

18. Topographical maps are inexpensive and relatively easy to obtain. Write to the Map Information Office, U.S. Geological Survey, Washington, D.C. 20242, and request a copy

of the "Index to Topographic Mapping" for the state in which the city that you wish to study is located. As an outline map of the state that you request, the Index will show the topographic map coverage for that area and will give directions for ordering individual maps. Often two maps of different scale and date will be available, thus enabling the historian to compare different time periods. All topographic sheets published by the U.S.G.S. since the 1880s have recently been reproduced on microfilm, on a state basis. For information and prices on this "Historical File," write to the National Cartographic Information Center, U.S. Geological Survey, 507 National Center, Reston, Virginia 22092.

19. All Chicago maps hereafter referred to this essay can be assumed to be deposited in the Map Collection of the Chicago Historical Society unless otherwise noted. Reference librarians Grant Dean and Frank Jewell and research associate Gerald Danzer at the Chicago Historical Society were all of immense assistance to me in conducting my research, and profited greatly from their generous advice and thoughtful critique.

20. Compare Rollin D. Salisbury, *Geography of Chicago and Its Environs* (Chicago: Geographical Society of Chicago; 1899), p. 55, and William C. Alden, *Geologic Atlas of the United States* (Chicago Folio: Washington, D.C., 1902) with U.S. Topographic Map Series (1963), Section 2; also see Robert Knight and Lucius H. Zeuch, *The Location of the Chicago Portage of the Seventeenth Century* (Chicago: University of Chicago Press, 1920) and George B. Cressey, *The Indiana Sand Dunes and Shorelines of the Lake Michigan Basin* (Chicago: Geographical Society of Chicago, Bulletin no. 2, 1901).

21. See, for instance, numerous quarry sites on the Rees and Rucker *Map of Chicago and Vicinity* (1849); H. B. Wilman, *Summary of the Geology of the Chicago Area,* Circular no. 40 (Urbana, Illinois: Illinois State Geological Survey, 1971); also consult J. Harlem Bretz, *Geology of the Chicago Region* (Urbana, Illinois: Illinois State Geological Survey, Bulletin no. 65, 1939).

22. Philip Hansen, *Chicago Area Geology: A Discovery Unit from Field Museum of Natural History* (Chicago: Field Museum of Natural History, Department of Education, 1978).

23. Wilman, *Summary of Geology of Chicago Area,* maps on pages 39, 43, 53.

24. Compare, for instance, the Albert Scharf manuscript maps of Indian travel routes in the Chicago region with any contemporary road map of the same area. The Scharf maps can be found in the A. D. Scharf and C. Dilg Map Collection, Chicago Historical Society. Also review F. M. Fryxell, *The Physiography of the Region of Chicago* (Chicago: University of Chicago Press, 1927).

25. Urban histories that make particular use of topographic data as historical evidence include Walter M. Whitehill, *Boston, a Topographical History,* second edition (Cambridge, Mass.: Belknap Press of Harvard University, 1968); Reyner Banham, *Los Angeles: The Architecture of Four Ecologies* (New York: Harper and Row, 1971); and Peirce F. Lewis, *New Orleans: The Making of an Urban Landscape* (Cambridge, Mass.: Ballinger Co., 1976); and James E. Vance, "Geography and the Study of Cities," *American Behavioral Scientist* 22, no. 1 (September 1978): 131–149.

26. John Fraser Hart and Karl B. Raitz, *Cultura Geography on Topographical Maps* (New York: John Wiley and Sons, 1975), pp. 83–136.

27. Norman J. W. Thrower, *Maps and Men: An Examination of Cartography in Relation to Culture and Civilization* (Englewood Cliffs, N.J.: Prentice-Hall, 1972), pp. 9–22.

28. F. J. Marschner, *Land Use and Its Patterns in the United States,* Agriculture Handbook no. 153 (Washington, D.C.: Department of Agriculture, 1959); John Fraser Hart, "Land Division in America," in *The Look of the Land* (Englewood Cliffs, N.J.: Prentice-Hall, 1975), pp. 45–66; Glenn T. Trewartha, "Types of Rural Settlement in Colonial America," *Geo-*

graphical Review 36 (1946): 568–596; Marshall Harris, *The Origin of the Land Tenure System in the United States* (Ames, Iowa: Iowa State College Press, 1953); and Constance Perin, *Everything in Its Place: Social Order and Land Use in America* (Princeton, N.J.: Princeton University Press, 1977).

29. John Reps, *Cities of the American West: A History of Frontier Urban Planning* (Princeton, N.J.: Princeton University Press, 1979); also see Hildegard B. Johnson, *Order Upon the Land: The U.S. Rectangular Land Survey and the Upper Mississippi Country* (New York: Oxford University Press, 1976).

30. William D. Pattison, *Beginnings of the American Rectangular Land Survey System, 1784–1800,* Research Paper no. 50 (Chicago: University of Chicago Department of Geography, 1957) has traced the idea of rectangular land survey back to the Roman scheme of centuriation, which is described in some detail in George Kish, "Centuratio: The Roman Rectangular Land Survey," *Surveying and Mapping* 22 (1962): 233–244, but Norman J. W. Thrower, *Original Survey and Land Subdivision: A Comparative Study of the Form and Effect of Contrasting Cadastral Surveys,* American Association of Geographers Monograph no. 4 (Skokie, Illinois: Rand, McNally, 1966), p. 8, argues that the first towns in the Indus Valley had even earlier gridiron plans.

31. See bibliography in Pattison, *Beginnings of the American Rectangular Land Survey System,* pp. 235–248 as well as in Hart, *Look of the Land,* pp. 56–66. In brief, the township system worked as follows: The 1785 ordinance required that, before public lands could be sold or settled, they had to be surveyed and mapped. The survey lines were to follow a national pattern and were to run in the cardinal directions—north, south, east, and west. The land was to be divided into square townships six miles long and six miles wide, each one thus containing 36 square miles. These dimensions were thought to be the ideal size for a local farming community. Each township, in turn, was subdivided into 36 sections, each one a mile long and a mile wide. Each section contained 640 acres. Ordinarily, that was too large for a family farm, so the land was further subdivided into half-sections (320 acres), quarter-sections (160 acres), half-quarter-sections (80 acres) and quarter-quarter-sections (40 acres). The quarter-section of 40 acres was thought to be the smallest useful division for a single family farmstead. About three-fourths of all the land in the United States was first divided according to that township system.

32. An example of the way this might be done, using a current Chicago road/street map, is detailed in Exercise II of the Appendices.

33. Grady Clay, *Close-Up: How to Read the American City* (New York: Praeger, 1972), pp. 42–52.

34. An excellent finding aid for work in landownership maps is Stephenson's *Land Ownership Maps: A Checklist of Nineteenth-Century United States County Maps in the Library of Congress* (Washington, D.C.: Library of Congress, 1967) which, in addition to listing 1,449 maps in the Library of Congress's Geography and Map Division, has an excellent introductory essay on the origin, production, and significance of the U.S. county landownership map; also see J. S. Adams, "Residential Structure of Midwestern Cities," *Annals of Association of American Geographers* 60 (March 1970), pp. 37–62.

35. "Addison Township Map," in Thompson Brothers and Burr, *Combination Atlas Map of DuPage County, Illinois* (Elgin, Ind., 1874).

36. Gerald Danzer, "Addison Township Map: An Inquiry Approach," cartographic exercise presented at Research Colloquium, Chicago Historical Society, Chicago, Illinois, April 5, 1978.

37. See composite Chicago annexation maps for 1893 and 1915, drawn from various

municipal annexation maps in Harold Mayer and Richard Wade, *Chicago: Growth of a Metropolis* (Chicago: University of Chicago Press, 1969), pp. 177, 251.

38. See David Ward, *Cities and Immigrants: A Geography of Change in Nineteenth-Century America* (New York: Oxford University Press, 1971), pp. 105–145; Otis Dudley Duncan and Beverly Duncan, *The Negro Population of Chicago: A Study of Residential Succession* (Chicago: University of Chicago Press, 1957); Humbert S. Nelli, *The Italians in Chicago, 1880–1930: A Study in Ethnic Mobility* (New York: Oxford University Press, 1970); and Department of Development and Planning, *Historic City: The Settlement of Chicago* (Chicago: City of Chicago, 1976).

39. Walter W. Ristow, "U.S. Fire Insurance Maps, 1852–1968," *Surveying and Mapping*, 30 (March 1970): 19–41; also see Gary W. Rees and Mary Hoeber, *A Catalogue of Sanborn Atlases at California State University* (Santa Cruz, Cal.: Western Association of Map Libraries, 1973) and Philip R. Hoehn, *Union List of Sanborn Fire Insurance Maps Held by Institutions in the United States and Canada* (Santa Cruz, Cal.: Western Association of Map Libraries, 1976).

40. The principal midwest producer of insurance maps in the latter decades of the nineteenth century was the Rascher Map Company of Chicago. In addition to a series for Chiago, Rascher also published, between 1887 and 1893, insurance maps of Detroit and Muskegon, Michigan; Duluth, Minnesota; and Kansas City, Missouri. The Alphonson Whipple Company and its predecessor, Oliver and Whipple, mapped St. Louis and some southern Illinois communities for insurance purposes during the years 1874 to 1898.

41. The Davis brothers argued: "Maps issued to the insurance companies covering the different cities of the Commonwealth [of Massachusetts] when taken in connection with the correction slips, furnish a complete history of the growth and progress of these places." Colonial Socety of Massachusetts, *Transactions* 3 (1895–1897): 67–71.

42. David Weitzman, *Underfoot: An Everyday Guide to Exploring the American Past* (New York: Charles Scribner's Sons, 1976), p. 182; Robert J. Hayward, "Sources of Urban Historical Research: Insurance Plans and Land Use Atlases," *Urban History Review* [Canada], 1973, pp. 2–9.

43. Sanborn Map Company, *Description and Utilization of the Sanborn Map* (New York: Sanborn Map Company, 1953), p. 3.

44. Model analyses can be developed from Harland Bartholomew's *Land Uses in American Cities* (Cambridge, Mass.: Harvard University Press, 1955).

45. Write to Sanborn Map Company, 629 Fifth Avenue, Pelham, New York, 10803.

46. Martin Reinemann, "The Pattern and Distribution of Manufacturing in the Chicago Area," *Economic Geography* 3 (1960): 139–144. Also of use here is G. Alexanderson, *The Industrial Structure of American Cities* (Lincoln, Neb.: University of Nebraska Press, 1956).

47. Brian J. L. Berry, *Commercial Structure and Commercial Blight: Retail Patterns and Processes in the City of Chicago*, Research Paper no. 85 (Chicago: Department of Geography, University of Chicago, 1963).

48. John Reps, *Cities on Stone: Nineteenth-Century Lithographic Images of the Urban West* (Fort Worth, Texas: Amon Carter Museum, 1976), p. 35.

49. The 1892 Currier and Ives lithograph appears to be a reprint of the 1874 version with a token attempt to bring the cityscape up to date for sale to visitors to the 1893 World's Fair.

50. John R. Hébert, *Panoramic Maps of Anglo-American Cities: A Checklist of Maps in the Collections of the Library of Congress* (Washington, D.C.: Library of Congress, 1971).

51. Mayer and Wade, *Chicago*, pp. 52–53.

52. R. B. Wilcox, "The River and Harbor of Chicago," *Journal of Western Society of Engineers* 5 (November-December 1900): 499–535; George M. Wisner, "A Description of the Opening of the Chicago Drainage Canal," *Journal of Western Society of Engineers* 5 (January-February 1900): 8–11.

53. David Solzman, *Waterway Industrial Sites: A Chicago Case Study*, Research Paper no. 107 (Chicago: University of Chicago Department of Geography, 1966).

54. Because of this fact, Hart and Raitz center their Chicago map exercise (no. 16) on this railroad corridor on a current (1963) topographical map of the city; see *Cultural Geography of Topographical Maps*, pp. 15–16, 99. For an excellent survey of the impact of the railroad on a city such as Atlanta, see Dana F. White and Timothy I. Crimmins, " How Atlanta Grew," *Atlanta Economic Review* 28, no. 1 (January/February 1978): 7–15.

55. J. D. Fellman, "Pre-Building Growth Patterns in Chicago," *Annals of the Association of American Geographers* 47 (1957): 59–82; also see G. M. Smerk, "The Streetcar: Shaper of American Cities," *Traffic Quarterly* 21 (1967): 569–584; Sam Bass Warner, *Streetcar Suburbs: Process of Growth in Boston* (Cambridge, Mass.: Harvard University Press, 1962).

56. John R. Borchert, "American Metropolitan Evolution," *Geographical Review* 57 (1967): 303–332, outlines four periods in American history in which changes in transportation and industrial technology have had significant effects on urban growth and development. His four periods are identified as Sail-Wagon, 1790–1830; Iron Horse, 1830–1870; Steel Rail, 1870–1920; and Auto-Air-Amenity, 1920–Present.

57. A sampling can be gleaned from Alan R. Lind, *Chicago Surface Lines: An Illustrated History* (Park Forest, Illinois: Transport History Press, 1974).

58. Rand McNally's *Map and Guide to Chicago Containing Bird's-Eye Views of the City* (Chicago: Rand, McNally, 1893).

59. Federal Writers Project, *Catalog: American Guide Series* (Washington, D.C.: United States Government Printing Office, 1938).

60. For additional information, write to John Fondersmith, AIP, American Urban Guides, Post Office Box 186, Washington, D.C. 20044.

61. Walter W. Ristow, "American Road Maps and Guides," *Scientific Monthly* 62 (May 1946): 397–406.

62. See chapter 9, "Above-Ground Archaeology: Discovering a Community's History Through Local Artifacts" and Appendix II.

63. Hart and Raitz, *Cultural Geography*, p. 130.

64. Karl B. Raitz, "Ethnic Settlements in Topographic Maps," *Journal of Geography* 72 (1973): 29–30.

65. Hart and Raitz, *Cultural Geography*, pp. 132–134.

66. See engraving from S. E. Warner's real estate promotional brochure, "Ashland Avenue at Madison Street in 1892," as reproduced in Meyer and Wade, *Chicago*, p. 64. An invaluable resource for Chicago street-name research is Edward Paul Brennan's *Chicago Street-Numbering System and Nomenclature, 1866–1948*, a file-card collection in the Chicago Historical Society, Chicago, Illinois.

67. For more clues on deciphering urban parks as historical evidence, see Michael P. McCarthy, "Politics and the Parks: Chicago Businessmen and the Recreation Movement," *Journal of the Illinois State Historical Society* 65, no. 2 (1972): 158–172; Peter Trowbridge, "The Recognition of Large-Scale Designed Municipal Parks," in *Public Space: Environmental Awareness in America during the Later Nineteenth Century* (Cambridge, Mass.: Harvard University Department of Landscape Architecture, 1975), pp. 18–29.

68. See Albert D. Scharf and Charles Dilg Map Collections, Map Division, Chicago Historical Society, Chicago, Illinois.

69. Residents of Hull House, *Hull-House Maps and Papers: A Presentation of Nationalities and Wages in a Congested District of Chicago* (New York: Thomas Y. Crowell, 1895).

70. Other settlement houses such as Graham Taylor's Chicago Commons were equally taken with the idea of careful geographical observation and cartographic survey work. See, for example, *A Map of the Social Influences in the Chicago Commons Neighborhood* (1912).

71. Thomas R. Winpenny, "The Nefarious Philadelphia Plan and Urban America: A Reconsideration," *Pennsylvania Magazine of History and Biography* 101 (January 1977): 103–113.

72. John Reps, *Monumental Washington: The Planning and Development of the Capitol Center* (Princeton, N.J.: Princeton University Press, 1967).

73. John Reps, *Town Planning in Frontier America* (Princeton, N.J.: Princeton University Press, 1965).

74. Victoria P. Ranney, *Olmstead in Chicago* (Chicago: The Open Lands Project, 1972); Thomas J. Schlereth, "Nathan Francis Barrett, 1845–1919," in *The Town of Pullman* (Chicago: Pullman Civic Organization, 1974), pp. 40–43.

75. See also Carl Condit, "The Chicago Plan," in his *Chicago, 1910–1929; Building, Planning and Urban Technology* (Chicago: University of Chicago Press, 1973), pp. 59–85 and *The Plan of Chicago: 1909–1979*, edited by John Zukowsky (Chicago: The Art Institute of Chicago, 1979).

76. D. W. Meinig, "The Continuous Shaping of America: A Prospectus For Geographers and Historians," *American Historical Review* 83 (December 1978): 1186–1205.

77. Quoted by J. B. Harley, "The Evaluation of Early Maps: Towards a Methodology," *Imago Mundi* 21 (1967): 62.

78. Harley, "Evaluation of Early Maps," pp. 62–80. Also consult Denis Wood, "Now and Then: Comparisons of Ordinary Americans' Symbol Conventions with Those of Past Cartographers," *Prologue* 9, no. 3 (1977): 151–161.

79. C. Koeman, "Levels of Historical Evidence in Early Maps," *Imago Mundi* 22 (1968): 75–80; also see Ralph E. Ehrenberg, "Taking the Measure of the Land," *Prologue* (Fall 1977), pp. 28–150.

80. J. A. Williams, *The Voyages of John and Sebastian Cabot* (London, 1937), p. 7.

81. Marc Bloch, *The Historian's Craft* (New York: Vintage, 1953), p. 68.

82. For information on geographical libraries and map collections, see John Wolter, "Geographical Libraries and Map Collections" in *Encyclopedia of Library and Information Science* 9 (New York: Marcel Dekkor: 1973); 236–266, and *The Geography and Map Division: A Guide to Its Collections and Services*, revised edition (Washington, D.C.: Library of Congress, 1975). Professor George Kish of the University of Michigan has prepared a set of two hundred 35mm. slides, instructor's notes, and audio tape ("The Discovery and Settlement of North America, 1500–1865: A Cartographic Perspective") available from Harper and Row College Media, Hagerstown, Maryland.

83. James Lemon, "Approaches to the Study of the Urban Past: Geography," *Urban History Review* [Canada] 1973, (2): 13–19.

Chapter 5

1. "The Challenge of the Artifact," in James H. Rodabaugh, editor, *The Present World of History: A Conference on Certain Problems in Historical Agencies Working in the United States* (Madison, Wis.: American Association For State and Local History, 1959), p. 68.

2. Linda F. Place, *et al.*, "The Object as Subject: The Role of Museums and Material

Culture Collections in American Studies," *American Quarterly* 26, 170–3 (August 1974): 281–294; John L. Cotter, *Above Ground Archaeology.* (Washington, D.C.: U.S. Government Printing Office, 1972); Wilcomb E. Washburn, "Manuscripts and Manufacts," *American Archivist* 27, no. 2 (April 1964): 245–250; John A. Kouwenhoven, "American Studies: Words or Things?" in Marshall Fishwick, editor, *American Studies In Transition* (Philadelphia: University of Pennsylvania Press, 1964).

3. For a descriptive directory of the major historic museum villages in the United States, see Nicholas Zook, *Museum Villages, USA* (Barre, Mass.: Barre Publishers, 1971), which discusses sites topically and lists one hundred and twenty villages in its "Directory of Museum Villages," pp. 126–135; and Irvin Haas, *America's Historic Villages and Restorations* (New York: Arco Publishing Co., 1974), which summarizes the aspects of fifty villages according to their regional distribution. Also useful is *Restored Village Directory: An Illustrated Directory Listing Restored, Recreated, and Replica Villages of Historic Interest in the United States and Canada,* 3rd edition (New York: Quadrant Press, Inc., 1973), Mitchell R. Alegre, *A Guide to Museum Villages: The American Heritage Brought to Life* (New York: Drake Publishers, 1978), and Alice Cromie, *Restored Towns and Historic Districts of America* (New York: E. P. Dutton, 1979).

4. My debt to Peter Cousins, Curator of Agriculture, Department of Mechanical Arts; to Craig Morrison, Architectural Historian; to Larry Lankton, formerly Assistant Curator, Power and Shop Machinery, Department of Mechanical Arts; to David Glick, Manager, Adult Education Division; and to Kenneth Cochran, Audio-Visual Department, is extensive.

5. In material culture analysis, whether of a single artifact or an entire museum site, documentary evidence is never to be neglected. The excellent resources of Greenfield's Robert Hudson Tannahill Research Library have been invaluable for all dimensions of our work at the village. For a helpful introduction to the library's collections, see Jerome J. Smith, *Robert Hudson Tannahill Research Library* (Dearborn, Mich.: Edison Institute, 1974).

6. "Henry Ford: Symbol for an Age," in *The Nervous Generation: American Thought, 1917–1930* (Chicago: Rand McNally, 1970), pp. 153–163.

7. As a reference source for this type of analysis, we employ Frederick L. Rath and Merrilyn Rogers O'Connell, *Guide to Historic Preservation, Historical Agencies, and Museum Practices: A Selective Bibliography* (Cooperstown, N.Y.: New York State Historical Association, 1970); Philip D. Spiess, *Historical Agency Operation: A Basic Research Bibliography* (Washington, D.C.: National Trust for Historic Preservation, 1974); Freeman Tilden, *Interpreting Our Heritage,* rev. ed. (Chapel Hill, N.C.: University of North Carolina Press, 1957, 1967); and Edward P. Alexander, *Museums in Motion: An Introduction to the History and Functions of Museums* (Nashville: American Association for State and Local History, 1979) and "Selected Bibliography on History Site Programming," in *Programs for Historic Sites and Houses,* edited by Susan N. Lehman (Washington, D.C.: Center for Museum Education Sourcebook No. 3/George Washington University, 1978), pp. 68–69, 73–96.

8. Reyner Banham, *Los Angeles: The Architecture of Four Ecologies* (New York: Harper and Row, 1971); Laurence Lafore, *American Classic* (Iowa City: State Historical Society, 1975); Thomas J. Schlereth, *The University of Notre Dame: A Portrait of Its History and Campus* (Notre Dame, Ind.: University of Notre Dame Press, 1976); and Carl Anthony, "The Big House and the Slave Quarters, Part 1. Prelude to New World Architecture," *Landscape* 20, no. 3 (Spring 1976): 8–19.

9. A sample of the reference documentary resources we consult would include works such as Jill Grossman, *Revelations of New England Architecture* (New York: Viking Press,

1975); Henry C. Forman, *The Architecture of the Old South: The Medieval Style, 1585–1850* (Cambridge, Mass.: Harvard University Press, 1948); and Wilbur D. Peat, *Indiana Houses of the Nineteenth Century* (Indianapolis: Indiana Historical Society, 1962).

10. Here the principal primers are John J.-G. Blumenson, *Identifying American Architecture: A Pictorial Guide to Styles and Terms, 1600–1945* (Nashville: American Association for State and Local History, 1977); Marcus Whiffen, *American Architecture since 1780: A Guide to the Styles* (Cambridge, Mass.: MIT Press, 1969); John E. Richert, "House Facades of the Northeastern United States: A Tool of Geographic Analysis," *Annals of the Association of American Geographers* 57, no.2 (June 1967): 211–238.

11. Useful in this context is John Jakle's *Past Landscapes* (Monticello, Ill.: Council of Planning Librarians, 1974); John Fraser Hart, *The Look of the Land* (Englewood Cliffs, N.J.: Prentice-Hall, 1975); Ervin H. Zube, editor, *Landscapes, Selected Writings of J. B. Jackson* (Amherst, Mass.: University of Massachusetts Press, 1970); and Grady Clay, *Close-Up: How to Read the American City* (New York: Praeger Publishers, 1972) and John T. Vance, *This Scene of Man* (New York: Harper's College Press, 1977).

12. Craig Morrison, "Greenfield Village Evaluation of Sites and Structures: Environments," manuscript study (Department of Architecture Files, Greenfield Village, n.d.).

13. An excellent primer that acquaints historians with the concepts, resources, teaching strategies, and learning objectives to be employed within a historic residence is the Winter 1975 edition of *Almanac* published by the Museum Education Center, Old Sturbridge Village, Sturbridge, Massachusetts. Also applicable in this context would be this book's chapter 4, "Historic House Museums: Seven Teaching Strategies."

14. Within Greenfield Village, for example, there are four civic sites, three education sites, thirteen business or commercial sites, twenty-eight industrial sites, and one religious site.

15. Henry Nash Smith, *Virgin Land, The American West in Myth and Symbol* (Cambridge, Mass.: Harvard University Press, 1950); John William Ward, *Andrew Jackson, Symbol for an Age* (New York: Oxford University Press, 1955); Leo Marx, *The Machine in the Garden, Technology and the Pastoral Ideal in America* (New York: Oxford University Press, 1964).

16. Deetz, *Invitation to Archaeology* (Garden City, N.Y.: Doubleday, 1967), p. 8; also see chapter 9, below, "Above-Ground Archaeology: Discovering a Community's History through Local Artifacts."

17. David Lowenthal, "The American Way of History," *Columbia University Forum* (Summer 1966), p. 31.

18. Some of these interpretive difficulties are noted in Thomas J. Schlereth, *It Wasn't That Simple* (Washington, D.C.: American Association of Museums, 1977).

Chapter 6

1. Dee Brown, *The Year of the Century: 1876* (New York: Charles Scribner's Sons, 1966); William Randel, *Centennial; American Life in 1876* (Philadelphia: Chilton Book Company, 1969); John Maass, *The Glorious Enterprise, The Centennial Exhibition of 1876 and H. J. Schwarzmann, Architect-in-Chief* (Watkins Glen, N.Y.: American Life Foundation, 1973); John Brinckerhoff Jackson, *American Space, The Centennial Years, 1865–1876* (New York: W. W. Norton, 1972); Lally Weymouth, *America in 1876, The Way We Were* (New York: Vintage Books, 1976); Robert C. Post, *1876: A Centennial Exhibition* (Washington, D.C.: National Museum of History and Technology, Smithsonian Institution, 1976); Gore Vidal's *1876, A*

Novel (New York: Random House, 1976); and articles such as Lynne V. Cheney, "1876: The Eagle Screams," *American Heritage,* April 1974, pp. 15–34, 98–99; Robert A. Trennert, Jr., "A Grand Failure: The Centennial Indian Exhibition of 1876," *Prologue,* Summer 1974, pp. 118–129; H. Craig Miner, "The United States Government Building at the Centennial Exhibition, 1874–77," *Prologue,* Winter 1972, pp. 202–218; and Arlene Swidler, "Catholics at the 1876 Centennial," *Catholic Historical Review,* July 1976, pp. 349–365.

2. The counter-hypothesis can be tested by comparing Brown *(The Year of the Century),* Randel *(Centennial),* and Weymouth *(America in 1876)* with Thomas Fleming, *1776: Year of Illusions* (New York: W. W. Norton, 1975), and Marshall Davidson, *The World in 1776* (Marion, Ohio: American Heritage, 1975).

3. Such a course (American Studies 485) was offered at the University of Notre Dame during the fall semester, 1975; see Thomas J. Schlereth, "Material Culture of America—The Centennial Years," Seminar Syllabus, Program in American Studies, Fall 1975.

4. On March 3, 1871, Congress so established the official name of the 1876 event. The terms *Centennial Exhibition* and *Centennial Exposition* were commonly used by contemporaries, as was the phrase *the Philadelphia World's Fair.* The popular term *World's Fair* for an international exposition was coined in 1851 by William Makepeace Thackeray in the humorous poem "Mr. Molony's Account of the Crystal Place."

5. Merle Curti, "America at the World's Fairs, 1851–1893," in *Probing Our Past* (New York: Harper and Row, 1955), pp. 246–277. David F. Burg has applied Curti's insight in a full-length monograph on the Chicago Columbian Exposition of 1893. See his *Chicago's White City of 1893* (Lexington, Kentucky: University of Kentucky Press, 1976).

6. Henry Adams's *Democracy, An American Novel* (New York, Henry Holt, 1880) can be effectively contrasted with Vidal's new fiction. Juxtaposing the work of these two historical novelists yields insight not only into the historical era that they both survey, but also into the evolution of the American historical novel as literary genre. See Thomas J. Schlereth, "Fictions and Facts: Henry Adams's *Democracy* and Gore Vidal's *1876,*" *The Southern Quarterly* 16, no. 3 (April 1978): 209–222.

7. *Guide des visiteurs a l'Exposition de centenaire et a Philadelphe* (Philadelphia, 1876); *Official Catalogue of the British Section, United States Centennial Exposition* (London: George E. Eyre and William Spottiswoode, 1876); *Redogorelser for verldsutstallningen i Filadelfia, 1876,* 2 volumes (Stockholm, 1877); *Comisaria regia, Exposicion universal de Filadelfia, 1876 . . . Lista preparatoria del catalogo de los expositores de Espana, y sus provincias de utramar, Cuba, Puerto Rico y Filipinas: Formade para uso del jurado* (Philadelphia: Campbell, 1876).

8. U.S. Foreign Trade (in the millions of dollars):

Year	Imports	Exports	Balance
1875	533	499	−34
1876	461	526	+65
1877	451	590	+139

9. J. S. Ingram, *The Centennial Exposition, Described and Illustrated* (Philadelphia: Hubbard Brothers, 1876); James D. McCabe, *The Illustrated History of the Centennial* (Philadelphia: The National Publishing Company, 1876); T. Bentley, *The Illustrated Catalogue and History of the Centennial Exposition, Philadelphia, 1876* (New York: John Filmer, 1876); E. C. Bruce, *Century, Its Fruits and Its Festival: Being A History and Description of the Centennial Exhibition With a Preliminary Outline of Modern Progress* (Philadelphia: J. B. Lippincott, 1877); Francis A. Walker, *The World's Fair, Philadelphia, 1876, A Critical Account* (New York: A. S.

Barnes, 1877); and P. T. Sandhurst, *et al.*, *The Great Centennial Exhibition Critically Described and Illustrated* (Philadelphia: P. W. Ziegler and Co., 1876).

10. See, for example: *Burley's United States Centennial Gazette and Guide, 1876* (Philadelphia: Burley Co., 1876); *Magee's Centennial Guide of Philadelphia* (Philadelphia: R. Magee and Son, 1876); F. H. Norton, *Illustrated Historical Register of the Centennial Exhibition, Philadelphia, 1876, and of the Exposition universelle, Paris, 1878* (New York: American News Company, 1879); W. C. Ulyat, *The Centennial City: Philadelphia* (New York: A. C. Coffin, 1876); and T. Westcott, *Centennial Portfolio: A Souvenir of the International Exhibition at Philadelphia* (Philadelphia: T. Hunter, 1876).

11. U.S. Centennial Commission, *International Exhibition, 1876*, Official Catalog (Philadelphia: John R. Nagle, 1876); Francis A. Walker, ed., *International Exhibition, 1876, Reports and Awards*, 9 vols. (Philadelphia: Lippincott & Co., 1879; Washington: Government Printing Co., 1880); *International Exhibition, 1876, Report of the Director-General*, 2 vols. (Philadelphia: Lippincott & Co., 1879; Washington: Government Printing Co., 1880); *International Exhibition, 1876, Appendix to the Reports of the Director General*, 2 vols. (Philadelphia: Lippincott & Co., 1879; Washington: Government Printing Co., 1880); *International Exhibition, 1876, Reports of The President, Secretary and Executive Committee* (Philadelphia: Lippincott & Co., 1879, Washington, Government Printing Co., 1880).

12. Daniel Boorstin, *The Americans: The Democratic Experience* (New York: Random House, 1973), pp. 165–224.

13. Although Henry Adams did not stay long at the Centennial (see his correspondence with his English friend, Charles Milnes Gaskell, Adams Papers, Massachusetts Historical Society), his trenchant reflections on the World's Columbian Exposition of 1893 and the Paris Exhibition of 1900 are also most appropriate commentaries on many of the Centennial's cultural themes. In *Education of Henry Adams*, his famous chapters on "Chicago" (chapter 22) and "The Virgin and the Dynamo" (chapter 25) are useful to compare to Howells's "Sennight of the Centennial," *Atlantic Monthly*, 38 (July 1876): 91–107.

14. John Kouwenhoven, "American Studies: Words or Things?" in Marshall Fishwick, editor, *American Studies in Transition* (Philadelphia: University of Pennsylvania Press, 1964), pp. 1–16; Harold Skramstad, "American Things: Neglected Material Culture," *America Studies, An International Newsletter*, Spring 1972, pp. 11–22.

15. Richard S. Latham, "The Artifact as a Cultural Cipher," in *Who Designs America?* (Garden City, N.Y.: Doubleday, 1965), pp. 257–281; Henry Glassie, "Artifacts: Folk, Popular, Real, Imaginary," in Marshall Fishwick and Ray B. Browne, editors, *Icons of Popular Culture* (Bowling Green, Ohio; Bowling Green University Press, (1970), pp. 103–119; E. McClung Fleming, "Artifact Study, a Proposed Model," in *Winterthur Portfolio* 9 (1974): 153–172.

16. Robert C. Post, editor, *1876, A Centennial Exhibition* (Washington, D.C.: National Museum of History and Technology, Smithsonian Institution, 1976), "Editor's Note: On 1876 and Other Things," p. 24.

17. Post, *Centennial Exhibition*, p. 25.

18. Memorial Hall (now a recreational center) and the Ohio Building (now a security guard house) are the only two Centennial buildings that still stand *in situ* in Fairmount Park. After the Exposition a number of buildings were sold and re-erected elsewhere; a few of these survive.

19. Alan Trachtenberg, *The Brooklyn Bridge, Fact and Symbol* (New York: Oxford University Press, 1965) and Marvin Trachtenberg, *The Statue of Liberty* (New York: Viking Press,

1976). The most prominent piece of public sculpture at the Centennial was the towering arm and torch of the "Statue of Independence" by the French sculptor Bartholdi, an ardent admirer of the United States. The complete statue, better known as the "Statue of Liberty," was unveiled in New York Harbor in 1886.

20. Maass, *The Glorious Enterprise*, pp. 12–24.

21. Leo Marx, *The Machine in the Garden, Technology and the Pastoral Ideal in America* (New York: Oxford University Press, 1967).

22. Maass, *The Glorious Enterprise*, pp. 74–93; also see L. Skidmore, "Expositions Always Influence Architecture," *American Architect*, May 1932, pp. 26–29, 78–80; D. Gardener, *Grounds and Buildings of the Centennial Exposition* (Philadelphia: J. Lippincott, 1878); "Centennial Exposition, 1876," *American Architect and Building News* (1876); and C. Lancaster, "Philadelphia Centennial Towers," *Journal of Society of Architectural Historians*, March 1960 pp. 11–15.

23. Jackson, *American Space*, pp. 239–240.

24. See, for instance, Elizabeth Cady Stanton, *Eighty Years & More: Reminiscences, 1815–1897* (reprint ed., New York: Schocken Books, 1971).

25. Robert A. Trennert, Jr., "A Grand Failure: The Centennial Indian Exhibition of 1876," *Prologue*, Summer 1974, pp. 118–129.

26. Vincent Scully in his 1955 edition of *The Shingle Style* (New Haven: Yale University Press, 1955) erroneously claimed the "the colonial revival appeared in 1876 as the chief characteristic of popular feeling about the Centennial" (pp. 19–21). A more accurate conclusion appears in the careful study by Rodris Roth, "The Colonial Revival and 'Centennial Furniture,' " *The Art Quarterly* (1964), pp. 57–82, proving that no Colonial Revival furniture was shown at the Centennial. The Colonial Revival in architecture and artifacts was largely a development of the 1880s.

27. By geographic scope, as of mid-1975, 4,623 projects and 2,240 events were local; 1,558 projects and 771 events were statewide; 314 projects and 299 events encompassed more than one state; 1,149 projects and 925 events were national; and 437 projects and 255 events were international. *Bicentennial News* (Washington, D.C.: American Revolution Bicentennial Administration, n.d.), p. 2.

28. Usually known by its acronym, ARBA was created under Public Law 93–179 to replace the mismanaged American Revolutionary Bicentennial Commission originally created by the Congress in 1966.

29. The PBC, headed by economist Jeremy Rifkin, began in 1972 when it was organized as a nonprofit public foundation in the District of Columbia. The national organization's primary claim was that the American Revolution brought democracy to government, and that the Bicentennial should do the same for the economy.

30. For a sample of the type of historic preservation projects undertaken, see Geoffrey C. Upward, " '76 Plans For the Bicentennial," *Preservation News*, July 1975, pp. 6–7.

Chapter 7

1. See, for example, Heinrich Marzell's *Volksbotanik Die Pflauze im deutscheu Brauchtum* (1935) and *Die Planzen im deutschen Volksleben* (1925).

2. Penelope Lively, *The Presence of the Past: An Introduction to Landscape History* (London: William Collins Sons, 1976); Maurice Beresford, *History on the Ground, Six Studies in Maps*

and Landscapes, revised edition (Metheuen, 1971); W. G. Hoskins, *The Making of the English Landscape* (London: Hodder and Stoughton, 1955, 1963).

3. Two journals, *Forest History* and *Environmental Review* regularly explore these topics; also consult James Tretethen, *The American Landscape: 1776–1976, Two Centuries of Change* (Washington, D.C.: Wildlife Management Institute, 1976).

4. Archer B. Hulbert, *Soil: Its Influence on the History of the United States* (New Haven: Yale University Press, 1930); K. S. Quisenberry and L. P. Reitz, "Turkey Wheat: The Cornerstone of an Empire," *Agricultural History* 48, no. 1 (January 1974): 98–110, and Raymond Baker, "Indian Corn and its Culture," *Agricultural History* 48, no. 1 (January 1974): 94–97; James T. Lemon, *The Best Poor Man's Country: A Geographical Study of Early Southeastern Pennsylvania* (Baltimore: Johns Hopkins University Press, 1972).

5. John Leighly, editor, *Land and Life: A Selection from the Writings of Carl Ortwin Sauer* (Berkeley and Los Angeles: University of California Press, 1963); Carl Sauer, "American Agricultural Origins: A Consideration of Nature and Culture," in *Essays in Anthropology Presented to A. L. Kroeber* (Berkeley: University of California Press, 1936), pp. 279–297; John Fraser Hart, *The Look of the Land* (Englewood Cliffs, N.J.: Prentice-Hall, 1975); Fred Kniffen, "The Physiognomy of Rural Louisiana," *Louisiana History* 4, no. 4 (Fall 1963): 29–99.

6. J. B. Jackson edited *Landscape* magazine from 1952 until 1967, and the back issues of this influential journal are a rich lode of insight for the above-ground archaeologist. Several of Jackson's famous essays have been republished by MTT Press in an anthology (*Landscapes: Selected Writings of J. B. Jackson,* edited by Erwin Zube (1970). Grady Clay, also an editor *(Landscape Architecture),* has done an important primer, *Close-Up: How to Read the American City* (New York: Praeger, 1972).

7. Thomas J. Schlereth, "The Town as Artifact: Discovering a Community's History through Above-Ground Archaeology," paper presented at Indiana Historical Society 1978 Spring Conference, Madison, Indiana, May 12, 1978. For a bibliography for the approach, see chapter 9, "Above-Ground Archaeology."

8. In formulating this approach, I have borrowed extensively, if eclectically, from two books by James Deetz: *Invitation To Archaeology* (Garden City, N.Y.: Natural History Press, 1967) and *In Small Things Forgotten: The Archaeology of Early American Life* (Garden City, N.Y.: Anchor/Doubleday Press, 1977) and various colleagues, particular James O. Bellis (Department of Anthropology, University of Notre Dame) in the Society for Historical Archaeology. The society's most recent publication, *Historical Archaeology and the Importance of Material Things,* edited by Leland Ferguson, Special Publications Series, 2 (1977), has also been useful.

9. John G. Evans, *An Introduction to Environmental Archaeology* (Princeton, N.J.: Princeton University Press, 1978); G. W. Dimbleby, *Plants and Archaeology* (London: John Baker, 1967); Audrey Noel Hume, *Archaeology and the Colonial Gardener* (Williamsburg, Va.: Colonial Williamsburg Foundation, 1974).

10. I am indebted to John Stilgoe for bringing this phenomenon to my attention and for furnishing me with a slide transparency of it.

11. Friedrich Ratzel, *Politische und Wirtschafts-Geographie der Vereinigten Staaten von Amerika* (Muenchen: R. Oldenbourg, 1893), p. 413. Most handbooks written for European immigrants to the United States in the nineteenth century contained at least one full chapter explaining the significance of the different hardwood tree species as indicators of soil quality, and no less than fifty extensively illustrated pages are devoted to that topic in C. L. Fleischmann, *Der Nordamerikanische Landwipth: Ein Handbuch fur Ansiedler in den Vereinigten Staaten* (Frankfurt: C. F. Heyer Verlag, 1852), pp. 21–71.

12. Wayne E. Kiefer, *Rush County, Indiana: A Study in Rural Settlement Geography,* Geographic Monograph Series, 2 (Bloomington, Ind.: Indiana University Department of Geography, 1969): 47–48, footnote 8.

13. Eric Sloane, *Our Vanishing America.* (New York: Ballatine Books, 1974), p. 29.

14. A natural feature of the terrain along Barlow Pass in the Mt. Hood National Forest in Oregon are the tall firs on the top of Little Laurel Hill. These trees were used to control the descent of the covered wagons down a three-hundred-foot incline or chute. In practice, a rawhide rope was wrapped around a fir trunk with the wagon snubbed to the other end of the rope, thus providing a drag to brake or slow the wagon down the steep slope. Some of the rope-burned snub-trees still stand on Laurel Hill. They are about five miles east of the community of Rhododendron, on the south side of the Mount Hood Loop Highway (U.S. 26).

15. Leslie D. Bruning, "Early Road Signs" *Americana,* July-August 1977, p. 64.

16. Charles E. Randall and Henry Clepper, *Famous and Historic Trees* (Washington, D.C.: American Forestry Association, 1976) lists six tree sites associated with Jackson.

17. W. Lloyd Warner, *The Living and the Dead, A Study of the Symbolic Life of Americans* (New Haven: Yale University Press, 1959), chapter 4.

18. Since 1865, a tree, usually an aspen, has been growing out of the roof of the courthouse of Decatur County in southern Indiana. The current local landmark, the eleventh such tree since the 1860s, is considered a major historical monument and duly recorded as such on most Indiana state roadway maps.

19. David Lowenthal, "The Bicentennial Landscape: A Mirror Held up to the Past," *Geographical Review* 67, no. 3 (July 1977): 253–267.

20. Randall and Clepper, *Historic Trees,* p. 70.

21. May T. Watts, *Reading the Landscape of America* (New York: Collier/Macmillan, 1975), pp. 15–16, first published as *Reading the Landscape: An Adventure in Ecology* (New York: MacMillan, 1957); especially useful for historical landscape and garden analysis is her playful essay, "The Stylish House, Or, Fashions as an Ecological Factor," pp. 320–346.

22. Thomas J. Schlereth, *The University of Notre Dame: A Portrait of Its History and Campus* (Notre Dame, Ind.: University of Notre Dame Press, 1976), pp. 111–112.

23. See, for example, Roderick Nash, *The American Environment: Readings in the History of Conservation,* second edition (Reading, Mass: Addison-Wesley, 1976) and Doublas H. Strong, *The Conservationists* (Reading, Mass.: Addison-Wesley, 1971).

24. Phoebe Cutler, "On Recognizing a WPA Rose Garden or a CCC Privy," *Landscape,* Winter 1976, pp. 3–9.

25. George R. Stewart, *U.S. 40: Cross-Section of the United States of America* (Boston: Houghton Mifflin, 1953), p. 303.

26. Ronald L. Baker and Marvin Carmony, *Indiana Place Names* (Bloomington, Ind.: Indiana University Press, 1975). Also see Ronald L. Baker, "Locational and Descriptive Settlement Names in Indiana Flora," *Newsletter of the Indiana Place Name Survey* 5 (1975): 6–7.

27. Robert Alotta, *The Street Names of Philadelphia* (Philadelphia: Temple University Press, 1975).

28. George R. Stewart, *Names on the Land: A Historical Account of Place-Naming in the United States* (Boston: Houghton Mifflin, 1958), pp. 104–105.

29. Robert Venturi, *Signs of Life: Symbols in the American City* (New York: Aperture, 1978), p. 56.

30. Meredith Sylles and john Stewart, "Historic Landscape Restoration in the United

States and Canada: An Annotated Source Guide," *A.P.T. Bulletin* 4, no. 3–4 (1972): 114–158; John Stewart and Susan Bugger, "The Case for Commemoration of Historic Landscapes and Gardens," *A.P.T. Bulletin* 7, no. 2 (1975): 99–123; David Streatfield, "Standards for Historic Garden Preservation and Restoration," *Landscape Architecture* 59, no. 3 (Aril 1969): 198–200.

31. Dumbarton Oaks Research Library and Collection, *Preservation and Restoration of Historic Gardens and Landscapes* (Washington, D.C.: Dumbarton Oaks, 1976).

32. John T. Stewart, "Landscape Archaeology: Existing Plant Material on Historic Sites as Evidence of Buried Features and as Survivors of Historic Species," *A.P.T. Bulletin*, 9, no. 3 (1977), pp. 65–72; John Stewart, *Historic Landscapes and Gardens* (Nashville, Tenn: American Association for State and Local History: 1974); Donald H. Parker, "What You can Learn from the Gardens of Colonial Williamsburg," *Horticulture* 44, no. 28 (1975). Stewart's use of "landscape archaeology" should not be confused with Michael Aston and Trevor Rowley, *Landscape Archaeology: An Introduction To Field Work Techniques on Post-Roman Landscapes* (London: David & Charles: 1974)

33. John R. Stilgoe, "Jack-o-lanterns to Surveyors: The Secularization of Landscape Boundaries," *Environmental Review* (1976): 14–32; "Documents in Landscape History," *Journal of Architectural Education* 30 (September 1976): 15–17; "The Puritan Townscape: Ideal and Reality," *Landscape* 20 (Spring 1976): 3–7; and "Colonial Space: Landscape as Artifact," paper presented at American Studies Association National Meeting, Boston, Massachusetts, 28 October 1977.

34. E. N. Anderson, Jr., "On the Folk Art of Landscaping," *Western Folklore* 31 (1972): 179–188; James P. Duncan, Jr., "Landscape Taste as a Symbol of Group Identity: A Westchester County Village," *Geographical Review* 63(July 1973): 334–355; David Lowenthal and Hugh C. Prince, "English Landscape Traits," *Geographical Review* 55 (1965): 186–222.

35. Jay A. Anderson, "Foodways Programs at Living Historical Farms," *ALHFAM Annual Proceedings* 1 (1975): 21–23; Roger L. Welsh, "Sowbelly and Seedbanks: The Living-History Museum as a Process Repository," *ALHFAM Annual Proceedings* 1 (1975): 23–26; Edward L. Hawes, "Historic Seed Sources and the Future," *ALHFAM Annual Proceedings* 1 (1975): 28–32.

36. Darwin P. Kelsey, "Historical Farms as Models of the Past," *ALHFAM Annual Proceedings* 1 (1975): 33–38; Edward L. Hawes, "The Living Historical Farm in North America: New Directions in Research and Interpretation," *ALHFAM Annual Proceedings* 2 (1976): 41–60; Daryl Chase, "Keeping Living Historical Farms Alive and Their Methods of Teaching Innovative and Creative," *ALHFAM Annual Proceedings* 3 (1977): 43–47.

37. Eugene Kinkead, *Wildness is All Around Us: Notes of an Urban Naturalist* (New York: Dutton, 1978); Neil Jorgensen, *A Sierra Club Naturalist's Guide to Southern New England* (San Francisco: Sierra Club Books, 1978).

Chapter 8

In both this essay and the notes that accompany it, the author has used asterisks to indicate works available in soft-cover editions.

1. See examples of this interest in specific American cultural areas in American Studies programs at the University of Pennsylvania and Michigan State University in Robert F. Lucid, editor, "Programs in American Studies," *American Quarterly* 22, part 2 (Summer 1970).

2. Ray Ginger, *Altgeld's America: The Lincoln Ideal Versus Changing Realities** (New York: Funk and Wagnalls, 1958) and Hugh D. Duncan, *Culture and Democracy: The Struggle for Form in Society and Architecture in Chicago and the Middle West during the Life and Times of Louis H. Sullivan* (Totowa, N.J.: Bedminster Press, 1965).

3. Joseph Kirkland, *The History of Chicago*, 3 vols. (Chicago: Dibble Publishing Co., 1892–1894); Lloyd Lewis and Henry Smith, *Chicago: The History of Its Reputation* (New York: Harcourt, Brace and Co., 1929); Edgar Lee Masters, *The Tale of Chicago* (New York: G. P. Putnam's Sons, 1933); Wayne Andrews, *Battle for Chicago* (New York: Harcourt, Brace and Co., 1946); Emmett Dedmon, *Fabulous Chicago* (New York: Random House, 1953); Bessie Pierce, *A History of Chicago*, 3 vols. (New York: Knopf, 1937–1957); Edward Wagenknecht, *Chicago* (Norman, Okla.: University of Oklahoma Press, 1964); Finis Farr, *Chicago: Personal History of America's Most American City* (New Rochelle, N.Y.: Arlington House, 1973); Stephen Longstreet, *Chicago, 1860–1919* (New York: McKay, 1973).

4. (Chicago: University of Chicago Press, 1966). The University of Chicago Press, a cultural agency itself, has been a major publisher of data and studies about Chicago since 1894.

5. Arthur M. Schlesinger, Sr., *The Rise of the City, 1878–1898** (New York: Macmillan, 1933); Constance Green, *American Cities in the Growth of the Nation** (New York: Harper and Row, 1957); Daniel Boorstin, *The Americans: The National Experience** (New York: Random House, 1965); Howard Mumford Jones, *The Age of Energy: Varieties of American Experience, 1865–1915** (New York: Viking, 1970).

6. (DeKalb, Ill.: Northern Illinois University Center for Governmental Studies, 1972).

7. Second edition (Chicago: University of Chicago Press, 1968). The University of Chicago Press, also published the first edition, in 1947.

8. Joel A. Tarr, *A Study in Boss Politics: William Lorimer of Chicago* (Urbana, Ill.: University of Illinois Press, 1971); Claudius O. Johnson, *Carter Henry Harrison I, Political Leader* (Chicago: University of Chicago Press, 1928); Alex Gottfried, *Boss Cermak of Chicago: A Study of Political Leadership* (Seattle, Wash.: University of Washington Press, 1962); Mike Royko, *Boss: Richard J. Daley of Chicago** (New York: Dutton, 1971).

9. Lloyd Wendt and Herman Kogan, *Lords of the Levee: The Story of Bathhouse John and Hinky Dink* (Indianapolis: Bobbs-Merrill, 1943); retitled *Bosses in Lusty Chicago** (Bloomington, Ind.: Indiana University Press, 1967).

10. Carter Harrison, *Stormy Years: The Autobiography of Carter Henry Harrison, Five Times Mayor of Chicago* (Indianapolis: Bobbs-Merrill, 1935) and *Growing Up with Chicago* (Chicago: R. F. Seymour, 1944).

11. Charles E. Merriam, *Chicago: A More Intimate View of Urban Politics* (New York: Macmillan, 1929).

12. Joan S. Miller, "The Politics of Municipal Reform in Chicago during the Progressive Era: The Municipal Voters League as a Test Case, 1896–1920" (M.A. thesis, Roosevelt University, 1966); Bruce Grant, *Fight for a City: The Story of the Union League Club and Its Time, 1880–1955* (Chicago: Rand McNally, 1955); Mark Haller, "Urban Vice and Civic Reform: Chicago in the Early Twentieth Century," in *Cities in American History*, edited by Kenneth T. Jackson and Stanley Schultz (New York: Knopf, 1972), pp. 290–305.

13. Jane Addams, *Twenty Years at Hull House** and *Second Twenty Years at Hull House, 1909–1929*, both published by Macmillan, in 1910 and 1930, respectively; Francis Willard, *Glimpses of Fifty Years: The Autobiography of an American Woman* (1889; reprint ed., New York: Source Book Press, 1970); Clarence Darrow, *The Story of My Life* (New York: Scribner's, 1932); Louise deKoven Bowen, *Growing up with a City* (New York: Macmillan,

1926); Eugene Debs, *Walls and Bars* (Chicago: Socialist Party of America, 1927); Alice Hamilton, *Exploring the Dangerous Trades* (Boston: Little, Brown, 1943); Graham Taylor, *Chicago Commons through Forty Years* (Chicago: Chicago Commons Association, 1936).

14. (New York: Arno Press and *New York Times,* 1970). Allen Davis and Mary Lynn McCree have edited a marvelous anthology, *Eighty Years at Hull House* (Chicago: Quadrangle Books, 1969) that nicely complements the *Maps and Papers.* On Addams's male counterpart, see Louise C. Wade, *Graham Taylor, Pioneer for Social Justice, 1851–1938* (Chicago: University of Chicago Press, 1964).

15. Florence Kelley, *Some Ethical Gains through Legislation* (1905, 1910, 1914; reprint ed., New York: Arno Press, 1969); Louise deKoven Bowen, *Speeches, Addresses, and Letters of Louise deKoven Bowen, Reflecting Social Movements in Chicago,* 2 vols. (Ann Arbor, Mich.: Edwards Brothers, 1937).

16. Harvey Zorbaugh, *Gold Coast and Slum: A Sociological Study of Chicago's Near North Side* (Chicago: University of Chicago Press, 1929); Louis Wirth, *The Ghetto* (Chicago: University of Chicago Press, 1928); Nels Anderson, *The Hobo: The Sociology of the Homelss Man* (Chicago: University of Chicago Press, 1923); Homer Hoyt, *One Hundred Years of Land Values in Chicago: The Relationship of the Growth of Chicago to the Rise in Its Land Values, 1830–1933* (Chicago: University of Chicago Press, 1933).

17. See, for example, Humbert S. Nelli, *The Italians in Chicago, 1880–1930: A Study in Ethnic Mobility* (New York: Oxford University Press, 1970); Andrew J. Townsend, *The Germans of Chicago* (Chicago: University of hicago Press, 1932); Ulf Beijhom, *Swedes in Chicago: A Demographic and Social Study of the 1846–1880 Immigration* (Stockholm: Laromedelsforlaget, 1971); Philip P. Bregstone, *Chicago and Its Jews: A Cultural History* (Chicago: Privately printed, 1933); Edward W. Levine, *The Irish and Irish Politicians: A Study of Cultural and Social Alienation* (Notr Dame, Inc.: University of Notre Dame Press, 1966).

18. St. Clair Drake and Horace R. Clayton, *Black Metropolis** (New York: Harcourt, Brace, 1945; Harper Torchbook edition, 1962).

19. William Tuttle, *Race Riot: Chicago in the Red Summer of 1919** (New York: Atheneum, 1970); Carol Sandburg, *The Chicago Race Riots, July 1919* (1919; reprint ed., New York: Harcourt, Brace, 1962); The Chicago Race Relations Commission, *The Negro in Chicago: A Study of Race Relations and a Race Riot* (Chicago: Chicago Commission on Race Relations, 1919).

20. On Pullman, also see Almont Lindsey, *The Pullman Strike: The Story of a Unique Experiment and of a Great Labor Upheaval** (Chicago: University of Chicago Press, 1942), and Colston Warne's sourcebook, *The Pullman Boycott of 1894: The Problem of Federal Intervention** (Boston: D. C. Heath, 1955).

21. William Adelman, *Touring Pullman** (Chicago: Illinois Labor History Society, 1972).

22. Bessie Pierce, *A History of Chicago,* 3 vols. (New York: Knopf, 1937–1957).

23. Harper Leech and John Carroll, *Armour and His Times* (New York: Appleton-Century, 1938); Morris Werner, *Julius Rosenwald: The Life of a Practical Humanitarian* (New York: Harper and Brothers, 1939); John Tebbel, *The Marshall Fields: A Study in Wealth* (New York: E.P. Dutton, 1947) and *An American Dynasty: The Story of the McCormicks, Medills, and Patterson* (1947; reprint ed., New York: Greenwood Press, 1958); Forest McDonald, *Insull* (Chicago: University of Chicago Press, 1962); Siegfried Giedion, *Mechanization Takes Command: A Contribution to Anonymous History** (1948; reprint ed., New York: Oxford University Press, 1969).

24. Ernest W. Burgess and Charles Newcomb, *Census Data of the City of Chicago* (Chicago: University of Chicago Press, 1931); Homer Hoyt, *One Hundred Years of Land*

Values in Chicago (Chicago: University of Chicgo Press, 1933); Evelyn Kitagawa and Philip M. Hauser, *Local Community Fact Book for Chicago* (Chicago: University of Chicago Press, 1953).

25. Bernard Duffey, *The Chicago Renaissance in American Letters* (East Lansing, Mich.: Michigan State College Press, 1954); Hugh Duncan, *The Rise of Chicago as a Literary Center from 1885 to 1920: A Sociological Essay in American Culture* (Totowa, N.J.: Bedminster Press, 1964); Dale Kramer, *Chicago Renaissance: The Literary Life in the Midwest, 1900–1930* (New York: Appleton-Century, 1966); and Henry May, *The End of American Innocence: A Study of the First Years of Our Time, 1912–1917** (New York: Knopf, 1959).

26. See Robert E. Spiller's introduction and notes, *Crumbling Idols: Twelve Essays on Art Dealing Chiefly with Literature, Painting, and the Drama* (Gainesville, Fla.: Scholars' Facsimiles and Reprints, 1952) or a more recent edition edited by Jane Johnson for the Belknap Press (Cambridge, Mass.: Harvard University Press, 1960).

27. Hamlin Garland, *A Daughter of the Middle Border* (1921); *Roadside Meetings* (1930); *Companions on the Trail* (1931), all published by Macmillan.

28. Theodore Dreiser, *A Book about Myself* (1922); *Dawn: A History of Myself* (1931), both published by Liveright.

29. Sherwood Anderson, *A Story-Teller's Story* (New York: B. W. Huebsch, 1924); *Tar: A Midwest Childhood* (1926; reprint ed., Cleveland, O.: Press of Case Western Reserve, 1969); *Sherwood Anderson's Memoirs* (1942; reprint ed., Chapel Hill, N.C.: University of North Carolina Press, 1969).

30. Carl Sandburg, *Always the Young Strangers* (New York: Harcourt, Brace, 1953); Eunice Tietjens, *The World at My Shoulder* (New York: Macmillan, 1938); Edgar Lee Masters, *Across Spoon River* (New York: Farrar and Rinehart, 1936); Harriet Monroe, *A Poet's Life: Seventy Years in a Changing World* (New York: Macmillan, 1938); Floyd Dell, *Homecoming: An Autobiography* (New York: Farrar and Rinehart, 1933).

31. Ben Hecht, *A Child of the Century** (New York: Simon and Schuster, 1954); Melville Stone, *Fifty Years a Journalist* (Garden City, N.Y.: Doubleday, 1921); Burton Rascoe, *Before I Forget* (Garden City, N.Y.: Doubleday, 1937); Arthur Meeker, *Chicago with Love: A Polite and Personal History* (New York: Knopf, 1955).

32. Slason Thompson, *Eugene Field: A Study in Heredity and Contradictions*, 2 vols. (New York: Scribner's, 1901), and *Life of Eugene Field, the Poet of Childhood* (New York: Appleton, 1927).

33. Jean Shepherd, *The America of George Ade, 1866–1944: Fables, Short Stories, Essays** (New York: Putnam, 1961).

34. Louis Filler and Robert Hutchinson, *Mr. Dooley: Now and Forever* (Stanford: Academic Reprints, 1954); *Mr. Dooley on Ivrything and Iverybody** (New York: Dover, 1963). On Dunne, also see his autobiographical fragments and an interpretive commentary by Philip Dunne, *Mr. Dooley Remembers: The Informal Memoirs of Finley Peter Dunne* (Boston: Little, Brown, 1963).

35. Maxwell Geismar has edited *The Ring Lardner Reader** (New York: Scribner's, 1963) pp. 112–135.

36. Edmund Wilson, "Henry B. Fuller: The Art of Making It Flat," *The New Yorker*, 23 May 1970; Guy Szuberla, "Making the Sublime Mechanical: Henry Blake Fuller's Chicago," *American Studies* 14, no. 1 (Spring 1973): 83–93.

37. Henry Blake Fuller, *With the Procession** (Chicago: University of Chicago Press, 1965); *The Cliff-Dwellers* (Ridgewood, N.J.: Gregg Press, 1968); and *Under the Skylights* (New York: Garrett Press, 1969).

38. Clara Kirk and Rudolf Kirk, "Edith Wyatt: The Jane Austen of Chicago?" in *Chicago History* 1, no. 3 (Spring 1971): 172–178; David Henry, *William Vaughan Moody: A Study* (Boston: Little, Brown, 1934).

39. Blake Nevius, *Robert Herrick: The Development of a Novelist* (Berkeley: University of California Press, 1962); Kenneth Jackson, "Robert Herrick's Use of Chicago," *Midcontinent American Studies Journal* 5 (1964): 24–32.

40. Surveys that place the Chicago writers in a national context include Larzer Ziff, *The American 1890s: The Life and Times of a Lost Generation** (New York: Viking, 1966); Jay Martin, *Harvests of Change: American Literature, 1865–1914* (Englewood Cliffs, N.J.: Prentice-Hall, 1967); Warner Berthoff, *The Ferment of Realism: American Literature, 1884–1919* (New York: Free Press, 1965). Also useful is Lennox B. Grey, "Chicago and the Great American Novel: A Critical Approach to the American Epic" (Ph.D. diss., University of Chicago, 1935).

41. Also see Louis Utermeyer, *The New Era in American Poetry* (New York: Holt, 1919) and Charles Blanden and Minna Mathison, *The Chicago Anthology: A Collection of Verse from the Work of the Chicago Poets* (Chicago: Roadside Press, 1916).

42. Karl Detzer, *Carl Sandburg: A Study in Personality and Background* (New York: Harcourt, Brace, 1941); Ann Massa, *Vachel Lindsay, Fieldworker for the American Dream* (Bloomington, Ind.: University of Indiana Press, 1970).

43. Francis Browne, *The Dial* (Chicago: Jansen, McClurg, 1881–1918; New York: Dial Publishers, 1918–1929).

44. *The Chapbook: A Miscellany and Review of Belles Lettres* (Chicago: Stone and Kimball, 1894–1896; Herbert S. Stone and Co., 1896–1898).

45. *The Little Review: Literature, Drama, Music, Art* (Chicago: M. C. Anderson, 1914–1929).

46. Margaret Anderson, *My Thirty Years' War, an Autobiography: Beginnings and Battles to 1930* (1930; reprint ed., New York: Horizon Press, 1969). Miss Anderson's anthology is *The Little Review Anthology* (New York: Heritage House, 1953).

47. For a contemporary illustrated portrait of the 1893 Exposition, see the Bounty Books reprint of volume one of Hubert Howe Bancroft's multivolume *The Book of the Fair: An Historical and Descriptive Presentation of the World's Science, Art and Industry, as Viewed through the Columbian Exposition at Chicago in 1893.* There are also insights in the periodical literature: Merle Curti, "America at the Worlds' Fairs, 851–1893," *American Historical Review* 55 (1950): 833–856; and Justus D. Doenecke, "Myths, Machines and Markets: The Columbian Exposition of 1893," *Journal of Popular Culture* 6 (Spring 1973): 535–549.

48. Most studies of Chicago and the fine arts are quite uneven, but ideas can be gleaned from Charles E. Russell, *The American Orchestra and Theodore Thomas* (Garden City, N..: Doubleday and Page, 1927); Lorado Taft, *The History of American Sculpture* (New York: Macmillan, 1930); Edward C. Moore, *Forty Years of Opera in Chicago* (New York: H. Liveright, 1930). Anna Morgan's *My Chicago* (Chicago: R. F. Seymour, 1918) is one place to begin for the Little Theater movement that has also been studied by Constance D. MacKay, *The Little Theatre Movement in the United States* (New York: Holt, 1917).

49. George D. Bushnell, Jr., "When Jazz Came to Chicago," *Chicago History* 1, no. 3 (Spring 1971): 132–141.

50. Chadwick Hansen, "Social Influences on Jazz Style: Chicago, 1920–1930," *American Quarterly* 12, no. 4 (Winter 1960): 493–507.

51. Richard Storr, *The Beginnings of Graduate Education in America* (Chicago: University of Chicago Press, 1953).

52. Robert Farris, *Chicago Sociology, 1920–1930* (San Francisco: Chandler Publishers,

1967); James Short, Jr., *The Social Fabric of the Metropolis: Contributions of the Chicago School of Urban Sociology* (Chicago: University of Chicago Press, 1971); Thomas V. Smith and Leonard Whit, *Chicago: An Experiment in Social Science Research* (Chicago: University of Chicago Press, 1929).

53. Laurence Veysey, *The Emergence of the American University* (Chicago: University of Chicago Press, 1965).

54. Donald Flemming, *The Mechanistic Conception of Life* (Cambridge; Mass.: Belknap Press, 1964).

55. Lloyd J. Averill, *American Theology in the Liberal Tradition* (Philadelphia: Westminster Press, 1967).

56. R. M. Barry, "A Man and a City: George Herbert Mead in Chicago," in *American Philosophy and the Future: Essays for a New Generation*, edited by Michael Novak (New York: Charles Scribner's Sons, 1968).

57. L. L. Bernard and J. Bernard, *Origins of American Sociology: The Social Science Movement in the United States* (New York; Crowell, 1943).

58. Thorstein Veblen, *The Higher Learning in America** (1918; reprint ed., Stanford: Academic Reprints, 1954); Ida B. DePencier, *The History of the Laboratory Schools, the University of Chicago, 1896–1965* (Chicago: Quadrangle Books, 1967).

59. Joseph Dorfman, *Thorstein Veblen and His America*, revised ed. (New York: Viking Press, 1961); Laurence Cremin, *The Transformation of the School: Progressivism in American Education, 1876–1957** (New York: Knopf, 1961).

60. Hugh C. Miller, *The Chicago School of Architecture** (Washington D.C.: Department of the Interior, 1973), p. 1.

61. Carl Condit, *American Building Art: The Nineteenth Century** and *American Building Art: The Twentieth Century** (New York: Oxford University Press, 1960 and 1961, respectively); *The Chicago School of Architecture: A History of Commercial and Public Building in the Chicago Area, 1875–1925*, Chicago, 1910–1929: Building, Planning, and Urban Technology*, and *Chicago, 1930–1970: Building, Planning, and Urban Technology** (Chicago: University of Chicago Press, 1964, 1973, and 1974, respectively).

62. Siegfried Giedion, *Space, Time, and Architecture: The Growth of a New Tradition*, fifth ed., rev. (Cambridge, Mass.: Harvard University Press, 1967); Lewis Mumford, *The Brown Decades, a Study of the Arts in America, 1865–1895** (New York: Harcourt, Brace, 1931); Mark Peisch, *The Chicago School of Architecture: Early Followers of Sullivan and Wright* (New York: Random House, 1964); William Jordy, *American Buildings and Their Architects: Academic and Progressive Ideals at the Turn of the Century** (Garden City, N.Y.: Doubleday, 1972); *The Rise of an American Architecture,** edited by Edgar J. Kaufman (New York: Praeger, 1970).

63. Harriet Monroe, *John Wellborn Root* (1896; reprint ed., Prairie School Press, 1966); Donald Hoffman, *The Architecture of John Wellborn Root* (Baltimore: Johns Hopkins University Press, 1973); Charles Moore, *Daniel H. Burnham, Architect, Planner of Cities* (Boston: Houghton, Mifflin, 1921); Julius Fabos, et al., *Frederick Law Olmsted, Sr., Founder of Landscape Architecture in America* (Amherst, Mass.: University of Massachusetts, 1968); Henry Russell Hitchcock, *The Architecture of H. H. Richardson and His Time*, revised ed. (Hamden, Conn.: Archon Books, 1961).

64. Ira Bach, *Chicago on Foot: An Architectural Walking Tour,** revised second ed. (Chicago: J. Philip O'Hara, Inc., 1973); Arthur Siegel, *Chicago's Famous Buildings: A Photographic Guide,** second ed. (Chicago: University of Chicago Press, 1969).

65. For slides available, see William H. Pierson, Jr., and Martha Davidson, editors, *Arts of the United States: A Pictorial Survey* (New York: McGraw-Hill, 1960).

66. (New York: Documents of Modern Art: George Wittenborn, Inc., 1968).

67. Hugh Morrison, *Louis Sullivan, Prophet of Modern Architecture** (1935; reprint ed., New York: W. W. Norton & Company, Inc., 1962).

68. Frederick Gutheim, *Frank Lloyd Wright on Architecture: Selected Writings, 1894–1940** (New York: Duell, Sloan, and Pearce, 1941). For a helpful checklist of Wright's separately published first editions, see Kenneth Starosciak, *Frank Lloyd Wright: A Bibliography* (New Brighton, Minn.: Privately printed, 1973).

69. Martin Pawley, *Frank Lloyd Wright: Public Buildings* (New York: Simon and Schuster, 1970); Yukio Futagawa and Edgar Kaufman, *Frank Lloyd Wright: The Early Work* (New York: Horizon Press, 1968).

70. Duncan, *Culture and Democracy*; Szuberla's dissertation, "Urban Vistas and the Pastoral Garden: Studies in the Literature and Architecture of Chicago, 1893–1909," was done at the University of Minnesota, 1972.

71. On Chicago's role in urban planning, see John W. Reps, *The Making of Urban America: A History of City Planning in the United States* (Princeton: Princeton University Press, 1965) and Mellier G. Scott, *American City Planning Since 1890* (Berkeley: University of California Press, 1969).

72. Jones, *The Age of Energy: Varieties of American Experience, 1865–1915** (New York: Viking, 1970).

73. While the majority of the titles included in this supplement carry a publication date between 1975 and 1980, I have also added a few earlier studies that I have since read but of which I was unaware in 1975.

74. (Chicago: Chicago Historical Society, 1976). Duis, along with Glen Holt, writes an illustrated feature column, "Chicago as It Was," in the monthly *Chicago Magazine* and often includes general articles on topics in the 1871–1919 period.

75. In addition to analyzing the Loop, Holt and Pacyga analyze the Stockyards and the Central Manufacturing District, plus the neighborhoods of Douglas, Oakland, Kenwood, Hyde Park, Grand Boulevard, Washington Park, Armour Square, Bridgeport, Back-of-the-Yards, Canaryville, McKinley Park, Brighton Park, and Gage Park.

76. Victor Dyer, *Prairie Avenue: An Annotated Bibliography** (Chicago: Chicago Architectural Foundation, 1977); Jean F. Block, *Hyde Park Houses: An Informal History, 1856–1910* (Chicago: University of Chicago Press, 1979).

77. (Cambridge, Mass.: Harvard University Press, 1970). For the impact of an event such as the Haymarket Riot of 1886 on a neighboring community (Union Park), see Sennett's article, "Genteel Backlash, Chicago—1886," *Transaction* 7, no. 3 (1970): 41–50.

78. William Adelman, *Haymarket Revisited** (Chicago: Illinois Labor History Society, 1976) and his *Pilsen and Chicago's West Side** (Chicago: Illinois Labor History Society, 1980). Just as the Chicago Pullman Strike of 1894, with its wealth of documentation and secondary literature, can be studied as crucial case-study in urban violence and labor relations, so too can the Haymarket crisis be employed in an urban history course. Here too excellent new sources should be included in the materials to examine—Herman Kogan's short study of "William Perkins Black: Haymarket Lawyer," *Chicago History* 5, no. 2 (1976): 85–94, and Carolyn Ashbaugh's biography on *Lucy Parsons: American Revolutionary** (Chicago: Charles H. Kerr, 1976). Inasmuch as the police were a controversial component in all of these urban disturbances, Mark Haller's "Historical Roots of Police Behavior: Chicago, 1890–1925," *Law and Society Review* 10, no. 2 (1976): 303–323, provides helpful background. Haller's research deserves to be extended backward into the 1870s.

79. For Posadas's complete methodology, see her dissertation, "Community Structures of Chicago's Northwest Side: The Transition from Rural to Urban, 1830–1889" (Northwestern University, 1976); here also consult the dissertation of James E. Clark, "The

Impact of Transportation Technology on Suburbanization in the Chicago Region, 1830–1920" (Northwestern University, 1977).

80. For additional suggestions for cartographic exercises using Chicago as the geographical focus, see Chapter 2 of this book, "Past Cityscapes: Uses of Cartography in Urban History."

81. *Polish-American Politics in Chicago* (Chicago: University of Chicago Press, 1975); "Minyans for a Prairie City: The Politics of Chicago Jewry, 1850–1940" (Ph.D. diss., University of Chicago, 1974); Charles H. Shanabruch, *Toward an American Catholic Identity: The Chicago Experience* (Notre Dame, Ind.: University of Notre Dame Press, 1980).

82. David Hogan provides another perspective in his assessment of "Education and the Making of the Chicago Working Class, 1880–1930," *History of Education Quarterly* 18, no. 3 (Fall 1978): 227–270.

83. On the Chicago Irish, see the prolific work of Charles Fanning: *Finley Peter Dunne and Mr. Dooley: The Chicago Years* (Lexington, Ky.: University of Kentucky Press, 1979); *Mr. Dooley and the Chicago Irish: An Anthology* (New York: Arno Press, 1976); "Varieties of Irish-America: The New Home, Chicago" in *Varieties of Ireland, Varieties of Irish-America,* edited by Blanche Touhill (St. Louis: University of Missouri at St. Louis, 1976); "Mr. Dooley's Bridgeport Chronicle," *Chicago History* 1 (Spring 1972): 47–57. Also consult Barbara C. Schaaf, *Mr. Dooley's Chicago* (Garden City, N.Y.: Anchor Press, 1977).

84. Kenneth L. Kusmer, "The Functions of Organized Charity in the Progressive Era: Chicago as a Case Study," *Journal of American History:* 60, no. 3 (December 1973): 657–678; Kristin S. McGrath, "American Values and the Slums: A Chicago Case Study" (Ph.D. diss., University of Minnesota, 1977); Thomas Philpott, *The Slum and the Ghetto Neighborhood Deterioration and Middle-Class Reform: Chicago, 1880–1930* (New York: Oxford University Press, 1978).

85. Guy Szuberla, "Three Chicago Settlements: Their Architectural Form and Social Meaning," *Journal of the Illinois State Historical Society:* 70 (May 1977): 114–129.

86. For instances of other American studies scholars using Chicago literary works in this fashion, consult the various course syllabi on "Chicago Studies/Regional Studies" filed with the Regional American Studies Information Clearinghouse, the American University, Program In American Studies, Washington, D.C.

87. Ann Douglas, "Studs Lonigan and the Failure of History in Mass Society: A Study in Claustrophobia," *American Quarterly* 29, no. 5 (Winter 1977): 487–505; Charles Fanning, "James T. Farrell and Washington Park; the Novel and Social History, *Chicago History* 8, no. 2 (Summer 1979): 80–91; Anthony Grosch, "Social Issues in Early Chicago Novels," *Chicago History* 4, no. 2 (Summer 1975): 68–77; Carl Smith, "Fearsome Fiction and the Windy City: Or, Chicago in the Dime Novel," *Chicago History* 7, no. 1 (Spring 1978): 2–11.

88. Jonathan Yardley, *Ring: A Biography of Ring Lardner* (New York: Random House, 1977); Robert Conrow, *Field Days: The Life, Times, and Reputation of Eugene Field* (New York: Charles Scribner's Sons, 1974).

89. (Westport, Conn.: Greenwood Press, 1974); (Urbana, Ill.: University of Illinois Press, 1977).

90. "The Chicago Business Elite, 1830–1930: A Collective Biography," *Business History Review* 50, no. 3 (Autumn 2976): 288–328.

91. Thomas J. Schlereth, "Mail-Order Catalogues as Resources in Material Culture Studies," *Prospects: An Annual of American Cultural Studies* (forth-coming: 1980).

92. Lawrence P. Bachmann, "Julius Rosenwald," *American Jewish Historical Quarterly* 66 no. 1 (1976): 89–105.

93. Thomas J. Schlereth, "Big Money and High Culture: The Commercial Club of Chicago and Charles L. Hutchinson," *Great Lakes Review: A Journal of Midwest Culture,* 3, no. 1 (Summer 1976): 15–27. Thomas J. Schlereth, "A 'Robin's Egg Renaissance': Chicago Culture, 1893–1933," *Chicago History* 8, no. 3 (Fall 1979): 144–154. Helen Lefkowitz Horowitz, *Culture and the City: Cultural Philanthropy in Chicago from the 1880s to 1917* (Lexington, Ky.: University of Kentucky Press, 1976).

94. Paul Finkelman, "Class and Culture in Late Nineteenth-Century Chicago: The Founding of The Newberry Library," *American Studies* 16, no. 1 (1975): 5–22; Perry Duis, " 'Where is Athens Now?' The Fine Arts Building, 1898–1918," *Chicago History,* pt. I, 6, no. 2 (Summer 1977): 66–78 and part II, 7, no. 1 (Spring 1978): 40–53; Donald F. Tingley, "The 'Robin's Egg Rennaissance': Chicago and the Arts, 1910–1020," *Journal of the Illinois State Historical Society* 63, no. 1 (Spring 1970): 30–35.

95. See, for example, essays by Helen Horowitz, Erne and Florence Frueh, and Peter Marzio in the special issue of *Chicago History* 8, no. 1 (Spring 1979), devoted to the institute, along with Vera Lenchner Zolberg's doctoral dissertation "The Art Institute of Chicago: The Sociology of a Cultural Organization," (University of Chicago, 1974).

96. James T. Carey, *Sociology and Public Affairs: The Chicago School* (Beverly Hills, Cal.: Sage Publications, 1975); Fred H. Matthews, *Quest for an American Sociology: Robert E. Park and the Chicago School* (Montreal: McGill-Queens University Press, 1977); Winifred Rauschenbush, *Robert E. Park: Biography of a Sociologist* (Durham: Duke University Press, 1979); and Steven J. Diner, *A City and its Universities: Public Policy in Chicago, 1892–1919* (Chapel Hill, N.C.: University of North Carolina Press, 1980).

97. Frank L. Ellsworth, *Law on the Midway: The Founding of the University of Chicago Law School* (Chicago: University of Chicago Press, 1977).

98. Katherine Mayhew, *The Dewey School: The Laboratory School of the University of Chicago, 1896–1903* (New York: Columbia University Press, 1966). A figure that predates Dewey both in progressive education concepts and work in Chicago is *Colonel Francis W. Parker: The Children's Crusade,* the topic of a well-researched life by Jack K. Campbell (New York: Columbia University Press, 1967).

99. Francis Schussler Fiorenza, "American Culture and Modernism: Shailer Mathew's Interpretation of American Christianity," in *America in Theological Perspective,* edited by Thomas M. McFadden (New York: Seabury Press, 1976), pp. 163–186.

100. Barry D. Karl, *Charles E. Merriam and the Study of Politics* (Chicago: University of Chicago Press, 1974).

101. Dorothy M. Livingston, *The Master of Light: A Biography of Albert A. Michelson* (New York: Scribners, 1973).

102. Perry Duis, "Bessie Louis Pierce: Symbol and Scholar," *Chicago History* 5, no. 3 (Fall 1976): 130–140.

103. *The Idea of the University of Chicago: Selections from the Papers of the First Eight Executives of the University of Chicago from 1891 to 1975,* edited by D. J. R. Bruckner and William Michael Murphy (Chicago: University of Chicago Press, 1976).

104. *Dreams in Stone: The University of Chicago,* edited by D. J. R. Bruckner and Irene Macauley (Chicago: University of Chicago Press, 1976); Harold F. Williamson and Payson S. Wild have collaborated to do a detailed (403-page) institutional history—*Northwestern University: A History, 1850–1975* (Evanston, Ill.: Northwestern University, 1976)—that also uses some historical photography.

105. Jack Tager, "Partners in Design: Chicago Architects, Entrepreneurs, and the Evolution of Urban Commercial Architecture," *South Atlantic Quarterly* 76, no. 2 (Spring

1977): 204–218. Two dissertations exploring the dissemination of architectural theory and practice among architects and clients are Robert Prestiano, "The *Inland Architect: A Study of the Contents, Influence, and Significance of Chicago's Major Late-Nineteenth-Century Architectural Periodical*" (Northwestern University, 1973), and Eillen M. Nichols, "A Developmental Study of Drawings Published in the *American Architect* and in the *Inland Architect*" (University of Minnesota, 1978).

106. David Lowe, *Lost Chicago** (Boston: Houghton Mifflin, 1975), and *Chicago Interiors: Views of a Splendid World* (Chicago: Contemporary Books, 1979).

107. Oswald Grube, Peter Pran, and Franz Schulze, *100 Years of Architecture in Chicago: Continuity of Structure and Form** (Chicago: J. Philip O'Hara, 1976), and Stuart E. Cohen, *Chicago Architects: Documenting the Exhibition of the Same Name Organized by Laurence Booth, Stuart E. Cohen, Stanley Tigerman, and Benjamin Weese** (Chicago: Swallow Press, 1976).

108. For a more thorough discussion of the debate, see my review essay on both books in *The Old Northwest: A Journal of Regional Life and Letters* 3, no. 3 (September 1977): 319–323, and Nory Miller's appraisal, "Man of Ideas: Chicago's Battle of Architecture," *Inland Architect* (March 1976), pp. 8–14.

109. William Allin Storrer, *The Architecture of Frank Lloyd Wright: A Complete Catalog*, second edition (Cambridge, Mass.: MIT Press, 1978).

110. John Vinci, *The Stock Exchange Trading Room** (Chicago: The Art Institute of Chicago, 1977); James O'Gorman, "The Marshall Field Wholesale Store: Materials toward a Monograph," *Journal of the Society of Architectural Historians* 37, no. 3 (October 1978): 175–194; Harry Price, *The Auditorium Building: Its History and Architectural Significance** (Chicago: Roosevelt University, 1976).

111. For additional information, write Commission on Chicago Historical and Architectural Landmarks, Room 800, 320 North Clark Street, Chicago, Illinois 60610.

112. *City House: A Guide to Renovating Older Chicago-Area Houses,** compiled by Linda Legner (Chicago: Commission on Chicago Historical and Architectural Landmarks, 1979).

113. Jackson, "Chicago," in *American Space: 1865–1876: The Centennial Years** (New York: W. W. Norton & Company, Inc., 1972), pp. 72–86; also valuable in this context is Richard W. Shepro's B. A. thesis, "The Reconstruction of Chicago after the Great Fire of 1871" (Harvard University, 1974).

114. Cutler, *Chicago: Metropolis of Mid-Continent,** second edition (Dubuque, Ia.: Kendall/Hunt Publishing Company, 1976); *Chicago: Transformations of an Urban System*, edited by Brian J. L. Berry (Cambridge, Mass.: Ballinger Publishing Company, 1976).

115. Thomas Hines, *Burnham of Chicago: Architect and Planner** (New York: Oxford University Press, 1974); Cynthia Field, "The City Planning of D. H. Burnham" (Ph.D. diss., Columbia University, 1974).

116. Michael P. McCarthy, "Chicago Businessmen and the Plan," *Journal of the Illinois State Historical Society* 63, no. 3 (Autumn 1970): 228–256; Carl Condit, *Chicago, 1930–1970: Building, Planning and Urban Technology** (Chicago: University of Chicago Press, 1974); Michael Simpson, "Two Traditions of American Planning: Olmsted and Burnham," *Town Planning Review* 47 (April 1976); Paul F. Barrett, "Mass Transit, the Automobile, and Public Policy in Chicago, 1900–1930" (Ph.D. diss., University of Illinois at Chicago Circle, 1976); James E. Clark, "The Impact of Transportation Technology on Suburbanization in the Chicago Region, 1830–1920" (Ph.D. diss., Northwestern University, 1977).

117. Galen Cranz, "Changing Roles of Urban Parks: From Pleasure Garden to Open Space," *Landscape* 22, no. 3 (Summer 1978): 9–18; Leonard K. Eaton, *Landscape Artist in America: The Life and Work of Jens Jensen* (Chicago: University of Chicago Press, 1964);

Michael P. McCarthy, "Politics and the Parks: Chicago Businessmen and the Recreation Movement," *Journal of the Illinois Historical Society* 65, no. 2 (1972): 158–172.

118. David Burg, *Chicago's White City** (Lexington, Ky.: University of Kentucky Press, 1974); R. Reid Badger, *The Great American Fair: The World's Columbian Exposition and American Culture** (Chicago: Nelson-Hall, 1979).

119. Also see, however, William D. Andrews, "Women and the Fairs of 1876 and 1893," *Hayes Historical Journal* 1, no. 3 (Spring 1977): 173–184; Margaretta Darnall, "From the Chicago Fair to Walter Gropius: Changing Ideals in American Architecture" (Ph.D. diss., Cornell University, 1975); Elizabeth Brown, "American Paintings and Sculpture in the Fine Arts Building of the World's Columbian Exposition" (Qh.D. diss., University of Kansas, 1976).

120. Cathy and Richard Cahan, "The Lost City of the Depression," *Chicago History* 5, no. 4 (Winter 1976–77): 233–242; Lenox R. Lohr, *Fair Management, the Story of a Century of Progress Exposition* (Chicago 1952); August Mier and Elliott M. Rudwick, "Negro Protest at the Chicago World's Fair, 1933–34," *Journal of The Illinois State Historical Society* 59, no. 2 (Summer 1966): 161–171; F. T. Rihlstedt, "Formal and Structural Innovations in American Exposition Architecture: 1901–1939" (Ph.D. diss., Northwestern University, 1973).

Chapter 9

1. Ray Allen Billington, *Frederick Jackson Turner: Historian, Scholar, Teacher* (New York: Oxford University Press, 1973), pp. 122–131; Finley Peter Dunne, *Observations by Mr. Dooley* (New York: R. H. Russell, 1902), p. 271.

2. W. G. Hoskins, *The Making of the English Landscape* (London: Hodder and Soughton, 1955, 1963), p. 14.

3. *Landscape* I, no. 1 (Spring 1951): 5.

4. "Introduction," *The Interpretation of Ordinary Places*, edited by D. W. Meinig (New York: Oxford University Press, 1979), p. 6.

5. Borrowing from archaeologist John L. Cotter's slightly similar use of the term in an essay titled "Above-Ground Archaeology" (*American Quarterly* 26, no. 3 [August 1974]: 266–280), I first argued for the methodology in a short study, "The City as Artifact" (*American Historical Association Newsletter* 15, no. 2 [February 1977]: 7–9). In this context, also see Bert Salwen, "Archaeology in Megalopolis," in *Research and Theory in Current Archaeology*, edited by Charles L. Redman (London/New York: John Wiley and Sons, 1973), pp. 151–163; David R. Goldfield, "Living History: The Physical City as Artifact and Teaching Tool," *The History Teacher* 8, no. 4 (August 1975): 535–556.

6. Definitions of these three archaeological perspectives on three major chronological periods can be found in James B. Griffin's "The Pursuit of Archaeology in the United States," *American Anthropologist* 61 (1959): 379–388; Douglas Schwartz, "North American Archaeology in Historical Perspective," *Actes de Congres International D'Historie de Sciences* 2 (Warsaw and Cracow, 1968): 311–315; Gordon Wiley and Philip Phillips, "Method and Theory in American Archaeology, II: Historical-Developmental Interpretations," *American Archaeologist* 57: 723–819; and Gordon R. Wiley and Jeremy A. Sabloff, *A History of American Archaeology* (San Francisco: W. H. Freeman, 1974).

7. Perhaps the most useful introduction to the principles, practices, and problems of

modern archaeological study is James Deetz's *Invitation to Archaeology* (Garden City, N.Y.: Doubleday/Natural History Press, 1967).

8. Grahame D. Clark, *Archaeology and Society* (London: Methuen, 1947); James Deetz, "Archaeology as a Social Science," *Bulletin of American Anthropological Association* 3, no. 3, part 2: 115–125.

9. James Dalibard, "Architectural Recording as Above-Ground Archaeology," *Abstracts*, Third Annual Meeting, Society for Historical Archaeology, Bethlehem, Pa., 1970, p. 15; Bert Salwen, "Archaeology In Megalopolis," pp. 151–154; Cary Carson, "Doing History with Material Culture," in *Material Culture and the Study of American Life*, edited by Ian M. G. Quimby (New York: W. W. Norton & Company, Inc., 1978), pp. 41–64.

10. Peirce Lewis, "Axioms of the Landscape," *Journal of Architectural Education* 30 (September 1976): 8.

11. For example, Michael Aston and Trevor Rowley, *Landscape Archaeology: An Introduction to Field Work Techniques on Post-Roman Landscapes* (London: David and Charles, 1974); Henry Glassie, *Patterns in the Material Folk Culture of the Eastern United States* (Philadelphia: University of Pennsylvania Press, 1968); David Weitzman, *Underfoot: An Everyday Guide to Exploring the American Past* (New York: Charles Scribner's Sons, 1976); David Kyvig and Myron Marty, *Nearby History* (Arlington Heights, Ill.: AHM Publishing Corporation, 1980).

12. Penelope Lively, *The Presence of the Past: An Introduction to Landscape History* (London: William Collins and Sons, 1976); Maurice Beresford, *History on the Ground: Six Studies in Maps and Landscapes*, revised edition (London: Methuen, 1971); and W. G. Hoskins, *The Making of the English Landscape* (London: Hodder and Stoughton, 1955, 1963).

13. Grady Clay, *Close-Up: How to Read the American City* (New York: Praeger, 1973); John Leighly, editor, *Land and Life: A Selection from the Writings of Carl Ortwin Sauer* (Berkeley: University of California Press, 1963); John Fraser Hart, *The Look of the Land* (Englewood Cliffs, N.J.: Prentice-Hall, 1975); Fred Kniffen, "Louisiana House Types," *Annals, American Association of Geographers* 26 (1936): 179–193; Peirce Lewis, *New Orleans: The Making of an Urban Landscape* (Cambridge, Mass.: Ballinger Publishing Co., 1976); John R. Stilgoe, "Jack-o-Lanterns to Surveyors: The Secularization of Landscape Boundaries," *Environmental Review* (1976), pp. 14–32.

14. Don Yoder, *American Folklife* (Austin: University of Texas Press, 1976); May T. Watts, *Reading the Landscape of America* (New York: Collier/Macmillan, 1975), first published as *Reading the Landscape: An Adventure in Ecology*; Eugene Kinkead, *Wilderness is All Around Us: Notes of an Urban Naturalist* (New York: E. P. Dutton, 1978).

15. See Thomas J. Schlereth, "History Outside the History Museum: The Past on the American Landscape," in *Twentieth-Century Popular Culture in Museums, Archives and Libraries*, edited by Fred E. Schroeder (Bowling Green, O.: Bowling Green University Press, 1980).

16. Peirce F. Lewis, "Physical Geography and the Location of Cities," in *The Local Community: A Handbook for Teachers* (New York: Macmillan, 1972), pp. 551–552.

17. Marion Steinmann, "Fossil Hunters Find Treasures in Manhattan Buildings," *Smithsonian* 9, no. 6 (September 1978): 143–151.

18. See, for instance, the recent scholarship of Roderick Nash, *The American Environment: Readings in the History of Conservation*, second edition (Reading, Mass.: Addison-Wesley, 1976), and the literature published in *Environmental Review*, the quarterly journal of the American Environmental History Society.

19. Galen Cranz, "Changing Roles of Urban Parks: From Pleasure Garden to Open Space," *Landscape* 22, no. 3 (Summer 1978): 9–18.

20. Phoebe Cutler, "On Recognizing a WPA Rose Garden or a CCC Privy," *Landscape* 20, no. 2 (Winter 1976): 3–9.

21. Richard Francaviglia, "The Mormon Landscape: Existence, Creation, and Perception of a Unique Image in the American West" (Ph.D. diss., University of Oregon, 1970).

22. John P. Baumgardt, "The Osago Orange," *Horticulture* 50, no. 26 (1972): 47.

23. "The Osage Orange as a Botanical Artifact," *Pioneer America* 2, no. 3 (August 1979): 134–141.

24. Walter Prescott Webb, *The Great Plains* (New York: Grossett and Dunlap, 1931), p. 292.

25. Winberry, "Osage Orange as a Botanical Artifact," p. 139.

26. George R. Stewart, *Names on the Land: A Historical Account of Place-Naming in the United States* (Boston: Houghton Mifflin, 1958), pp. 104–105.

27. Ronald L. Baker and Marvin Carmody, *Indiana Place-Names* (Bloomington, Ind.: Indiana University Press, 1975), p. 7.

28. George R. Stewart, *American Place-Names: A Concise and Selective Dictionary for the Continental United States of America* (New York: Oxford University Press, 1970).

29. Grady Clay, *Alleys: A Hidden Resource* (Louisville, Ky.: Grady Clay and Company, 1978); also see James Borchert, "Alley Landscapes of Washington, D.C.," *Landscape* 23, no. 3 (1979): 3–10.

30. Anthony Vidler, "The Scenes of the Street: Transformations in Ideal and Reality, 1750–1871," in *On Streets* (Cambridge, Mass.: MIT Press, 1978), pp. 29–112; Bernard Rudofsky, *Streets for People: A Primer for Americans* (Garden City, N.Y.: Doubleday, 1969).

31. Indianapolis Historic Preservation Commission, *Historical Roads of Marion County* (Indianapolis, 977).

32. Sam Bass Warner, *Streetcar Suburbs: The Process of Growth in Boston, 1870–1900* (Cambridge, Mass.: Harvard University Press, 1962), pp. 15–21.

33. Clay, *Close-Up*, pp. 42–50; also see chapter 3 of *this* book.

34. See Deetz, *Invitation to Archaeology*, p. 26.

35. Several recent publications are quite useful in deciphering the antiquity and building history of domestic structures. See, for instance, David M. Hart, *How to Date a House: Part One and Two* (reprint from July and November (1976) issues of *Yankee*; and David Iredale, *Discovering Your Old House* (London: Shire Publications, 1977).

36. The best available discussion of the classification of house types is R. W. Brunskill's *Illustrated Handbook of Vernacular Architecture* (London: Faber and Faber, 1971). Another excellent discussion is Henry Glassie's "The Types of the Southern Mountain Cabin," Appendix C of Jan H. Brunsvand's *The Study of American Folklore* (New York: W. W. Norton & Company, Inc., 1968), pp. 338–370.

37. Wilbur Zelinsky, *The Cultural Geography of the United States* (Englewood Cliffs, N.J.: Prentice-Hall, 1973), p. 88.

38. Kenneth Hudson, *A Handbook for Industrial Archaeologists, A Guide to Fieldwork and Research* (London: John Baker, 1967), and J. P. M. Pannell, *The Techniques of Industrial Archaeology* (London: David and Charles, 1974).

39. John D. Tyler, "Industrial Archaeology and the Museum Curator," *Museum News* 47, no. 5 (January 1969): 30–32; Robert M. Vogel, "Industrial Archaeology—A Continuous Past," *Historic Preservation* 19, no. 2 (April-June 1967): 68–75.

40. T. Allen Comp and Donald Jackson, "Bridge Truss Types: A Guide to Dating and Identifying," AASLH Technical Leaflet No. 95, in *History News* 32, no. 5 (May 1977); Fred E. H. Schroeder, "Victorian Breweries: High-Rise in Industrial Architecture," paper pre-

ting of the Popular Culture Association, April 22, 1978, Cincinnati; Larry Lankton, The 'Practicable' Engineer: John B. Jervis and the Old Croton Aqueduct," *Essays in Public Works History* 5 (September 1977); Ross Holland, Jr., *America's Lighthouses* (Brattleboro, Vt.: Stephen Greene Press, 1972); Terry Jordan, "Evolution of the American Windmill: A Study in Diffusion and Modification," *Pioneer America* 5, no. 2 (1973): 3–12.

41. Robert Vogel, editor, *A Report of the Mohawk-Hudson Area Survey: A Selective Recording of the Industrial Archaeology of the Mohawk and Hudson River Valleys in the Vicinity of Troy, New York, June-September, 1969,* (Washington, D.C.: Smithsonian Institution Press, 1973); Theodore A. Sande, *Industrial Archaeology: A New Look at the American Heritage* (Brattleboro, Vt.: Stephen Green Press, 1976); Donald E. Sackheim, *Historic American Engineering Record Catalog* (Washington, D.C.: National Park Service, 1976).

42. James T. Flink, *The Car Culture* (Cambridge, Mass.: Harvard University Press, 1975); Marshall McLuhan, *Understanding Media: The Extension of Man* (New York: New American Library, 1964), p. 201; also see John B. Rae, *The Road and the Car in American Life* (Cambridge, Mass.: Harvard University Press, 1971).

43. Howard H. Peckham, *Indiana: A Bicentennial History* (New York: W. W. Norton & Company, Inc.; Nashville: American Association for State and Local History, 1978), pp. 112–113.

44. For further documentation of this argument, see Kathy Mack, *American Neon* (New York: Universe Books, 1977), and Dextra Frankel, *Neon Signs and Symbols,* Art Gallery Catalogue, California State University at Fullerton (February 23, 1973–March 15, 1972).

45. Robert Venturi, Denise Scott Brown, and Stephen Izenour, *Learning from Las Vegas* (Cambridge, Mass.: Massachusetts Institute of Technology Press, 1972); for an extended review of this provocative book, see Sigrid H. Fowler, "Learning from Las Vegas," *Journal of Popular Culture* 7, no. 2 (1973): 425–433.

46. Bruce A. Lohof, "The Service Station in America: The Evolution of a Vernacular Form," *Industrial Archaeology* 2, no. 2 (Spring 1974): 1–13; John A. Jackle, "The American Gasoline Station, 1920–197," *Journal of American Culture* 1, no. 3 (Fall 1978): 520–542; James B. Schick, "Vehicular Religion and the Gasoline Service Station," *Midwest Quarterly* 19 (October 1977); David I. Vieyra, *Fill 'Er Up: An Architectural History of America's Gasoline Stations* (N.Y.: Macmillan, 1979).

47. John Baeder, *Diners* (New York: Harry N. Abrams, 1978); Richard Gutman, "The Diner from Boston to L. A.," in *Environmental Communications* (Venice, Cal. 1976), p. 24; Richard J. S. Gutman and Elliot Kaufman, *The America Diner* (New York: Harper & Row, 1979).

48. Reyner Banham, "Unrecognized American Architecture: The Missing Motel," *Landscape* 15, no. 2 (Winter 1965–1966): 4–6; Warren J. Belasco, "Americans on the Road: Autocamping, Tourist Camps, Motels, 1910–1945" (Ph.D. dissertation, University of Michigan, 1977).

49. Neil Harris, "American Space: Spaced-Out at the Shopping Center," *The New Republic,* December 15, 1975, pp. 23–26; William Kowinski, "The Malling of America," *New Times,* May 1, 1978, pp. 29–55.

50. Marshall Fishwick, "Introduction,' *The World of Ronald McDonald* (Bowling Green, O.: Bowling Green Popular Press, 1978), p. 341.

51. See, particularly, Kenneth I. Helphand, "The Landscape of McDonald's," pp. 357–362, and David Orr, "The Ethnography of Big Mac," pp. 377–386.

52. Chester Liebs, "Remember Our Not-So-Distant Past?" *Historic Preservation* 30, no. 1 (January/March 1978): 30–35; *Proceedings,* First Annual Conference, Society for Commercial Archaeology, Boston, November 15, 1977 (Burlington, Vt., 1979).

53. Sam Bass Warner, "An Urban Historian's Agenda for the Profession," in *History and the Role of the City In American Life* (Indianapolis: Indianapolis Historical Society, 1972), pp. 56–58.

54. Marwyn S. Samuels, "The Biography of Landscape: Cause and Culpability," in *The Interpretation of Ordinary Landscapes,* edited by D. W. Meinig (New York: Oxford University Press, 1979), p. 77.

55. D. W. Meinig, "Reading the Landscape: An Appreciation of W. G. Hoskins and J. B. Jackson," in *The Interpretation of Ordinary Landscapes,* p. 236.

Chapter 10

1. Nicholas Zook, *Outdoor Museum Villages* (Barre, Mass.: Barre Publishers, 1971); Irvin Haas, *America's Historic Villages and Restorations* (New York: Arco Publishing Co., 1974).

2. For an overview of these developments, see the experimental text *Museum Studies Reader: An Anthology of Journal Articles on Open-Air Museums* (Noblesville, Ind.: Privately printed, 1979) developed by Ormond Loomis and Willard B. Moore at the Museum Studies Institute held at the Conner Prairie Pioneer Settlement, Noblesville, Indiana, June 12–30, 1978.

3. For this approach, I am indebted to David Hackett Fischer, *Historians' Fallacies: Toward a Logic of Historical Thought* (New York: Harper, 1970).

4. Calvin Trillin and Edward Koren, "The Inquiring Demographer; This Week's Question: What Are You Doing to Celebrate the Bicentennial?" *New Yorker,* May 10, 1976, p. 34–35; and Israel Shenker, "U.S. Bicentennial Cures History's Wants," *International Herald Tribune,* July 5–6, 1975, p. 5, as quoted by David Lowenthal, "The Bicentennial Landscape: A Mirror Held up to the Past," *Geographical Review* 67, no. 3 (July 1977): 259.

5. Ruth M. Elson, *Guardians of Tradition: American Schoolbooks of the Nineteenth Century* (Lincoln, Neb.: University of Nebraska Press, 1964); Frances Fitzgerald, *America Revised: History Schoolbooks in the Twentieth Century* (Boston: Little, Brown: 1979).

6. See, for example, Robert Bellah, *The Broken Covenant: American Civil Religion in a Time of Trial* (New York: Seabury Press, 1975) for the most recent analysis of the phenomenon; and Russell E. Richey and Donald G. Jones, *American Civil Religion* (New York: Harper and Row, 1974) for a bibliography and the best summary of the discussion to date.

7. Thomas R. Adam, *The Civic Value of Museums* (American Association for Adult Education, 1937), p. 8.

8. Margot Hornblower, "Would You Side with the British?," *International Herald Tribune,* December 10, 1975, p. 5.

9. " 'Bicentennial Schlock' Given Its Due in U.S. Exhibition," *International Herald Tribune,* October 15, 1976, p. 5; D. Lowenthal, "Bicentennial Landscape," p. 263–264.

10. Robert M. Newcomb, "The Nostalgia Index of Historical Landscapes in Denmark," in W. P. Adams and F. M. Helleiner, editors, *International Geography,* 2 vols. (Toronto: University of Toronto Press, 1972), I: 441–443.

11. David Lowenthal, "Past Time, Present Place: Landscape and Memory," *The Geographical Review* 65, no. 1 (January 1975): 6.

12. Michael Lesey, *Wisconsin Death Trip* (New York: Pantheon Books, 1973); Laura Ingalls Wilder, *The Little House on the Prairie* (New York: Harper and Row, 1971).

13. Louis Hartz, *The Liberal Tradition in America* (New York: Harcourt, Brace, 1955); Daniel Boorstin, *The Genius of American Politics* (Chicago: University of Chicago Press,

l Potter, *People of Plenty: Economic Abundance and the American Character* niversity of Chicago Press, 1954).

14. Russell G. Handsman, "Muddles in the Movement: The Preservation of Masks in Litchfield, Connecticut," *Artifacts* 6, no. 2: 6–7; also see his extended analysis, "Machines and Gardens: Structures in and Symbols of America's Past," an unpublished paper presented at the Annual Spring Meeting of the American Ethnological Society, Laval University, Quebec City, March 19, 1978.

15. Linda Grant Depauw and K. Conover Hunt, *Remember the Ladies* (New York: Viking, 1976); Phyllis Arlow and Merle Froschl, "Women in High School History Textbooks," in *Women in the High School Curriculum* (Old Westbury, N.Y.: Feminist Press, 1975).

16. Thomas J. Schlereth, "It Wasn't That Simple," *Museum News* 56, no. 3 (January 1978): 36–44.

17. Kevin Lynch, *What Time Is This Place?* (Cambridge, Mass.: MIT Press, 1972), p. 53.

18. Walter Muir Whitehall, "Cerebration versus Celebration," *The Virginian Magazine of History and Biography* 68, no. 3 (July 1960): 259–270.

19. Robert Swierenga, "Rural Studies in America," in *Farming in the Midwest, 1840–1900*, edited by James W. Whitaker, (Washington, D.C.: Agricultural History Society, 1974), p. 42.

20. *Recycling the Past: Popular Uses of American History*, edited by Lelia Zenderland (Philadelphia: University of Pennsylvania Press, 1978), "Introduction," pp. viii–x; Christopher D. Geist, "Historic Sites and Monuments as Icons," in *Icons of America*, edited by Ray B. Browne and Marshall Fishwick (Bowling Green, Ohio: Popular Press, 1978) pp. 57–65; David Lowenthal, "Bicentennial Landscape," pp. 261–262.

21. John Maass, "Architecture and Americanism, or Pastiches of Independence Hall," *Historic Preservation* 22 (April–June 1970): 17–25.

22. Peirce F. Lewis, "The Future of the Past: Our Clouded Vision of Historic Preservation," *Pioneer America* 6, no. 2 (July 1975): 5.

23. Thomas H. Pauley, "In Search of 'The Spirit of '76'," in *Recycling the Past: Popular Uses of American History*, edited by Leila Zenderland (Philadelphia: University of Pennsylvania Press, 1976), pp. 29–49.

24. David Lowenthal, "The American Way of History," *Colombia University Forum* 9, no. 3 (Summer 1966): 27–32.

25. Lewis, "The Future of the Past," p. 5; Lowenthal, "The Bicentennial Landscape," p. 259, and "The American Way of History, pp. 27–32, as well as his essays "Past Time, Present Place," pp. 1–36, and "The Place of the Past in the American Landscape," in *Geographies of the Mind: Essays in Historical Geosophy in Honor of John Kirtland Wright*, edited by David Lowenthal and Marilyn H. Bowden (New York: Oxford University, 1976), pp. 89–117.

26. Thorstein Veblen, *The Theory of the Leisure Class* (New York: Macmillan, 1899); Erving Goffman's *The Presentation of Self in Everyday's Life* (Garden City, N.Y.: Doubleday, 1959); Roland Barthes, *Mythologies*, translated by Annette Lavens (New York: Hill and Wang, 1972); Daniel Boorstin, *The Image: A Guide to Pseudo-Events in America* (New York: Harper and Row, 1961); Edward T. Hall, *The Hidden Dimension* (New York: Anchor, 1969) and *The Silent Language* (New York: Anchor, 1973); *Icons of America*, edited by Ray Browne and Marshall Fishwick (Bowling Green, Ohio: Popular Press, 1978); Russell E. Richey and Donald G. Jones, *American Civil Religion* (New York: Harper and Row, 1974); W. Lloyd Warner, *The Living and the Dead: A Study of the Symbolic Life of Americans* (New Haven: Yale

University Press, 1959); *Recycling the Past: Popular Uses of American History,* edited by Leila Zenderland (Philadelphia: University of Pennsylvania Press, 1978); Dean MacCannell, *Tourist: A New Theory of the Leisure Class* (New York: Shocken, 1976); Gene Wise, *American Historical Explanations* (Homewood, Ill.: Dorsey Press, 1973); J. P. Hexter, *The History Primer* (New York: Basic Books, 1971).

27. C. R. Elton, *The Practice of History* (London: Collins, Fontana Library, 1969), p. 152.

28. Schlereth, "It Wasn't That Simple," pp. 41–42; also see E. McClung Fleming, "The Period Room as a Curatorial Publication," *Museum News* 50, no. 10 (June 1972): 39–43.

29. See, for example, the audiovisual materials section of the journal, *The History Teacher* (Long Beach, Cal., 1967); and the newsletter *Film and History,* published by the Committee on Film and Historians (Newark, N.J.: Newark University, 1972–   ).

30. Linda F. Place, *et al.,* "The Object as Subject: The Role of Museums and Material Culture Collections in American Studies," *American Quarterly* 26, no. 3 (August 1974): 281–294.

31. For the analogue of architecture, film production, and museum exhibition, I am indebted to Harold Skramstad's fine essay "Interpreting Material Culture: A View from the Other Side of the Glass," in *Material Culture and the Study of American Life,* edited by Ian Quimby (New York: W. W. Norton & Company, Inc., 1978), pp. 184–185.

32. To date, we have devised programs using the concept of the "city as artifact" for the Indianapolis Museum of Art (1978), the Chicago Historical Society (1979), the Cincinnati Historical Society (1980), and the Delaware Museum of Art (1980).

33. John L. Cotter, "Above-Ground Archaeology," *American Quarterly* 26, no. 3 (August 1974): 266–280; Thomas J. Schlereth, "The City as Artifact," *American Historical Association Newsletter* (February 1977), pp. 7–9.

34. Isak Dinesen [Baroness Karen Blixen], *Out of Africa* (London: Putnam, 1937), p. 402.

35. John Steinbeck, *The Grapes of Wrath* (New York: Viking Press, 1939), pp. 117 and 120.

General Index

Authors' names appear in SMALL CAPITAL letters; titles of works are in italics; subjects discussed are listed in roman (or text) type.

ANDREWS, DEBORAH, and WILLIAM ANDREWS, 54, 103
Anthony, Susan B., 139, 141
Architectural history, 61, 63, 92, 138, 168–170, 186
Art history, 157, 186
Association for Living Historical Farms and Agricultural Museums (ALHFAM), 158

BAKER, RONALD, and MARVIN CARMODY, *Indiana Place-Names*, 192
Baltimore, 93–94
BARNARD, GEORGE, 21, 22
BARTHES, ROLAND, 218
BEECHER, CATHERINE, and HARRIET BEECHER STOWE, *The American Women's Home*, 96, 103
BELL, WHITFIELD, 117, 118
—*A Cabinet of Curiosities*, 118
BELLAH, ROBERT, 209
BERESFORD, MAURICE, 147, 186
BERRY, BRIAN, *Chicago: Transformation of Urban System*, 181
Bicentennial, 130, 132, 140–142, 151, 173
BICKELL, A. J., *Specimen Book of One Hundred Architectural Designs*, 63
BLOCH, MARC, 86
—*The Historian's Craft*, 5
BLUMENSON, JOHN J.-G., 111
—*Identifying American Architecture*, 114
BOORSTIN, DANIEL, 20, 48, 59, 133, 161, 212, 218
—*The Americans: The National Experience*, 104
—*The Americans: The Democratic Experience*, 104
Boston, 70–71
BOURKE-WHITE, MARGARET, 21
—and ERSKINE CALDWELL, *You Have Seen Their Faces*, 33
BOTEIN, STEPHEN, *Experiments in History Teaching*, 103

BOWRON, BERNARD, *Henry B. Fuller on Chicago*, 176
BROOKS, H. ALLEN, *The Prairie School*, 170
BROWN, RALPH, *Historical Geography of the United States*, 107
BRYANT, WILLIAM CULLEN, *A Lifetime*, 131
—*The Flood of Years*, 131
BRYCE, JAMES, 170
—*The American Commonwealth*, 136
Building types, 36
Burnham, Daniel, 84, 169, 170, 182

CALDWELL, ERSKINE, and MARGARET BOURKE-WHITE, *You Have Seen Their Faces*, 33
Calumet Sag Channel, 70
CARMODY, MARVIN, and RONALD BAKER, *Indiana Place-Names*, 192
CARSON, CARY, 185
Carte de viste, 18–19
Cartography, historians' use of, 66–86, 106–107, 122; limitations as historical evidence, 85–86
CATHER, WILLA, *The Professor's House*, 111
CATLIN, GEORGE, *Illustrations of the Manners, Customs, and Condition of the North American Indians*, 139
Chicago, 1, 24, 36, 53, 57, 62, 63, 64, 68, 69–86, 150, 151, 155, 160, 162–183, 184, 188, 189, 193, 194, 195, 197, 211
Chicago Historical Society, 28, 50, 61, 80, 164, 171, 172
Chicago Sanitary and Ship Canal, 70
Chicago School of Architecture, 168–170
Chicago, University of, 167–168, 177
Cincinnati, 70
City plans. *See* Town plans
Civilian Conservation Corps (CCC), 155
CLAY, GRADY, 108, 148, 186
—*Close-Up: How to Read the American City*, 72, 106, 192, 193
COHEN, LIZABETH, 103, 119
COLEMAN, LAURENCE, 117, 118
—*The Museum in America*, 118
Colonial Williamsburg (Va.), 121, 122
Commercial archaeology, 198–201

289

Winterthur Museum, 103
WITTLIN, ALMA, 117, 118
—*Museums*, 118
Women's history, 59, 61, 103, 105, 139
Works Progress Administration (WPA), 51,
  81, 157, 190
World fairs, 62, 81–82, 130–142, 166–76,
  182, 184
World's Columbian Exposition of 1893,
  166–167, 184

Wright, Frank Lloyd, 169, 180, 183

YERKES, CHARLES, *Atlas of Chicago
  Warehouses, Docks, and Freight Depots*, 77

ZELINSKY, WILBUR, 197
—*The Cultural Geography of the United States*,
  106
ZUKOWSKY, JOHN, *The Plan of Chicago*, 182